TEXAS RANGER
N. O. REYNOLDS
THE INTREPID

The best known photograph of N. O. Reynolds, 1875. Photographer unknown.

Courtesy the late Ed Bartholomew.

TEXAS RANGER
N. O. REYNOLDS
THE INTREPID

CHUCK PARSONS
AND DONALY E. BRICE

Foreword by Leon Metz

Number 14 in the Frances B. Vick Series

University of North Texas Press
Denton, Texas

Printed in the United States of America.

10 9 8 7 6 5 4 3 2 1

Permissions:
University of North Texas Press
1155 Union Circle #311336
Denton, TX 76203-5017

The paper used in this book meets the minimum requirements of the American National Standard for Permanence of Paper for Printed Library Materials, z39.48.1984. Binding materials have been chosen for durability.

Library of Congress Cataloging-in-Publication Data

Parsons, Chuck, author.
Texas Ranger N.O. Reynolds, the Intrepid / Chuck Parsons and Donaly E. Brice ; foreword by Leon Metz. -- Second Edition.
pages cm -- (Number 14 in the Frances B. Vick series)
ISBN 978-1-57441-572-8 (cloth : alk. paper) -- ISBN 978-1-57441-585-8 (ebook)
1. Reynolds, N. O. (Nelson Orcelus), 1846-1922. 2. Texas Rangers--Biography. 3. Frontier and pioneer life--Texas. 4. Crime--Texas--History--19th century. 5. Peace officers--Texas--Biography. 6. Soldiers--Texas--Biography. 7. Texas--History--1846-1950. I. Brice, Donaly E., author. II. Title. III. Series: Frances B. Vick series ; no. 14.
F391.R47P37 2014
363.2'09764092--dc23
[B]

2014017090

Texas Ranger N. O. Reynolds, the Intrepid is Number 14 in the Frances B. Vick Series
The electronic edition of this book was made possible by the support of the Vick Family Foundation.

Dedicated to our helpful, understanding and patient wives, whose encouragement drove us to devote so much time to this project: Pat Parsons, and Clare Brice.

CONTENTS

FOREWORD

by Leon C. Metz

Chuck Parsons and Donaly E. Brice are unique among biographers. Most writers of their genre, with this skill and background knowledge, would have chosen well-known Texas characters to immortalize, individuals perhaps like John Wesley Hardin, Sam Bass, Bill Longley, King Fisher, John Ringo or even Sam Houston.

But Parsons and Brice picked a little-known figure like N. O. Reynolds, a man so apparently unimpressed with his first name that he seldom wrote it. Reynolds, decisive in almost every respect, also vacillated regarding his place of birth (Pennsylvania or Missouri) and the date of his birth. The authors never resolved the variances either, but they gave the question their best research shot.

Of more significance, they answered the question of just who was N. O. Reynolds. Why was his life worthy of a biography?

First, they acknowledged that he possessed the wit and abilities to have been a successful farmer or rancher. He might have been a businessman or a professional such as a doctor, lawyer, or member of the clergy.

This former Union soldier opted to become a Texas Ranger, eventually the commander of Company E of the Frontier Battalion. With this selection, he deliberately chose an occupation of hardship and danger. Although the modern world regards the Rangers in legendary, romantic terms, the realities were harsh. The Rangers often slept on the ground, spent long hours in the saddle, dug for water, prayed for rain and a good horse, and hoped those occasional bullets buzzing past their ears never carried their name scratched in soft lead.

Although N. O. Reynolds is little known today (this is his first biography), his work brought him into contact with the most wicked warriors in Texas. Many were Indians, although by Reynolds' time the Comanche and others had been reduced to small raiding parties now and then terrorizing remote settlements, seldom striking larger settlements.

Outlaws comprised the primary reason for Reynolds' career. With Texas recovering from Reconstruction, with night-riders criss-crossing the brush covered landscape, and vigilantes saving numerous communities the expense of legal executions, Reynolds cast his long shadow across the twisting pathways of lawlessness.

His career brought him into collision with gunmen such as Scott Cooley, John Ringo and the Dublin brothers. He captured the Horrell brothers, and forced a peace treaty between them and the Higgins bunch. He escorted desperado and acclaimed man-killer John Wesley Hardin back and forth from jail to court, and then from jail to prison. Reynolds rode day and night, practically ruining what was already shaky health, trying to reach Round Rock, Texas in time to help intercept the Sam Bass gang. The lawman missed the fight by a couple of hours.

Even so, the authors all but positively identified the actual slayer of Bass. It could have been Ranger Dick Ware or Ranger George Herold. Parsons and Brice evaluated a large assortment of evidence.

Several figures famous in Texas history crossed the path of N. O. Reynolds. Major John B. Jones, commander of the Frontier Battalion, spent time riding with Reynolds and assisted his rise through the ranks. James B. Gillett served personally under Reynolds for several months. The Reynolds biography includes information not found in his famous book, *Six Years with the Texas Rangers*.

Serious writers and readers of Texas history will be familiar with Chuck Parsons and Donaly Brice. Parsons has written numerous books and articles dealing with lawmen, Texas Rangers and outlaws. He has been particularly adept at defining many puzzling aspects of John Wesley Hardin's bloody career. Parsons had for a number of years edited the *Quarterly* and *Newsletter* of the National Association for Outlaw and Lawman History (NOLA) and for seventeen years was "The Answer Man" for *True West* magazine.

Brice has supervised reference services at the Texas State Archives in Austin. It is virtually impossible to seriously investigate Texas history without being indebted to the vast knowledge and immense patience of Donaly Brice.

The authors selected N. O. Reynolds as a subject for co-authorship because he epitomized the quiet, dogged, legendary determination of Ranger commanders. Reynolds had his frailties but they primarily involved his health. He never backed away from a mob; he never relinquished a prisoner; he never gave up on the trail; and only once did he lose a Ranger to opposing gunfire.

Parsons and Brice examined the ponderables and the imponderables with the tenacity of a hound dog working his way through briar patches. They have taken the career of an extraordinary man, woven in the people involved, and have produced a saga about crime, outlawry, bravery, suffering, inhumanity, and how dauntless men rise above travail and do their job not because the pay is good, but because they have no other conscionable options.

Through the exploits of N. O. Reynolds, the authors have described law enforcement during a particularly bitter portion of Texas history, the smoky 1870s and 1880s. In doing so, Parsons and Brice have avoided television heroics, concentrating instead on the man's patient, dedicated tenacity.

They have realized that Nelson Orcelus Reynolds merited a greater tribute than what's ordinarily found in dusty, seldom analyzed reports filed in impersonal cabinets. The exploits of Reynolds warranted something better than vague recollections of local citizens.

This account assembles and evaluates the life and labors of a gifted and generally neglected man who patiently wandered—and sometimes shot his way—across central and west Texas. Certainly he never thought of himself as a superstar. When he laid down his sword and shield, he went on to other trades, never looking back, never considering that the state or the citizens owed him a living, or a retirement, or even a paragraph of recognition.

The authors have resurrected an American hero. In a simple, quiet, honest way, they have narrated the story of a just, honest, and steadfast man, an intrepid Texas Ranger, N. O. Reynolds.

ACKNOWLEDGMENTS

Without the invaluable assistance of many other researchers, writers, historians and descendants of N. O. Reynolds and other Texas Rangers this work would have remained a miniscule biography. The following represents those who provided assistance; our apologies to any individual we may have overlooked.

California: Harold L. Edwards, Bakersfield.

Florida: Thomas C. Bicknell.

Georgia: The late James A. Browning, Douglasville.

Illinois: Walter L. Brieschke, History Office, Illinois Department of Corrections, Menard.

Indiana: Dave Johnson, Zionsville.

Kansas: Ms. Wanda Christy, Lawrence; Coffey County Genealogical Society, Burlington.

Montana: Hallie Woods, Dillon.

New York: Pat Buck, Endicott.

Ohio: Carol W. Bell, Warren; Robert K. DeArment, Sylvania.

Texas: Bob Alexander, Maypearl; Dorothy Allison, Cameron; John Anderson, Texas State Archives; Michael Bailey, Angleton; the late Ed Bartholomew, Fort Davis; the late David Baskins, Texas State Library; John W. Bell, San Antonio; the late Leona Bruce and her granddaughter, Sue Porter, Austin; Gene and Donnie Coleman, Junction; the late Bernard Davis, San Perlita; Joe B. Davis, Former Texas Ranger Foundation, Fredericksburg; Stephen Reynolds Davis, Kingsville; William

C. "Bill" Dowdy, Round Rock; George Easterling, Angleton; Pansy Gillett Espy, Fort Davis; Jim Green, San Marcos; Dora E. Guerra, DRT Library, the Alamo; Jeff Jackson, Lampasas; Darrell Jepson, Angleton; the late Harry and Bernice Lear, Junction; Dan Lengefeld, Johnson City; the late Al Lowman, San Marcos; Dennis McCown, Austin; Don C. Marler, Woodville; Leon C. Metz, El Paso; Rick Miller, Harker Heights; Kris Mize, La Porte; Jamie Murray, Angleton; Bill O'Neal, Carthage; Mike Peck, Cameron; the late Diane Davis Rieter, Center Point; Peter R. Rose, Austin; Dorothy Schwartz, Alverado; Jean Schroyer, Marble Falls; Robert W. Stephens, Dallas; Frederica Burt Wyatt, Junction; the staff of the Texas State Archives, Austin; and the staff of the Briscoe Center for American History, Austin.

1

CONTINUING THE WARRIOR TRADITION

"Private in Company B, 147th Illinois Volunteer Infantry."
—Orcelus Reynolds

Moonlight rays fell on the sentinel's Winchester, creating glimmers of light in the camp of the sleeping men. A young Texas Ranger paced the ground nervously, realizing the urgency of his guard. He had to protect the horses and the other Rangers, but he also had to prevent the mobs from taking the prisoner . . . and more importantly prevent him from escaping. John Wesley Hardin was the prisoner guarded so closely, the man-killer for whose capture Rangers John Armstrong and Jack Duncan earned a reward of $4,000. Hardin had been the most wanted man in Texas, but now he was a prisoner in the camp of Lieutenant N. O. Reynolds. It was abundant glory for the Rangers, but what if Hardin should escape? What if he was mobbed by friends of his victims? Who would pay for the carelessness?

Texas Ranger Lt. N. O. Reynolds, known as the "Intrepid" by fellow Ranger James Buchanan Gillett and history, is not among the better known of the nineteenth-century lawmen. No other biographies have appeared before, and the few articles discussing his most noted exploits reveal him only in the reflected light of the outlaws he pursued and captured. During his lifetime, however, especially during the 1870s and 1880s, he was widely recognized as an intrepid lawman. He had risen steadily on the ladder of law enforcement, beginning as a jail guard, then serving as a sergeant in the Frontier Battalion of the Texas Rangers, then rising to the rank of Lieutenant Commanding of Company E. Later he was city marshal of Lampasas and then sheriff of Lampasas County. His experiences were extensive, and during his career he earned the respect of countless Texans, the lawless and the law-abiding alike.

N. O. Reynolds never attempted to enhance his legacy or to even seek publicity. On the contrary, the man generally known as Major Reynolds, or simply "Mage," intentionally clouded his beginnings. Even though he avoided the fame that some other Rangers eagerly sought, his actions in reducing the number of outlaws established his reputation for generations to come. He earned glory in Texas and the nickname "The Intrepid" for his resolute fearlessness, his fortitude and "true grit," but his roots reached back to the cradle of American Independence, Pennsylvania. He could claim a Revolutionary soldier among his forebears.

Although his career as a Ranger can be traced fairly completely, his early years remain elusive. The standard Texas certificate of death reveals he was born in Pennsylvania on November 21, 1846, the son of Hiram Gillett and Betsy D. Taylor Reynolds. His widow, Irene Temperance Nevill Reynolds, was the source of this information.[1]

However, Reynolds himself wanted his companions to believe he was a southerner, not a "Yankee," in spite of having fought for the "Yankee" cause during the American Civil War. When joining the Frontier Battalion in 1874 he provided information differing from what his widow gave for the official record. The May 1874 Company D muster roll shows Reynolds as being twenty-five years of age, suggesting a birth year of 1849. As for birthplace, he gave Bradford County, Missouri. The muster roll of Company E prepared by Lieutenant Reynolds himself in September 1877, on the other hand, shows him as being twenty-nine years old, suggesting a birth year of 1848, and again the birthplace is listed as Missouri. One year later Reynolds was lieutenant commander of Company E. He is shown to be thirty years of age, suggesting a birth year of 1847, and again his birthplace is given as Missouri.

Three years later, in 1880, Reynolds was a resident of Hays County, Texas, and the census shows him again as a native of Missouri. For the first time, we have information on his parents' birthplaces. His father's birthplace is given as Kentucky and his mother's as Pennsylvania. Here he gave his age as thirty-one, once again suggesting a birth year of 1849. Two decades later, while a resident in Lockhart, the seat of Caldwell County, Texas, the census shows him as being fifty-four years of age, born in November 1845 in Missouri. A further discrepancy is that both his parents are now shown to be natives of Kentucky. A decade later in Orange County, Texas, Reynolds is shown to be sixty-four years old, suggesting a birth year of 1846, and from Missouri. His parents are now shown to be born in the United States.

In 1920 Reynolds was still in Orange County, renting a house in the city of Orange. Nelson O. Reynolds is shown to be married but living alone in a dwelling on Front Street. He is enumerated as a seventy-three-year-old white male, suggesting a birth year of 1847; his occupation is given as time keeper in an unidentified paper mill. Surprisingly Reynolds indicated he had been born in Pennsylvania but his parents were both born in Kentucky. Obviously there are discrepancies in the records, which he himself, or family members, provided over the decades. As if the differences in birth year weren't confusing enough, Bradford County, Missouri, doesn't exist.[2]

Ranger James Buchanan Gillett, who served six years in the Ranger force and later as sheriff of Brewster County, Texas, greatly admired his commander. When asked about his early life, Reynolds told him that he was "a Missourian by birth, a bootmaker by trade, and that his early history could interest no one."[3] Reynolds was indeed a boot maker for a brief period of time, but he was not born in Missouri and contrary to his statement, there is today great interest in his life.

Reynolds' parents are found on the 1850 Bradford County, Pennsylvania (not Missouri), census, although the name of Nelson or N. O. Reynolds has not been found on any census of 1850, the earliest year in which he could have been enumerated. That year, Hiram Gillett Reynolds, born in Virginia about 1821, resided in LeRoy Township with his wife Betsy, born in Pennsylvania in December 1827. In 1850 Hiram Reynolds was twenty-nine years old, farming with real estate valued at $2,000. Housewife Betsy was twenty-four, also a native of Pennsylvania. There is but one child in this family, identified as Franklin on the census, seven months old in August when the family was enumerated. This child was born in February 1850.[4] Presumably Nelson was overlooked by the census enumerator. Reynolds' most complete obituary, that of the *San Antonio Express* of March 5, 1922, stated that he was born in 1849 and was a native of Pennsylvania. This suggests the seven-month-old Franklin could be the future N. O. Reynolds, and the census enumerator simply erred in identifying the child. Was the entry of the name of Franklin instead of Nelson merely an error on the part of the census enumerator? Presumably the obituary information was provided by his widow Irene or other members of the immediate family, but differs in three years from the information provided on the standard certificate of death. If Nelson and Franklin are not the same person, then Franklin likely died young as no further record is known of his existence. Also, he is not listed as a survivor to his mother when she died in 1912.

Family sources reveal that his mother, Betsy Dorleska Taylor Reynolds, was the daughter of Levi and Louisa Holcomb Taylor. Betsy, born in Granville Center, died on March 26, 1912, at the home of her daughter, Mrs. Edla A. Rockwell, in Troy, Pennsylvania. She was survived by four daughters, a son (N. O.), and a brother, Volney Taylor of Granville. Her grave in the Granville Cemetery is marked, the stone reading simply, "Betsy D. Reynolds 1827–1912."[5] Her husband Hiram G. Reynolds had died years before on November 7, 1866, at the family home in Coleta, Whiteside County, Illinois.[6]

In the 1850 census there is adjacent to the Hiram Reynolds family a couple in their sixties, Joshua Reynolds and his spouse. Five dwellings later the census taker visited the residence of one *Nelson Reynolds*. His wife was named Clarissa, and presumably these Reynoldses are relatives of Hiram Reynolds.

Although he may have considered himself a Missourian, listing that state as the place of his nativity, on Texas Ranger muster records as well as three different census records, it is accepted that he was born in Bradford

County, Pennsylvania, on November 21, 1846. As there are inconsistencies in the record of Hiram and Betsy Reynoldses' only son who survived to adulthood, there is little information regarding his siblings as well, all sisters. In 1853 Louisa was born, followed six years later by Emma in 1859. Ella Alvira was born in July 1861, followed by Edla Davis, or Eddie, in 1863.[7]

Family tradition states that when Ella was about two years of age—or in early 1863—the family began a move west. By later 1863 the family was located in Whiteside County, Illinois, located nearly straight west of Chicago and bordering on the Mississippi River. They established their new home in Coleta, a small community known first as Crum's Store after John Thompson Crum who had established the first business. The name was later changed to Clayton, but due to dissatisfaction with both names the citizens elected to call it Coleta. By 1868 community members had established a Methodist Episcopal Church, and by 1869 the United Brethren Society had established a church, followed by the establishment of a Christian Church soon after. As churches and the school flourished a Masonic Lodge was established whose membership gradually increased.[8]

Hiram G. Reynolds owned land in the northwest quarter of the northwest quarter of section thirty-five, township twenty north in range six. After the death of her husband, Betsy sold this land on June 20, 1867, to David A. Bisby. Most interesting is not that she sold the land the family had lived on and farmed, but the identity of her son is listed in the official records: he is here identified as *Orcelus N. Reynolds*. In later years he occasionally signed his name as Orcelus. Obviously when in Texas, Reynolds preferred to be known as Nelson O. or simply N. O. Reynolds. No doubt his legal name given at birth was Orcelus Nelson Reynolds, a name which he apparently disliked.[9]

As the Reynolds family grew during this decade, the country experienced its greatest upheaval. Young Reynolds experienced combat in the struggle, although in a very limited capacity. The tragedy of the nation was reflected in the Reynolds household as well as it was during this decade that the family lost its patriarch. Hiram G. Reynolds died in 1866, although the cause of his death is unknown. But by then his son, Orcelus

N. O. Reynolds' sisters as adults. From left: Emma, born 1859, who married Marble Benninger; Louisa Wilbur, born 1863; Ella, born 1861 who married Elbert I. Santee; and Edla born 1863 who married Edward Alan Rockwell. *Courtesy Kris Mize.*

Reynolds, was off on his own. With her husband gone and her son seeking his own life on the frontier, there was little to hold the widow Reynolds in Coleta. The Reynolds family left a sparse "paper trail" in Illinois records. By 1870 the widow Reynolds was back in Pennsylvania living with her father Levi Taylor and his third wife, Sarah Campbell.

Levi Taylor, born in 1797 in Massachusetts, was now seventy-two years of age. He and his first wife, Louisa Holcomb, daughter of Sterling and Elizabeth (Stone) Holcomb, had given four children to the world: Alvira, Sterling, Betsy, and Volney. After the death of his first wife, Taylor married Mary Landon. Apparently this marriage was short as there were no children born from the union and by 1850 he was married a third time, now to Sarah Campbell. To this union three sons were born: Milan, Hollis H., and Fred. They perhaps only knew Nelson Orcelus from hearing other family members speak of him.

In 1870 in Granville Township, Bradford County, Pennsylvania, Levi Taylor was the head of the household, a farmer with real estate valued at $15,000 and personal estate valued at $2,900. Sarah was fifty-four, eighteen years younger than her husband. Living with them were Hollis and Fred, Betsy Reynolds, now forty-three, the mother of Orcelus, and her daughters Louisa, now seventeen; Ella, nine; and Edla, six years old. Betsy Reynolds claimed real estate valued at $800 and personal estate valued at $200. Intriguingly, her daughter Emma, now thirteen, is not listed as living with them. She was still living in Illinois with the Samuel D. Perry family. Emma suffered from deafness and an inability to speak, described as "deaf & dumb" by the census enumerator. As an infant she had fallen from a high chair, which resulted in her becoming deaf. Presumably either Samuel D. Perry or his wife was a teacher, and a teacher of the deaf Emma. Curiously Mrs. Reynolds did not take her daughter back to Pennsylvania for whatever education she could receive there.[10]

How often N. O. Reynolds the Texan ever returned home to visit family members in Bradford County is uncertain. From the war's end until his own death he spent his years primarily in Illinois, Missouri, and Texas. Letters and other documents that would reveal the man's personal life, his feelings towards his sisters, and the experiences of the war, seemingly do not exist. Living in Texas his normal reference to being a Missourian by birth suggests that he wished to avoid any possibility of being labeled a Northerner.

With these humble beginnings, the conflicting dates of his birth, variously listed as 1845, '46, '47, '48, and '49, the name change from Orcelus Nelson to Nelson O., the man Reynolds created the guise of being a Southerner, a Missourian. An obituary from the *San Antonio Daily Express* reported that he had arrived in Texas "at an early day" but with no further clarification. A later publication provided information that he had served in the Civil War for three years and then went to Texas, arriving in 1872. This is only partly correct, as he did serve during the war but not for the Confederacy as many Texans believed he had done.[11] This deception worked on Gillett who recorded his adventurous memoir, but it also adds an air of mysterious deception about his career, causing us to wonder what he did between the end of the war and his first arrival in Texas in 1873.

The recollections of Texas Ranger James B. Gillett provide only a glimpse into the service of Reynolds during the Civil War. Gillett wrote that when Reynolds was mustered in as commander of Company E, Frontier Battalion on September 1, 1877, he was about thirty years of age, and was "vigorous in mind and body, and had a massive determination to succeed as a ranger . . . a native of Missouri, and who was always known as Major or 'Mage' Reynolds." Gillett supposedly learned that Reynolds, though "a mere boy," had served with the Confederates in the latter years of the war. Reynolds was one of a party that captured a troop of Federal cavalry, the major of which was well supplied with clothing. As the captors were very scantily clad Reynolds appropriated the major's uniform, hence his nickname. Reynolds and Gillett must have maintained their friendship after their service in the Frontier Battalion, as in "later years, when I had grown intimate with him and was probably closer to him than any other," Gillett brought up the story about the origin of his nickname. Reynolds could have been less secretive about his earlier years, but his answer then did remain with Gillett when he was recording his own memoir. So recalled Gillett years later after the Ranger years were well behind him.[12]

Gillett was correct in at least one respect, that he was well known as Major Reynolds. On the Hays County 1880 census one year after Reynolds resigned from the Frontier Battalion, he was listed as a boarder in a San Marcos hotel, thirty-one years of age and a native of Missouri. When Assistant Marshal Calvert Wilkins enumerated the former Ranger he was not identified as Nelson or N.O., but *Major Reynolds*. The "rank" of major was obviously the name by which he was best known. In numerous newspaper articles from the decade after his Ranger service he was referred to as Major Reynolds, as if that was his accepted title, with no question as to it being a genuine rank or an honorary title.

James Buchanan Gillett on horse "Dusty" in 1875. *Courtesy Former Texas Rangers Foundation.*

But Gillett was wrong on one important point: Reynolds did not serve as a Confederate soldier during the war. He did serve, but as a private in the Union Army. Gillett would not have erred through carelessness in such an important distinction when writing of his beloved commander. N. O. Reynolds, the Intrepid Texas Ranger, intentionally misled his Texas contemporaries into believing he had fought for the Southern Cause.

Regardless of what Reynolds may have told the various census enumerators or his Ranger companions he undoubtedly was as accurate as he could be when he appeared before Orange County Judge O.R. Sholars on July 2, 1912, making his declaration to receive a pension. He gave his name as Orcelus Reynolds, sixty-six years of age, that he had enrolled at Dixon, Illinois under the same name on either February 6 or 8, 1865, as a private in Company B. 147th Illinois Volunteer Infantry. He claimed to have been honorably discharged at Springfield, Illinois, on January 20 or 25, 1866. He recalled that at the time of enlistment he was five-foot-nine inches tall, his complexion dark, his eyes blue, his hair brown and his occupation a blacksmith. He gave as his birthplace Bradford County, Pennsylvania, born there on November 21, 1846. According to the Pension Act approved May 11, 1912, to a person who had "reached the age of sixty-six years and had served ninety days, fifteen dollars per month [would be allowed]; six months, fifteen dollars and fifty cents per month; one year, sixteen dollars per month."[13] At that point in time the old lawman could look forward to sixteen dollars per month.

Additional documentation in Reynolds' pension file reveals his birthplace in Granville Center, Bradford County. It may be only a coincidence but Reynolds called himself a boot maker "by trade." Was this a recollection of his youth? While growing up in Granville Center, in 1857, a tannery had been established. Because of that industry the community grew into a flourishing village. Prior to his enlistment on February 8, 1865, at Dixon, he had lived in Hume Township, Whiteside County, Illinois, post office then Sterling. He gave both blacksmithing and farming as his occupation. Since his discharge at Springfield he had lived at Coleta three years, then Roscoe, Missouri, for three years, then Nicaragua, Central America, for one year, San Marcos, Texas, for three years and had then served in the Texas Rangers for five years.

The Civil War record reveals little. Orcelus Reynolds, eighteen years old when enlisting on February 8, 1865, at Dixon, Illinois—hardly "a mere boy" as Gillett recalled—certainly realized that the war was nearly over. He was present at each two-month muster roll, the final dated at Savannah, Georgia, on January 20, 1866. He had earned $76.33 but was paid only $33.33 due to a stoppage of $43 for having lost some unidentified ordnance.[14] The official record provides only a glimpse of his unit's activities. In late February the 147th Illinois Infantry Volunteers were ordered to Dalton, Georgia, arriving there on the twenty-eighth. Their responsibilities included defending the garrison and protecting the railroad and garrison between Dalton and Ringgold. Reynolds experienced limited action; Dalton, located in the foothills of the Blue Ridge Mountains, had been a mere footnote to a more bloody battle such as Chickamauga. Colonel

Hiram F. Sickles reported that early on the morning of March 13 a group of guerrillas had captured the railroad hands only a mile from his line. Sickles mounted all the mules and horses he could and sent them in pursuit of the guerrillas. These troops did see action, as Sickles ended his report saying he had "Killed 2 of the cusses, captured 1. I am sorry they did not kill him also. What shall I do with him?"[15] On the very next day Sickles sent out a small detachment under Major Giles H. Bush who met up with seventy mounted Rebels. A fight followed in which several were killed or wounded. One prisoner was taken "from Lee's rebel army, Virginia."[16]

A group of Rebel guerrillas commanded by Maj. Thomas Polk Edmondson frequently demanded the attention of Reynolds' unit. He may have been more brutal than his better known contemporary William Clarke Quantrill, as a letter from Maj. Benton D. Fox to Maj. Gen. James B. Steedman, written on October 20, 1864, from Dalton, contained these lines: "There is a man by the name of Edmonson [*sic*] about this country, hanging and killing men and women. He has about seventy-five men with him."[17]

Thomas Polk Edmondson was the son of wealthy parents, farmer James and Virginia Rebecca Edmondson, born at Spring Place, Murray County, Georgia, in August 1844. When the war began he was one of the first to enlist in the "Murray Rifles" as a private on July 3, 1861. He was all of seventeen years old. The Murray Rifles went into the Confederate service as Company C, 11th Regiment, Georgia Volunteer Infantry, enlisting at Atlanta for the duration of the war. Nine days later Edmondson was detached to a Colonel Anderson's staff as a clerk in regimental headquarters. He was there until February 7, 1862, when he was transferred to recruiting duties.

Edmondson's blood was too hot to not see action and thus he paid a bounty for an unidentified man to replace him. He re-enlisted as a 2nd Lieutenant in Company C, 10th Georgia State Troops on May 16, 1862. He found the action he craved, participating in such engagements as Perryville and Stone River. He was promoted to the rank of captain on July 31, 1864 and then in the same year promoted to the rank of major.

By Match 1865 Edmondson was in his home area of Spring Place, in charge of a group of men known as the "North Georgia Scouts." He raided and harassed Union forces, and fought against citizens known to be sympathetic to the Union cause. His reputation now included killing women as well as men. His guerrilla-like warfare was so successful Major Fox as well as other Federal officers intensified their efforts to track him down.[18]

On the first of April Reynolds was one of a three-hundred-man expedition of the 147th, along with eighty cavalrymen of the 6th Tennessee, which engaged Confederate guerrillas. Major Bush was in command when on the next day the opposing forces occasionally fired shots at each other but inflicted only minor damage. That day Bush, with three companies of the infantry regiment and one of cavalry, moved up the river to find a crossing place. Meanwhile Col. Werner W. Bjerg, with the balance of the command, moved south for the same purpose. Bjerg's command found a crossing place at Pullen's Ferry and located a boat hidden on the opposite side. Two men swam across and despite being fired on secured the boat and found a quantity of forage and provisions, indicating the place as headquarters for guerrillas. Leaving Capt. Frank Clendenin with companies B and H, and twenty cavalry troops to guard the ferry, Colonel Bjerg with the balance of the command proceeded to find Major Bush. Returning with him they were attacked by an estimated 150 to 200 guerrillas. Clendenin's command was hit twice but the guerrillas were repulsed. During this exchange commander Major Edmondson, personally leading the charge, was killed. Also, "from 12 to 15 are known to have been killed or wounded." Edmondson received two wounds, one in the face and one in the neck. The body of Major Edmondson was turned over to his fellow Confederates, but his saddle and gun—and his coat—were kept by the Federals. Today he lies in the Spring Place Cemetery alongside his mother and father, a small tombstone informing the viewer he was born in August of 1844 and was killed in action, April 3, 1865.[19]

On the fourth Clendenin crossed the river and after a five-mile march camped his men for the night. On that day they "were saluted with a few harmless shots from the guerrillas" but suffered no damage.[20] The engagement in which Maj. Thomas Polk Edmondson was killed marks the final action experienced by Orcelus N. Reynolds during the Civil War.

When Reynolds enlisted in the 147th he was residing at Hume, Illinois, and was mustered in on February 8, 1865. On January 20, 1866, he was mustered out at Savannah, Georgia. Other Hume boys who were mustered out on the same day, and who were certainly by then companions of Reynolds, included Pvts. David Hess, Charles O. Morse, and John C. Rogers. Company B had been recruited from Whiteside County. A summary of the actions of the 147th shows it continually engaged in action against guerrillas. Three days after being mustered out, on January 23, the regiment started for Springfield, Illinois, via Augusta and Nashville, arriving at their destination on the thirty-first. Final payment and discharge was made on February 8, 1866. Reynolds must have quietly returned home to his family after war's end.[21]

Over half a century later Gillett wrote the following song of praise about his commander N. O. Reynolds, that the lieutenant was a native of Missouri, "and was always known as Major or 'Mage' Reynolds."

> It was said that Reynolds, though a mere boy, had served with the Confederates in the latter part of the Civil War. He was one of a party that captured a troop of Federal [*sic*] cavalry, the major of which was well supplied with clothing. The captors, however, were very scantily clad and Reynolds appropriated the major's uniform, hence his nickname "Mage." In later years, when I had grown more intimate with him and was probably closer to him than any other, I mentioned this story. He neither affirmed nor denied it, declaring he was a Missourian by birth, a bootmaker by trade, and that his early history could interest no one.[22]

Undoubtedly Reynolds did not wish to be questioned too closely on those early years. His later contemporaries in the Frontier Battalion believed he had fought for the South, a false belief but one which nevertheless could work to his benefit. Certainly the tale of the major's uniform being appropriated by Reynolds, resulting in a nickname which would last his lifetime, had its origin in this engagement in which Maj. Thomas Polk Edmondson was killed. Ironically his Texas contemporaries believed the coat was of an unidentified Federal major, but in truth "Mage" Reynolds was the Federal soldier, and the coat belonged to a Confederate guerrilla, Major Thomas Polk Edmondson.[23]

2

Joining the Frontier Battalion

"[O]nly sound young men without families and with good horses will be received."
—Adj. Gen. William Steele, May 6, 1874

Orcelus Reynolds was mustered out of the Union Army at Springfield, Illinois, in late January 1866. He then traveled 100 miles north to join his family in Coleta where he resided for three years. It must have been a happy reunion; many families suffered the loss of a son or father, or a brother, but the Reynolds family was whole once again. Unfortunately father Hiram Reynolds died in November of 1866, of unknown causes. With the head of household gone, there was little to hold the family together. The widow Reynolds and daughters Louisa, Ella, and Edla moved back to Granville Center, Pennsylvania. Emma remained in Illinois, but brother Orcelus relocated in Roscoe, St. Clair County, Missouri.[1]

Why Reynolds chose to move to Roscoe, some eighty miles southeast of Kansas City, is unknown. From 1869 to 1872 he did reside in Missouri, hence in later years it was easy for him to say he was "from Missouri." St. Clair County was in the heart of the home country of the notorious Younger brothers—Cole, Jim, Bob, and John—whose fame as brigands would only be eclipsed by the James brothers with whom they would share notoriety. During Reynolds' residence there he may have become acquainted with members of the Younger family, although he did not live there on March 17, 1874, when a gun battle between the Youngers and Pinkerton agents cost the lives of John Younger and two detectives. By then Reynolds had moved on but he certainly read of the battle as it received considerable newspaper coverage at the time.

Although one can only speculate if Reynolds at least knew members of the James-Younger gang at this point in his life, the early seventies, one fact, only recently discovered, gives evidence there was some acquaintance among them. In 1886 there was a military encampment held in Lampasas when Reynolds was a resident there. The newspaper coverage was extensive, and among individuals noted as being present, although not a player in the military aspect of the encampment, was the notorious Alexander Franklin "Frank" James, brother of the leader of the gang. Jesse James, the gang's leader, had been killed in 1882; Frank had surrendered and then been pardoned for his various crimes. As he was indeed in Lampasas it is very likely that N. O. Reynolds did meet Frank James on this occasion. The question remains: what did Reynolds do in Missouri following the end of the war, but also why did Frank James visit Lampasas, Texas, in 1886? Very likely Reynolds and James had been acquaintances back in Missouri, and perhaps the two got together and talked about "the old days" back in Missouri ion this occasion.[2]

From Roscoe, Reynolds spent a year in Nicaragua, Central America. Just as there is no contemporary documentation showing his activities during the three years spent in St. Clair County, Missouri, nothing has been found to document his activities in Nicaragua. Perhaps it was a business venture that attracted him there. A commercial treaty between that country and the United States guaranteeing citizens the right of transit between the Atlantic and the Pacific oceans through Nicaragua was in effect. In addition to citizens being able to travel freely, the transportation of merchandise was guaranteed, free from duties. Munitions of war and mail were also guaranteed safe passage. Reynolds may have been involved in any one of these aspects of commerce. All that is known with certainty is that Reynolds claimed to have spent a year in Central America before heading for Texas.[3]

Texas was considered the land of opportunity for hordes of soldiers, farmers, planters, pioneers, opportunists, and men wanting to simply start anew after their defeat in the war. The land was vast and the opportunities were limitless, but danger was ever present as well. During the Civil War and subsequent period of unrest, Indian raiding parties had wrecked havoc with settlers on the fringes of the frontier with their increased marauding. In the early 1870s the western half of the state was still wild frontier. Protection was provided by whatever local law existed and the Texas State Police, a force that many Texans deeply resented as many of the policemen were former slaves suddenly given authority over them. The Texas State Police was "[o]ne of the most hated organizations—and one of the most misunderstood—in the history of Texas" according to one historian.[4] The Comanchero trade was suppressed significantly and with white buffalo hunters destroying the Indian food supply some semblance of rest descended upon West Texas. But occasionally raids by Comanche, Kickapoo, Lipan, and Kiowa still took place; the defeat of the powerful Comanche tribe at Adobe Walls was not until 1874. When Reynolds arrived in Texas the state was in the last days of Reconstruction and final days of Indian warfare.

Reynolds established himself early at San Marcos, county seat of Hays County in Central Texas, some thirty miles south of Austin, although no reason has been determined as to why he chose that particular location over any of a hundred other settlements. He may have intended to open a business and become an active member of the community. Evidence to support this is in the form of a petition *against* the incorporation of San Marcos as a city. In early 1873, when the town's population was less than a thousand, many citizens petitioned for incorporation but others petitioned against it,. A petition to senators and legislators of the 13th Legislature read, in part:

> We the undersigned citizens and property holders of the town of San Marcos, learning that some of our citizens have petitioned your honorable body to encorporate [*sic*] our town, and being already overburdened with taxes, would most respectfully enter our protest against being encorporated, and request that your honorable body do not encorporate said town, and thereby subject the citizens thereof to an additional tax which they are but ill prepared to pay, and for which the advantages to be derived from the encorporation, if any, would be no adequate compensation.

Fifty-four citizens signed the anti-incorporation petition, one of whom was "O. Reynolds." Another was John W. Herndon.[5] These two men were later guards for the county sheriff, Zachariah P. Bugg.

Reynolds began his law enforcement career as a guard for the March 1873 term of district court, an inauspicious beginning but nevertheless a start in what would become a lengthy career enforcing the law. The only contemporary document corroborating Reynolds' early activity as a lawman is found in the minutes of the San Marcos police court for April 1, 1873. Sheriff Bugg employed men to guard prisoners during the March 1873 term of district court and presented bills so they would receive payment for that duty. They were H. A. McMeans,[6] George Ward,[7] John Hill,[8] J. M. Jennings,[9] I. F. J. Banta, C. Hill, Alexander Jennings, and Reynolds. These guards were to be paid two dollars per day; Reynolds earned ten dollars for five days' worth of "guard & Board." At the same meeting the sheriff presented a bill for eighteen dollars for "rent of house for jail." This amount was issued to John W. Herndon, the fifty-nine-year-old speculator who had earlier signed the petition against incorporation with Reynolds.[10] Was the makeshift jail in reality Herndon's house?

Bugg was considered an above average individual for the position of Hays County sheriff. Born in Giles County, Tennessee, he had served as a private in James Callahan's company of Rangers from San Marcos. He was first elected sheriff on June 5, 1858, and again on July 16, 1860. During the war he served as a 2nd Lieutenant, Company H, 23rd Regiment Texas Cavalry, C.S.A. He was elected sheriff again on November 8, 1872, and served until September 14, 1874, when he resigned. He and his jailer, John Hill, kept the jail "safe, and secure and well arranged" according to a later grand jury report.[11]

But by then Reynolds had moved on. Occasionally in the years of 1874 and 1875 postmaster Alfred Vom Stein published a list of unclaimed letters, and at least twice there were letters for "Orestes Reynolds," an obvious misreading of the name Orcelus.[12]

Guarding Hays County prisoners represented Reynolds' first, rather unglamourous, experience as a lawman. He would serve in many capacities, from jail guard to Ranger sergeant to the rank of lieutenant commanding, then serving as the city marshal of Lampasas and then sheriff of Lampasas County. Later in his twilight years he served as a deputy in Orange County. His career in law enforcement reached into the early years of the twentieth century.

Acting as a jailer may not have sounded impressive enough, as a later report identified Reynolds' first service as a *deputy sheriff* rather than a mere jail guard.[13] His trade of making boots was not satisfactory to newspaper reporters, either. But the boot maker by trade claim is documented as is the first known use of his "new" name, N. O. Reynolds. In the *San Marcos Times* of September 27, 1873, appeared this brief notice:

> WANTED.—A couple of journeymen shoe makers. Ready and permanent employment given. For particulars address N. O. Reynolds, San Marcos.[14]

Reynolds could not have realized it at the time but he was then in the geographical area that would have a great impact on his life and career. Lockhart, the seat of Caldwell County, where he would later reside and manage a saloon, was some twenty miles to the east; Austin, the seat of Travis County and the state's capital, which he would visit many times in his official capacity delivering prisoners, was to the northeast; Center Point, Kerr County, where he would live out his final years, was to the west; and Lampasas, seat of Lampasas County, where he would serve as the city marshal and then county sheriff, was one hundred miles to the north. The outlaws and desperate men he would come in direct contact were also in this general area. Men such as Sam Bass, John Wesley Hardin, James Madison Brown, Scott Cooley, John Ringo, and the Horrell brothers were all troublesome and dangerous men causing problems for lawmen of Central Texas and the Hill Country.

But before leaving San Marcos and looking for new experiences in Texas, Reynolds made a visit home to Bradford County, Pennsylvania. The brief notice in the local newspaper included an important line, stating that Orcelus Reynolds visited "his native home." We don't know if it was a matter of simply missing the comfort of home or if there was some other reason now unknowable.[15] Reynolds would enjoy those presumed comforts of home for only a short period, as his life would be radically different back in Texas.

As described above, a state of near emergency existed in Texas. Four years of war followed by five years of misrule had ground Texas into a chaotic state of affairs by 1870. The governor declared martial law in several counties and created the Texas State Police force, an organization that largely proved to be unacceptable to the average Texan. Accusations against the police included the breaking up of legal political meetings, stuffing ballot boxes, entering private dwellings without warrants, and making false arrests. Frequently the police were accused of killing prisoners in their custody out of convenience, then claiming the prisoner had to be killed as he "attempted to escape." Further disgrace fell upon the state when in 1872 Adjutant General James Davidson allegedly absconded to Belgium with over $37,000 of state funds, never to be returned. The act creating the force was repealed on April 22, 1873, after a Democratic majority was elected to the legislature.[16] N. O. Reynolds was certainly aware of the accusations made against the police force and scrupulously avoided any accusations that he ever engaged in such acts.

Richard Coke took over the governor's office in 1874 and among his first concerns was bringing a solution to the lawless situation. To replace the former police force, Coke created the Frontier Battalion, its objective both to protect the frontier line and to restore law and order within the interior. Six companies of seventy-five men each made up the Battalion, each one commanded by a captain; the force was placed under the command of Civil War veteran John B. Jones. He served with the rank of major and earned the respect of Texans everywhere, as well as winning the admiration of his men.

Jones was born in Fairfield District, South Carolina, December 22, 1834. He moved to Texas with his parents as a boy, and when the Civil War broke out he gave up stock-raising and joined the Confederate Army. After being appointed adjutant of the 15th Texas Infantry he served in the Trans-Mississippi Theater until war's end. He then returned to his farm in Navarro County, Texas.[17] An unidentified reporter sang his praises in the *Austin Statesman*, describing him as "scrupulously exact in

Major John B. Jones, from *The Encyclopedia of the New West*.

the discharge of his multifarious and onerous duties, a good disciplinarian, and one of the coolest and most daring men that ever faced a battery or met a bayonet charge." Jones further brought "military experience, unflinching courage and indomitable energy as earnests of success in the future."[18] After his service as major of the Frontier Battalion he was appointed adjutant general of the state.

On May 7. 1874, Jones wrote General Order No. 1, which provided the oath for officers, to whom necessary arms and ammunition would be sent, established the general location of each of the six companies, and made a general statement that captains were to use discretion "to the end that their commands may be as effective as possible for the protection of the frontier." An accurate account of all depredations and number of settlers killed and carried off was to be kept. In addition the amount of property stolen and the amount of property recovered, the number of Indians killed and the distance traveled on scouting expeditions was to be recorded and then reported to headquarters via monthly reports.[19]

The initial geographical assignments for the six companies were designated to provide a buttress of civilized Texas in the eastern half against Indian incursions from the western half. Company A, under John R. Waller, was stationed near the western corner of Erath County and was to patrol the country north to Stephens County and southwest into Brown County. Company B, under George W. Stevens, was to patrol from the area of Belknap—a community located less than a mile

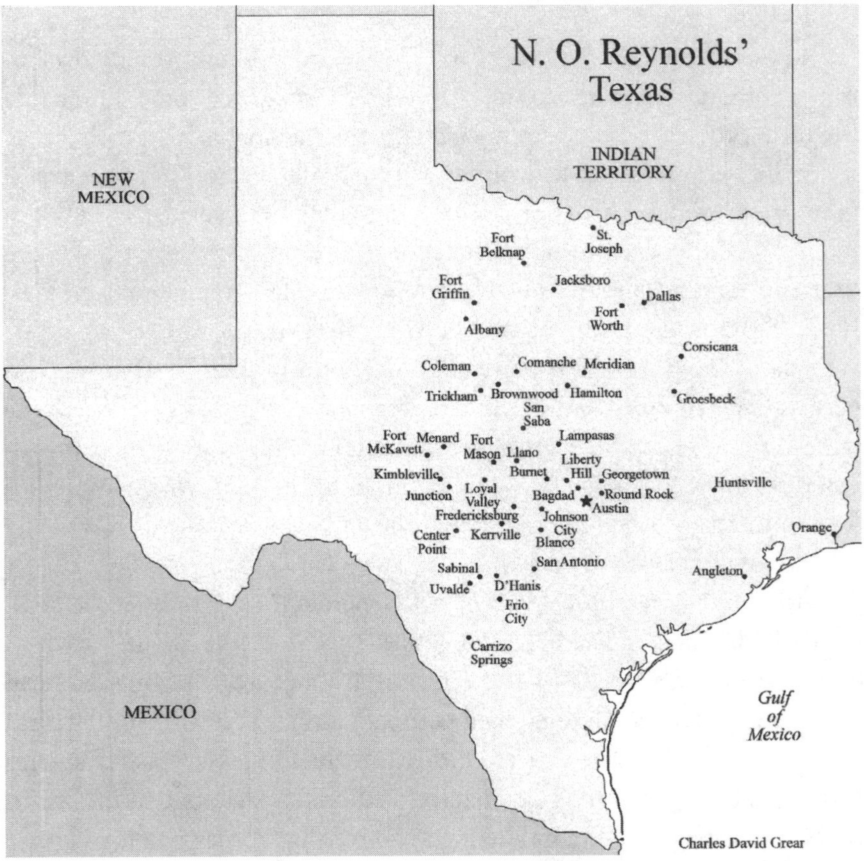

N. O. Reynolds' Texas. *Map by Charles David Grear.*

from Fort Belknap—into the northeast, halfway to Buffalo Springs and south to the center of Stephens County. Company C, under the command of E. F. Ikard, was to patrol north to the Red River and southwest halfway to Fort Belknap. Cicero Rufus Perry, commander of Company D, was stationed near Mason and was to patrol north to Brady's Creek and south to the southern line of Kimble County. (Reynolds would first serve under Perry.) Company E, under William Jefferson Maltby, was stationed in the vicinity of Santa Anna Peak in Coleman County and was to patrol northeast into Brown County and south to Brady's Creek. Company F, under Neal Coldwell, was stationed in Bandera County and was to patrol north to Kimble County and southwest to the Nueces River.[20]

In theory the "line" of troops as established by Jones presented a barrier against raiding parties. Major Jones visited the six companies along the line with several men from each company acting as his escort. In so doing he became better acquainted with his officers and to some extent the men, preventing many problems before they became costly in lives or money. To supervise the entire Battalion, Governor Coke named William Steele as adjutant general. The New York native had graduated from West Point in 1840 at the age of twenty. He experienced combat in fighting Indians in the Southwest, particularly in South Texas. In 1848 he had earned the rank of captain for his service in the Mexican War. When the Civil War broke out Steele resigned his commission to serve the Confederacy. At war's end he returned to Texas and entered the mercantile profession in San Antonio, working there from 1866 to 1873, before being appointed adjutant general.[21]

Adjutant General Steele prepared General Order No. 2 on the sixth of May. He stated his expectations clearly and to the point: "As it is expected that this force will be Kept actively employed during their term of Service only Sound young men without families and with good horses will be received. Persons under indictment or of Known bad character or habitual drunkards will be rejected."[22] If you were alone in the world there would be no parent or spouse to report the sad news to if you were killed in the line of duty.

Captain Perry wasted no time in mustering in Company D, as by May 25 he was in command of seventy-five men. William H. Ledbetter, formerly an attorney in Fayette County, Texas, and George Freeman were named as Perry's lieutenants, but by May 25 Daniel Webster Roberts had replaced Freeman who had resigned. Lieutenant Ledbetter and Roberts were second in command while Newton H. "Plunk" Murray,[23] Paul Durham, C. L. Deggs and N. O. Reynolds held the rank of sergeant. J. W. Blackwell, William Scott Cooley, J. P. Wynn, and Joseph O. Allen were corporals while the remaining sixty-one men were privates. Perhaps Reynolds was able to begin his service with the rank of sergeant because of his previous brief duties as a jail guard. Captain Perry swore the command in on May 25 at Blanco City.[24]

Captain Perry, a native of Montgomery County, Alabama, was then fifty-three years old, five-foot-ten-inches tall, dark complexioned with gray hair and eyes. Besides his farming and stock raising responsibilities, in January of 1874 Blanco County voters had elected him Hide and Animal Inspector. His experiences in Texas had been varied: he had taken part in the siege of Bexar under Ben Milam in 1835, had fought Indians off and on for years, had been with John H. Moore in the expedition against the Comanches in 1839, and had joined Jack Hays' company of Rangers in 1844.[25] On learning that Perry was named a captain in the newly formed Frontier Battalion the Austin's *Statesman* reported he had "spent an ordinary life-time on the frontier of Texas, and knows the character and habits of the Indians—their mode of conducting their expeditions, the time to anticipate their coming and their route in getting out of the settlements." Perry was termed a good trailer of Indians, and "his love of border warfare ensures the region . . . he is sent to watch over perfect protection."[26]

Lieutenant Roberts was keenly aware of the Indian threat as his family had suffered losses during 1874. Raiders had stolen horses and destroyed fences belonging to his father, Alexander "Buck" Roberts. Many other citizens had lost horses to raiding parties.[27]

N. O. Reynolds began his Ranger career as 4th sergeant of Company D on May 25, 1874. Whereas the census enumerator accepted whatever data was given by whoever was home at the time, when providing information for the muster and pay roll, Reynolds himself gave his personal description. He described himself as twenty-five years old, five-foot-ten-inches tall, dark complexioned, with blue eyes and light colored hair. He gave *Bradford County, Missouri,* as his place of nativity. Like many others he gave his occupation as farmer, no longer thinking of himself as a boot maker. Fellow sergeant Paul Durham was also from Hays County. He had earlier served in the Frontier Forces, mustered in at Austin on September 6, 1870, by Adj. Gen. James Davidson for a twelve-month period. He had served in Capt. James A. Swisher's Company P from September 6 to October 21, 1870, then as corporal from October 22, 1870 to February 5, 1871.[28] Durham and Reynolds may have become acquainted in Hays County prior to becoming members of Captain Perry's Company D, but no documentation has been found to verify this. Becoming a member of the Frontier Battalion assured a regular monthly salary as well as the opportunity to experience the excitement of fighting marauding raiders.

From this personal data provided by Reynolds it is obvious that he was willing to be truthful about the *county* but not the *state* of his origin. Informing Captain Perry he was twenty-five at the time he joined would mean a birth year of 1849, whereas for his pension application he gave the year as 1846. It is now impossible to explain the inconsistencies of these varying dates, other than to admit that Reynolds intentionally misled others about his past. He was now N. O. Reynolds, a Texas Ranger, a sergeant in Company D of the Frontier Battalion under the command of veteran Indian fighter Cicero Rufus Perry. It was as a Texas Ranger that he would find his place in the sun.

3

Removal of Cattle from their Accustomed Range

"I sent Sergeant N. O. Reynolds . . . to quell the intended riot."
—Captain C. R. Perry, October 24, 1874.

Governor Coke received many reports of Indian sightings in the months prior to the organization of the Frontier Battalion. The settlers were pleased at the prospect of the protection of Rangers when they saw Captain Perry establishing his first permanent camp at Celery Springs, six miles northwest of Menardville (now Menard) in Menard County. He was to operate generally north to the Colorado River and south to the mouth of Bear Creek on the North Llano River.

Captain Perry and the men of Company D experienced numerous engagements with hostiles during 1874 although the company saw no action during the month of June. Daniel Webster Roberts, now promoted to the rank of 2nd lieutenant after George Freeman declined the appointment,[1] was absent from camp with a squad from June 14 to 19. He returned after a 120-mile march on the South Llano and its tributaries but reported finding no recent sign of Indian activity. During the same period Lt. William H. Ledbetter and a squad were scouting on Brady Creek; after a march of 118 miles they gave up on finding any recent Indian sign.[2]

Although the Rangers spent a great deal of time and effort searching for hostiles, events were developing in the Mason County area that would have a profound effect on certain members of Company D. Cattle theft was becoming more than an irritant and some citizens were ready to deal with suspected marauders without benefit of the court system. On June 25 Wilson Hey, presiding justice of Mason County, wrote to Governor Coke complaining that "parties from Llano & Other Counties" were "Continually depredating upon the Cattle" of citizens in Mason County. He identified one Roberts (no relation to D. W. Roberts) as being in charge of men who "in open Violation of law" had been gathering and driving cattle from Mason County "without having them inspected as the laws direct." The man was Allen G. Roberts, who allegedly had hired the cattle thieves and was working with a dishonest cattle inspector identified as William Z. Redding. Having little confidence in the local authorities, Hey hoped the Rangers would assist the sheriff in breaking up the ring of thieves. A week previously, on the nineteenth, he had written Captain Perry, then conveniently camped some twenty-five or thirty miles away, requesting him to station all or part of his force at Mason, "to assist the Sheriff in serving processes issued by the proper authorities." But Governor Coke's response was totally opposite to what Hey had hoped, as "Since then I am informed that Capt. Perry Under Orders has moved his Command to Menard County above Menardville, a distance of 45 miles."[3] Sheriff John Clark, having been elected only six months before on December 31, 1873,[4] certainly experienced a degree of frustration as well, upon learning there would be no Ranger protection. Hey almost predicted mob violence as he further wrote that Rangers would have been able to "prevent the citizens from protecting their hard Earnings by taking the Law into their own hand[s]."[5] The men of Company D would not become involved in the Mason County difficulties for some months when the vigilante violence hinted at by Justice Hey became a reality.

Frontier Battalion Maj. John B. Jones was continually on the march to inspect his companies and meet with citizens as needed. He did not travel alone, but chose half a dozen men from each company as his escort, providing protection as he rode the Texas frontier line. In addition to being able to travel safely Jones could also better understand the quality of the men making up the battalion.

Major Jones and a portion of his new company did find themselves in a desperate struggle against overwhelming odds in July. The young men showed courage and enthusiasm in fighting the hostiles, but suffered casualties as well. It was in Lost Valley in Jack County, some twenty miles west of Jacksboro, that Jones and his escort had their first engagement with hostiles. The battle remains one of the most noteworthy actions of the Ranger force; in addition to being the first contact with hostiles, it placed Jones and his escort under fire, enabling the commander to see first-hand the quality of men. Also it allowed the young Rangers—some hardly out of their teens—to see how a Ranger should conduct himself under fire by observing Major Jones in action.

Two days prior to the Lost Valley engagement, about thirty Indians had attacked the J. C. Loving ranch in Jack County, some fifteen miles from Jacksboro. The group, which may have numbered as many as fifty, engaged a party of white men, leaving a cowboy named John Heath dead as well as stealing several horses. A squad of cavalry galloped after them but failed to catch up with them.[6]

The Lost Valley engagement took place on July 12, 1874, less than two months after the organization of the force. Jones' escort, still untried and consisting of young men with virtually no previous combat experience, was composed of officers Lieutenant J. T. Wilson and Capt. George W. Stevens and thirty-three men. Lieutenant Wilson had discovered a fresh Indian trail and Jones immediately started in pursuit. He initially estimated the group numbered about fifty warriors. In tracking them he allowed part of his force to become separated with a creek in between them. Now, while the Rangers were divided, about one hundred Indians charged. As Jones explained in a lengthy communication to Adjutant General Steele, he

> fell back two or three hundred yards when we were joined by the rest of our men, charged them, repulsed them, and drove them about two miles, when they took refuge among the rocks and caves of a mountain ridge. Several of our men having been dismounted in the charge, having only twenty eight present, all told, we were unable to dislodge them

> from their position, but formed in a ravine and continued firing at them until they ceased firing, and abandoned their position.[7]

Two Rangers lost their lives in this engagement: Privates D. W. H. Bailey and William A. Glass, both of Captain Stevens' Company B. In addition two men were wounded, Lee Corn of Captain Coldwell's Company F and George Moore of Captain Maltby's Company E. Thirteen horses were killed or seriously wounded in the fight and two slightly. The Rangers killed at least three of their attackers and wounded three others, but this was only an estimate as no doubt others were carried off. The escort did capture one horse, blankets, moccasins, bows and arrows, and other accoutrements. The fight lasted between two and three hours, with the Indians numbering between 125 and 150 warriors. In case Adjutant General Steele was not yet convinced, Jones further wrote that the hostiles were "beyond doubt, strictly on the war-path, and all well armed with improved breech loading guns . . . all well mounted, and painted, and decked out in gay and fantastic style." Not surprisingly one of Jones' men was scalped and his body "mutilated in a horrible manner, and shot full of arrows." When it was safe to examine the field of battle, Jones determined the attacking warriors were Kiowa, Apache, and Comanche.[8]

Major Jones was fortunate that his losses were not greater; having divided his force and apparently not thinking the odds were against him because there could be many Indians hidden in the ravines, he indeed was lucky that day. Nevertheless in his report to his superiors the "spin" he presented was that he and his Ranger escort were victorious. Historian Rick Miller in his biography of Major Jones described Jones' treating the results as "too succinctly" but nevertheless "Jones' esteem among his men was forged that day" and every Texan who read of the fight no doubt believed Major Jones was just the man to hand the hostiles the defeats they needed. After all, many a Texan, especially those who had lost loved ones or livestock to raiding parties, continued to believe that the only "good Indian" was a dead one. Continuing in his discussion of the Lost Valley engagement, Miller wrote that Major Jones' "lack of military-type discipline in approaching the Lost Valley led to his men being ambushed and placed in a difficult defensive posture."[9] This is certainly true, and it is indeed Jones' luck that prevented a greater loss of life, of either men or horses. Another historian, Robert M. Utley, provided the reason perhaps that Jones allowed himself to get into that dangerous position: stating that he was "a neophyte at Indian warfare" even though the Indians, led by Kiowa Lone Wolf, felt they were the victorious ones. But because Texans accepted Major Jones' interpretation, the version presented by Jones of the battle at Lost Valley "helped validate the existence of the Frontier Battalion."[10]

Was N. O. Reynolds one of the Rangers in this Lost Valley engagement? Jones did not prepare a roster of the men making up his escort, unfortunately; the company muster rolls only recorded the number of men absent on scout or on detached service with no identification, except

Members of Company D at a Ranger reunion, 1928. Standing from left: Ed Conn, W. W. Lewis, James Bomar, Henry Rishworth, and Will Traweek. Seated from left: Captain D. W. Roberts and Thomas Gillespie. Photo probably by Noah H. Rose.

Courtesy Former Texas Rangers Foundation.

in rare cases. The names of several who did participate in this engagement however, have been learned from contemporary sources as well as from the memoirs of the participants. Besides Jones, from Company A there were Zachary T. Wattles and J. T. Wilson; from Company B there were William A. Glass, David W.H. Bailey, Captain Stevens and Mel W. Porter; from Company D there were John P. Holmes, D. R. James, William W. Lewis, Horatio Grooms Lee, Walter M. Robertson, John V. Wheeler, and Edward B. Carnal; from Company F were George Moore and Lee Corn. Frontier Battalion Dr. E. G. Nicholson was also present. Others who possibly were there include S. P. Elkins and John O. Allen of Company D, Ira Long, James McIntire, Hugh E. Conn, William Scott Cooley, and Nelson Orcelus Reynolds. [11]

Captain Perry's monthly return, prepared on July 27 at Menard, shows a command of sixty-four privates, four corporals, four sergeants, two lieutenants, and himself. Of this aggregate of seventy-five men, nine were on detached service while thirty-two were on scout and one was listed as sick. Were the nine men on detached service with Major Jones making up part of his escort? Seemingly so as from Company D the following are believed to have been with Jones: Carnal, Elkins, Holmes, Wheeler, Robertson, Lee, and Lewis. It is *probable* that the other two with Jones were W. S. Cooley and N. O. Reynolds.

S. P. Elkins considered Scott Cooley such an effective fighter because as a child he had lost his parents—his "people"—to Indians in Palo Pinto County, and was held captive by them for a time. Later recovered, he had developed a great hatred of Indians, "and when he got a chance he fought them hard and close. Cooley had no fear and had a blood thirst for the Comanches."[12]

Although Elkins no doubt believed what he wrote, he did err in saying that Cooley had lost his family to Indians; his mother died during the decade of the sixties and his father was killed in 1870 by a white man who was in turn killed by the Cooleys.[13] There may have been a Cooley family who lost some of the family members to Indians but it was not the immediate family of W. S. Cooley. No record yet found suggests that Cooley and Reynolds had known each other prior to their joining the Frontier

Battalion only two months before. If during the Rangers' baptism of fire at Lost Valley, Cooley had proved himself to be an admirable fighter, a hero, one who conceivably had saved Reynolds' life, that would provide a reason for Reynolds in the following year *to resign from the Ranger service rather than pursue Scott Cooley, by then a fugitive from justice.* On the other hand, although it is intriguing to speculate why Reynolds preferred resignation rather than pursuing Scott Cooley, the fact that none of the Rangers later recalled Reynolds or Cooley by name in their reminiscences about the Lost Valley fight suggests that the pair, who were both to soon achieve a great degree of fame, may have been elsewhere when Major Jones and his men were fighting for their lives in the Lost Valley of Jack County.

One reason citizens normally gave a warm welcome to the Rangers when they camped in their vicinity is that there was little confidence in the regular United States troops. In the latter part of July, Captain Perry ordered Lieutenants Ledbetter and Roberts on a fifteen-day scout. He hoped they would come in contact with hostiles during that moon, although he had heard of none in the immediate vicinity. It was because Perry had established camp in the Menard area that the regular troops from Fort McKavett had begun scouting, but he noted, "their force does not amount to much."[14]

Austin became a scene of considerable excitement when a man from Blanco came into the city on the twenty-third and reported that some of Perry's company had gotten into a fight amongst themselves and eight of them had been killed. The word quickly spread and was apparently believed by many, enough so that Ranger Private Thomas P. Gillespie felt compelled to contradict the rumor: "Nothing of the kind he says has happened," reported the *Statesman* of Austin "and that everything with them is serene and lovely."[15]

Serene and lovely—among fighting Rangers!

Menard County officials also heard the rumor and reacted with a communication both serious and light hearted. District Clerk Thomas Cunningham, Justice of the Peace T. H. Mires and Sheriff William C. Martin advised the *Statesman* of Ranger activities.

Rangers of the 1870s: James B. Gillett (standing) and Thomas Gillespie.
Courtesy Pansy Gillett Espy

We noticed in your issue before the last, the report of a "chap" from Blanco, relative to a serious difficulty purporting to have occurred among Capt. Perry's men stationed in Menard county, and he, the disappointed appointee, kills eight of Capt. Perry's men in that report, though Capt. Perry says, they have answered roll call every morning since, and have drawn rations thrice, once a week. We have noticed a similar malicious report from the same locality, published in a Bexar [County] journal, and we felt it our duty, owing to the peaceable, gentlemanly deportment of Capt. Perry and his men, and on account of the inestimable service he, Capt. Perry, has so often rendered the civil authorities in suppressing crime by the example of gentlemanly

> deportment, set not only by himself, but his entire command without an exception, and arresting lawless characters and bringing them to justice, to impress the public mind with the truth, by saying that Capt. Perry and his men are, without any idle boast, worth being proud of on the frontier, where they want law and order maintained, and their homes and lives protected from the unfeeling and relentless savages.[16]

The *Statesman* failed to report any event which might have caused this rumor to gain credence, and dropped the matter after printing Cunningham's letter with no additional comment.

Rumors may have provided some distraction for the men but more meaningful results were noted in the August record of scouts, although Reynolds' name was not yet recorded individually. Captain Perry and ten men aided the civil authorities in bringing Felix Mann and several accomplices to justice on July 29.[17] Due to the loss of early Menard County court records it is impossible to determine what acts Mann and his pals were accused of but most likely they were guilty of nothing more than "treeing" the town of Menard. Ranger S. P. Elkins recalled the event years later while writing his memoir: one day a half dozen "outlaws" shot up the town. Sheriff William C. Martin asked for help from Captain Perry who "detailed six men to go and capture them. We had no trouble capturing them as we found them all asleep."[18] Less delicately, Ranger historian Bob Alexander also accepted their offense was no more serious than their "treeing the town" and wrote that the "inebriates were roused out of their stupor at gunpoint and safely jugged in Menard County Sheriff William C. Martin's lockup."[19] Mann was born in Smith County, Tennessee, and came to Texas in 1855, settling in Tarrant County. During those two decades before being arrested in a "stupor" he had begun his lifelong career in the cattle industry. He was considered a "patriarch of the cattle industry" and was described as a "pioneer Indian fighter and trail driver and Union veteran of the Civil War." Leaving Menard County in 1900 he began anew in Tom Green County and lived there until his death on October 14, 1925.[20]

On the following day, July 30, Thomas Hopper was arrested. Nothing is known of Hopper other than the fact that he was considered "a noted character" when he was arrested by Sgt. Newton H. Murray and several civil authorities. He may have been one of the men shooting up the town along with Mann. Hopper was released only after giving bond of $1,000 and paying a fine of twenty-five dollars.[21]

By mid-August it was apparent that the situation in neighboring Mason County was deteriorating further. Major Jones found the people "a good deal excited in regards to the cow thieves and rumors coming in now and more depredations of the Same kind. Will look into it and go after them if I find there is anything in it." In the same communication to Captain Perry he ordered him to move to "Soldier Camp" on the north side of the river above Pegleg Crossing as the water, grass, and wood were better there. Jones allowed perhaps a trace of levity in this letter to Perry, advising him that he would be only twelve miles below Menard and could send small parties up there occasionally "to let them know that they have not been turned over to the tender mercies of the Savages."[22]

Not all of the men who enlisted with Reynolds in May were able to continue their duties; some were honorably discharged, some dishonorably discharged. On September 15 Major Jones prepared his Special Order No. 15, which gives an indication of the variety of men with whom Reynolds worked. Second Sergeant Paul Durham requested "to be placed in the ranks as a private soldier for reasons best known to myself." The request was granted. Third Sergeant C. L. Deggs and Privates Michael Hill, John O. Allen, and James W. Patterson were honorably discharged on Dr. James Odiorne's certificate of disability. Private John Columbia was dishonorably discharged for harboring a deserter and for insubordinate conduct. Private Morton Sublette was dishonorably discharged "for being found asleep while on post as a sentinel."[23]

It was in the matter of Morton Sublette that Ranger Reynolds' name first appears in the Ranger records. Sublette, a twenty-two-year-old private who had been mustered in along with Reynolds on May 25, was from Clay County, Missouri, the same state that Reynolds claimed he hailed from. He was the son of Thomas and Catherine Sublette, and had been born in 1852.[24] Morton Sublette was guilty of falling asleep on duty but his Ranger companions must have respected him highly as they petitioned Major Jones to reinstate him to duty:

> We the members of Capt. C. R. Perrys Co D, Frontier Battalion, do ask the favor of you, to allow Morton Sublette to remain as a member in Co. D. He was drinking at the time, and not able for duty. The Corporal was not aware of the fact [and] he pledges himself to remain a sober man, & not touch intoxicating liquors while in the Service. [Sublette] Also pledges himself to perform faithfully his duties, while in the Company—We the undersigned Petitioners do ask That he be allowed to remain in the Company among us.

Among other signatures were those of Captain C. R. Perry, N. O. Reynolds, and W. S. Cooley.[25] Following their signatures the petition concluded: "Morton Sublette regrets very much having been under the influence of Liquor, and vows never to touch it again while in the Company. All of the Company signed [the] petition that were in Camp. [He] was always ready heretofore to perform his duties. And is ever willing to obey the orders of the officers above him."[26]

On September 16 Major Jones revoked Sublette's dishonorable discharge. He took "pleasure in restoring said Sublette to all his rights and good standing as a member of Said Company." But a little over two months later, on November 20, Morton Sublette let down all his Ranger companions by deserting. The muster roll carried no explanation, nor does it provide any clue as to whether he left the weapons belonging to the state of Texas in camp or took them with him. His actions were hardly fitting after the men had made the effort to get him reinstated in the company. Sublette's subsequent actions after his November 9 desertion have not been determined.[27]

Reynolds is mentioned in Captain Perry's October 28 letter to Major Jones written from Camp Elm, describing Reynolds' involvement in a possible riot. The presiding justice from Fort Mason had come to camp on the thirteenth "soliciting aid" from the company, stating that a "Vigilant Committee" was organizing. Mason County authorities had called on

Perry several times before and this time he reacted no differently. The captain had confidence in Sergeant Reynolds and on the day after the judge's visit he sent him with a squad of five men "to quell the intended Riot" or to assist the sheriff if requested. Reynolds returned to camp nine days later on the evening of October 22, and reported "all quiet in Mason Co. to the best of his knowledge." Apparently no written report was made of exactly what Sergeant Reynolds did. He certainly met with Sheriff Clark to identify potential trouble makers; possibly his quintet was sent to sites where trouble makers were known to congregate. Or possibly the scout made camp close to the jail, and with their high visibility all potential trouble makers remained out of sight. Although at the time things appeared to have quieted down, Sheriff Clark would soon have a great deal of trouble in his county. A number of the Rangers themselves would also experience concerns over the worsening situation in Mason County.[28]

Although it was not recorded which five Rangers made up Reynolds' scout on this occasion, Nick Ware and Scott Cooley were probably two of them as the monthly return noted their horses as well as Reynolds' mount were subsequently unserviceable. If Reynolds and Cooley had not participated in the Lost Valley fight, then perhaps their friendship was cemented on this scout to Mason.[29]

On the night of November 15 a dozen Indians passed near the Ranger camp but their trail was not discovered until the next morning, by Reynolds himself. He gathered up eight men and went on a hastily formed pursuit up the Big Saline. Although at times they believed they were close they couldn't catch up near enough to engage them. When their horses gave out they had no choice but to slowly return to camp. Perry, concluding his report, wrote that: "it was useless to follow them further [as] the boys['] horses being about given out [so they] returned to Camp November 21st 1874."[30]

On the very same day a band of Comanche warriors was sighted; this time Lieutenant Roberts with several others took up the chase. The Indians had descended Elm Creek in Menard County and passed within a few miles of camp, accidentally running into Rangers Scott Cooley and

William B. Traweek who were out on a beef detail. The band of Indians now gave chase to the two white men, who now needed help from their companions. Both sides exchanged ineffectual shots, but the gunfire brought out a number of Rangers and the chase began. Occasionally the warriors would stop to make a stand, but the Rangers' superior firepower quickly forced them to continue their flight. In all, five Indians were killed and scalped; one was captured after his horse was shot out from under him. After running a short distance on foot he saw he had no chance of escaping and turned to face his enemy. He fell to his knees and threw up his hands, shouting "bueno amigo." Had not Roberts been there the Indian would have been killed and scalped like his companions, as many a Texan believed in the adage that "the only good Indian was a dead Indian." Lieutenant Roberts took charge of the wounded warrior and saved his life.[31]

The wounded Comanche, So-no-ya-na, or "Little Bull," was taken into camp while his five dead companions presumably were left to rot on the rocky ground. Rather than turn the prisoner over to county authorities he was delivered to Austin to be sent to the State Penitentiary at Huntsville. A half dozen Rangers escorted Little Bull to Austin where he was paraded up Congress Avenue, the main street in the capital city, dressed in his "wild Indian costume, strapped to a mule." Large crowds followed the strange group up to the capitol grounds where hundreds gathered to stare. The *Statesman* pointed out that the "boys brought back some fresh scalps with them, and they report that Scott Cooley, who was fired at and run into camp, not only cut a wounded Indian's throat, but stripped a large piece of skin from his back, saying that he would make a quirt out of it."[32] Besides Cooley, participants in this notable fight included lieutenants Dan W. Roberts, L. P. Beavert, Corporal Newton H. Murray, J. V. Wheeler, G. W. Bryant, and W. B. Trayweek. Scott Cooley was riding Quartermaster Martin M. Kenney's horse, which was shot in the knee. Wheeler's horse was wounded in the jaw and Roberts' horse was wounded in the shoulder. Preventing the killing and scalping of So-no-ya-na, or Little Bull, made Roberts an exception among white men on the frontier. Mutilation was no stranger to Scott Cooley, on the other hand. As early as January 1872 three of the Cooley men had fought four Indians in Wise County, killing two, "one of whom they scalped."[33]

Little Bull was placed in the Travis County jail until he could be transported to Huntsville. On Saturday, November 28 a reporter from the *Statesman* and Adj. Gen. William Steele visited the jail, intending to interview him. A Mexican who had been held captive among the Comanches was found who could act as interpreter. Other than determining that Little Bull belonged on the reservation at Fort Sill, Indian Territory, not much was learned. On the following day he was placed on exhibit at the Opera House without Steele's knowledge. Handbills were printed announcing that such an exhibition would be made again, due to a business arrangement between the Rangers who had brought him in and liveryman Duncan J. Murchison. Adjutant General Steele learned of the plan and promptly put an end to the enterprise.[34] Little Bull eventually found companionship in Huntsville with Kiowa chieftain Satanta, incarcerated there for atrocities against the whites, but he soon developed consumption in confinement and died in prison about 1876.[35]

Cooley resigned from the service not long after. His discharge is dated December 9, 1874, showing only that he was mustered in on May 25 and honorably discharged. The state of Texas owed him $152 but he was indebted to the state for $86, so his final approved payment was only sixty-six dollars. The record gives no explanation as to why he left the service.[36]

Reynolds missed the engagement that resulted in the capture of Little Bull as he was out on a different scout. He returned to camp on November 21. Sergeant Murray, who frequently prepared Perry's monthly reports, wrote of this unsuccessful scout:

> [W]ithout affecting any thing after a hard chase of five days, horses wearied [*sic*] down, [having] followed trail of Indians for 3 days Through toughest Country on The breaks of [the] Llano, did all in his power to Capture the party he was in pursuit of, but failed in accomplishing his intentions.[37]

On December 17 frontiersman Rance Moore trekked the four miles from his ranch house to the Ranger camp and reported Indians had stolen some of his horses. Roberts sent out Sergeant Reynolds and a detachment of twenty-three men immediately but due to the "very hard mud" most of the horses wore down quickly. Only three Rangers were able to continue the pursuit: Corporal James Hawkins and Pvts. John Capp and William Springer.

Company D Ranger James Hawkins, proudly showing his Winchester, 1875.
Courtesy Pansy Gillett Espy.

They caught up with the Indians on the divide between the Big Saline and Elm Creek. When within shooting distance the pursuit began in earnest. Over the lengthy fight Hawkins killed one and scalped him while Springer killed one as well. Capp and Springer each wounded one. The starving Indians were able to hold on to their weapons, several needle guns, bows and arrows and lances, and made their escape. From the point where the trail was struck and where the last one was killed was a distance estimated at forty miles.[38]

This engagement resulted in considerable publicity for Roberts' group, not only being reported in the *Statesman* of Austin, but the *Daily Telegraph* of Houston as well.[39] The latter concluded its report: "Two Indians were killed and two wounded, and fifteen horses captured. Major Jones' command 'gets away' with the red butchers every time an engagement takes place."[40]

Roberts no doubt reviewed his own report prepared in 1874 when writing his reminiscences published as *Rangers and Sovereignty*, almost forty years later.

> Sergeant Reynolds had come into camp late in the evening and reported the last he had seen of the three men they were still in pursuit of the Indians. At nightfall everything in camp was deathly still. . . . Finally one man said he heard the sound of horses coming, and human voices, and still all was anxiety. When they came up to the corral one of them sang out "all's well." Then the yell in camp went up which paid for all our anxiety.[41]

One of the sixteen horses recovered belonged to rancher Rance Moore.[42]

At year's end orders came to reduce the size of the various companies due to inadequate appropriation from the legislature. Captains Perry, Maltby, Ikard, and Stevens and Lieutenant J. T. Wilson were all discharged as well as each company reduced numerically. Daniel Webster Roberts was named lieutenant commanding to replace Perry. Roberts' command, now composed of two sergeants, three corporals, and only twenty-five privates, was expected to accomplish what a few months before Captain Perry was to do with seventy-one.[43]

Reynolds continued with Indian scouting as his main responsibility. From January 12 to 16, 1875, he led a detachment of fourteen men searching the tributaries of the Llano and the divide between the San Saba and the Llano Rivers, marching to the head of the Big Saline, then to the head of Gentry Creek, down Gentry to the Llano at the mouth of Cedar Creek, a distance of 175 miles, searching continually for recent Indian sign. Roberts no doubt wrote with pride in his January report that some fifteen or twenty families had recently emigrated to that section and settled on the Llano River.[44] The Comanche and Kiowa menace was being greatly reduced due to the efforts of Company D.

A trio of Texas Rangers. This image is from the original tintype in the collection of James B. Gillett. The man seated at left is probably William Scott Cooley. Figure seated on right possibly N. O. Reynolds. *Courtesy Pansy Gillett Espy.*

4

A White Man Takes a Scalp

". . . whereupon the fiend mounted his horse and rode off."
—Fredericksburg Freie Presse, August 17, 1875

Fort Mason had been established in 1851 on Post Hill in Mason County by Brevet Major H. W. Merrill. Through the years the fort had been abandoned and then reoccupied, before being abandoned for the last time on March 23, 1869. In 1936 the state erected a State Historical Marker which made only a brief allusion to the violence the fort had witnessed, which once flared between white men and Comanche, between American soldiers of differing ideology, and then between the feuding factions designated as "Anglos" and "Dutch": the followers of Sheriff John Clark and the friends and associates of William Scott Cooley, one-time Ranger of Company D and friend of N. O. Reynolds.[1]

There was no single cause for the difficulties that have become known as the Mason County War, or "Hoo Doo" War, but the problems were exacerbated by the ethnic differences between the Germans and the Americans. The former had supported the Union in the late war and the hard feelings between them and southern-sympathizing Texans had not entirely subsided even a decade later. As cattle theft increased, hard feelings turned to violence and men formed mobs to protect their property due to the ineffectiveness of the local law. The most violent action of the feud was the lynching of several prisoners, arrested for cattle theft, who were taken from the Mason jail in February 1875. An additional important "spark" was the killing of Tim Williamson on May 13 of the same year. Lieutenant Roberts investigated and concluded that the killing was committed by the Germans. Other cattlemen, less than honest in their own dealings, took advantage of this turmoil "to excite the Americans against the Germans." This, in Roberts' opinion, amounted to the causes of the Mason County War.[2]

Although the threat of Indian activity still remained a reality in 1875, of greater immediate concern—at least to the stockmen of Mason and the surrounding areas making up the Hill Country—was the increasing amount of cattle rustling. To eradicate the problem many men joined mobs to administer their own brand of justice.

Lucia Holmes, wife of attorney Henry M. Holmes, was an astute observer of events in Mason and confided her thoughts and activities in her diary as they occurred. She wrote that on Saturday, February 15, 1875, Sheriff Clark arrested and brought to the jail nine men who were charged with stealing cattle. Mrs. Holmes identified only one in her diary—a Mr. Barkas [*sic*][3]—suggesting he was the only well known prisoner of the group. On Thursday, February 18, some three dozen mob members raided the jail and forced jailer Wohrle to surrender the keys to the cells. Wohrle, the deputy sheriff on duty when the mob made its forced entrance, was a twenty-nine-year-old Union army veteran who had earned the rank of corporal before being discharged at Fort Craig, New Mexico Territory. From there he went on to Mason and settled down to family life, having married Helena Geistweidt on August 5, 1872.[4] On the night of the jail delivery Wohrle at first bravely refused to surrender the keys, but members of the mob choked him and knocked him around. Seeing the treatment the mob was giving her husband, Mrs. Wohrle became hysterical. This stress upon the pregnant woman caused her to miscarry seven days later.[5] The unnamed baby was the fourth victim of the feud's violence. Although deputy Wohrle refused to give up the keys, the mob stormed the jail itself and forcibly took the prisoners out of the cells.

Five prisoners were taken out and marched some distance from the jail where ropes were thrown around their necks. Attorney Henry M. Holmes, an occasional contributor to the *San Antonio Daily Herald*, wrote that about midnight "a mob of . . . mounted men came to the jail . . . took five of the prisoners out, and about three quarters of a mile from town hung three [,] shot one and one escaped."[6] Elijah "Lige" Baccus (as his name is properly spelled according to Dave Johnson) and his cousin Peter Backus, Charles Johnson, Abe Wiggins, and Tom Turley composed the quintet taken from the jail. Sheriff Clark and Lieutenant Roberts were both in Mason and attempted to gather a posse to combat the mob in hopes of saving the prisoners. Before Roberts and his half dozen men could arrive on the scene some members of the lynch mob started shooting at the prisoners to finish them off. Roberts and Clark mistakenly thought they were the ones being shot at—or so they claimed—and fired back at the mob. The exchange of gunfire produced no results as there were no casualties among the mob, so far as known, nor were Roberts or any of his posse hit. The arrival of Clark and Roberts and their quick action did cause the mob to break and run.

In spite of the efforts of Roberts and Clark, the mob's work was partly successful. The Backus cousins were both dead, hanging from ropes. Abe Wiggins was severely wounded and died the following day. In the confusion caused by the exchange of shots between the mob and Roberts and Clark, Charles Johnson managed to pull the noose off his shoulders and flee the scene. Tom Turley was close to death but survived the ordeal.[7] He was again placed in jail but when rumors started to circulate that the mob intended to return and finish the work they had started Turley managed to escape. Noted desperado Caleb Hall, incarcerated with him, seized the opportunity to escape and left the area as well.[8] Holmes, Roberts, and others in Mason believed that Sheriff Clark simply had not done his duty in protecting the prisoners, an attitude that was shared by many citizens of Mason as well.[9]

This remains one of the deadliest acts of mob violence in Texas history. The mob had others to eradicate, as four days later Lucia Holmes noted that the body of a dead man was found on the road with a note pinned to his shirt, saying: "he wouldn't stop killing cattle" so he was therefore killed.[10]

Shortly after this mob action, a man named William Wages was killed, presumably by members of the same mob that had participated in the hanging of the Backus cousins. Wages' only known criminal activity was killing cattle other than his own, for their hides, an offense for which he was fined twenty dollars in early December 1874.[11] Lieutenant Roberts was aware of the Wages killing but apparently made no effort to determine who the guilty individuals were, or if he knew chose to do nothing. Possibly Wages had been involved in cattle theft, or was one of those acting "suspicious," as Roberts considered the work of the mob as beneficial to the community. He concluded one report to his superiors, discussing the social conditions of Mason County, by saying of the mob, "As yet—theyv [*sic*] harmed no good man."[12] Roberts did not explain how he had determined if Wages was a good man or bad, although in Roberts' mind the fact that he had been convicted of killing cattle may have automatically marked him as a "bad" man. This lack of objective investigating, or at least providing any record of it, remains frustrating to historians. We must assume that Roberts did learn much about the workings and membership of the mob and the other county officials who sanctioned it, but he made no explanation as to how he determined who was good or bad. A few other men were ordered to leave the country or else be given the same treatment as Wages.

Strangely, Lieutenant Roberts made no report to Major Jones or Adjutant General Steele of his involvement in resisting the mob's action that night in Mason. Possibly he chose not to do so because of his own ineffectiveness; Sheriff Clark's own actions were equally unworthy of an elected official. From Camp Saline on March 1 Roberts communicated to Major Jones that "everything quiet" in that immediate section. He did write of William DeLong's unprovoked attack on a quartet of Indians, however. DeLong had been out hunting on Bois d'Arc Creek, a tributary of the Llano River, when he saw the four Indians. He whistled to attract their attention and then shot one down. As the others ran off he fired again, hitting one. DeLong later found the dead Indian and "considerable quantity" of blood on the trail where the remaining pair had carried off their wounded companion.[13] Seemingly Roberts was eager to report actions against Indians but chose to avoid discussing in detail the work of the mob in Mason County.

As yet Sergeant Reynolds had had no direct involvement in the Mason County War. On March 8 he was scouting on the Llano River with a fourteen-man detachment, searching as far north as the mouth of Bear Creek, and then scouting up Bear Creek, Gentry Creek, and the Big Saline. In addition to looking for recent Indian sign he intended to capture Tom Turley and Caleb Hall, the two prisoners who had escaped from the Mason jail the night of the seventh of March. Three days later, after covering seventy-five miles of the Hill Country, Reynolds had to report he had failed "to find any trace of Savages" nor had he captured Turley or Hall.[14] Reynolds was insightful enough to realize that the Indian menace was diminishing and the energies of the Frontier Battalion would be focused more and more on white desperadoes.

Roberts had gone to Austin, perhaps to lobby for his company, and left Sgt. Newton H. "Plunk" Murray in charge. Twenty-five years old when he was mustered into the Frontier Battalion on May 25, 1874, the same day as Reynolds, the Clay County, Missouri, native began his service career as a sergeant, as did Reynolds. His enlistment was for a three-month period.[15] While nominally in charge, Murray received a telegram from Mason County Judge I. N. Everett asking for help to preserve order during district court. Murray sent a detachment of nine men to assist the sheriff, which squad was out until March 13. "All quiet as far as I know in this vicinity" was the report. Obviously Murray was kept in the dark as far as recent events in Mason County were concerned. This was a remarkable statement in view of the recent lynching of three men, the mysterious killing of William Wages, a jail break, and some individuals fleeing the country under threat of similar violence. Probably the mob was quietly biding its time, knowing the Rangers could not remain there indefinitely.[16]

In spite of the optimistic "all quiet," on March 26 Reynolds with a nine-man detachment was sent to Mason to assist Sheriff Clark as needed. They returned to camp three days later after determining that the "malice" existing between the sheriff and other parties had been "Compromised." One wonders if Reynolds had arranged a meeting between Sheriff Clark and his opponents to iron out that "compromise." Reynolds failed to provide any details of this meeting, unfortunately. Roberts had learned

A general view of Mason where much of the violence of the "Hoo Doo" war occurred. Photo by McArthur Cullen Ragsdale in 1878. *Courtesy Jan Appleby and the Mason County Historical Commission.*

that there had been complaints against several unidentified men and so sent Reynolds to investigate.[17] In a communication dated April 1 Roberts calmly reported "everything quiet in regard to the Mason trouble."[18]

Although outwardly Mason County may have seemed tranquil, in late March Thomas Gamel, a rancher and veteran of Company L, 3rd Frontier Battalion from the Civil War period and one-time member of Governor E. J. Davis' Texas State Police force, believed he was a marked man and gathered his followers together for protection. Gamel had earlier been associated with Sheriff Clark, but when he (Gamel) refused to participate in the killing of prisoners he was marked for death by the mob. He had some sixty-two men in Mason, all Anglo. Clark's followers were essentially German and with the Americans behind Gamel the disputes over cattle were now developing more and more into an ethnic feud.[19]

During much of April Reynolds was away from camp on scouting duty. He began one scout on April 4 with fourteen men, reconnoitering in the vicinity of Kerrville, Kerr County. A week later they remained after covering two hundred miles without finding any recent Indian sign and everything quiet. Obviously the Indian threat had moved much farther west, and a temporary peacefulness existed in Mason County.[20]

Roberts wrote to Major Jones on April 15, again reiterating that Mason County was quiet. The "excitment among the stock men of Mason County—seems to have subsided" he reported, "all gone to work & quit quarreling." Roberts optimistically expressed his belief that the "nest of thieves" that had congregated around the mouth of Johnson's Fork on the Llano River had left; in fact he denied there being a "considerable band of loafers" anywhere on the Llano. Those who had encamped there during the winter had apparently all "left for other quarters."[21]

In addition to the increased activity of Anglo outlaws, Major Jones had another concern, that of the legislature reducing the appropriation for frontier defense. Jones had to inform Roberts that due to a 50 percent reduction, "we will not be able to recruit our numbers any, and may have to disband a portion of the force now in the field."[22] The reduction was to be significant.

To add to the potential of outright warfare—in spite of the various reports attesting to the tranquility in Mason County—the town of Mason was rapidly taking on the semblance of an armed camp. When both groups of armed men were in Mason together, the followers of Gamel and those sympathetic to Clark, they managed to remain peaceful, and finally agreed that there would be "no more mobs or hangings."[23] It was an admirable intent, but on May 13, Tim Williamson, a prisoner in the custody of Sheriff Clark, who happened to be a close friend of former Ranger William Scott Cooley, was killed. Williamson and Carl Lehmberg, a Llano County cattleman, were with Sheriff Clark when, according to a garbled Fredericksburg report, they were "attacked by a disguised mob . . . and that Tim Williamson was literally riddled with bullets. Sheriff Clark escaped, but Mr. Carl Lehmberg, who is a prominent merchant of Llano county, has not been heard of." [24] Certainly Clark had nothing to fear from the assassins, and his reported "escape" was for appearances only.

The Fredericksburg report was picked up by numerous other newspapers, which gave further notoriety to the troubles of Mason County. The murdered Timothy P. Williamson was a cattleman and had made several trips to Kansas markets. In either 1872 or 1873 Williamson brought back Scott Cooley with him. In 1875 when he was killed, he was about thirty-three years of age. He left a ranch, a wife (a cousin of Charles Johnson who had narrowly escaped death by the mob in February) and five children.[25]

Attorney Henry M. Holmes provided important details:

> [Williamson] again was in the hands of the law, in the person of deputy sheriff John Whorlia [*sic*], disarmed, and on the road to Mason to renew a bond for his appearance at the District Court. I have learned that a good bond was offered for him at Lehmberg's, where the re-arrest was made, but was not accepted, for what reason I know not but certain it is that whilst on the road to Mason with his surety Chas. Lehmberg he was set upon by 10 or 12 men with their faces blacked and foully murdered. No effort whatever so far as known was made by the authorities to endeavor to discover the perpetrators of this outrage further than to hold a coroner's inquest over the remains.[26]

While these important events were taking place, Reynolds was on the trail of fugitives elsewhere. On June 15 he and an eight-man squad left for Fort McKavett in search of Burt Powell, charged with cattle theft, and another fugitive identified only as Jones. Three days later they returned without having found the pair. Roberts complained in his report that the fugitives had learned the Rangers were coming "& dispersed in every direction[,] the largest squad in direction of [the] Nueces [River]. Burt Powel was reported with the band—I think they were regular thieves—though they [have] stolen nothing on Llano [River] that I know of." Then from June 25 to 27 Reynolds with ten men was searching for other fugitives on the Llano but again returned to camp without having made any arrests. But even while concentrating on white outlaws, one had to be aware of the possibility of Indian depredations. A woman was supposedly attacked and "shot with a gun" in mid-June, but Roberts was unable to determine the truth of the report.[27] Indians were definitely in the area as marauders raided the horse herd of Rance Moore and made away with several head; at least it was the common belief the raiders were Indians.[28]

In spite of the several earlier reports describing the outward quietness of Mason County the conflict between groups of white men intensified. While Reynolds was on a seven-day scout during the first part of July, Lieutenant Roberts and six men went to Mason to assist the authorities while district court was in session. More trouble had been anticipated by some and the Rangers had been called upon to assure court would be held without interruption.[29] Lieutenant Roberts was called to testify before the grand jury about the night the jail was mobbed, but, strangely, refused to reveal what he knew. Later he claimed that he was evasive with the truth as he suspected that some members of the jury had been members of the mob. Attorney Holmes was also on the scene, but expressed in his correspondence a degree of disappointment, writing that "in spite of the admirable charge of the Judge any efforts that the Grand Jury may have made were fruitless as far as bringing any of the murderers to justice."[30]

On July 21 someone fired on a group of stock hunters only ten miles west of Mason. There was considerable uncertainty as to whether Henry Doell, who was killed, and August Keller, who was wounded, had been attacked by white men or Indians. Lieutenant Roberts expressed the opinion that the two men were victims of the latter. Roberts, examining the trail prior to the rain washing it away, estimated that there were fifteen hostiles in the party.[31]

Attorney Holmes wanted it to be perfectly clear that the Indian menace was still a reality in Mason County.

> This murder [of Henry Doell] was at once assumed by the supporters of the sheriff to be the work of white men in revenge for the death of [Tim] Williamson. . . . was not a scintilla of evidence pointing to any conclusion that other than Indians did it except their own imagination. . . . [Doell and Keller] were camped on high open ground, no cover for any lurking foe, an impossibility for any one to distinguish between forms laying on the ground unless they had followed the party up, and seen where they slept, which it would have been impossible to do undiscovered, and further their horses [were] stolen and driven out of the country and not heard of since, and no tracks but those of moccasins.[32]

Scott Cooley had been honorably discharged from Company D on December 9, 1874.[33] What the friend of Sergeant N. O. Reynolds—and friend of the murdered Tim Williamson as well—did after leaving the Rangers is uncertain; he may have worked the land with farmer John "Humpy" Jackson. Whatever he did he was not going to ignore the death of his friend Williamson.[34]

According to Ranger James Buchanan Gillett,[35] Cooley did remain in the immediate area, and even attended district court where he learned the part John Wohrle had played in the Williamson killing. It was not long before he decided on how best to deal with his enemies: he would treat them as he had treated Indians not long before. He had learned the names of two men involved in the death of his friend: John Wohrle and Peter Bader, the former for shooting Williamson's horse, the latter for shooting Williamson. His personal trail of vengeance started with John Wohrle, the deputy sheriff who prevented Williamson from escaping the mob.

Cooley found him on August 10, 1875. Wohrle, Charles "Doc" Harcourt, and a third man known to history only as Harcourt's "Yankee" were digging a well near the heart of Mason. During their work Cooley, described as "a young man of about twenty-four years of age" approached on horseback and stated that he was looking for two horses. Wohrle was taken off his guard at the friendliness of the stranger and they conversed. Cooley asked for a piece of leather with which to fasten his gun to his saddle, a request with which Wohrle complied. While the stranger was fixing the leather to his saddle, Wohrle began lowering Harcourt to the bottom of the well. When his head was below the surface, Cooley calmly asked: "Wohrle, why did you kill Williamson?" He answered, "Because I had to." Cooley then answered: "For the same reason I am killing you." He then shot Wohrle in the head. "Yankee" jumped over the dying man and ran, ignoring Harcourt who tumbled to the bottom where he remained senseless for some time. "The murderer then fired six shots into the body of Wohrly [*sic*], stabbed it in four places with his knife, and finally took his scalp, whereupon the fiend mounted his horse and rode off." The *Fredericksburg Freie Presse* may have seen the official coroner's report enabling it to provide such a detailed description. There was little confidence in the law ever capturing the killer, as the reporter concluded: "It is probable that the murder[er] will evade all earthly punishment as he is evidently the paid assassin of men who will back him up."[36]

Henry M. Holmes described the Wohrle killing as "the last horrible tragedy," at least up to that point in time, but denied the rumor that Cooley had acted as a paid assassin. "I deny that it is the general belief that Scott Cooley was paid. The day the news of Williamson's murder came to the Ranger camp, to which force Cooley at one time belonged, he sat down and cried with grief for the loss of the one who he said was his best friend in the world, and declared then, that he would have revenge, and this before it was possible he could have had any communication with any of Williamson's friends."[37]

Up to this time Scott Cooley's victims were Indians with scalping and mutilation as a matter of course. Now his victim was a white man, a deputy sheriff, and Wohrle too became a victim of scalping and mutilation. Whereas killing Indians may have made Cooley a popular figure among his peers, killing a white man made him a fugitive from justice. On September 6, Governor Coke offered a reward of $300 for anyone who could arrest and then deliver Cooley to the sheriff of Mason County. All one had to do was to deliver him to the jail. The reward notice described Cooley as having a dark complexion, dark hair, and small black eyes. It stated he was five-foot six inches tall, had legs rather short in proportion to his body, a "mincing walk," and claimed to be half Indian. The notice further pointed out that Cooley had been a Ranger under Major Jones in 1874.[38] Wohrle had been killed on August 10; nine days later Cooley thought he had located his second victim, Peter Bader, and shot him as he worked in his field. Cooley erred in his choice of victims this time, as it was not Peter that he killed but his brother Karl. It was Peter Bader who had killed Tim Williamson, although Karl may have been one of the mob members present.

Since Reynolds and Cooley had been close associates during the days of 1874 it is probable that the pair continued to remain in communication with each other, even after Cooley became a fugitive. Events would prove their loyalty was deep. Cooley was out of the immediate area avoiding

Ranger patrols, but Reynolds and Cooley could still have remained in close contact with each other.

From July 2 to 12 Reynolds was on a scout on the Llano River but failed to find any sign of Indian presence.[39] On August 27 Major Jones wrote to Roberts informing him of an "important scout" planned in September; he specifically wanted Sergeant Reynolds and twenty men from Company D.[40] The fact that Jones requested Reynolds rather than another clearly reveals that the sergeant was earning a reputation for his leadership abilities.

On September 6 Reynolds left the Las Moras camp with a squad of twelve men for a scout on the Llano; they returned on the fifteenth. Ten days later he and a twenty-nine man detachment left camp to join up with Captain Neal Coldwell of Company F, intending to intersect with Major Jones' escort. Jones then received orders from Adjutant General Steele to return to camp but retained Reynolds and eight men to accompany him to Fort Mason.[41] It was as he was on detached duty with Major Jones that N. O. Reynolds was placed in the middle of the violence of Mason County.

Earlier that month correspondent Holmes had written another letter, only this time to Governor Coke himself. He now told of a shooting on September 6 in which Mose Baird was killed and his companion George Washington Gladden was severely wounded. The men "were alone and were Killed by a large number of Germans with Mr. Jno Clark, Sheriff of the County at their head. The Germans claim that Beard [*sic*] and Gladden began the fight firing about fifty shots at ten or twelve paces from Mr. Clark. No one was hurt however except the two men Beard and Gladden." One wonders who believed the report that two men had first fired fifty shots from ten or twelve paces without hitting anyone. Because Baird, the slain man, was a "man of large connxions [*sic*] in Burnet County" Holmes feared if something was not done "a civil war will be inaugurated. The County authorities are completely paralyzed and can do nothing." He reported that a town meeting had been held not long before in which Clark and other county officers were requested to resign. Clark refused, and remained in effect the leader of "a band composed exclusively of Germans." Although Clark was the county sheriff Holmes accused him of being a fugitive from justice, claiming that there were indictments against him for robbery and false imprisonment.[42] Indeed Clark, although the sheriff, did have a black spot on his record, having been indicted in August 1874 for robbery.[43] He had at least fifty men at his disposal and, according to Holmes, "all those who do not belong to the mob are in danger and quiet can hardly be restored until Some Steps are taken to bring the late murders (10) to justice, and this cannot be done in this county by any jury Grand or petit Summoned from the vicinage."[44]

Now Governor Coke did take notice. He conferred with his adjutant general who ordered Major Jones to send a lieutenant and at least thirty men to Mason County to preserve the peace. They were to remain there until receiving further orders and were subordinate to the civil law.[45] Jones had been planning to march up the line of Ranger camps but had to abandon that idea due to the Mason County feudists. He hoped to have "a friendly interview with them and if possible reconcile the difficulty and induce both parties to disband and return quietly to their homes."

Moses Baird's original headstone; he was a victim in the "Hoo Doo" War of Mason County. *Courtesy Dave Johnson.*

Major Jones and a detachment of only twenty men, including Reynolds, arrived at Mason on September 29. The group had narrowly missed a fire fight with one of the feuding parties, as while passing Keller's store en route to Mason, Jones saw fifteen or twenty men armed with Winchesters and pistols "rise up from behind a stone fence, in a fighting attitude." He halted his command in order to communicate with the group, learning that they were ready to defend themselves against the Gladden and Baird party. The men feared that they were coming to Mason either that day or that evening with the intention to "burn out the Dutch."

The town of Mason, Jones found on further investigation, was far from peaceful. "I find the homes closed [and] a death like stillness in the place and an evident suspense if not dread in the minds of the inhabitants. Every man is armed."[46] The day before his arrival Daniel Hoerster, county brand inspector, had been ambushed and killed on the town's main street. Jones believed the shootists were John Baird, George Gladden, and Scott Cooley. The trio attempted to kill Peter Jordan and Henry Pluenneke as well but the pair escaped to find refuge in the Mason hotel. The two men exchanged shots with the killing trio who in turn shot into the hotel, causing great alarm to the women and children within. They then mounted their horses and rode out of town. Sheriff Clark made a token effort to pursue them but returned empty handed.[47]

Clark may indeed have gone after them with good intentions, but L.M.P., a *San Antonio Daily Herald* correspondent, had no confidence in the Mason authorities. He described the killing of Hoerster, adding that another man had been wounded and another thrown from his horse. "The murderers remained in town some time after the killing, then rode off triumphantly to the hills, their place of safety, where they no doubt will plan another raid on the Dutch." L.M.P. identified the killers only with initials: "J.-, G. – and S. – " but he only hid the identity of the killers with a thin veil, everyone realizing that they were John Baird, George Gladden and Scott Cooley. "The murderers . . . are the worst men on the frontier of Texas, and would not hesitate to do anything to gratify their prejudice and passions." L.M.P. added wistfully, "the sooner they are put out of the way the better it will be for the country. They have always been

George Gladden, a feudist who survived his wounds during the "Hoo Doo" War. *Courtesy Dave Johnson.*

drawing their revolvers on some quiet citizen. So you see it is good riddance of bad rubbage [*sic*] when one of them is picked off."[48]

Jones intended to search for the three killers but doubted there was much chance of arresting them due to the number of friends they had. Realistically he could only hope to restore quiet to the community as the Americans did not "yet manifest any disposition to assist in the arrest of the perpetrators . . . or any particular desire to have them arrested." Jones ascertained that by the time he had arrived in Mason there had been fifteen men killed since the commencement of the feud.[49]

On September 30 Reynolds and a squad of ten men left Mason and scouted to Bluff Creek twenty miles away, where they camped. The following day they scouted thirty miles southeast to the Llano River. On

October 2 they scouted some fifteen miles and returned to Mason, in all a sixty-five mile scout on the lookout for outlaws, but finding none.[50]

The internal conflict within Reynolds—whether to honor his oath and pursue fugitive Scott Cooley or resign—and others came to a resolution in Mason County at this time. All Rangers had taken an oath to uphold the laws of the State and to obey the orders of their commanding officers. Cooley had resigned his position in the force, but events were to prove that he was not just another Ranger. Several of the men sympathized with Cooley, and Major Jones finally decided that a drastic change had to be made.

Jones, upon learning that some of his men could no longer remain neutral, realized that the so-called efforts to arrest Cooley were really a sham. James B. Gillett wrote that Jones finally admitted that nearly the whole of his command, especially those men of Company D who had served alongside Cooley, were in sympathy with him and were "making no serious attempt to locate or imperil him. It was even charged that some of the Company D Rangers met Cooley at night on the outskirts of Mason and told him they did not care if he killed every damned Dutchman in Mason County who formed part of the mob that had murdered Williamson."

Still, according to Gillett, Jones then drew up his entire force of forty men and made them an elaborate speech about the pride he took in the Frontier Battalion, that he was aware of the friendly feeling that many of his command bore towards Scott Cooley, but at the same time could not allow the situation to continue. He promised every man who wished to leave the ranks an honorable discharge if they did not feel they could pursue their duty. According to Gillett, "The major paused and about fifteen men stepped to the front." These men were then issued an honorable discharge.[51]

What Gillett wrote was undoubtedly what he believed had happened after more than forty years of separation from the frontier line. However, the official record shows that far fewer than fifteen men had stepped forward to receive their honorable discharge. Only three members of Company D elected to leave the service at that point: Paul Durham, James P.

Day, and Nelson O. Reynolds. Jones must have felt there were others who were unwilling to resign, as he replaced Roberts' entire company with that of Lieutenant Ira Long. Jones explained that Long's men had "no personal acquaintance with the people here, no knowledge of the troubles heretofore and no predjudice [*sic*] for or against either party."[52]

Major Jones now prepared Special Order No. 47 at Mason. It read:

> At their own request, approved by the Company Commander, Sergt. N. O. Reynolds and private Jas. P. Day of Co. "D." are hereby discharged from the Service of the State for the reason that they say they can no longer conscientiously discharge the duty to which they have been assigned.[53]

Four days later Major Jones discharged Paul Durham by Special Order No. 48 for the reason "he says he cannot conscientiously discharge the duties to which he had been assigned."[54] He had earned the rank of 2nd sergeant but then requested to be returned to the ranks back in September. Now he was resigning fully from the service. Virtually nothing is known of the man; the 1870 Travis County census shows him as a nineteen-year-old boarder living in Austin. Part of the census page is missing thus his occupation is not available, but he probably gave his occupation as "laborer." Later, during the fall term of District Court of Tom Green County, a Paul Durham was convicted of stealing a gelding and sentenced to a term of five years in the state penitentiary. Durham, on December 10, 1877, was issued a full pardon by Gov. Richard B. Hubbard due to his being a "victim of bad associates."[55] Apparently this man convicted of horse theft and the Paul Durham of Company D were the same man.

Reynolds' carbine was purchased from him and then issued to William Griffin. His position was filled by Lamar P. Sieker who was appointed 2nd Sergeant.[56]

In late October Major Jones wrote a lengthy letter to Adjutant General Steele in which he discussed the disturbing situation in Mason County. He had brought with him Lieutenant Ira Long's company and eight men of Lieutenant Roberts' company, Jones wrote, the latter because they had been there before and were well acquainted with the country. He "became convinced that it would only aggravate the trouble" if he left Roberts' men there "for the reason that the sympathies of his men were entirely with one of the parties to the feud, that the notorious murderer Scott Cooley having at one time been a member of the company had many friends among the men who were in sympathy with him and his party and entertained a violent predjudice [*sic*] against the Sheriff Clark and the German population." Jones wrote that he found that the feeling "became so manifest" that he discharged three of them and felt compelled to remove Roberts' company entirely.[57]

In spite of fugitive Cooley's notoriety he did not attempt to remain in seclusion. From Austin Adjutant General Steele wrote Major Jones that Cooley had been there a few days before and talked quite openly of his actions, bragging that there were not enough men in Texas to keep him from killing Sheriff Clark. Cooley was not alone as John Baird and George Gladden were with him. After enjoying themselves in Austin they went to Burnet.[58]

If we can believe Gillett's account then following the discharge of Reynolds, Day, and Durham, the Ranger force "went to work with a new vigor" and soon brought the ethnic animosities to an end. Although the open warfare decreased, the hard feelings continued for several generations.

Gillett reported a very interesting exchange from about this time, which very likely was based on fact. Soon after Cooley killed "John Worley" [*sic*], Norman Rodgers got permission from Captain Roberts to go over to Joe Franks's cow outfit to exchange his horse for a better one. When Rodgers rode into the cowboy camp he noticed a man resting under a tree. The stranger called one of the cowboys and asked him who Norman was. As Rodgers left camp the man followed him and asked if he were one of Roberts' Rangers and if he knew Major Reynolds. Rodgers replied that he knew Reynolds very well.

The man then identified himself as Scott Cooley, then reached into his pocket and pulled out the scalp of John Worhle. "You take this to Major Reynolds with my compliments, but don't you tell anybody you saw me." Rodgers dutifully did deliver the scalp to Reynolds who cautioned him to say nothing about the matter. Forty years later, at an old settlers' reunion in Sweetwater, Nolan County, Norman Rodgers mentioned this incident in a speech. He had kept his promise to Cooley and Reynolds all those years.[59]

Sheriff John Clark did escape from Mason County and the wrath of Scott Cooley who had sworn to kill him, but only because of his superior ability to run from his enemies. His activities after fleeing Mason County and what he later did with his life are controversial. The John E. Clark who died in May 1888 and is buried in the Wohrle Cemetery near Doniphan, Ripley County, Missouri, is no doubt the former sheriff of Mason County. He had successfully run away from his past, and the men who sought to avenge the death of Tim Williamson by killing him.[60]

Reynolds' first experiences with the Texas Rangers were successful. He had joined in May of 1874 and left the service in October of 1875 in a *crise de conscience*, but only after gaining valuable experience in trailing hostiles and pursuing white desperadoes. He may have participated in the Lost Valley engagement. Although as yet he had had no experience that would bring him real recognition, he had learned valuable lessons in dealing with good men and bad. After this brief interlude out of the service he would return, and would earn statewide fame.

Thomas Mead, dressed in the typical Ranger attire of the 1870s. In 1876 Mead went to the Black Hills and "was never heard from again" according to Ranger J. B. Gillett.
Courtesy Pansy Gillett Espy.

5

Death of the Avenger

"But for God['s] sake don't take the Rangers away."
—George W. Todd to Major Jones, December 14, 1875.

Major Jones, writing from Mason on October 25, ordered Neal Coldwell of Company F to make a scout to the Upper Llano where "some fifteen men, very suspicious looking fellows" had been seen. If they were not found there he was to continue scouting for them on the Nueces, further south. He was specifically told to keep a "sharp lookout" for Scott Cooley and George Gladden, who, it was believed, intended to rendezvous there with other outlaws.[1] They, along with John Baird, were considered the leaders of the Cooley faction.

Although some believed that Cooley and his closest associates had left the area, Lieutenant Roberts continued to send scouts out in hopes of running them down. "Desperadoism has somewhat ceased" he wrote to Major Jones in mid-November from Menard. Then he told of an "old man" identified as Miller, who somehow had feudist Coke in custody, and had been shot at in his house in Mason. He was possibly wounded, "but was not killed." Supposedly a man named Johnson, possibly Charles Johnson, had been the man who shot Miller. Roberts continued his report saying that Cooley had been seen in Menard a few days before, had called at the blacksmith to have his horse shod and wanted it done quick. "[U]pon being informed he was in Menard I started in pursuit of him and by trailing his horse I found he went West—in the direction of Llano. I could not follow his track far [fast?] enough to overtake him."[2] A month later

Cooley was reported to have been seen in the town of Mason itself with a dozen others, one of whom was James Polk Mason[3], who, with Wesley Johnson, had shot and killed well-known pioneer rancher Rance Moore a year before, on December 12, 1874, in a dispute over cattle. Both were now on the list of fugitives from justice.

Sergeant Reynolds would get to know Rance Moore, by reputation as a fighting man if not personally, as he would later be one of many who tried to run down the men who killed him. In many ways Rance Moore was an exemplar of the frontier Texan and his loss was felt deeply. Moore had fought for his rights and the safety of his family for years. During the Civil War he had provided protection from raiding parties while his family remained in Milam County. In 1862 he purchased land on Bear Creek, five miles from where it flows into the mouth of the North Llano River. In 1867 he relocated his family temporarily to Mason where they could enjoy relative security from the hardships of the frontier. On the night of February 5, 1867, Moore accidentally shot and killed his son Daniel, thinking the figure in the dark was an Indian attempting to steal his horses. The boy was five days shy of his fifteenth birthday. Today the remains of Daniel Moore, along with his parents, rest in the Koocksville Cemetery near Mason.[4]

Indians raided Moore's ranch in late November 1870, killing a Mr. Harris, who was the only male present at the time. Harris was shot as he approached the safety of the ranch house, and was shot again and fell dead within four feet of the front door. Mrs. Moore, wearing a man's hat and coat, came out with a double-barreled shotgun and fired on the Indians, driving them away.[5] In early 1872 a party of fifty Indians raided in Kimble County, killing one James H. Sewell and several stock animals. They were feasting on the beef when attacked by a party of nine settlers led by Rance Moore. In the exchange the settlers killed four Indians, but sixty-five-year-old James Bradberry lost his life.[6] Commented the *San Antonio Daily Herald*, "Mr. Rance Moore was the leader of the brave and intrepid nine who had the courage to attack fifty Indians but of course they did not know that the Indians were so well armed [all with Winchester rifles]."[7] With Mrs. Moore assuming the guise of a man to fight off raiders, and her husband leading a group of settlers although vastly outnumbered by the hostiles, one can appreciate the bravery of the white settlers who established their homes on the Texas frontier. In 1870 there were but a dozen families living in Kimble County. In the Moore household there were enumerated Rance, his wife, and nine others with the name of Moore and a stock hand, a twenty-two-year-old laborer by the name of Charles F. Miller.[8]

Wesley Johnson would eventually be arrested, stand trial, be found guilty, and sentenced to five years in the penitentiary for his part in the killing of Rance Moore. During the 1880 census he was incarcerated in the Travis County jail, thirty-one-years-old, single, claiming to be a native of Missouri.[9] James Polk Mason, on the other hand, was never tried for his part in the killing and his fate remains uncertain.

Whether the Cooley faction was still present or not there was still an element of fear among many citizens of the Hill Country as a result of the numerous killings. George W. Todd, a merchant and cattleman who also practiced law in Mason, communicated his fears to Major Jones in late 1875, beginning his letter stating the times "in and around Mason" seemed to be becoming more dangerous. Cooley and his "party" had been in town the night before, some estimating eleven men. A few days before, the group had been in Loyal Valley and were "becoming more bold every day." Lieutenant Ira Long "is the right man and in the right place but he has not force sufficient to do what the emergency of the Case demands[.]" Todd was aware that Ranger Long had two scouts out and had left only a few men in town, "not enough to cope with the 11 outlaws which were in Town last night." Attorney Todd could write only a few more lines: "Now Major I am in great haste and will have to close But for God['s] sake don't take the Rangers away. But Send more for I know they are needed worse here Than any where else."

Todd concluded his letter by saying that while in Austin "Cooley & Co." made their headquarters at McDonald's, an Austin merchant who provided Mason saloons with their liquor.[10] County clerk George W. Todd was a man who was very familiar with frontier violence. He had lost a servant girl, his wife had also been killed, and his daughter had been

Attorney George W. Todd, a leading figure during the Mason County "Hoo Doo" War.
Courtesy Jan Appleby and the Mason County Historical Commission.

taken captive by Indian raiders and never recovered. In addition to his personal tragedies due to the Indian menace, Todd was keenly aware of the danger from white desperadoes.[11]

Scott Cooley was not on the loose for long. In late December 1875 he and companion John Ringo were arrested by Sheriff John Clymer and his deputy John J. Strickland and placed in the Burnet County jail. Fearing a jail delivery, Deputy Strickland and a squad of nearly a dozen men delivered the pair to the Travis County jail in Austin for safe keeping until district court met later that month. Prior to delivering the pair to the jail the party stopped for lunch at the fashionable restaurant of William H. Salge, and a crowd, including a reporter from the *Daily Democratic Statesman*, gathered to see the notorious outlaws. "The prisoners," he later wrote, "were apparently cool and reserved, and chatted as freely as any of the guard, and each recognized a person or two in the crowd." The reporter was obviously aware of the leading prisoner and noted that Cooley, "who is said to have been a very quiet man until about a year ago" was a short solid man, appearing to be about twenty-eight years old (he was closer to twenty-four) "and looks like he might have some Cherokee blood in him." John Ringo was described as "taller and perhaps older than Cooley, is said to have taken an active part in the Mason county war, and he and Cooley are charged with having threatened the lives of Sheriff Clymer . . . and his deputy Strickland."[12]

The arrest of Cooley and Ringo did result in some quiet returning to Mason County. Of the "American faction" Cooley and Ringo were behind bars, Moses Baird was dead, and George Gladden and John Baird were hiding out, avoiding Ranger patrols. By mid-April Major Jones was able to report to Adjutant General Steele that he "found everything quiet and peaceable in Mason county and a better feeling among the people than has existed there for more than a year past."[13]

Cooley and Ringo obtained a change of venue to Lampasas County. During the night of May 4 they were delivered from that jail by a group of men including Ed Brown, James Polk Mason, brothers Bud and Champ Farris, Andrew Murchison, John Carson, and William T. Cavin. Brown and Mason were later arrested for their part in the jail break, and they in turn later escaped. Cavin turned state's evidence and was released. Their jailer, William S. Gilliam, was later charged with allowing the prisoners to escape.[14]

It remains a mystery as to Reynolds' actions prior to his rejoining the company on April 13, at Camp Jones, Menard County. He was now among men who wanted to rejoin, as Roberts had inquired how many could be accepted, having numerous applications almost daily from young men. Roberts perhaps anticipated the need for additional Ranger protection as Kimble County had just been organized and had a "set of Buckskin officials in full blast."[15] Frequently a judge attempting to hold district court required a Ranger presence, especially in the outlying counties. With Reynolds again in the service he now shared the responsibilities of Company D, composed of four sergeants—himself, James B. Gillett, James B. Hawkins, and Newton H. Murray—three corporals and twenty-six privates. The new recruits were issued pistols and other accoutrements on April 14. Sergeant Hawkins led a detachment up Bear Creek and returned six days later, reporting everything quiet there.

Within a week Reynolds was given an opportunity to exert his leadership abilities. On April 21 he led a twelve-man detachment scouting the Colorado River via Salt Gap. Five days later he returned, reporting he had seen no recent sign of Indian activity or any sign of white outlaws.[16]

Sometimes reports came in of Indian sightings that proved to be erroneous, costing much time and energy. On May 6 a report came in that Indians had been seen on the Big Saline. Sergeant Reynolds and ten men started immediately in pursuit but the tracks proved to be nothing more than the tracks of an earlier scouting party led by Lieutenant Roberts. Nine days later Reynolds and three men left for the Nueces to arrest James Polk Mason. The quartet found the man so identified but on further investigation determined he was someone other than the noted fugitive.[17]

William Scott Cooley the avenger did manage to escape capture but did not live long to enjoy his liberty. If he had had his wish he would have met death in a clash with Indians or a gunfight with law officers, but the end came much more prosaically. One report stated that "the notorious Scott Colley" had died of "congestion of the brain" near Fredericksburg on June 10. Galveston's *Daily News*, picking up a report from San Antonio, informed its readers that Cooley had died at the home of Daniel Maddox, nine miles from Blanco City, of "brain fever." Austin's *Statesman* of August 17, apparently wishing to establish the correctness of earlier reports that may have been questioned, reported: "The Blanco stage driver says the report published some time ago in this paper that Scott Cooley was dead, is correct. He died of disease, which is not generally the case with desperadoes. Those who kill almost invariably are killed themselves."[18]

Gillett also recorded that Cooley had died of "brain fever" and "though tenderly nursed, shielded by his friends, he died without ever being brought to trial for his killings."[19] Although there were numerous reports of Cooley's death at the time, there is a consistent oral tradition within the family that he survived his Texas difficulties and went west to New Mexico or perhaps north to Oklahoma, where he died of natural causes. More likely he did die in the mid-1870s, the reported "brain fever" being a non-medical term for the effects of the poisoning which also was given as a cause of his death, although whoever administered the poison has never been identified.[20]

The reported "brain fever" may have been given out only to mislead his friends to prevent their avenging his death. If indeed he was poisoned then his name rightly belongs on the death roll of victims in the Mason County feud. His grave is in the Miller Creek Cemetery, a few miles southeast of Johnson City in Blanco County. A crude stone with his name scratched on it once marked his final resting place, but now a large flat slab bears his name and years of his life and the words that seem to be terribly out of place: "Texas Ranger."[21]

Although Lieutenant Roberts was certainly aware of the death of his former Ranger, he made no written reference to his passing, no doubt due to greater concerns. On June 18 he wrote to Major Jones discussing various matters, concluding with the following: "I send Reynolds with nineteen men—making twenty himself, with all the ammunition they can carry—in their belts—or all they can pack [to meet and act in concert with Company A]." Reynolds and his detachment left on the eighteenth to become part of Jones' escort. They returned on July 14 and reported all was quiet on the frontier.[22] At this time Roberts planned to leave the service, as in a letter he indicated that for "reasons of private nature" he would have to resign, the resignation to take effect on August 31, 1876, the end of the fiscal year. Roberts would later be recalled and did serve again, from September 29, 1877, until the end of February 1879.[23]

Reynolds and his ten men left on the night of August 27 for Menard to assist the sheriff in arresting McDowell and Lloyd for murder. They had, allegedly, killed two black United States soldiers at Jackson's Crossing in Menard County McDowell and Lloyd "invited the negroes to drink with them, and then shot and killed them because they did so," according to one report.[24] The pair could not be located and the detachment returned to camp the following day. On October 29, 1876, Reynolds and his ten men went out to assist Mason County sheriff Jesse W. Leslie in arresting a party of cattle thieves. Again they returned to camp without finding any one for whom they carried capiases, but the trek was not a total waste of effort as they did recover some stolen cattle.[25]

At the end of the fiscal year, on August 31, the force again had to be reduced in strength "by expiation term of service." General Order No. 10

ordered company commanders to give discharges and final statements of accounts to all their men by August 31. The reorganization of the Frontier Battalion would take place on September 1. Each company was to be reduced to two sergeants, two corporals, and sixteen privates. Major Jones reminded his commanders that the men enlisted had to be "sound, able bodied unmarried men of good character" and no drunkard nor person against whom there was an indictment pending could be allowed. The horses as well had to be "of good size and Sound and Serviceable."[26]

With the reorganization on September first, six men were placed in Lieutenant J. M. Denton's Company A: Sergeant Reynolds, James B. Gillett, William O. Tompkins, Charles L. Nevill, Henry W. Merrill, and Thomas P. Gillespie. Tompkins showed great promise to the service. D. W. Roberts had written to Major Jones recommending him highly: "Mr. Thompkins [*sic*] comes with my squad to see if you design put[t]ing any men in place of [Nick] Donnally and [J. W.] Bell, if not he proposes to go with you—any way—provided you have no objection. I know Thompkins—he is a good young man—and if you wish to fill the vacancies in my company—you would oblige me to enlist him." A decade later William O. Tompkins, then the second elected sheriff of La Salle County, was involved in a conspiracy to murder his successor, a former Ranger himself, Charles Brown McKinney.[27]

With some regret Major Jones forwarded the resignation letters of commanders Neal Coldwell and D. W. Roberts to Adjutant General Steele. With the earlier resignation of Capt. Ira Long, accepted and to take effect on the fifteenth, considerable changes were taking place in the command. Jones immediately recommended 1st Lieutenant J. M. Denton to take command of Company A, Pat Dolan to take command of Company F, and Frank M. Moore to be 2nd Lieutenant of Company D.[28]

In spite of Major Jones' careful planning, on August 29, he issued to Lieutenant Roberts Special Order No. 67 for his "guidance." Company D was to remain on the San Saba and Company F was to go to the Nueces, "instead of as indicated in Gen. Order No. 10." This was done so that the property of Company D would not have to be moved. He wanted the two Sieker brothers—Lamartine P. and Edward A.—as well as eight others to be enlisted in Frank M. Moore's Company D. Reynolds, Gillett, Tompkins, Nevill, Merrill and Gillespie were to be enlisted in Company A.[29] John M. Denton was to be the new commander of Company A with the reorganization and resignation of Coldwell and Roberts. Whereas others chose to leave the service at this time, Reynolds saw the opportunity to continue and became a member of Major Jones' escort.

The first order for the detachment was to proceed to Kerrville without delay to meet with Major Jones. "Sergt. Reynolds and the men for Co. A must start down the next day after receipt of this. [T]hey need not wait until the first of Sept. and come to Kerrville, without delay where I will wait for them. They will pass up the line some time next month and need not bring all their Baggage now."[30]

Jones would continue his practice of stationing his companies along the edge of the frontier, with Company A continuing to be his escort, "to operate on the whole line of Frontier." Company B would be stationed on the Brazos River in the northeast corner of Throckmorton County; Company D would be on the Nueces River in the northeast corner of Uvalde County; Company F would be stationed on Jim Ned Creek in the southwest corner of Callahan County; Company F would be stationed on the San Saba River midway between Menard and Fort McKavett in Menard County. No mention was made of orders for Company C in this general order. Jones gave a final reminder to his commanders: they were to give "particular attention to the maintenance of Law and Order, and to the arresting of criminals and fugitives from Justice." In a few days "Large lists" of fugitives and criminals with orders for their arrest would be forwarded to each commander. Captain John C. Sparks would be the new commander of Company C, "especially for duty in the interior counties." The company would be stationed in Burnet County and would operate in Llano, Lampasas, Hamilton, Bell, and Williamson counties.[31] Now the primary concern was no longer the threat of Indian raiding parties but of white desperadoes.

Major Jones was continually on the scene of potential action by spending his time on the frontier line rather than seated at a desk in Austin. As he patrolled the frontier line he had with him an escort of Rangers, not only being aware of the needs of his men but even taking part in dangerous engagements with Indians or outlaws. He had faced hostiles at Lost Valley in June of 1874 and again in May of 1875. He later was in Lampasas County with the feuding Horrells and Higgins parties. In July of 1878 he would be in Round Rock exchanging shots with the Sam Bass gang in their failed attempt to rob the bank. Sergeant Reynolds, Gillett, Tompkins, Nevill, Merrill, and Gillespie—since September 1, 1876 a part of Major Jones;' escort—headed for the San Antonio area where camp was established on Salado Creek. A month later, along with Dr. E. G. Nicholson, the official surgeon of the Frontier Battalion, the escort began the line of march to inspect all Ranger companies.

Little is known of John M. Denton and the time he was in charge of Company A. The September muster roll placed the group near San Antonio in Bexar County with Denton as lieutenant commander. George W. Arrington was 1st sergeant and N. O. Reynolds still 2nd sergeant. Physically Reynolds was described as twenty-eight years old, five-feet-ten-and-one-half inches tall, light colored hair, blue eyes, and fair complexion. The roll shows his birth place as Missouri, and having been mustered in Menard County by Daniel W. Roberts. Each of the company's horses was evaluated also. Of the twenty-six mounts, Denton's was evaluated the highest at $165; three, including Reynolds', were evaluated at $154 while the remaining all evaluated at lesser amounts.[32]

During this period Reynolds and the escort covered a considerable expanse of the Texas frontier. His October scouting record showed that between October 2 and 5 they had traveled from Bexar County to Uvalde County, then established camp on the Nueces River. From there the escort moved up to Edwards County, arriving there by October 1.[33]

November was spent traveling up the line, leaving camp on the headwaters of the Nueces in Edwards County and moving to the headwaters of the South Llano on the first day's march. The group continued, crossing the North Llano, passing through Fort McKavett where Company D was camped. Then on November 7 the command crossed the Concho River at Paint Rock Crossing, then continued on to Company E in Callahan County. Leaving Company E they went on to camp on the waters of the Clear Fork of the Brazos, passing through Fort Griffin in Shackelford

County, crossing the Salt Fork of the Brazos, arriving at the camp of Company B in Young County. On November 25 the command left Company B, camping that night nine miles north of Fort Griffin. By the next day camp was made on the waters of Hubbard Creek near Albany, Shackelford County. The escort camped on Jim Ned Creek with Company E in Callahan County at the end of November.[34]

Gillett recalled this period of his Ranger service with great fondness. He remembered Dr. Nicholson always being present in case he was needed. There were also several Rangers who provided musical entertainment to pass the idle hours in camp. Vernon Coke Wilson played the guitar; Private Callaway, who Gillett identified as Columbus but who is identified as W. D. Callaway in the muster rolls, played the banjo, and William T. Clements played the violin. Major Jones provided a seine, and when camped on a big creek or river the boys would unroll the net, make a haul, and sometimes catch enough fish to supply the men several days, as Gillett recalled. A typical day's travel was twenty-five miles, the group traveling in a line with the men divided into groups of four: Jones and Dr. Nicholson in front, followed by the captain and orderly sergeant, then the men in double file. At the rear came the wagons. Two men preceded the column about one-half mile ahead. Four men, or flankers, two on each side, rode parallel to the company a half mile or so distant. With a non-commissioned officer and a guard covering the rear of the column with the pack mules it was nearly impossible for anyone to stage a surprise attack.[35]

At November's end Lieutenant Denton was forced to resign due to failing health, his resignation accepted as Special Order No. 79 dated December 1, 1876.[36] Neal Coldwell was called back into service to replace the ailing Denton, "subject to the approval of the Governor." His appointment was accepted and Coldwell took command of Company A, Frontier Battalion. Dr. Nicholson also chose to resign at this point.[37] The final roll for Denton's company, prepared in Callahan County, showed Reynolds had earned $150 for the previous three months' service. He had a stoppage of fifty-five cents for loss of horse shoes and nails.[38] Reynolds left camp on the twenty-seventh with nine men for a scout up the Sabinal River.[39] The glory years for N. O. Reynolds were just ahead.

6

Rangers Against the Confederacy

"I find that Kimble County is a thiafs [sic] stronghold. [T]he two Llanos and all tributaries are lined with them."

—Private H. B. Waddill, Company C, February 27, 1877

The beginning months of 1877 must have seemed terribly uneventful for Reynolds and the boys of Company A, stationed at Camp Hubbard in Frio County—named after Gov. Richard B. Hubbard, who had succeeded to the governorship upon the resignation of Richard Coke—as scout followed scout in the same general area with very little probability for action. On December 27, 1876, Captain Coldwell sent Reynolds with a nine-man squad up the Sabinal River, reaching Sabinal post office, some sixty miles west of San Antonio, the next day. They remained there for three days and then went to the small settlement of D'Hanis, a stage stop on the road between San Antonio and the Rio Grande. They remained there but one day and although they were unaware of it at the time a party of Indians had just passed through the country; when the Rangers learned of their presence it was too late to follow the trail. The squad returned to camp on the evening of January 2, having marched a total of eighty-two miles.[1]

January was an idle month for the entire command as well, not a single arrest being recorded and but one attempt made. The house of James Gatlin, wanted on a charge of horse theft in Hays County, was surrounded the night of January 23, but on investigation it was found to be empty.[2] On the next day Reynolds and a six-man squad left camp for another scout up the Sabinal, arriving at the Sabinal post office the following day. For four days they patrolled the area between the Sabinal and Seco Creek, but finding no sign of Indians or any fugitives from justice returned to camp by January 30, having covered one hundred-twenty miles.[3]

But the inactivity in pursuing Indians or wanted fugitives allowed the men to hunt and practice their shooting skills: the decrease of public property for Coldwell's Company A in January amounted to 130 carbine cartridges and 130 pistol cartridges, "Expended for game, and target practice."[4] Coldwell further reported that the health of the company was good, but the horses were not gaining to his satisfaction in spite of having good grass available. Unusual for South Texas, the "weather has been very cold, with Several heavy frosts."[5] Several days later he wrote again, this time complaining about the arms his men had. William O. Tompkins and L. W. Rogers were requesting Winchester carbines or rifles rather than the heavier single-shot Sharps. Coldwell added: "In fact nearly every man in the company is anxious to get a Winchester, but the two are particularly anxious. Sergeant Reynolds Says that he must have one, but will wait to See if he can get one from the State, before he buys one elsewhere."

A personal note was added to this communication, rare in Ranger correspondence:

> I like the company very well. I find them easy to control and have had only two of them ([Vernon Coke] Wilson and [A. J.] Bridges) on extra duty. Every one of them Seems to think that his personal reputation as a Ranger, depends on our catching a party of Indians and "getting away with them."[6]

But occasionally the service was too much for a man and an honorable discharge was the only way out. Walter P. Callaway was such an example. On February 1 he wrote to Major Jones requesting an honorable discharge, giving two reasons: for the past three weeks his bronchitis was bothering him, from which he had "suffered a great deal for the last 3 years." Secondly his horse had been "snagged" on a scout in December and was "now worthless for this business." Callaway knew he could not "stand the service after this disease has obtained a hold on me."[7] Coldwell agreed that the horse was "hardly able for Service."[8] Coldwell may never have gained recognition for deeds of bravery, but he did earn the respect of his men. Private Robert H. Eanes praised him in a letter to Jones, although the reason for the letter was his request to be discharged from the company. "It is not because I am dissatisfied in the least with the company for I have never been better Satisfied Since I have been ranging, than I am now," confided Eanes. He liked "all the boys first rate, and I am well pleased with our officers, especially Captain Colwell [*sic*], in fact all have worked agreeably ever Since we have been here. I never expect to find a company conducted better any where."[9] Coldwell could not "fully" endorse his request as he was disturbed by the idea that the men in the command were seemingly of the idea that they could quit the service whenever it seemed convenient, "which I think, impairs the discipline and ifficiency [*sic*] of the command." Eanes, who had been mustered into Coldwell's company September 1, 1876, received his honorable discharge on March 12, as requested. He later became a doctor.[10]

Captain Coldwell had learned of John Baird possibly being in the Dry Frio area and on February 5 began a scout after the well-known fugitive.[11] Baird, the brother of Moses Baird slain in the Mason County feud, was one of the few remaining feudists who had not been killed or imprisoned. John Baird, according to the sheriff's report from Burnet County, was wanted not only for the killing of Mason County's brand inspector Daniel Hoerster, but also for the theft of a mule committed on December 15, 1875, but not indicted until February 4, 1876. He was described by Burnet County authorities as thirty-eight years old, light complexioned with gray hair, almond shaped eyes and weighing one hundred-fifty pounds. Mason County authorities also provided a description, which differed somewhat, describing him as five-foot-eight inches tall, only twenty-eight years old, and with a "fair complexion" and "spare built." No doubt the conflict in physical descriptions of fugitives resulted in the wrong man occasionally being arrested. Ranger Gillett noted in his copy of the fugitives list that a reward of $500 was offered for Baird.[12] Lieutenant Pat Dolan of Company F also wanted to catch up with the fugitive and complained to Major Jones that "Baird is either gone or is hiding all the time. McNellys men gave him a scare that made him wild." Dolan was also anxious to catch up with Mason County mob member and cattle rustler Caleb Hall, his partner Bronson, Doc and Steve McLane and T. Goodman.[13]

The command experienced little action in February, but although the weather was disagreeable there was a little rain, which improved the available water. No definite reports of Indians were made although someone reported seeing a quartet of warriors on the Frio on February 2. Coldwell doubted the veracity of the report. He wrote at month's end that he had "nothing of interest to report at this time."[14] Sergeant Reynolds and a nine-man squad were scouting the country between Sabinal and D'Hanis on Seco Creek at this time, searching for Indian sign. He had left camp on the twenty-fourth and did not return until March 5, having made a march of one-hundred twenty-five miles. During the next three days the same men patrolled the same area.[15]

February's only real action occurred on the tenth when Sergeant G. W. Arrington and a nine-man squad arrested John R. Burleson at his home on Carrizo Creek in Dimmit County. He was wanted for an old murder and delivered to Frio County Sheriff J. B. Vinton, then released on bond of $12,000.[16] Ten years earlier Lampasas County authorities had charged Burleson with sixteen indictments for capital offenses, "and lately escaped from county jail. Is a desperate fellow."[17] And John Baird still remained at large.

By March 12 Coldwell and his eleven-man scout had returned from Carrizo Springs and the country around Pendencia Creek. He had intended to go west to Presidio County but the grass was so bad he could go no further, forcing him to return by way of Fort Inge. He reported that all was quiet except for an occasional horse being stolen. Citizens he visited complained that the stealing of live stock was "about equally divided between the white and Mexican thieves." In fact most of the complaints he heard were against King Fisher and his crowd. For the second consecutive month the company reported but one arrest: Burleson in February

Texas Ranger Capt. George W. Arrington, the Ranger with a hidden past darker than that of N. O. Reynolds. *Courtesy Former Texas Rangers Foundation.*

and now in March hard-case Green Ridgeway, wanted by authorities in both Travis County and San Patricio County. He was charged with assault with intent to murder and assisting a prisoner to escape in Travis County; in San Patricio he was charged with assault to murder.[18] The Rangers arrested him in Frio County and turned him over to authorities but he eluded justice and continued to be a trouble maker for several more years until he was gunned down in La Salle County.

The boredom and inactivity experienced in South Texas was to end with a grand scheme of Major Jones to "clean up" newly organized Kimble County. The county was created in 1858 from Bexar County, then in 1875 attached to Menard County for judicial purposes, then in 1876 organized with the election of county officials. Dr. Ezekial K. Kountz's home was the temporary county seat of Kimble, declared so by a proclamation of Governor Coke on February 21, 1876.[19] Also in 1876 the towns of Kimbleville and Junction were founded; now Kimbleville became the county seat. Not long afterwards it was moved to Junction and soon the village of Kimbleville dwindled away. Citizens elected Frank Latta to be the first sheriff on February 15; he served until October 4 when he chose to resign.[20] On that date commissioners appointed J. M. Reynolds to succeed him with E. K. Kountz, M. J. Denman and Jordan A. Burt his sureties. J. M. Reynolds served in that dual position as sheriff and tax collector until he resigned on May 3, 1877.[21] Other county officials included William Potter as county judge, E. K. Kountz as county and district clerk, M. J. Denman as county surveyor, Jordan A. Burt as inspector of hides and animals, and N. Q. Patterson as county treasurer.[22] Although the new officials may have had the best of intentions Kimble County soon became a haven for thieves, murderers, and desperadoes of all sorts, a virtual "no-man's land" for an honest pioneer.

Major Jones' grand scheme to clean up Kimble County did not include his riding in with guns blazing; rather it began with his sending in spies to determine what individuals posed threats to honest law-abiding individuals. He picked several men to be his spies, one of whom was H. B. Waddill, then serving under John C. Sparks in Company C. He had entered the county and then "settled" and then in truth became a detective. By February 27 he had sufficient information; not trusting completely anyone in Kimble County he went to Fort Mason and composed his document, which contributed to Major Jones' so-called Kimble County Roundup.[23] He boldly began his statement that he had found Kimble County a "thiafs stronghold" and then named names. The two Llano Rivers and their tributaries were "lined with them." Among those who harbored thieves were Thomas Doran, Judge John Potter, "Old

Man" Dublin, "Black Burt" who could be termed the "head man of the thieves," Justice of the Peace Squire Anderson, and Robert McKiver. Waddill even named the widow of Rance Moore as harboring thieves.

Then Waddill began to name the fugitives who were in the county. They included a man named Coburn, a heavy-set dark complexioned man who "wants to kill every stranger that comes into the neighborhood fearing that he is a detective"; the Dublin brothers—Richard and John Sheldon "Del"—Black Burt, Thomas Doran, Frank Burk, John Burleson, Caleb Hall, who had a $400 reward for him, Bill Deal, McGrue, one Allison, Bob and John McKeiver, "and numerous others that I could name are in the county." A number of settlers were afraid for their lives as they had been threatened. Waddill pointed out that he thought it was useless to arrest anyone as Sheriff Reynolds would accept anyone as bondsman. The cattle thieves even made forays into other counties, stole cattle, and rebranded them as their own. Curiously Waddill was perfectly satisfied that John Wesley Hardin was in Texas and made Creed Taylor's home his headquarters. Certainly this was another man using the name of the notorious man killer, as Hardin was then hiding out in Florida and Alabama using an assumed name. From his detective work Waddill was able to determine several citizens who could be trusted. They were William Franklin Gilliland, a Missourian by birth who lived and married in nearby Brown County prior to moving to Kimble. (Apparently after the "Roundup" the county became crowded and by 1887 the Gilliland family left and headed as far west as New Mexico Territory.[24]) Dr. Ezekial Keyser Kountz could also be trusted. He was a Virginian, but perhaps more importantly to the community was a medical doctor. He had fought for the Confederacy during the war and had arrived in Kimble County "to sort out the country for a likely place to bring his family," and did. He purchased the former Bradberry place on the South Llano. He was respected in the community, perhaps almost automatically due to his medical knowledge. He was elected the first county and district clerk of the county and Mrs. Kountz became the first post master with the "office" in the Kountz home. Certainly his feelings against Indian raiders were similar to every other white man's as he had lost two sons to them.[25] John

E. Temple was also placed on Waddill's list of trustworthy individuals. After settling in Coryell County the family feared for their safety from the numerous Indian raiding parties and thus relocated closer to Austin in Travis County. In the 1870s they moved to Kimble County and settled on the North Llano River, close to the settlement of Junction.[26] There was one more name on the trustworthy list: Benjamin Franklin Pepper. This West Virginia native had the yearning to move west and led a wagon train of settlers to settle in Texas, arriving there in 1874 and settling on the North Llano.[27] Mr. Burton even went so far as to recommend where the Ranger companies should be placed. He asked "for a company to be placed at the junction of the Llanos or Llano and Johnson [Creeks]" for if placed there "they will have full sway at the surrounding country, will be within a days ride of any one of the theives [*sic*]."[28]

The name of H. B. Waddill has been mainly forgotten but obviously he was not afraid to do such undercover work alone, knowing that if any of the thieves who made Kimble County their base learned his true purpose he would be killed. It is not known if Waddill had any previous experience as an undercover detective or when he came to Texas. We do know that he was born in Louisiana about 1854. He enlisted in Corsicana, where Major Jones lived, and returned there after his resignation from the Rangers. Waddill's Ranging career began on October 1, 1876, as a private in Capt. John C. Sparks' Company C. When mustered in he gave his age as twenty-two and his occupation as "clerk" with no further details. He served the state honorably until his discharge on July 24, 1879, by Special Order No. 22. In addition to serving under Captain Sparks he served under Capt. George W. Arrington.[29]

While the Waddill letter was being delivered to Major Jones, Sergeant Reynolds and his detachment of nine men were scouting from the Sabinal post office to D'Hanis on the Seco River, searching for recent Indian sign. None was found and the squad was back in camp on March 28, having covered one hundred twenty-five miles.[30]

For the first three months of 1877 Coldwell's command had called Camp Hubbard in Frio County home. Rumors began circulating that the company would be moving soon and in an effort to prevent that from happening Frio County officials and ordinary citizens petitioned Governor Hubbard to keep the Rangers there. The April 8 petition, signed by over fifty county residents, claimed there was "a disturbed state of Society on the part of the frontier caused by the actions of lawless characters and the frequent incursions of Indians prior to the Coming of said Company amongst us and the subsequent security of both life and property." When Company C came to the area this danger was removed. The Frio County petitioners claimed they had "suffered so much, more in fact than any other frontier community" and therefore the men of Captain Coldwell's company, "being cool, clear headed and well behaved" would guarantee protection in the future. Almost to reinforce the feeling of urgency among the Frio County citizens, as the petition was being circulated the courthouse was burned "by a party of lawless characters who must have been interested in the destruction" of district court papers.[31]

Governor Hubbard referred the matter to Steele who referred the matter to Major Jones who responded on April 12. Jones explained that he had to reject their request "for the reason that—although the statements in the petition are true and the Company has been, and could by remaining here be of great benefit to this section of the country—being well informed of the condition of the whole frontier, I know there is greater and more pressing necessity for this company in another locality."[32] Jones complained that the force was too small to respond to even "half the calls of this character" and therefore had to deny the request. In order to give the Frio County citizens some satisfaction, Jones assured them that he intended to station a portion of the company there in a few weeks, as soon as men could "be spared from an expedition which I have immediately in view."[33] The expedition was the Ranger invasion of Kimble County.

The letter from H. B. Waddill was not the only factor causing Major Jones to make the decision he did, however. William A. Blackburn, Judge of the 17th Judicial District, wrote from Burnet in early April that he was "most anxious to hold Court in Kimble, and will do so, unless prevented by force, which is threatened, I am credibly informed." Blackburn also indicated the court in Kimble was scheduled to begin on April 30. He would hold court the preceding week at Fredericksburg, Gillespie

County, and would be "thankful indeed for an escort." He did not feel it safe to travel in that section of Texas without a Ranger escort, and he knew he could not hold court without Ranger assistance.[34]

In preparation for the Ranger raid on Kimble County, Jones requested Adjutant General Steele to have thirty improved Winchester carbines and sufficient cartridges shipped to Fort McKavett in care of general merchant William Lehne. Jones was ready to move to Kimble with men of Moore's, Coldwell's, and Pat Dolan's companies. Jones had learned that the outlaws had purchased all the ammunition in Kimble and adjoining counties, "and have not yet as much as they want."[35] Whatever lack of action Reynolds and the others had experienced in the preceding months would be more than made up for in Kimble County.

Ben Anderson was another spy or informant in Kimble County who reported to Lieutenant Moore of Company D. The list of names forwarded to Major Jones by Moore was entitled "Names of Parties interested in Stealing in Kimble and Joining Counti[e]s as Given by Ben Anderson" and identified thirty-nine names. Most remain unknowns today, but several had gained notoriety—or would later gain notoriety—and perhaps were in Kimble County where they would be safer among others of their kind. One was Bill Taylor, who perhaps was the same Bill Taylor who gained notoriety in the Sutton-Taylor feud of the DeWitt County area; another was Porter Lancaster, who became part of the outlaw group who fought against the Earps in the Tombstone area in the early 1880s, but under the name of "Pete Spence." Paul Durham's name was included, who may have been the same Paul Durham who had served with Reynolds but chose to resign rather than pursue Scott Cooley. Of course the names of the Dublin brothers were included.[36]

But there was work for Reynolds to do before the Kimble County Roundup began. On April 2 he and a seven-man squad were on Black Creek hunting for fugitives, returning on April 9 with five prisoners suspected of being horse thieves, although four of them were ultimately released as there were no complaints made against them. The other was W. L. Berryman, arrested in Frio County on a charge of murder committed in Madison County. Berryman was turned over to Atascosa County

Sheriff George W. M. Duck.[37] On April 13 Reynolds arrested W. H. Davis in Uvalde County for theft committed in Blanco County. Davis was turned over to Uvalde County Sheriff George Johnson.

On April 16 Reynolds joined up with Company F and marched up the Nueces River and camped on its headquarters. Two days later the group marched across the divide and camped on the headwaters of the South Llano, a distance of twenty-seven miles. On the nineteenth Reynolds was in Junction City, now the county seat of Kimble County, where he immediately began hunting fugitives.[38]

The April Monthly Return lists several dozen men arrested for crimes ranging from theft to murder. A supplement to the April "Record of Scouts" identifies some of Reynolds' accomplishments. He and five others arrested John Walton and James Ponton, both escapees from the Lavaca County jail,[39] and James Potter on April 19–20. At the same time Sergeant Arrington and his seven-man squad were on the scout and arrested Bill Allison, charged with theft and being an accessory in the murder of Jim Williams. On April 20 Captain Coldwell and a dozen Rangers arrested J. Ruff, Sam Monroe and Eugene Hensley, the latter another escaped convict. Private George Nelson arrested Frank Potter on the same day, charged with theft in Menard County. On the twenty-third Corporal W. W. Bates and five others arrested Columbus Rowley and H. McMichael in Menard County, both of whom were charged with theft, and on the same day Reynolds went out again with another quintet and arrested J. B. McIver, charged with theft in Burnet County. Arrington and three others arrested Rol Dublin, William Collins, and Jack Hall on the twenty-ninth. On April 30 Capt Coldwell arrested Nathan McFaddin, who, along with N. Q. Patterson on October 4, had signed as securities on the bond of Sheriff J. M. Reynolds. McFaddin was charged with theft in Menard County.[40]

The Kimble County Roundup was accomplished with no shots fired. Several gun battles between quick-shooting Rangers and evil thieves and murderers would have made excellent reading, and no doubt would have initiated debate among historians for years to come. Such did not occur, however, due to Major Jones' careful planning. From the initial meeting when Jones gave the men their assignments, they followed orders like professionals. The Rangers were divided into four detachments and then systematically scoured the drainage basins of the North and South Llano Rivers, everywhere a fugitive might think it safe to hide. Every man—or woman—they met who could not explain their presence or provide an occupation were considered a suspicious person and arrested. The work was difficult, as the Rangers never could determine if a person they met was friend or foe. The terrain as well was unfriendly, as the area was virtually a wilderness, with small streams and slippery banks, thick brush and dense cedar breaks—all proved a challenge to a man on horseback. No man gave any serious resistance, realizing the young Rangers were intent on carrying out orders and all too willing to shoot first and deal with ramifications later. All detachments were to converge at Junction City the evening of April 9. The prisoners were shackled and confined in a makeshift "bull pen."

The arrival of the Rangers in Kimble County had been a complete surprise to the residents, law-abiding or outlaw. Only three people in the county knew of their coming, and they had been notified only two days previously. Good men then came to Jones' camp once they realized a clean-up was in progress, offering their assistance. Jones reported to Steele with great confidence that he had "reason to believe" that he had caught "every man who was in the county at the time of my arrival against whom I have charges except three, and two of those left the country before I knew of the charges against them." Jones regretted that four of the "worst men in the county" committed a murder three days before his arrival. "Three of them left the county immediately. The other was the first man I arrested and is now in jail in Menardville."[41]

The murder Jones referred to was committed on April 16 by Lewis Cathey and Richard Dublin. When Kimble County authorities later sent in their list of fugitives from justice for Adjutant General Steele's published list, Cathey and Dublin were two of those named; John Elliot, James Polk Mason, and Stark Reynolds were the other three.[42]

The arrested men were at first taken to Junction City and confined in shackles in a place called the "bull pen." Judge Blackburn was able to hold court under a live oak tree, and as if to give color to this primitive court of justice in the wilderness, a swarm of wild bees were working in the tree

Two desperadoes of Kimble County in 1875: James Roland "Roll" and brother John Sheldon "Dell" Dublin. *Courtesy Kimble County Historical Commission.*

under which were assembled judge and jury, lawyers and witnesses. Instead of delivering the prisoners over to a secure jail such as the one in Travis County, they were turned over to civil authorities in Kimble County.

The significance of Jones' round-up of outlaws was that Judge Blackburn could now initiate regular court sessions in an area that before was totally lawless. Court opened with Judge Blackburn presiding and Rangers guarding the judge, the prisoners and the witnesses. Everyone was orderly and not the slightest disturbance occurred during the entire week. Twenty-five bills of indictment were presented; more could have been had had there been sufficient witnesses.[43] Indictments were found even against the county sheriff and the county judge. J. M. Reynolds, sheriff since October of 1875, now chose to resign. Lieutenant Moore recorded in his April return that he had sent Sergeant Sieker and some men to arrest the sheriff who had been charged with the fraudulent inspection of cattle and willfully allowing prisoners to escape.[44] Judge William Potter, father of the Potter boys, resigned as well. The former sheriff, and presumably the former judge as well, were delivered to jail in Menard by Corp. Isham H. Rhodes and two other Rangers who then guarded the jail. Members of the grand jury appointed men to replace the sheriff and judge.[45]

Jones stated that the outlaw organization was "pretty well broken up now" yet elected to station Lieutenant Moore's company there for the next few months to prevent any outlaws from reassembling or reorganizing or forming new combinations and "to catch any that may come into the county hereafter." Jones shared his ideas with Steele in a letter that was printed in the influential *Galveston Daily News*. The *News* headlined it "Raiding Upon Outlaws"—thus providing the work of the Rangers statewide publicity.[46] Major Jones went on to Fort McKavett and on May 6 telegraphed Steele: "Have finished in Kimble. Arrested forty-one lawbreakers. Court passed off quietly. Good grand jury. Twenty-five indictments. No trials for want of qualified jurors. All quiet there now." But there was still another concern on the frontier, as Jones concluded his report that Indians had passed through the southern part of the county three days before. Three detachments were ordered out, following the trail into Gillespie County before rain destroyed the tracks.[47]

The results of the Rangers' work proved that only with effective leadership could organized outlawry be conquered. Not only had Major Jones made numerous arrests, but not a shot had been fired. There were no pitched battles between Reynolds' squad and the Potter boys, or Arrington's detachment and the likes of Bill Allison. All this was accomplished without a courthouse existing in the county. And not only did the Rangers get considerable positive publicity, but there appeared a thread of encouragement to people who might be considering moving into Kimble County. As the *Lampasas Dispatch* expressed it:

> We have reports from Kimble County of a favorable nature. The rascals over there are being thinned out materially. . . . Kimbleville, a small place of no great pretentions, is the county seat. The county has a good

> average share of excellent land and numerous running streams, some of which are free stone or soft water. The better class of the citizens of the county are beginning to see their way out of the difficulties under which they have been resting for some time, and are determined to bring the county to a prosperous condition.[48]

The Rangers experienced only small problems. Jones described their work as "very fatiguing" as much of it had to be done at night. Several parties were caught by Rangers surrounding their house or finding a camp in the woods. "Sometimes we came in contact with their women and were terribly tongue-lashed by them for searching their houses and arresting the men." But in spite of such tongue-lashings "not one instance came to my knowledge of any man of the command failing to come cheerfully and promptly up to his duty, or of them failing to give prompt consideration and good treatment to those with whom they came in contact. Each man seems to take a personal interest and pride in catching every one he is ordered to arrest."[49]

A Texas State Historical Marker provides Major Jones with the recognition for his accomplishments. The legend is devoted primarily to a stopping place on the Fort Clark–Fort McKavett military road and is located on U.S. Highway 377 at Paint Rock Springs, twenty-one miles northeast of Rock Springs in Edwards County. In part it reads: "Here, too, Maj. John B. Jones' Frontier Battalion assembled in 1877 to begin the famous outlaw roundup, to make this area safe for settlement by ranchers." Although the message is misleading in that only portions of the battalion were involved it does provide suitable recognition for Jones and his work.[50]

Although Major Jones could justifiably boast of his nearly fifty arrests without any gunfire, some felt his action was unjustified. M. J. Denman, serving as county surveyor since his election on February 15, 1876, wrote that the county had been organized twelve months before Jones' raid, and "its officers had done much in bringing offenders to a responsibility before the law." This perhaps was news to Major Jones. Denman further claimed that when Jones "arrived there were twenty-five citizens on duty with the deputy sheriff and Lieutenant Moore, making arrests. A great many of the arrests made by Jones were of the best citizens of the community, unknown to him, who were soon turned loose, and it was natural that such wholesale arrest[s] would throw discredit upon the county." Denman claimed that all the bad men had left the county, and that it was then one of the most orderly in the state.[51] In part he was correct as such fugitives as Bill Taylor, Lark Ferguson, and Stark Reynolds had gone prior to the roundup.

A few months later a lengthy letter appeared in the *Galveston Daily News* in which Jones' work was discussed, after there had been considerable time for reflection. "Tranquility in Kimble County" was the subheadline. It contained such praise for Jones and his men that they may have actually been embarrassed. The unidentified letter writer opened his work by reminding all that it had been "some few months" since Jones and a company of his Frontier Battalion raided the county and made about forty arrests of "outlaws, murderers and thieves and run off perhaps as many more. When he went into the county the citizens and officers were so thoroughly bulldozed by the outlaws that they would not only not give him any information, but were afraid to be seen talking to him or his men." The outlaws had so intimidated everyone that the judge could not hold court; and any person considering moving into Kimble County was foolhardy. After the "raid" by Jones, district court was held but cases were continued due to lack of juries. Due to the work of the major and his Rangers, "the people remember Jones in their prayers, and are rejoiced to meet and take care of his men . . . and they say to the Adjutant General that the protection of the State troops is not needed at the next term." It was certainly a well composed letter giving due praise to the commander of the Frontier Battalion.[52]

Strangely, J. B. Gillett, whose work is considered by many to be a Texas Ranger classic, gave little attention to the Kimble County affair, although he gave some details of importance. "When the major reached the headwaters of the South Llano River," Gillett wrote, "he halted his escort and detailed several small scouting parties of five or six men each, with orders to arrest every man who could not give a good account of himself" but mistakenly recalled that some fifty or sixty men were arrested and brought in. "Many of the suspects were released upon examination, but I remember one scout brought in two escaped convicts who had been captured on Copperas Creek. We bagged several men wanted for murder and some horse and cattle thieves. Old Kimble County had never had such a clean-up of bandits in her history."[53]

The men Gillett "bagged" were later identified in the press. Sheriff John Walter and deputy sheriff Kleck with six guards delivered them from Gillespie County to the jail in Austin. Travis County Sheriff Dennis Corwin added their names to the jail roster for the night prior to their continuing to Huntsville. The *Statesman* identified them as John Walton and Jim Ponton from Lavaca County, Hensley, an escaped convict from Washington County, Wellington Latimer, accused of murder in Dallas County, and Brauns McKee of Burnet County. Others were J. R. Donoho, J. D. Jones, W. C. L. Jones, Jack Fowler, and William Blantcul from Gillespie County.[54]

In his lengthy report Major Jones perhaps without realizing it provided the reason for the success of the Ranger raid. "Each man," he wrote, "seems to take a personal interest and pride in catching every one he is ordered to arrest." Historian Peter R. Rose expressed his thoughts on why the Roundup worked so successfully, beyond merely Major Jones' planning. He wrote that the young Rangers had frontier skills such as tracking, good marksmanship (although no shots were fired), good horsemanship, and they all wanted to serve the state in a positive manner.[55] These qualities Major Jones observed in his command were similar to those within N. O. Reynolds' own personality and character. They were why he was eminently successful as a leader of men and why "Major" Reynolds would also be remembered as "The Intrepid."

7

A Single Shot Ends a Feud

"[The Horrells were] the most dangerous band of men that ever lived."
—James Buchanan Gillett, 1921

There was virtually no time for the Rangers to rest after their work in Kimble County. On April 29 Reynolds left camp to arrest J. E. Burt and Jack Jones. He scouted from the head of Copperas Creek on the Llano River to Fort McKavett and Menard but failed to find them. By May 4 he was back in camp with no prisoners, but rode out the next day hoping to locate a party of Indians reported to be on Celery or Scalp Creek in Menard County. Reynolds and his ten-man squad went as far as the head of Brady Creek in McCulloch County where they found the trail but were unable to track them down. After a march of ninety miles there was nothing to do but return to camp, now at Kickapoo Springs, reaching there on the seventh.[1]

Two days later Major Jones headed for Coleman County in pursuit of cattle thieves. During that sixty-mile scout they met with some success, capturing J. H. Curtis and Pete Cassimer. Cassimer had escaped from the Burnet County jail. Curtis was one of three men wanted for the murder of Lewis Stone in Kimble County on August 9, 1876. J. H. Curtis, William M. Curtis, and Samuel Williams were all charged with the murder two days later. J. H. was easily recognizable: he was about forty-five years old and had been shot in the mouth. William M. was about twenty-five years old, "spair made" and of light complexion. Sam Williams was also about twenty-five years old, heavily built and of dark complexion. A reward of $250 for each of them had been offered on September 5, 1876.[2] Major Jones was keenly aware of the reward and reminded Brown County Sheriff R. B. Willson to be sure to give Reynolds a receipt for Curtis specific enough so that his description would result in the reward being paid.[3] Reynolds did receive the $250 reward after delivering Curtis to the Brown County jail in Brownwood. Cassimer was delivered there as well.[4] Other fugitives believed to be in the area and who were still high on the Rangers' wanted lists included rustler Caleb Hall, Lewis "Luke" Cathey,[5] charged with a murder in Kimble County on April 16, 1877, Richard Dublin, charged with murder and cattle theft in Kimble County, and Mac Potter. They were frequently not only the subject of Reynolds' scouts but other Ranger patrols as well.

At this point Lt. Berch S. Foster, commander of Company E, tendered his resignation. Whatever explanation he gave for resigning at this time was not preserved in the Ranger records. Instead of immediately replacing him Major Jones "temporarily attached" the company to Company A for duty, all members subject to the order of Captain Coldwell.[6]

On June 9 Major Jones selected Reynolds and eleven others to be his escort. They first marched to Trickham in Coleman County and then to Beasley's Ranch on the Colorado River, a distance of thirty miles. The next day the escort left Beasley's Ranch and camped on the San Saba River. Reynolds and a three-man squad left the escort to hunt for fugitive George Von Cannon and one McCarroll, both charged with murder. After a thirty-mile scout they determined the trail was too cold to continue and returned to Camp San Saba. On the eleventh they learned that Sergeant G. W. Arrington had already arrested Von Cannon and had him safely lodged in the Menard County jail. They could learn nothing of McCarroll. Noted hard-case Caleb Hall was rounded up, arrested in McCulloch County, and charged with cattle stealing in San Saba County. He was also placed in the Menard County jail. A Mason County reporter visited the jail and found reason for levity describing fiddle playing Von Cannon as a "dancing master, [who] adapts himself to the situation, drives away dull care and ennui by extracting melodious notes from an old violin, and teaching his comrades in crime the poetry of motion."[7] But capturing fugitives did not necessarily mean that a case was closed, as Caleb Hall burned a hole in a wooden portion of the courthouse where he was confined and escaped with three other prisoners. Caleb Hall managed to utilize the talents of "dancing master" Von Cannon to act as a decoy in the break. Von Cannon had been taken out of the jail and "was playing in the court-house where they had a ball." During the noise and confusion of the rustic concert Caleb Hall and the others escaped, or so reported the correspondent of the *Galveston Daily News*.[8]

Continuing on, Reynolds and his detachment rode down the San Saba River to the town of San Saba where they provided assistance to county authorities in scouting after horse thieves. Also, members of a Hardin family were reported in the area but Reynolds found none to arrest, apparently another false rumor, nor was McCarroll found whom they heard was in the area. On June 13 Reynolds and a four-man patrol left the command, again in pursuit of William H. Curtis. On reaching Curtis' ranch the next day they were informed that he had left the area and had gone to Coryell County. The Rangers returned to their camp on the fifteenth but then started out on another scout after two others, Sylvester Lockwood and Charles "Jack" Romines, charged with assault to murder and theft in Travis County, and C. C. Nairn, charged with theft in Travis County. Lockwood was not found but Romines and Nairn were arrested. Major Jones gathered up four Rangers to help him deliver the pair to the Travis County jail in Austin. Then Private J. W. Warren and three men were sent out on a scout after Alf Cornet, charged with cattle theft, and J. H. Curtis, who had apparently escaped his guard.[9] Curtis was arrested again, and Major Jones, communicating to Reynolds from headquarters in Austin, ordered Reynolds to have Curtis delivered "under guard of two good men. Have him well secured so as to run no risk of his escape." Jones advised that if Reynolds felt more than two guards were necessary, he could send more, but two should be sufficient "if he is properly secured." Jones, characteristically thinking of all possible concerns, advised also that if Curtis did not have his own horse he could ride one of the camp mules. Reynolds felt two men were sufficient and the two Rangers and prisoner Curtis left for Austin on the thirtieth where he was turned over to Travis County authorities.[10]

The leader of the Higgins faction in the Horrell-Higgins Feud, John Calhoun Pinkney "Pink" Higgins. *Courtesy Bill O'Neal.*

While these actions consumed time and effort, the differences between the Horrell and the Higgins factions in Lampasas County had reached the stage of ambushes and street battles. Ending the feud would result in considerable fame for the Rangers in general and Reynolds in particular. Major Jones had gained valuable experience working with desperate men in Mason County, and now had another opportunity to exhibit his leadership abilities in Lampasas County, but the troubles in Lampasas County would prove to be more vexing. Major Jones arrived in Lampasas, the county seat, on June 14 and immediately reported to Adjutant General Steele that the town was "in a great state of excitement and alarm in consequence of the conflict which occurred here between the Horrel[l] and Higgins parties a few days ago." On June 4 unknown men forced open the courthouse door and carried away all the records of the district court. Then three days later members of both factions started shooting at each other on the town square, a fiery exchange that resulted in the wounding of William Wren, the killing of James Buck Waldrip by Frank Mitchell of the Higgins faction, and the mortal wounding of Frank Mitchell by Mart Horrell. Jones intended to remain in Lampasas a few days to inquire into the condition of affairs "and see if anything can be done to quiet the disturbance and bring the offenders to justice." In truth, Jones feared little could be done as members of both factions had many friends and supporters. Jones wrote it was "difficult to find a man in the county who is not in open or secret sympathy with one or the other of the contending parties." Indeed, on the day of the shootout on the public square Sheriff Albertus Sweet had summoned thirty-one men to assist him in arresting the shootists but only three obeyed the summons.[11]

Third Street looking east from Western Avenue in downtown Lampasas. This image is from the decade following the Horrell-Higgins Feud. *Courtesy Jeff Jackson.*

Sergeant Reynolds did not immediately become involved in the feud. On the contrary, lesser known characters were the object of the Rangers' scouts, some of which resulted in arrests. On the twenty-fifth in Lampasas, Reynolds himself arrested Joe Fowler, charged with assault with intent to murder in Upshur County back in 1871. Fowler was released on bond.[12] Some other scouts were less successful: Sylvester Lockwood, Alf Cornet, and Dudley Buchanan were the objects of scouts led by Reynolds' men but these fugitives managed to avoid arrest. What Reynolds did not know was that Alf Cornet had already been arrested by Capt. John C. Sparks' Rangers. According to one report appearing in the *San Saba News* Cornet had been indicted in San Saba district court for unlawfully branding cattle back in August 1875. He had escaped but was arrested and returned to San Saba; in default of $500 bail he was committed to jail.[13] Capturing Dudley Buchanan would be a special *coup* for any lawman. He had killed Commodore Perry in Dallas County in late 1873; on December 19, 1875, Governor Coke offered a $200 reward for his capture. To make the pot even sweeter A. W. Perry, the murdered man's brother, offered an additional $500 reward for his arrest and safe delivery to authorities. Buchanan was described as "about twenty-five years of age, five feet ten inches high, florid complexion, sandy beard, light hair, blue eyes, and in general appearance rough looking."[14]

Elsewhere, on June 25, Erath County Sheriff James Martin and Napoleon "Bone" Wilson, alias S. Watson, became embroiled in a difficulty near Stephenville, which resulted in the sheriff's death. Martin had attempted to arrest Wilson, believing him guilty of stealing a horse. Wilson resisted with gunfire, killing the sheriff. Murderer Wilson soon became an object of Reynolds' manhunts as well. Earth County officials gathered up $750 to be paid for the arrest and safe delivery of Wilson inside the jail door. Wilson was described as standing fine feet ten inches tall, weighed about 160 pounds, was dark complexioned with dark curly hair and dark eyes, wore a mustache and "a small patch of whiskers on his chin." He was about twenty-four years of age. He may have been wounded in the exchange with Sheriff Martin. Wilson eluded justice until the morning of September 22, 1877, when Capt. Thomas M. Sparks and a squad of Rangers surrounded the camp where Wilson was hiding out. He resisted arrest again and was shot to death.[15]

Even with the various squads out pursuing fugitives in the Lampasas area, the Horrell and Higgins parties were still willing to wage war against each other. Men of the Horrell group were recognized as being "of the very worst reputation." As early as 1873 they were thought of as desperate men, accused of branding and skinning cattle other than their own. Their reputation was sufficiently dangerous that "one yell from them to 'hide out' is sufficient to close all doors within hearing."[16] On January 14 of that year Lampasas County Sheriff Shadrick T. Denson had attempted to arrest one of their associates, George Washington "Wash" Short. Short resisted arrest and shot the sheriff down, wounding him but not fatally.[17]

Although wounded by members of the Horrell party, Sheriff Shadrick T. Denson survived. *Courtesy Jeff Jackson.*

The wounding of the county sheriff brought a squad of State Police to Lampasas, commanded by J. M. Redmon, to restore order. But he could make no arrests because no one was willing to file charges. Redmon realized his presence could do little good and recommended that twenty-five good policemen would bring about good results, and if that did not happen then the governor should declare martial law.[18] Governor E. J. Davis did not declare martial law but he did send Capt. Thomas Williams to Lampasas. Without adequate planning Williams attempted to arrest one of the Horrells inside a saloon. He resisted and in the subsequent minutes a volley of shots was fired into the police, killing Captain Williams and three of his men. After the initial gunfire inside the saloon, the battle moved into the street where Tom and Mart Horrell were wounded. After this disastrous affray the Horrells made an apparent effort to find a more peaceful life and relocated to Lincoln County, New Mexico Territory. They were unable to avoid trouble, and after numerous killings they decided to return to Lampasas County. But conflict continued to surround the Horrells, and animosity between them and the Higgins faction continued to grow.[19]

On January 22, 1877, it was again time for shooting. Merritt Horrell was killed in a Lampasas saloon by John Calhoun Pinkney Higgins, commonly called "Pink," accompanied by Nat Arnold, Maybelline Lovejoy, George Ware, and William Tinker.[20] On March 26, the Horrells, supposedly on their way to court, were ambushed on the road along Battle Branch Creek. Tom and Mart Horrell were seriously wounded.[21] With this latest act of lawlessness Lampasas citizens requested help from Governor Richard Hubbard, but were initially informed that they would have to help themselves. "Sheriffs and deputies and constables must be made to do their duty," communicated the executive. Hubbard knew that the citizens of Texas wanted lawmen with courage and efficiency, and if some lawmen were in league "with knaves in some counties" then those people who elected such individuals to office "deserve to suffer."[22]

With the courthouse being burglarized, district court records being burned, and men shooting at each other on the town square, not to mention the reckless shooting at door knobs and windows of the *Dispatch*

Grave marker of Sheriff Shadrick T. Denson, rural Lampasas County.
Photograph by Parsons.

office and those of attorneys White and Gibson, it became obvious to businessmen that such actions would be a deterrent to economic growth. With such concern growing daily the editors of the *Lampasas Dispatch* prepared a glowing report of the county in hopes of attracting immigrants. It appeared in the influential *Galveston Daily News*, informing potential newcomers that the county population was in excess of seven thousand, that the town was "located in the beautiful valley of the Salt or Sulphur Fork of the Lampasas River, and is one of the most liveliest, handsomest and most flourishing towns in Southwestern Texas." There were sulphur springs located there, one in the northern and the other in the southern part of the city of Lampasas, which had a population of about two thousand. Businesses included six dry goods establishments, three grocery and family provision stores, two clothing stores, two drug stores, two "well conducted hotels," four saloons and lager beer vendors, three carriage and wagon makers, three blacksmiths, two boot and shoemakers, a tin shop, two saddlery and harness makers, a news dealer, a photographer's gallery, a printing office, builders and stonemasons, and other trades and professions, which contributed to the well-being of an industrious and thriving community. The makeup of the buildings themselves was not overlooked: the principal ones were made of "superior quality" limestone rock. A Baptist church and a Methodist church were both under construction. Preaching by various denominations was regular, along with a Sunday school attended by every class of Christians. The Masonic and Odd Fellows lodges each had a flourishing membership. There was even a temperance society "working manfully and successfully in the good cause."[23] In such an attractive setting it is a wonder that the population had not swelled many times more than what was reported. N. O. Reynolds now became aware of these wonderful attractions and after his ranging days he settled in Lampasas County—to become county sheriff and city marshal.

In the late 1870s the Rangers at times camped on Sulphur Creek.
From original postcard in Chuck Parsons Collection.

When Major Jones reported from Lampasas he could make no such song of praise for the community as it still was in a "great state of excitement and alarm" following the shooting on the town square on June 7. In fact, as he wrote to Adjutant General Steele a week later describing the community's problems, he realized he would have to stay there for an indefinite length of time to determine what had caused the difficulties and how to resolve them. He was also aware that few people would give him any assistance, knowing full well that few Lampasas residents were willing to go up against either the Higgins or the Horrell forces.[24]

Albertus Sweet had taken over where Sheriff Denson had failed. Gillett, who may have known both men from his pre-Ranger days, depicted Sweet as cowardly in his dealings with the feuding parties, stating that Sweet believed that no man could arrest the Horrells.[25] Major Jones was very conscious of the attention given the situation, not only by the general population of the state but by his superiors. "They give us credit for much good work and expect us to keep it up," Jones wrote. "We must not let them be disappointed." Jones knew he could not stay in Lampasas indefinitely so placed Sergeant Reynolds in charge of a detachment to be stationed there "for several weeks."[26] It would be a busy period of Reynolds' life, very dangerous and significant not only for his career but for the history of Lampasas County as well.

Reynolds began work immediately. He arrested J. B. Owen on July 8, charged with horse theft in Llano County and disturbing public worship in Kerr County. The next day he arrested Joseph R. Hemphill, who had been charged with theft in Bastrop County. Hemphill was released on bond. Two days later Reynolds and a squad started with a large group of prisoners to the Travis County jail for safe keeping. Besides Owen there were the Faris brothers—Robert Elihu "Bud" and Champion Newton "Champ"—Ed Brown, Andrew Murchison, John Carson, James Polk Mason, and William Thomas Cavin. They were all charged with having broken Scott Cooley and John Ringo out of the Lampasas County jail during the previous year. Cavin turned state's evidence and was released. The group, Reynolds with his squad of five Rangers and the prisoners, rode to Round Rock where they arrived on July 12. Then they took the train to Austin.[27]

Besides the prisoners, Reynolds also had a letter from Major Jones to be personally delivered to Adjutant General Steele. In it, Jones explained his frustration at working with members of the feuding factions. Jones complained that the Horrell-Higgins trouble was "one of the most perplexing to me that I have yet had to contend with." He admitted that putting the parties under bond for their appearance at court "will not prevent them from fighting if they meet." As this effort had already been tried and failed, Jones chose to take the responsibility "in the interest of peace and quiet, rather than in accordance with the dictates of the law, to intercede and endeavor to reconcile the difficulty and thus terminate this long continued feud." Jones was on good terms with both parties and hoped "to effect something towards the desired object in a few days." In the meantime he hoped that the mere presence of the Rangers would prevent members of either party from starting another shooting affray.[28]

While Major Jones planned to work for a peaceful solution to the Horrell-Higgins conflict, he experienced his own irritation with the law. Judge W. A. Blackburn issued a writ of habeas corpus to him on July 12. The eight prisoners then being delivered to Austin charged Jones with illegally restraining them of their liberty. But Judge Blackburn's order to release the prisoners had arrived a day late. Jones explained that the prisoners were already in the Travis County jail and thus out of his control. He also expressed his honest opinion that the purpose of the writ was to give their friends an opportunity to rescue them or have them placed back in the Lampasas County jail where they could be turned out as had been the case with Cooley and Ringo the year before.[29]

Reynolds and his squad were back in camp on July 14. They could be confident that the prisoners would not escape from the new Travis County jail in Austin, a great contrast to the insecure jails in numerous counties on the frontier line. With those men in jail, Jones and Reynolds were anxious to go out and make more arrests. Jones, perhaps with some exaggeration, considered the Olneys and the Faris brothers among "the most desperate characters in the State." He was aware of their large family connections in Llano, Burnet, and Mason Counties, and believed they would resort to any and all means possible for the release of prisoners who they felt should be free.[30]

On the fifteenth Reynolds and a six-man squad traveled to Hamilton County in search of Dee Bailey, charged with assault with intent to commit murder, then indicted in October 1874 in Comanche County.[31] Reynolds was certainly aware that Bailey and his brother James were now both also wanted for murder. The brothers were suspected of passing counterfeit money in Comanche County when Deputy United States Marshal M. R. "Boss" Greene attempted to arrest them some ten miles out of town. The pair resisted with their weapons and Greene was wounded, shot in the right jaw, the ball ranging upward. Greene was left to die, abandoned by the Baileys. Some women were nearby and heard his cries for help and rendered all the aid they could. In spite of all efforts to save him Greene died two days later. A Comanche correspondent known only as W. A. F. described Greene as being "one of our best citizens, and had always taken a prominent part in enforcing the laws and overcoming lawless men." He had been town marshal of Comanche for some time and had served admirably in that capacity, "to which is due, in a great measure, the reputation of the town for peace and order." The Bailey boys eluded the hundreds of men hunting for them, making it safely back to their home country, Denton County, where they may have associated with members of the Sam Bass gang of stage and train robbers. The state of Texas offered a reward of $400 for their capture. The Greene killing occurred on May 12 but they were not indicted until September 28, 1877. They would receive "justice" in late 1883, suffering death at the hands of a mob.[32]

Ault Ferguson was also on the "most wanted" list. Although Reynolds had failed in learning anything of the whereabouts of the Baileys or Ferguson, the squad did arrest William Scarborough, charged with theft in Lamar County and robbery in Fannin County. Robert Cardwell was arrested on a Bastrop County charge and John Huff was arrested on suspicion. Huff was released as no charges could be found against him. On the fifteenth Reynolds sent one of his men with a Lampasas County deputy to arrest Sam Williams, located at Sheep Springs, charged with the Lewis Stone killing. This time Williams was arrested.[33] On the nineteenth he escaped at Liberty Hill while on the way to Austin's jail. As yet no one could claim the $250 reward. The *Lampasas Dispatch* could only report he "made his escape before he reached that place."[34]

Although Jones and Reynolds expected men serving as Rangers to be gentlemen and to conduct themselves as such, occasionally some had to be disciplined. Henry Maltimore was dismissed for drunkenness, but his companions felt the loss deeply and requested Major Jones to reconsider his action. Charles L. Nevill penned the petition in camp on Sulphur Creek on July 16; it was first signed by seventeen Rangers, then by N. O. Reynolds himself. From reading the petition Major Jones may have felt that Henry Maltimore was the most valuable man in his command, as it stated that after reviewing "his past record for good and manly service as a Ranger we believe that it will be a difficult matter to supply his place with a better soldier and a better man." Maltimore had promised that his offense would not happen again. Henry Maltimore was a farmer's son from Greene County, Ohio. Capt. Dan W. Roberts had mustered him into the service on June 1, 1875, in Menard County. Jones reinstated him and he remained in the service until February 28, 1878.[35]

Of greater concern was how to end the Horrell-Higgins feud. Jones had managed to get on "good terms with both parties" —although he never revealed in writing how he managed to accomplish this—the two factions were always ready to fight against each other. A Higgins supporter—"a man named Graham"—was shot and killed the night of July 24, "shot from the brush." It was presumed he had fallen victim to the guns of the Horrells.[36] Major Jones identified the victim only by his surname; the *Lampasas Dispatch* identified him as Elihu Graham. He had been in his field threshing wheat that day, and when about dark he had left his field when he was shot "by parties in ambush." The shooting took place about fifteen miles from Lampasas near Townsen's Mill. Major Jones and a squad of Rangers went out to investigate the killing, but no one was ever identified as his slayer or why he was killed. Although Graham's death failed to invoke any retaliation, Major Jones was able to report that the principal members of the feuding parties were in jail, as well as other fugitives from Colorado, Goliad, Bastrop, and Lamar Counties.[37]

Major Jones had been responsible for laying the groundwork but it was Sergeant Reynolds who accomplished the actual arrest of "the most dangerous band of men that ever lived" in a daring early morning raid on July 28. Ironically the arrest resulted in so many prisoners that the concern then became too few guards to protect the jail from possible mob action. The arrest of the Horrells can best be described by Reynolds himself. In the weekly *Lampasas Dispatch* of August 2 appeared an account of the arrest, which contained certain inaccuracies that Reynolds felt obliged to correct. The August 2 issue has not survived so it is impossible to determine exactly what errors editor W. P. Beall committed, in Reynolds' opinion, but fortunately Beall's report was summarized in the *Galveston Daily News* in the state news columns of August 8. According to this version in the *News* the Horrells were at the edge of town when William Wren and Robert and Alonzo Mitchell of the Higgins party notified Major Jones of the fact. Major Jones then sent Sergeant Reynolds with six Rangers, the two Mitchells, and Wren to the Horrells' place. The next morning the group divided into two parties of five men each, and just after daylight charged upon the house from opposite directions. The Horrells were asleep, which allowed Reynolds and his men to enter the house with guns drawn without waking them. "The Horrells are brave, desperate and determined men" concluded the *News*, "but finding that resistance would be useless, they surrendered." There were eleven men in the Horrell party, but all of them were released, except Tom, Mart, and Sam Horrell.[38]

Reynolds read editor Beall's account and found fault with it; on August 4 he composed his own version of the remarkable event, which was printed in the *Dispatch* five days later. It reveals Reynolds' skill with language as well as his determination that accuracy be recorded.

> In your last number appeared a brief mention of the arrest of the Horrells on the 28th of July, in which occurs some slight inaccuracies which I believe you will be satisfied to correct by the publication of this letter. As I commanded the scout which made the arrest before mentioned none will doubt that I am posted in regard to it.

Samuel "Sam" Horrell, another tough feudist who survived the feud and almost became a centenarian. *Courtesy Jeff Jackson and Martin Horrell.*

As the sun was setting on the evening of the 27th ult., while in camps on the Sulphur Fork about a mile from your office, Major Jones received information from Mr. Bob Mitchell that the Horrells were on School Creek ten miles from this town. Accordingly under orders I started to that point with six men, leaving camp just at dark guided by the two brothers Mitchell, whose names are known in the late difficulties, and by William Wren. Afterwards acting upon later information, I changed the direction of the scout and proceeded towards the residence of Mart. Horrell, on Mesquite Creek still employing the same guides, who were to act as guides only, and to take no part in making the arrest. At an early hour, about five o'clock on the morning of the

> 28th ult., while a heavy rain was falling, we "rounded up" the house and charged into it, surprising the inmates asleep. The Horrells thus rudely aroused, and confused as to the nature of their early visitors, sprang to their weapons and for a few moments a desperate conflict was imminent. Sam. Horrell seized upon my Winchester, and in wrenching it from his grasp the weapon was accidently discharged which added to the excitement, but it is fair and just to the Horrells to state that, though assembled in force, (eleven in number), and in possession of their arms, they surrendered as soon as they learned and fully believed that we were Rangers.
>
> After all was quiet, I approached four friends of the Horrells to aid me as guides and returned to camp on the Sulphur Fork, bringing Sam, Tom and Mart. Horrell as prisoners, having released the others.
>
> None of the Higgins party entered Mart Horrell's house, nor did they aid in rounding it up. They were not seen by the Horrells until all was settled. Afterwards we removed our prisoners to the court house in the town and guarded them without trouble until all three were released on their bonds. I do not believe that force was necessary to arrest the Horrells, but that they were ready to surrender to proper parties at any time, provided they were guaranteed protection while unarmed.
>
> Since the arrest the Horrells have written a conciliatory letter to the Higgins party, which was becomingly answered, and the public may feel assured against a recurrence of the late disturbance.

He had given his version of the arrest, and boldly scrawled his signature, perhaps and justifiably with a note of pride, "N. O. Reynolds, 2nd Sergeant, Commanding Detachment."[39] If there was an error in reporting the work of his men, he wanted it corrected, and it was, in full.

Reynolds' report to Major Jones was considerably briefer: "Sergt. Reynolds and 6 men left camp in pursuit of Tom, Sam and Mart Horrell. Found them at their Ranche on Mesquite Creek, arrested them and 11 of their party on the 29th[*sic*]. Distance marched 25 miles."[40] In his report of July 31, Reynolds pointed out that he had rendered the civil authorities "assistance" in guarding prisoners. It was quite a group, as besides

James Martin "Mart" Horrell, tough feudist and victim of a mob in 1878.
Courtesy Jeff Jackson and Martin Horrell.

the three Horrells there was Pink Higgins, Bob Mitchell, and William Wren (arrested by Major Jones), also John Overstreet, Bob McBee, and John Davidson. Higgins, Mitchell, and Wren were able to give bond and were released from custody. His monthly "Statement of Arrests" merely listed the three Horrells had been arrested on July 28 on a charge of murder and released on bond; and Pink Higgins, Bob Mitchell, William Wren and Alberry Jackson "Bud" Higgins, younger brother of Pink, had been arrested on a charge of murder on July 31—and all were released on bond.[41] In all, sixteen men were arrested during July on charges ranging from acting in a suspicious manner to murder. Reynolds placed his detachment on the town square where the prisoners were guarded, a gesture as much for show to potential troublemakers as for practicality.

The letters exchanged between the two warring factions, essentially treaties of peace, were printed in full in the August 9 edition of the *Dispatch*. Reynolds' corrective letter appeared in column one of the second page, while in the adjacent column appeared in bold headlines "PEACE RESTORED TO LAMPASAS! THE HIGGINS AND HORRELL PARTIES HAVE LAID DOWN THEIR ARMS!!" Editor Beall pointed out that the agreement between the two parties would be "a cause of much rejoicing throughout the section. Many women and children now sleep quietly who a few days ago were startled at the rustling of a bush and were hourly expecting the assassination of some of their friends." Beall reported optimistically that the "hatchet" was buried, and the late "belligerents" had shaken hands and mutually given pledges to keep the peace, to offer no insult or injury, and to abide the action of the law. "Enough blood had been shed, too many children had been made orphans, and too many happy wives had been widowed. But we believe the troubles are over, and once more it can be said that Lampasas is free from local broils and her population is quiet and law-abiding."[42]

The actual letters were both probably composed by Major Jones, who no doubt insisted the leaders of each faction sign their names and then actually keep the promises expressed within the treaties. Certainly the language expressing the intent to preserve the peace was from an educated individual, hardly what any of the Horrells or the Higgins would use, although the handwriting appears to be of someone other than Jones. Thomas L., Samuel M., and James M. "Mart" Horrell signed their letter on July 30, addressed to Pink Higgins, Robert Mitchell, and William Wren. Major Jones signed as witness. On August 2, J. P. Higgins, R. A. Mitchell and W. R. Wren returned the promise to keep the peace.[43]

Ranger Gillett, who was not involved in the actual arrest but no doubt heard of it in Ranger camps, and who also greatly admired Reynolds and was subject to the use of superlatives in his writing, wrote of the capture. Hundreds flocked to Lampasas after it was learned of Reynolds' work, wanting to see "the man that had accomplished the impossible in rounding up the most desperate band of men that ever lived." Gillett also wrote that the arrest covered Reynolds' name with glory and "brought to the name imperishable renown."[44] Besides such intangibles as glory and renown—there were no rewards offered for any of the feudists—the arrest of the Horrells did result in Reynolds being issued a promotion.

Correspondent "Winchester" from Lampasas provided a report to the *Galveston Daily News* of local happenings. He not only praised the town as a resort for invalids, but also told of the truce being accomplished "through the instrumentality of Major Jones" which brought "great peace and quietude to the public mind." Winchester reported that the "cessation of hostilities" was believed to be genuine, and too much praise could not be given to Major Jones. According to Winchester the Horrell party made the first advance toward the reconciliation and "it was met in a brave and manly spirit" by the Higgins party with Jones being the mediator. "The destruction of life, the making of widows and orphans, it is hoped, ceased when these two parties laid down their arms a few days since, and quietly and peaceably mingled together on the public square, eating fruit and melons, and talking of the peaceful days of the bygone times." Winchester concluded his praise of Major Jones with a brief mention of his sergeant, stating that about twenty Rangers, under the command of Reynolds, were encamped there and had frequent calls to arrest law-breakers. Two detachments were out on scout at that moment, and "they may be heard from very soon, to the dismay of evil doers."[45]

Who were the men in Reynolds' squad who rode through the dark and the rain and entered into the cabin of the sleeping Horrells? Reynolds failed to identify them in his reports, but Gillett named Charles L. Nevill, L. W. "Shape" Rogers, Thomas Gillespie, Jack Martin, William Clements, and John Gibbs.[46] However, the *Lampasas Leader* of January 26, 1889, printed a lengthy history of the Horrell-Higgins feud in which the arrest was described. Here the names of the Rangers were given as Isham Harrison, Sam Henry, Henry Maltimore, Henry Warren, Vernon Wilson, William Clements, and Jack Martin. There is no indication of the source of these names.[47] Although Gillett named *six*, the *Leader* reported the arrest was made by Reynolds and *seven* men of the Frontier Battalion.

Major Jones reported to Adjutant General Steele that in all fourteen of the Horrell party had been arrested. Reynolds, in his "Operations of

Detachments" report, indicated he had six men in the squad that arrested eleven of the Horrell party. The *Leader*, giving the number of arrested as "about a dozen" added that besides the three Horrells the others arrested were Bill Fisher, Tom Bowen, Tom McBee, John Stanley, John Dixon, Bill Mitchell, and others. Besides this crowd in the cabin were reportedly two of the Horrell wives and two girls. If nothing else the cabin must have been extremely crowded. Of course we have no real idea as to the size of this dwelling.[48]

Strangely, Walter Prescott Webb, who wrote the first comprehensive history of the Texas Rangers, devoted considerable space—about nine pages—to the Horrell-Higgins feud, but *failed to even mention Sergeant Reynolds by name*. From reading *The Texas Rangers*, one would have to be impressed with Major Jones' ability to direct the operations of the Frontier Battalion and oversee the administration of so many strong-willed young men and the dangerous situations they had to deal with. But, according to Webb, Jones one day not only arrested the entire Horrell party—fourteen in all—but then three days later captured "the three leading spirits of the Higgins faction and four others as well."[49] Did Webb believe that by ignoring Sergeant Reynolds, who made the actual arrest of the Horrells, he would be creating an even greater image of his hero Major John B. Jones? It would seem so.

Capt. Daniel W. Roberts, Reynolds' former commander, also wrote of the Horrell-Higgins feud in his memoir. After discussing briefly the adventures of the Horrells in New Mexico he reviewed their Lampasas County difficulties. In describing this period and the Rangers being called in he wrote: "Major Jones went in person and took my old duty sergeant, N. O. Reynolds, with him, in command of the squad. I loved Major Jones, but he played an Irish trick on me when he took Reynolds from me. But I was compensated later when the Major secured a captain's commission for Reynolds." Reynolds did not ever receive a captain's command, nor did Reynolds use a young local boy J. M. Hawkins as a guide to the Horrells' house as Roberts wrote. But Roberts did add a great compliment to his former sergeant when he noted that after Tom Horrell realized there would be no use in resisting Reynolds: "Horrell had struck the one man in his life that was the finest of steel, and he appeared to like Reynolds from that moment. . . . When Reynolds parted with them at the jail the Horrel[l]s shed tears and told him they never expected to see him again [expecting to be lynched]."[50]

C. L. Douglas prepared a history of various feuds of Texas in which he incorrectly identified Reynolds as a captain but did stress an important aspect of his character in arresting the Horrells. Douglas wrote that Reynolds "displayed the bravery that has immortalized him forever on the rolls of the Rangers." There are errors in Douglas' account, such as stating that Reynolds fired his Winchester "as a warning gesture to prove he meant business" when the shooting was not intentional, and that he fired so close to the bedding that it burst on fire. The other Rangers quickly entered the room and found the Horrells fighting the flames.[51] Reynolds made no mention of any flames caused by the accidental discharge of his Winchester.

The Horrell-Higgins difficulty is one of the few Texas feuds that apparently did terminate by the two warring factions agreeing to end the struggle, although there would be more tragedy within the lives of the Horrell family. Mart and Tom Horrell were later charged with complicity in the murder of store keeper J. T. Vaughn and jailed in Meridian, Bosque County, Texas. This act had nothing to do with the feud, it is believed. On the night of December 15, 1878, a mob of at least fifty men entered Meridian and threatened to burn the jail. The guards weakened under this threat and allowed some of the mob to enter. Forcing one prisoner to hold a candle the mob riddled the Horrell brothers with bullets. A report from Waco stated that the "general supposition at Meridian is that they [the mob] were friends of Vaughn, who had determined to avenge his death, even by taking the law into their own hands. The Meridian people regret the forcing of their jail and murder of men who have not yet been proven guilty, but the general comment is the Horrells *were* guilty."[52] No one was ever brought to justice for this double murder, nor was it ever satisfactorily determined if the Horrell brothers indeed had anything to do with the murder of old man Vaughn.

Even though the Horrells and the Higgins had settled their differences, Major Jones still felt great pressure on the Frontier Battalion. Wary of leaving the country so quickly after such a dramatic arrest, he felt it necessary to keep a force there for an indefinite time. Jones needed to get to Austin to finalize re-organization of the battalion but left Reynolds in Lampasas with a detachment to assure that peace be preserved. The duty had been very onerous on the men, most of whom had been on guard duty every day for the previous two weeks. There were dangerous fugitives still avoiding capture: Joe Olney, Ault Ferguson, and the Bailey brothers were still loose, as was Stark Reynolds, all wanted for murder. Jones left for Austin to make a decision as to who would be the new commander of Company E, Frontier Battalion.

8

A Prisoner Lost in Indiana

"[Sergeant Reynolds is] . . . a man of splendid courage, active and energetic, has good control of men and has been remarkably successful both as a scout after Indians and in finding and arresting fugitives from justice."

—Major John B. Jones, August 20, 1877

Back in Austin, although he would have preferred to remain in the field working directly with his commanders to continually improve efficiency among the Frontier Battalion, Major Jones was forced to deal with administrative matters. With the fiscal years ending on August 31, not surprisingly the legislature had forced a reduction in the Battalion's strength. Each commander was ordered to reduce his company. Every man would be discharged on that day, then reorganized on September 1, with each commander choosing who he wanted to continue to serve the state, only now the company would consist of two sergeants, two corporals, and twenty privates. But the criminal element or Indian raiding parties did not concern themselves with such elements of Texas frontier existence. Of concern as well were such things as changes in other areas of law enforcement. The death of a sheriff or a controversial election could produce a violent situation, such as old feuds flaring up again. Such a fact of life became apparent in nearby Hamilton County, although Reynolds was not personally involved.

Hamilton County Sheriff David Smith died on the thirtieth of July 1877, having served in that capacity since his appointment in 1871 and then being elected in 1872 and re-elected in 1876. He died not from wounds received in a gun battle with outlaws but of "bilious fever" as reported in an Austin newspaper.[1] Serious trouble was anticipated by attorney Charles K. Bell who wrote an urgent letter to Major Jones, then at Lampasas, requesting several Rangers be sent to prevent any potential trouble, believing that their presence alone would have a "quieting effect." Although Bell did not mention it in his letter, there had earlier been a feud of some duration that the Rangers had quieted down,[2] but now with Sheriff Smith's death Bell feared the old hatreds would erupt in violence. Bell estimated that half a dozen Rangers would suffice "for a few of them might now keep down trouble which it would take years to stop if once started." Bell knew more than he revealed apparently, as he also urged Major Jones to keep secret how he learned they were needed; he also noted that Dr. Nicholson was "badly needed now" but did not go into details. Bell had known the doctor from a few years before when Dr. Nicholson had resided there. The good news in Bell's letter was that fugitive Ault Ferguson was down on the Leon River and possibly could be captured, but the bad news was that Bell felt "it would not be worth while to attempt his arrest by surprise."[3]

Jones responded in the affirmative and ordered Sergeant Reynolds, still attached to Neal Coldwell's Company A, to send Corp. Henry W. McGhee with five men to Hamilton and assist the authorities in maintaining law and order. McGhee was to consult with Bell and if the situation remained peaceful he was to return to Lampasas by August 20.[4] Former Ranger George Washington Wade was appointed sheriff on August 2 to replace Smith, and no doubt his prior experience as a Ranger and the presence of the half dozen from the Frontier Battalion prevented any of the troubles anticipated by attorney Bell. Wade served as sheriff until November 5, 1878.[5]

Jones had intended to leave for the frontier but due to the uncertainty following the Horrell-Higgins peace agreement felt either he or Reynolds should stay there until at least mid-September. Jones was not only capable of grasping the bigger picture but was cognizant of the individual needs of his men. J. B. Gillett had been serving the state without a leave, and now Jones saw an opportunity to give him some time at home. He ordered Coldwell to send him on to Lampasas, explaining that Gillett had "been in the service a long time without an opportunity to go home, his mother, a widow, is very anxious to see him and as I will need more men at Lampasas I promised to order him to that place."[6] Jones may have been especially anxious to accommodate J. B. Gillett because James S. Gillett, his father, had served as adjutant general of the state from November 24, 1851, until February 4, 1856, when the office was discontinued. He had also served in Captain W. H. D. Carrington's company during the late war. J. S. Gillett died in Lampasas in April 1874.[7]

Events were rapidly taking place leading to the reorganization of the Frontier Battalion. Major Jones issued General Order No. 16 requiring company commanders to discharge the men of their respective companies and furnish them duplicate pay certificates. Then on September 1 the companies were to be re-organized, each company to be reduced to two sergeants, two corporals and twenty privates. Enlistments were to be for twelve months unless earlier discharged. Jones reminded his commanders that their attention "is hereby called to orders heretofore issued . . . that no habitual drunkard [nor any] men of immoral character or against whom an indictment is found can be received." As with previous orders, the recruits also had to have a good horse.[8]

Reynolds, in command of the Company A detachment and not directly concerned with administrative details, concentrated on pursuing fugitives. On August 1 he and two others arrested "Dock" Civils, charged with assault to kill.[9] Major Jones and four other Rangers left camp to deliver him and two other prisoners to the Travis County jail. On the way, in Jollyville, J. W. Warren and three others arrested Steve Stroud, Wiley Holcolm, W. P. Moore and Salem Curtis (charged with theft of corn) at Stroud's farm on Bull Creek in Travis County; they were turned over to a Williamson County deputy sheriff. While in Round Rock, they arrested "Wild Bill" Owens, who was charged with murder in Wilson County. Private Charles L. Nevill was sent down to San Marcos where he arrested Sanders Griffin, an escaped convict. Civils, Robert Cardwell, Owens, Griffin, and a man named Wilson were all delivered to the Travis County jail. By the seventeenth the squad had returned to Lampasas, having traveled 175 miles.[10]

Sergeant Reynolds provided Major Jones with some good news in his correspondence of August 11. Ranger privates George M. Doolittle[11] and John H. Gibbs had captured John D. McRae, better known as Dee McRae, charged with the double-barreled shotgun slaying of R. S. Peteet on April 26, 1874 in Grimes County. McRae was in his late twenties, tall and slender, over six feet tall with gray eyes and dark hair. He had a scar on his left cheek and was "fond of drinking ardent spirits." Reynolds reminded Jones that the $500 reward offered for McRae should be divided with "the Same Understanding." It was not specified in Ranger correspondence but apparently when a reward was issued it was accepted that all who had been involved in the capture would receive his fair portion of the reward. A *Statesman* reporter stressed that fugitive McRae had the reward on his head and a "deal of truck on his back." The reporter further explained that where a reward was offered for the arrest of a man Major Jones divided the reward among the parties giving information leading to the arrest, and the Ranger or Rangers making the arrest. "This is certainly very proper" concluded the reporter. McRae attempted to escape while in custody of the Rangers, but "was intimidated by the shots flying thick and fast around him." Rangers Harrison and Gibbs delivered McRae to the jail in Austin, arriving there on August 13. McRae feared being mobbed and wanted protection. He was delivered safely to Navasota, Grimes County, and then admitted to bail in the amount of $10,000. A voucher in the amount of $500 was issued, made out to John H. Gibbs, which he no doubt shared with Harrison and Doolittle.[12]

Reynolds proudly informed Major Jones that his Rangers had also captured Alf Cornet and then lodged him in the jail at Lampasas. An unidentified Ranger and a Lampasas County deputy had made the arrest, although no details were provided. Cornet was lodged in the Lampasas jail while McRae was delivered to the Travis County jail. Although Cornet may have been wanted in counties other than Llano, his punishment came from Lampasas. At his trial on March 27, 1878, he pled guilty to three counts of cattle theft. Cornet was then a twenty-one-year-old Texan, and was sentenced to three terms of five, one, and two years on the cattle theft charges. Received at Huntsville on April 10, 1878, he managed to escape on October 26 of that year but was recaptured on July 25, 1892. He then was pardoned by Gov. James S. Hogg on September 16, 1893, having spent more time as an escaped convict than he had served as a prisoner.[13]

On August 8 Reynolds sent Pvt. Samuel A. Henry and three others scouting after Ault Ferguson, feeling confident he would be arrested this time. Ferguson, indicted for murder on September 20, 1876, in Hamilton County, was a man of dark complexion, sandy hair and "considerably speckled with smallpox." Another slightly contradictory description pointed out that his six-foot-tall frame was "spair made," that he was of light complexion, had blue eyes, and his left arm had been broken causing it to swing unnaturally from his body. He had knife scars on the back of his neck and on his face. Reynolds confidently wrote in his letter of August 10 that he would not be surprised to hear of Ferguson's capture soon, but the quartet returned to camp on the eleventh and Reynolds had to write, "nothing accomplished, distance marched 125 miles." In spite of his optimism Reynolds never caught up with Ferguson. He was wanted as late as 1892 and was then believed to be in the Clark and Pike County area of southwest Arkansas.[14]

Besides pursuing thieves and murderers, Corporal McGhee was also out looking for an illegal still "and the Parties that Are Running It." In spite of the distillers, murderers, and thieves in the area and the potential for the Horrells and Higgins groups to start shooting at each other again, Reynolds concluded his letter to Jones with an optimistic "All things quiet."[15]

On August 27 Reynolds had William Cantrell in custody, charged with horse theft in Falls and McLennan Counties and murder in Erath County. Reynolds believed he was also somehow connected to the illegal whiskey still operation. He had sent out a scout and six arrests had been made; all prisoners were turned over to the sheriff. With disappointment obvious from his report, he complained that they were all released on bond or some other charges that were against them. Nothing could be proven in regard to the "Whiskey Business" as the county attorney would not accept the evidence of witness Casper. Certainly Reynolds can be forgiven for expressing hard feelings regarding these prisoners being released.[16]

Charles L. Nevill, who followed Reynolds as commander of Company E.
Courtesy RG 0001–102–422. People Collection, Maps & Photographs Collection. Courtesy Archives & Information Services Division, Texas State Library and Archives (ARIS/TSLAC).

In spite of the successes Reynolds was experiencing, an occasional failure was inevitable. Such a case was not due to his weakness but to the apparent carelessness of one of his men: Charles L. Nevill, a Ranger with experience and Reynolds' future brother-in-law. It involved Ohio-born Winfield S. Tuttle. Tuttle was born about 1852 but in the late 1850s the family moved to Hancock County, Indiana. While still in his teens he joined the army and then relocated to California. As he was under age his father had him removed from the army on a writ of habeas corpus and he was returned to Indiana. Not long after, he left home and returned to

California where he married. Then after returning to Indiana the couple decided to visit two sisters of Mrs. Tuttle who resided in Brown County, Texas. Once in county seat Brownwood, Tuttle became a popular figure and was elected mayor at the town's organization. According to Tuttle's version of events, an outlaw gang led by J. C. McGrew resented the semblance of law and order as represented by Mayor Tuttle and threatened the town. Tuttle sent word to McGrew that the town would be protected from them. In the ensuing weeks McGrew and his men stole cattle from the Brownwood area and headed in the direction of Mexico. The thieves were overtaken many miles south, captured and returned to Brown County. Soon after it was determined that young Ed Reese was absent when the cattle were stolen and returned, and he was suspected of belonging to McGrew's gang. In late April of 1876 he was found hanging from a tree limb. Tuttle and several others, Deputy U.S. Marshal David Breckinridge, Brownwood Constable Harvey B. Yarborough, and detective George B. Holland were suspected of lynching Reese but when no solid evidence was produced against them they were released.[17] Tuttle took a subscription to the local newspaper to have it sent to him in Indiana and with his wife and child returned to his former home.[18]

But the *Brownwood Eagle* presented a different version of the death of Ed Reese than did Tuttle. Reportedly he was found hanging, strangled by a small rope made from a buffalo hide. "The affair" according to the *Eagle*, was "a most dastardly cold blooded murder, showing a malignant and abandoned heart in the offenders." Continuing in the same vein it was reported that the "atrocity has seldom if ever been equaled in Texas. The deliberation with which they went about their fiendish work is enough to chill the very life blood in our veins."[19] Rumors circulated that clues pointed to the identity of the murderers. Based on those clues Sheriff R. B. Willson and the authorities determined that Reese came to his death at the hands of W. S. Tuttle. A reward of $250 was offered for him by Governor Hubbard after Brown County attorneys convinced him there was sufficient evidence to convict Tuttle. Authorities learned—apparently from the newspaper editor—that Tuttle was in Indiana.[20]

During this same period Capt. John C. Sparks of Company C had arrested John Lackey, a fugitive from Mississippi.[21] Lackey had, sometime in the fall of 1876, in Lauderdale County, Mississippi, killed his aged father-in-law, eighty-three-year-old Bennett Edwards. Fearing pursuit Lackey headed west, possibly killed a man in Alabama whom he believed was following him, and finally reached Texas. How Sparks learned of Lackey's whereabouts is unknown, but after a lengthy pursuit he captured him in the little community of Saint Joseph in Montague County, delivering him to the Travis County jail on August 14. Previously, on July 13, Mississippi Governor J. M. Stone had issued a requisition for Lackey to be delivered back to justice. Sparks was assured of receiving the $1,200 reward offered for Lackey's capture.[22] Captain Sparks and Sgt. Charles L. Nevill left Austin via train to deliver Lackey back to Mississippi. Sparks was to return to Texas while Nevill was to continue to Indiana, arrest Tuttle and return him to Brown County justice. Apparently Reynolds had extraordinary faith in Nevill's abilities, or else he would have sent one or two others with him to assist in bringing back a man charged with murder.

The trip to Mississippi was uneventful. After Sparks delivered Lackey to Mississippi authorities, Nevill continued on alone, arriving in Hancock County, Indiana, on Friday, August 24, with requisition papers to return Tuttle to Texas. The next morning he met with Sheriff William Thomas and with Deputy William Thompson started for New Palestine where Tuttle lived. There they learned he was in adjacent Shelby County attending a church picnic, with Tuttle working at a peanut stand. After adding Shelby County Constable Richard Duvall to the group the lawmen arrested Tuttle without incident. Sheriff Thomas wanted to take Tuttle to Indianapolis before a circuit judge to prove his identity but the clever Tuttle agreed to waive all the legal preliminaries and convinced the officers to allow him to see his wife and child one last time. He was taken to his house where—surprisingly—the officers allowed him to be alone with his family. Once inside Tuttle "armed himself with a large needle revolver, such as are in use on the frontier. . . . . [and] armed by the aid of his wife, Tuttle opened the door, and passed out the rear way into the yard." Deputy Thompson and Nevill then attempted to run

Tuttle down but they lost him in a nearby cornfield, their shots fired at him doing no harm. Tuttle was on foot and it remained a mystery why the two lawmen could not easily track him down in the field. The Indiana newspapers, showing sympathy for Tuttle and his family, gave the arrest and subsequent escape considerable coverage. The *Indianapolis Journal* concluded its report with a caustic: "The Texas sheriff [*sic*] hied him homeward yesterday [August 30] without having bagged any game."[23]

Reynolds could do nothing but report the results of this costly endeavor. He recorded that Sparks "having turned Lackey over to Sheriff [of] Laudeville [*sic*] County Miss from whence Nevill went to Indiana arrested Tuttle and he making his escape [;] distance marched 2000 miles."[24]

Reynolds must have been both angry and disappointed. His man Nevill had covered two thousand miles and had nothing to show for it. Governor Hubbard now offered a reward of $300 for Tuttle on August 15, but there is no evidence any of it was paid out for Nevill's traveling expenses.[25] Tuttle's final fate remains unknown. One wonders why Nevill could not have remained longer in Indiana hunting for his escaped prisoner, rather than so quickly returning to Texas.

In spite of such embarrassments Reynolds lost no credibility as a leader in the eyes of his superiors. Major Jones wrote to Adjutant General Steele "to recommend and request" that N. O. Reynolds—2nd Sergeant of Company A—be promoted to the rank of 2nd Lieutenant of Company E to take effect on September 1. "Sergt. Reynolds has been one of my best Non-Commissioned officers for nearly three years" wrote Jones, describing him as "a man of splendid courage, active and energetic, has good control of men and has been remarkably successful both as a Scout after Indians and in finding and arresting fugitives from justice."[26]

High praise for Reynolds also appeared in the press once it was learned that he was in line for the promotion. The *Galveston Daily News* contained a report from Frio City discussing the Frontier Battalion, in which the following appeared:

> The major has made a wise selection in placing Capt. Col[d]well in command of Company A, and if the report be true that Sergeant

> Reynolds is to be Lieutenant of Company E, his selection is truly a good one, for two braver men in a service they are now performing could not be found. Sergeant Reynolds is now on a scout from Capt. Col[d]well's company in the upper country.[27]

On August 24 Gov. Richard B. Hubbard signed General Order No. 20 assigning Reynolds to the command of Company E, to take effect on September 1, 1877. The man who in 1875 had preferred to resign rather than pursue fugitive Scott Cooley now was in command of his own company.[28]

Three days later Reynolds and Major Jones went to Burnet to develop a plan to make the county jail more secure, returning to camp the following day. There was a rumor that a jail delivery was imminent. On the August 30 Jones and a thirty-four-man detachment returned to Burnet to assist the sheriff and arrest the jail breakers. Tom Sneed, brother of one of the prisoners, and William Van Winkle, both from Llano County, had offered Sheriff John J. Strickland $1,000 if he would allow certain prisoners to "escape." Jones advised Strickland to accept the bribe and to set a date for the delivery to take place. Fifteen Rangers were inside the jail with Strickland when riders approached at midnight. Sneed and Van Winkle were arrested, charged with bribery and placed in jail. Andrew Murchison was also involved in the jail breaking plot, and Private Warren and five Rangers went out and arrested him. Murchison was brought in along with one Vinyard, charged with cattle theft. In Austin the *Statesman* reporter commented that the "Llano crowd made a junction with the three [Sneed, Van Winkle and Murchison], [and] it is probable a fight would have ensued and the professional jail breakers of Llano would have been roughly handled and taught a good lesson." In Weatherford, news of the planned jail break was treated with some levity, its report ending thus: "Maj. Jones with a sufficient force was stationed inside the jail, and the parties walked right in to the trap so prettily laid and instead of reducing the number of occupants, they succeeded in augmenting the number to thrice more."[29]

During August the detachment under Reynolds arrested a total of twenty-one men on various charges ranging from operating an illegal whiskey still to murder. In addition the men had provided assistance to authorities in Hamilton, Bell, and Burnet Counties. From August 21 to 24 they had rendered assistance to the Lampasas Fair Association: the county authorities still feared that the Horrell and Higgins problems might erupt in violence again. However, in spite of these accomplishments, such fugitives as James Polk Mason and Ault Ferguson were still enjoying their freedom, both wanted on charges of murder.[30]

Reynolds prepared his first muster roll at Burnet on September 1, 1877. Enlistments were to last until August 31, 1878. Gillett wrote that Reynolds was authorized to pick which men he wished from other companies and "either discharge or transfer the remainder to other commands. No other officer in the battalion, I believe, was ever accorded this privilege." He recalled that Reynolds had a week or so to make his selection. Gillett, his visit home with his mother having ended, was then stationed out on the Rio Grande frontier and was "nonplussed" when he received the order to report to Austin to be placed in Reynolds' company. Gillett's recollection of his new commander was perhaps a reflection of the general attitude of the other men, as he described the company as the "most formidable body of men I had ever seen." Although Reynolds described himself as five-foot nine-inches tall when joining the army in 1865, Gillett viewed him as "over six feet tall" and weighing one-hundred seventy-five pounds. "He was a very handsome man, a perfect blond, with steel-blue eyes and a long, light moustache. At that time he was about thirty years of age, vigorous in mind and body, and had a massive determination to succeed as a ranger. His mind was original, bold, profound and quick, with a will that no obstacle could daunt. He was the best ranger in the world—there was never another like him."[31]

9

One Dublin Taken, One Dublin Escapes

"Get out . . . don't you see the Rangers have got me?"
—Dell Dublin to his brother Richard, November 21, 1877

On August 23, 1877, Dallas detective and Ranger Jack Duncan and Texas Ranger John B. Armstrong, with several Florida officials, captured John Wesley Hardin, the Texas man-killer wanted for more than a score of murders. Hardin, now with a reward of $4,000 for his taking, had enjoyed eight years of lawlessness since his first killing in 1868, eluding members of the Texas State Police, county sheriffs, detectives, bounty hunters, and Rangers for years. Occasionally he had been captured but always managed to escape, sometimes shooting his way to freedom. In mid-1874, after the killing of Brown County deputy sheriff and former Texas Ranger Charles M. Webb,[1] Hardin felt the increasing pressure of the law and fled to Florida where relatives of his wife lived. As "John H. Swain," Hardin may have lived out a quiet life if Armstrong and Duncan had not plotted his successful capture. In resisting the lawmen one of Hardin's companions was killed, but he was taken back to Texas alive.

Through the southern states Armstrong and Duncan moved their prisoner via the rails; at every depot crowds of people gathered to see the notorious gunfighter. Hardin, heavily ironed with leg shackles and handcuffs, never lost his air of defiance and arrogance. At Palestine, Texas, the two Rangers had to change trains; hundreds were at the depot when

The deadliest man-killer Texas ever produced, John Wesley Hardin, from the original tintype made in Abilene, Kansas, in 1871. *Courtesy the Robert G. McCubbin Collection.*

someone called out, "What have you got there?" Hardin, in chains but still on the offensive, tartly replied, "A Panther." Armstrong and Duncan arrived back in Austin on August 28 and placed the prisoner in the new Travis County jail, after five days continually guarding the man-killer.[2]

Still arrogant and confident Hardin may have believed he could escape or somehow beat the charge of murder for the Webb killing. When placed in his cell he was one of some eighty prisoners, of whom a few he called friends or relatives, but also several from DeWitt County who were among his enemies from back in the days when the Sutton-Taylor feud was at its worst. The jail was considered among the largest and most secure prisons in the state, according to one Austin reporter. Upon Hardin's arrival, the jailer, never identified, discovered that some of the prisoners had been cutting the bars of the iron cage. Rangers "took the whole lot out and examined them. The saw or knife used could not be found. The prisoners were put back and the jail is now watched by a detail of frontier troops. Hardin will be carried to Comanche the latter part of next week."[3]

What Reynolds could not realize at this point was that he would be responsible for the safety of Hardin during the next year, through his trial, his appeal, and finally his delivery to Huntsville state prison. But before those orders came there were other fugitives to hunt down.

The new commander of Company E lived up to the expectations of his superiors, constantly on patrol, sending out scouts, and searching for and arresting wanted men. For the first time in Reynolds' career there is a near daily accounting of his actions and whereabouts. This is in the form of a small ledger book which was kept by 1st Sergeant Charles L. Nevill with entries dating from September 1, 1877, through April 17, 1879. The record reveals continuous scouts and arrests made, jails guarded, fugitives arrested, and Indians pursued.

During the first three days of September, the camp was moved from Burnet to Running Branch Creek, a total distance of thirty-two miles. On the third day of September Corporal J. W. Warren and five others were sent to Austin to assist Sheriff Dennis Corwin in guarding the jail, mainly due to the arrival of the new prisoner Hardin. On the following day Sergeant Nevill and four others went to Cypress Creek in Travis County in pursuit of B. F. Armstrong and D. E. Wise, the former charged with assault to murder in Clay County and the latter charged with theft in Houston County. They were both arrested and then delivered to the new jail but had to be released when authorities could not definitely establish their identity. On the same day Sergeant Henry McGhee and three others were sent out to arrest George Nelson, charged with assault to murder in Hood County and numerous other crimes. Reynolds reported that Nelson had once lived in Corpus Christi and was a noted character there. Nelson ended up in jail.[4]

On September 6 Pvt. Lowe W. Rogers and three other Rangers arrested William Owens in the little community of Bagdad in Williamson County, situated on Brushy Creek. Then Bagdad was a thriving town site boasting a blacksmith shop, several stores, and a stage stop. When the railroad bypassed it there was little future for it and today it has become a part of Leander.[5] Reynolds sent Privates R. C. Ware and M. B. Davis with prisoner W. A. J. Owens to Travis County, as he believed there were indictments against him there. Reynolds described him as "a bad character to say the least" and wanted something found to give the authorities a reason to hold him. Owens claimed to have gotten away from everyone who ever arrested him. This was almost a personal insult to Reynolds, but again nothing substantial could be found and once again Owens had to be released. Reynolds had to be satisfied that this "bad character" had gotten away from him as well. On the ninth Ranger Nevill and one other were sent to Williamson County to arrest Sam Higgins, who had been charged with theft in Marion County. Andrew Lewis was also taken in for carrying a concealed weapon. Both Lewis and Higgins were transported to the Williamson County jail in Georgetown by Private Rogers where on the next day Lewis was fined $25 and had to forfeit the weapon. Higgins was delivered to the Travis County jail.[6]

Although Gillett praised his new commander for being "vigorous in mind and body," in truth Reynolds was suffering physically. He admitted being ill when he took over the command and his physical problems had not improved. He was again very ill the following year in July and ultimately had to resign due to health reasons. He had written a letter to Major Jones on September 5 at Brushy Creek in which he stated that he was not well and that he feared he would get worse. He needed a pack of Dr. Sage's "Cattarh Remedy"; he also thought he was suffering from "Neuralga" and hoped Major Jones could send him some kind of medicine that would give him some relief. We don't know exactly what ailed Reynolds, although it must have been very painful to affect such a tough Ranger as Reynolds was and he tried hard to prevent his men from learning about it.[7]

In spite of Reynolds' aches and pains it was time to deliver John Wesley Hardin to Comanche for his trial. Comanche County Sheriff Frank Wilson,[8] a Major Griffith, and the entire Company E left Austin with their valuable prisoner on the nineteenth of September. They arrived at Comanche five days later, averaging twenty-eight miles a day. Sergeant Nevill recorded: "Left Camp on South Leon [river] and camped in Commanche [*sic*] [and] placed J. W. Hardin in Jail to await trial." That trial lasted from September 24 until the thirtieth with the Rangers continually guarding him.[9]

The newspapers gave extensive coverage to Hardin's trial and occasionally recognition of Reynolds as well. The experience was remembered for years afterward, and Gillett described the events. He wrote that Sheriff Wilson came to Austin to convey Hardin to Comanche for his trial and requested the governor send him a Ranger escort. As Reynolds and his company were there at the time he was ordered to accompany Wilson and protect Hardin from mob violence. Further, Gillett remembered vividly the day they left Austin, writing that there were between one and two thousand people gathered about the jail to see the notorious prisoner. Gillett realized the historic importance of the event:

> The rangers were drawn up just outside the jail, and Henry Thomas and myself were ordered to enter the prison and escort Hardin out. Heavily shackled and handcuffed, the prisoner walked very slowly between us. The boy who had sold fish and game on the streets of Austin was now guarding the most dangerous criminal in Texas. It was glory enough for me.[10]

The *Statesman* commented on Hardin's departure, describing the "very large crowd gathered in the street to see this noted knight of the six-shooter as he passed from the jail to the carriage waiting for him." When Hardin first appeared on the stone steps of the jail entrance he appeared somewhat nervous, and "looked about as if to observe who were there, and if possible to rest his eyes upon a familiar face." But within moments Hardin "became complacent and appeared pleasant, conversing freely with the sheriff and guard who occupied the vehicle with him." As the carriage began its slow journey from Austin north on the Georgetown road the crowds pressed up close to get a "clear view" of the prisoner. Although Hardin had expressed apprehension about his safety in Comanche—with good reason, as mobs had lynched his brother and two cousins in the immediate aftermath of the Webb killing—the *Statesman* pointed out "we are satisfied that the officers in charge of him will see that no mob is allowed to molest him."[11]

The Rangers and their single prisoner passed through Lampasas on September 21. The *Dispatch* commented that more people had "rushed to see him than if he had been a rhinoceros, and he seemed not to be displeased with the eager attention shown him." Apparently Reynolds' accomplishment of having arrested the Horrells not long before had been forgotten by the reporter, as his name was not even mentioned in the brief news item. It is probable that members of the Horrell and Higgins

Lieut. N. O. Reynolds and his command spent a night in this building delivering John Wesley Hardin to Comanche for trial. *Courtesy Leona Bruce.*

families were amongst those spectators rushing to see Hardin. Pink Higgins, Robert Mitchell, and William Tinker, charged with the killing of Merritt Horrell in January of that year, were preparing for their trial before Judge William Blackburn on the twenty-sixth. They were all released on bond. [12] At Comanche "quite a multitude" gathered to see the notorious Hardin, one reporter noting that "the people crowded upon one another, like sheep in a pen."[13]

Reporter Knix of the *Dallas Weekly Herald* was in Comanche to cover the trial. When Hardin and the Rangers arrived about 10 o'clock in the morning "the town was under some excitement, as well as interest, on hearing that John Wesley Hardin was coming to town." Knix recorded that the news of Hardin's arrival "spread like lightning, and in a few seconds everybody had left their employment to get a glimpse of him. Crowds had gathered along the streets where he had to pass, eagerly waiting his arrival (I must say that your correspondent was among them). At last they came."[14]

Hardin, writing years later, recalled his experience as a prisoner. "I stayed in Austin jail until the latter part of September, and then a company of Rangers (No. 35) commanded by N. O. Reynolds and accompanied by Sheriff Wilson and his deputies escorted me to Comanche." Hardin, in contrast to the *Lampasas Dispatch*, at least remembered Reynolds' name. His explanation for such a strong guard was because the Rangers feared the "brutal mob" which had lynched his brother and cousins back in 1874 would try to lynch him as well, and they had to prevent any friends of Hardin attempting to rescue him from his guards. Hardin recalled that "the military appearance" created great interest in the towns from Austin to Comanche. He rode in a buggy with the sheriff, with most of the company in front and a smaller portion bringing up the rear. Reynolds and his men camped out every night and everything was done to keep Hardin comfortable although he was kept shackled and cuffed. At Comanche, "my escort marched up, waited for me to be carried into the jail, as I was too heavily shackled to walk. Reynolds placed a guard around the jail and went out to see what the situation was. He soon found that feeling was very violent against me and that there were 200 men camped two miles from town for the purpose of hanging me."[15]

Hardin, whose tone suggests that he was in command of the Ranger group rather than their prisoner, recalled telling Reynolds to put the citizen guard summoned by the sheriff outside the jail yard and the Rangers inside if he wished to save his prisoner, which Reynolds did. Although the guard may not have been the same every day, usually there were four Rangers on duty inside the jail and the remainder camped just in the rear of the prison.[16] "The brave Reynolds told me that if the mob attacked me or the jail he would arm me and let me out to rough it with him and his men. He would also arm the men in jail, of whom there were ten or twelve. He gave this out publicly and the mob never came."[17] As there is only Hardin's word for this action on Reynolds' part it is impossible to verify, although Reynolds could have made such a statement. Later George D. Hendricks added considerable color to the scene, writing that Reynolds "threatened a surging mob that he would hand over two full six-shooters to the desperado if they did not disperse. They dispersed."[18] One cannot help but wonder how Major Jones would have responded if Reynolds had indeed armed John Wesley Hardin to fight off a lynch mob. One thing is certain: N. O. Reynolds was not going to let anyone take his prisoner; in fact, no one ever took a prisoner from Reynolds, nor did a prisoner ever escape from him.

John Harvey, who claimed to be an ex-Ranger although the existing records fail to record his service, was interviewed at the time of Hardin's death about his experiences. He claimed he was a guard, although whether as a citizen guard at Comanche or when and where is not stated, and as he knew Reynolds "and the boys" and therefore "kept up with them for company." He claimed that when the verdict was brought in there were "men around who wanted to lynch Hardin and the rangers kept closely around the prisoner." The commander "was a nervy man, and he had twenty-two rangers under his command, every one of whom would die when it came his turn, but show the white feather never. It took just such men to save Hardin from the determined Coleman [*sic*, Brown and Comanche] county regulators, who wanted to shoot or hang him so bad they could not sleep."[19]

Hardin was found guilty of second degree murder for the killing of Charles M. Webb. During the trial and then during the appeal Hardin was escorted back and forth from Comanche to Austin to Comanche, guarded by Reynolds and his men. The Rangers left Comanche on October 1 and arrived back in Austin on the sixth. W.A.F., a reporter of the *Galveston Daily News* stationed in Comanche, provided this comment: "He was taken back Monday by Sheriff Wilson, aided by twenty Rangers under command of Lieut. Reynolds, back to the Travis county jail, where he was ordered for safe keeping. His removal has restored our village to its usual order and quiet."[20]

For a time Lieut. George W. Campbell of Company B was in Comanche to assist as needed during the trial. Neither Reynolds' nor Campbell's report indicates specifically why there was a need for additional Rangers, but possibly Reynolds at times was so ill another commander's presence was advisable. At the time Campbell was stationed only ten miles away so his presence there was convenient.[21]

The number of Rangers actually on guard varied somewhat from twenty to Hardin's count of thirty-five. When Reynolds prepared his monthly return at Comanche he showed the command consisted of himself, two sergeants, two corporals, and nineteen privates, making an aggregate of twenty-four. At times Corp. J. W. Warren and a detachment were in Austin guarding the Travis County jail; however, between September 21 and 30 Warren and a five-man detachment worked the Lampasas County Fair. Apparently the entire company acted as guards during the removal of Hardin from Austin to Comanche, but at other times the company was reduced significantly due to other concerns.[22]

One of Reynolds' Rangers—Mervyn Bathurst Davis—an articulate and observant man with an above average education and a veteran of the Confederate Army, took time to write long letters that were printed in the *Galveston Daily News.* This literate Ranger—who signed his letters simply "Mervyn" —wrote the following on September 25.

> Day before yesterday Lieut. Reynolds, commanding Co. E. of the Frontier Battalion, arrived at this place, guarding John Wesley Hardin.

> The Rangers were five days on the road with their prisoner. Hardin deported himself with the utmost decorum, evincing no restlessness though his patience was sorely tried by the gaping crowds who gathered at the noon and evening camps to stare him in the face, with a curiosity that knew no sense of delicacy. He was quite communicative, talking freely of his terrible adventures, expressing regrets for what he termed his errors, and hopes for the future. He is what the ladies would call a blond, about five feet ten inches high, wears his whiskers in the French style, and is fairly educated in English and the common school branches. He has been wounded in several places, and suffered with one old bullet wound on the trip hither. He is confined in the jail at this place, which is a small stone building thickly walled, heavily sealed on the inside, with oak, containing an iron cage. He is also ironed and guarded by Rangers, who remain within the prison walls both by day and by night. A company of Rangers are camped in the back yard of the prison, so that the public may rest assured that there is no possibility of the prisoner's escape on the one hand or suffering by mob violence on the other.

Being a guard many hours over several days Ranger M. B. Davis used the time to visit with the "communicative" prisoner, and shared some of their thoughts and concerns with each other, although Hardin's adventures certainly eclipsed those of Ranger Davis.

> Your correspondent has heard many stories of John Wesley Hardin, and can not but believe that a few of them were greatly exaggerated. Many have asserted that he is unable to sleep with any degree of comfort to himself or those within hearing of him; that, disturbed by appalling dreams he is wont to spring, howling like a mad man, from his bed to grapple with phantom foes or cower whimpering on the floor. . . . But I have guarded this wild man the report of whose bloody crimes has caused so much shuddering, whose name was a "bug bear" to the timid tourist in Texas. Yes, I have guarded him at midnight, when the moonlight was reflected in the dew drops of the prairie sedge, and in the tangled brush that skirts the cow-house. Alone and standing among the sleeping

rangers I have gazed on the face of him I guarded, John Wesley Hardin, the gentlest sleeper of them all. Sometimes a troubled look disturbed his countenance for an instant, once he murmured "Johnny," his little son's name, but in the main his sleep was calmer than the moonlit stream flowing past me to the sea. If any demons ever haunted his bedchamber, they kept aloof from his bivouac. Were the irons on his limbs the potent charms that awed them, or was it the cold blue gleam of the sentinel's Winchester? Perhaps some spiritualist can answer.[23]

Texas Ranger, naturalist and journalist Mervyn Bathurst Davis served briefly as a member of N. O. Reynolds' Company E. He provided numerous pen pictures of his experiences, one of which was guarding John Wesley Hardin.

Courtesy Carol Davis Wiener.

In October, with Hardin again in the Austin jail awaiting the result of his appeal, the men of Reynolds' command were daily hunting other fugitives—men wanted for a great variety of offenses against the law. On the ninth Corporal Warren and one other arrested Thomas M. Childers, charged with obtaining money under false pretenses. Childers had presented a receipt purporting to be from the sheriff of Limestone County for the delivery of a murderer and collected the reward of $300. The Secretary of State discovered the signature was a forgery and had him arrested. Released on bond Childers chose to leave the area, but was later arrested in Hearne, Robertson County. The next day Sergeant McGhee brought in George R. Freeman, indicted in Cherokee County for assault to murder. Both were turned over to Travis County Sheriff Dennis Corwin. On the nineteenth Privates Gillett and Tim McCarty arrested James McCullough, also charged with forgery. McCullough was able to give bond and was released. Three days later Reynolds re-arrested McCullough, who was charged with violating postal laws and delivered him to the United States Marshal. What must have been quite a ring was apparent as on the nineteenth Private Nevill arrested Dr. Thomas E. Tullis for forgery in Travis County. Tullis, "chief of the local land pirates" was indicated for forging Jacob de Cordova's name on a deed of land in Blanco County, as well as other names as witnesses to the de Cordova deed. He also gave bond and was released but was then arrested by Sergeant McGhee for violating postal laws and was turned over to a United States Marshal. On the same day Nevill and McCarty started for Dallas in pursuit of William McCullough, James' brother, who was also charged with forgery in Travis County. After covering a total of 575 miles through Dallas, Fort Worth, and Caddo they had to give up the chase.[24]

Enforcing the laws for white-collar crimes must have been a nice change from chasing down violent criminals for Reynolds' Rangers. Thomas E. Tullis had had a successful practice as a land agent in Austin in the early seventies. The 1872–1873 *Austin City Directory* shows him working with Dr. J. S. Stewart in the firm of Stewart & Tullis. Tullis was still listed as such as late as 1877. James and William McCullough were both listed as attorneys at law practicing in Austin. What happened to William McCullough is unknown, but James received a prison term. Austin's *Daily Democratic Statesman* enjoyed ridiculing his change of "profession," that of making chair bottoms in prison. His "weekly occupation is making shock chair bottoms, which is an intellectual and pleasing occupation for a lawyer who was never worth shucks." He also was teaching Sunday school, making himself an "officious teacher." The *Statesman* pointed out that McCullough would "read his title clear to mansions in the skies" even if it was a forgery! What eventually happened to the McCulloughs is unknown, but Tullis was found guilty of uttering a false instrument on December 28, 1877. As prisoner #6479 Tullis was described as fifty-one years old, born in South Carolina, and married. Although having a "common education" he gave his occupation as a physician.[25]

On the twenty-third of October the company left Austin to escort Bill Allison and Wes Johnson to Kimble County for trial, the latter charged with the murder of Rance Moore along with James Polk Mason. Wes Johnson managed somehow to elude the lawmen, but no details have been preserved as to how he accomplished his escape; but he was not a free man for long. By month's end William Crier and William Leonard were both arrested in Kimbleville, charged with "removing Live stock out of range," or more simply put, cattle theft.[26]

Judge William A. Blackburn, who had earlier held court successfully in Kimble County thanks to the Rangers, on November 4, with an escort of Corporal Warren and three additional Rangers, journeyed to Menard to hold court. That same day Gillett and a half dozen other Rangers scouted out to search for sign of Indians who reportedly had been seen in the area. That night Reynolds and Thomas Sieker,[27] on detached duty from Company D, overtook them and all returned to camp as the report of Indians proved to be unfounded.[28]

Ranger-correspondent Mervyn was with the squad escorting Judge Blackburn to Menardville. On November 5 he again wrote to the *Galveston Daily News*. It was through the courtesy of Menard County Sheriff J. H. Comstock and his friend Sam H. Wade, a former Ranger of F. M. Moore's Company D, that he was able to write "these hurried lines." He was out on a scout with Corporal Gillett following the trail of a band of Lipan Indians who had raided into Kimble County the previous week. According to Mervyn, the Indians got so close that they entered Junction City, the new county seat. "Court was in session, and the savages made wild work of the lawyers' horses. Judge [Alby O.] Cooley, of Fredericksburg, and a Mr. Denham, of Mason, are among those who lost their horses." Judge Blackburn disposed of some cattle stealing cases and then dealt with two men charged with murder: Wesley Johnson and James Grey, a thirteen-year-old boy. Both were "put under heavy bonds to answer charges of murder."[29]

On November 6 Reynolds sent Corporal Warren to Mason to assist Sheriff Jesse W. Leslie. What specific trouble may have been anticipated is unclear, the "Mason County War" being effectively ended.[30] It was important enough that even the *Galveston Daily News* gave space to the event, pointing out that with district court in session there were eight Rangers of Lieutenant Reynolds' company present, under the command of Corporal Warren. They had arrived in time to be present when court opened until it adjourned. It was "the same detachment who guarded John Wesley Hardin during his recent trial at Comanche."[31] It was apparent to those who may have paid attention to such things that certain events would define N. O. Reynolds, such as arresting the Horrells and keeping Hardin alive until delivered to Huntsville.

On November 8 Reynolds sent Pvt. Henry Maltimore with five others to Mason to assist Corporal Warren. On the same day Reynolds arrested H. F. Dial, charged with aiding prisoners to escape in Menard County. He was turned over to Sheriff Comstock. Three days later Reynolds and a squad went out in search of Charles Pickett, alias Charles Lewis, wanted for a Travis County murder. The man they arrested could not be satisfactorily identified and had to be released.[32]

On November 19 Corporal Warren and six men escorted the notorious John Ringo and others to the Travis County jail. Ranger Mervyn was inspired to write another letter, one of particular interest as it further reveals his appreciation for the natural beauty surrounding him. From Llanotown (now Llano) Mervyn wrote

> We halted on the banks of the Colorado, having crossed over to the Llano side just as the sun was setting on the evening of the 26th inst. The great glow gave a deeper tint of scarlet to the wild sumac, dyed with the tint of autumn and waving like red suction flags over all the flowers of bankrupt summer. Twelve men we numbered in our party: Seven Rangers, Sheriff (J. J.) Bozarth and Col. Wright, the livery man of Llano and 3 prisoners, Geo. Gladden, John Ringo and – Mitchell. The latter were heavily ironed. The purple skies faded, but our camp fires glowed brightly on the boughs of the trees, and we fell to work with a zest upon the fried bacon, bread, and coffee that bespoke the hungry men. Indeed, the day had been chilly. We had ridden long and hard, and were very hungry. At midnight your correspondent was aroused to go on guard. The waning moon was dancing on the rippling sheen of the Colorado as I took my post to watch the sleepers and the glowing coals beneath the big log.[33]

Once the prisoners were delivered to the Austin jail Warren and his squad returned to Llano. With such notorious prisoners as Ringo and Gladden in jail with him, Hardin now seriously contemplated his situation. He became acquainted with these men who had gained such notoriety due to their involvement in the Mason County War while he had been hiding out in Florida. In the new Travis County jail he and Ringo earned each other's respect. Hardin wrote, years afterward, in "that jail I met some noted men. Bill Taylor, George Gladden, John Ringo, Manning Clements, [Sam] Pipes and [Albert G.] Herndon of the Bass gang, John Collins, Jeff Ake, and Brown Bowen."[34] The men he recalled years later are surprising in some cases, as he had "met" several before in desperate situations. He served alongside Bill Taylor and to a lesser degree Brown Bowen during the shooting phase of the Sutton-Taylor feud. Clements was a first cousin who had helped break Hardin out of the Gonzales County jail a few years before. Brown Bowen of course was his brother-in-law.

But having such noted men behind bars did not satisfy the Rangers of Company E. On November 21 Reynolds and a ten-man squad left camp in pursuit of brothers John Sheldon "Dell" and Richard Dublin.

The Dublins, as well as other fugitives like their brother-in-law Bill Allison and Stark Reynolds, frequently used "Old Man" Dublin's place as their headquarters. According to Gillett, Richard Dublin had convinced his father to move there after discovering that the naturally brushy and tangled country of Kimble County would provide good cover for fugitives. Richard Dublin's record was impressive by any standard: a Kimble County killing on April 16, 1874; three cattle theft indictments in Kimble County; and a cattle theft indictment in Coryell County in August of 1873.[35] By reputation the Dublins had "committed more murders and robberies than any two men who have terrorized the Texas frontiers." Obviously whoever wrote that blood-and-thunder had forgotten the crimes of John Wesley Hardin.

The Dublin family had become a thorn in the Rangers' side, as three of the six sons became fugitives from justice, while two of the eight daughters also married men who became fugitives. James Dublin, generally referred to as "Old Man" Dublin to distinguish him from his numerous brood, was approaching the age of sixty years when Lieutenant Reynolds focused on ending the criminal activities of the Dublins, which included not only those with the Dublin name but also a son-in-law, Bill Allison.[36]

But on November 21 Gillett managed to "round up" one of the Dublins, "a daring cut-throat and renegade who has headed Indian raids into Kimble and Menard counties for the past seven years" as one reporter described him. The Rangers rode up to a cow-pen about four miles from Junction City and easily took James Roland "Dell" Dublin by surprise. After Dell was in custody, brother Richard rode up, unaware of the situation, and was himself almost captured as well, but Dell Dublin screamed, "Get out, you d—d fool, don't you see the Rangers have got me?" Two Rangers closely pursued him as he ran, emptying their carbines at him, but he managed to escape, leaving brother Dell to his fate. Two days later Dell Dublin was escorted to Llano County for a habeas corpus trial.[37] Gillett's description of the arrest was similar to the newspaper report. He recalled the arrest of Dell Dublin as uneventful, but said he became "fearfully angry when he found escape impossible. He tore his shirt bosom open and dared the rangers to shoot him. When he was being disarmed his elder brother,

Dick, rode out of the brush and came within gunshot of the ranch before he discovered the presence of the rangers." Then he "turned his horse quickly and made his escape, though the rangers pursued him some distance and fired many shots at him."[38] Gillett had known both brothers as cowboys while working on the Joe Franks spread in 1873.

With the year of 1877 in its closing weeks, the record reflects a flurry of Ranger activity, as if the new commander wanted to arrest all the fugitives before the new year dawned. Such names as Stark Reynolds, Caleb Hall[39] and Richard Dublin remained the frequent subject of Ranger scouts. Yet every day there were new men to pursue who had become fugitives for a crime of passion or an act of cold-blooded savagery. On the evening of December 3, in Wortham, Freestone County, three men, including Alf Rushing, argued with store keeper J. J. Stubbs, over a seventeen-dollar pistol that Stubbs accused the trio of stealing. When City Marshal Jackson Barfield attempted to settle the argument peacefully, Alf Rushing blasted him with a shotgun. Rushing, Harve Scruggs, and Frank Carter were able to get out of town but Carter was wounded and then captured. Rushing did not stay in Texas, for as late as 1898, Freestone County District Attorney O. C. Kinner, writing to Texas Governor Charles A. Culberson, stated that Rushing had been the leader of a gang of outlaws who "infested" the Mt. Pisgah country some seven or eight miles from Wortham, and who were "a terror" to the whole section. Some of the gang had been killed, others died or left the country, but Rushing, then the last of the gang, remained a fugitive, most of the time out of the state. Rushing indeed had become a long-time fugitive and was at times reported to be in such faraway places as California and the Wyoming territory, as well as Arkansas and the Indian Territory. Reynolds, as well as other Ranger commanders, frequently sent out squads to arrest him; all were well aware of the $1,000 reward for his capture. One description depicted him as six-foot two-inches tall, weighing about 175 pounds, his hair a dark sandy color with a red florid complexion and "*a wolfish look* [*and*] *is bold to recklessness*."[40] He was a genuine nineteenth-century giant of a Texas desperado who became the object of many Ranger patrols.

On December 7 Sergeant C. L. Nevill and a six-man squad went on scout to capture fugitive Stark Reynolds. He was not found but the squad did capture Luther Wilson, charged with theft of horses in Lavaca County. On the eighth, Pvt. John R. Banister and two others delivered him to the jail in Menardville. On the following day Gillett and four others went out again to capture Stark Reynolds, but again nothing was accomplished. Three days later Nevill again took out after Reynolds with the same results.[41] It was apparent that Stark Reynolds was hiding in the area but managed to elude the Ranger patrols.

On December 18 Sergeant McGhee and five men went out to capture Richard Dublin again but returned two days later with no prisoner. On that same day Banister and two others went out on a scout after Caleb Hall and other fugitives in Brown and McCulloch Counties. Lieutenant Reynolds, on the same day, investigated a report—which proved to be false—of an Indian sighting.[42] Even though the concern of marauding savages was essentially over, some still believed they were prowling around intending to do harm to white settlers.

On Christmas Eve Sergeant McGhee and four others went out with orders to capture Wesley Johnson, as he had escaped from the Kimble County jail. They failed to capture him but did arrest W. W. Collins and George Spear, charged with cattle theft in Mason County. Gillett recalled that it was on a scout on the Little Saline in Menard County, on Christmas Day, that the detail had a running fight with four men. They captured a man identified as John Collins who had stolen a yoke of oxen in Fredericksburg and brazenly drove them up to within two miles of the Ranger camp, and a man he identified as John Gray, wanted for murder "in one of the eastern counties." James Polk Mason, wanted for the murder of Rance Moore, was in the skirmish, but he managed to escape. John Gray was delivered to the Burnet jail while W. W. Collins and Spear were delivered to authorities in Gillespie County. Gillett did not identify the men with him, nor did he allude to the fact that on December 1 Sergeant Nevill had already arrested W. W. Collins and George Spear, but they had escaped from the Gillespie County jail. Nevill did record that on December 1 Privates John H. Gibbs and Thomas P. Gillespie were sent out in pursuit of the escaped thieves. Nevill could only record that "Collins made his escape and they returned to camp [.] dis[tance] marched 2 miles." On the same day Sergeant Nevill and a four-man squad went to Collins' house but again failed to find the fugitive.[43]

On the nineteenth Lieutenant Reynolds with eight men went in pursuit of Indians "supposed to be going up Llano information having come to camp to that effect [but] found report to be false." It had been a fruitless march of twenty-five miles. Two days later Reynolds took a squad out to again look for Collins and Spear but again failed to find the fugitives. But it was not a total waste of effort as they did manage to capture W. W. Collins and Spear. Also on that day Corporal Gillett and four men went out in pursuit of Richard Dublin and other fugitives but failed to find them, returning to camp on December 27.

During this time Kimble County Sheriff John B. Gorman[44] must have been doing his own sleuthing as he had located several thieves and requested assistance from the Rangers. Two days after Christmas, Pvt. Abram Anglin and six others went out with the sheriff and arrested Jordan A. Burt, J. K. Potter, and E. T. Denson for theft of hogs. They came across their quarry in Kimble County, meeting up with them with four headless hogs in their possession. Presumably the hogs had been decapitated as the markings on their ears would indicate they were stolen property. One of the thieves, apparently J. A. Burt, was also known as "Black Burt" and had escaped from the Menard County jail some time before.[45]

Elsewhere events were developing that would affect Reynolds and the men of Company E. On December 22 three men had robbed the Cleburne–Fort Worth stagecoach about nine miles west of Dallas. The mail was not disturbed but passengers were robbed. Although it was not known at the time it was the noted Sam Bass who led the trio. Then on January 26, 1878, the Fort Worth–Weatherford stage was robbed by two men, presumably Sam Bass and Frank Jackson. The highwaymen did better this time, taking between four and five hundred dollars in currency and three gold watches.[46]

By now Lieutenant Arrington had returned from Wortham, Freestone County, and reported his efforts to capture Ault Ferguson a failure.

Although Ferguson and Rushing, as far as known, did not associate with each other, Lieutenant Arrington may have been aware they were active in the same area and had hopes of arresting both. In this case, he failed. Rushing had many friends and relatives in the area who harbored and protected him. The Rushing gang had purchased all the guns they could find in the area, even trying to buy guns from the Rangers. Arrington's scout was not a total failure, however, as on the return he captured one Harry Cook who had deserted from the Rangers on July 15, 1877. He had taken with him arms belonging to the state of Texas.[47]

Sam Bass in the following year became somewhat of a folk-hero, even becoming one of the few Wild West desperadoes about whom a ballad was composed, sung by cowboys on the cattle trails. Although Bass became popular, other criminals never caught the attention of balladeers or poets, nor the legend-makers. Ault Ferguson, for example, remained a fugitive. Lieutenant Arrington, having gone to Wortham in Freestone County, failed to locate him. Alf Cornet, a fugitive who had many friends in the Wortham area, also managed to evade capture. Neither ever caught the attention of the public to become a folk-hero like Sam Bass.

10

A Killing in Scabtown

"[*Lieutenant Reynolds*] *of the rangers fears the consequences of his bloody work.*"

—**Widow Ida Miller, March 21, 1878**

By 1878, Menard County, once on the very edge of the frontier, was considered settled. The county had been organized in 1871 and in the following year a courthouse was erected in Menardville (now Menard). Former Frontier Battalion member William W. Lewis, who had joined Captain Perry's Company D at the same time Reynolds had back in 1874, operated a saloon there. Lewis' saloon, according to the *San Antonio Daily Express* traveling reporter Hans Mickle, displayed a large canvass sign depicting an imaginative steamboat going up the Salt River in which Lewis was a "distinguished passenger." The most prominent buildings were the two-story rock courthouse and Mr. Becker's store.[1]

The community of Menardville had organized around a military post established in 1852, which was named after Captain Henry McKavett, killed at the battle of Monterrey during the Mexican War. Fort McKavett originally boasted five companies of the 8th Infantry stationed there to protect incoming settlers and to push the frontier further west. By 1859 the Indian menace was considered minimal and the post was abandoned. Then during the Civil War with many able-bodied men serving in the eastern theaters Indian activity increased in the area. In 1868 the fort was re-established; at its peak in the 1870s four hundred troops were stationed there, including units from the 1st, 10th, 16th, and 22nd Infantry along with "Buffalo Soldiers" of the 24th Infantry and 9th and

A grouping of the men in Captain D. W. Roberts' Company D, a collage made by photographer M. C. Ragsdale in 1878. Top row from left: Doug Coalson, Ed Wallace, Ed Cook, George Hughes; second row: Nick Brown, William Sheffield, R.G. Kimbell, Tom Carson, R.R. Russell, L. C. Miller; third row: Ed Sieker, L. P. Sieker, Captain Roberts, Henry Ashburn, "Doc" Gourley; fourth row: Tom Sparks, Robert Roberts, William Clements, J. L. Rogers, George R. Bingham, James Renick; bottom row: James Moore, Sam Henry, E. J. Pound, Henry Thomas. This image originally appeared in Mrs. D. W. Roberts' book, *A Woman's Reminiscences of Six Years in Camp with the Texas Rangers.*

10th Cavalry. A variety of civilian establishments were there to provide services to the troops. After the Civil War, substantial homes were built and according to correspondent Mickle, there was "the air of comfort and convenience" everywhere.

The civilian settlement, located about a mile north of the post, was known as Lehnesburg by some, named in honor of early merchant William Lehne, but Mickle—perhaps in deference to William Lewis—identified it as Lewisville. To give additional color to the scene Mickle pointed out that "the boys" called the settlement "Scabtown." Lehne died in early 1877 but his widow continued to operate the general merchandise store, under the supervision of Mr. H. J. M. Bridge; the other was operated by Will Prescott. Besides the two stores, there were three saloons and places which "allowed the widest latitude and [were] Characteristic of a frontier town and post" as Mickle delicately described it.[2]

In late December 1877 Lieutenant Reynolds and a small squad stopped at Fort McKavett while pursuing fugitives. With Reynolds were Sergt. Henry McGhee, Privates Tom Gillespie, Richard Harrison, and Tim McCarthy, the latter detached from Captain Coldwell's Company A. They were not on the trail of any particular fugitive, or at least none were identified in the reports. Reynolds' Monthly Return merely indicates he and his scout went to Menard County "in pursuit of fugitives."[3] George Stevenson, the black cook, and Ben Johnson, the black teamster who had joined the command on October 23, 1877, accompanied the Rangers.[4] Camp was made at Fort McKavett on New Year's Eve.

Gillett, who was not present but certainly learned of the events at Fort McKavett from those who were there, explained that at "that time each frontier post had its Chihuahua or scab town, a little settlement with gambling halls, saloons, etc., to catch the soldiers' dollars." Fort McKavett was no different, and there "were many discharged soldiers, some of them negroes from the Tenth Cavalry. These blacks had associated with white gamblers and lewd women until they thought themselves the equals of white men, and became mean and overbearing."

On New Year's Eve there was a dance held at Scabtown, a dance that Gillett claimed was provided by ex-soldiers of the Tenth Cavalry, an all-black unit. Naturally only Stevenson, described as "a light mulatto, almost white, but well thought of by all the boys in the company" and Ben Johnson attended the dance from Reynolds' detachment. Gillett explained that it was George Stevenson's idea to attend. Stevenson and Johnson both obtained Reynolds' permission to leave camp, each one carrying a pistol to help enjoy the festivities which were being held at the house of ex-soldier Charles Miller.

Stevenson and Johnson were both admitted to the dance, but almost immediately trouble broke out. Although black, like Miller, they were both part of the Rangers who were "despised" by some of the ex-soldiers. Miller and others "jumped on" the pair, took their pistols and kicked them out. The luckless pair had no alternative other than to return to camp, weaponless. George Stevenson, who had borrowed a pistol from Tim McCarty, went to him and explained what had happened. McCarty then went to Lieutenant Reynolds to report that two pistols had been taken, both property of the state of Texas.[5] Reynolds was sleeping at Mrs. Lehne's merchandise store when McCarty awakened him. Reynolds gathered his Rangers and with the cook and teamster headed for Miller's dance hall where he demanded the return of the pistols. Miller had no appreciation of who he now had to deal with, for he answered: "Stand your ground you white livered sons of bitches" and shouted further insults. Reynolds demanded their surrender so he and his Rangers could search the house.

Miller must have anticipated gunplay and may have even wanted a fight, yelling out, "If we die we will die right in this house!" Or he may simply have been expressing drunken bravado. Mrs. Miller told her husband to give the pistols back to the Rangers, obviously trying to calm the situation before it escalated even further. She approached the door to return one of the pistols when Charles Miller took it away from her and fired at McCarty, but missed. McCarty fired back, and then the shooting "became General on Both Sides" as Reynolds described the affray. A bullet hit McCarty, plowing through his chest below the left nipple. He had the strength to holler out, "Lieutenant, I am killed!"[6]

No description is known to exist of the interior of Miller's house, but it must have been of considerable size if it could hold a dance for many people. Inside were Charles Miller and his wife Ida, Steve Saunders, Henry Clay, Mrs. Miller's little girl, and certainly a few other men and women as well.[7] Reynolds and his men poured in volleys of shot; when the smoke had cleared and the Rangers entered they found Miller, Saunders, and Clay stretched out dead, and one other body: the little girl of Charles and Ida Miller who had been unintentionally shot and killed. Gillett wrote that only one man escaped from the house during the exchange of gunshots, jumping out through a window into the darkness. McCarty survived the night. George Stevenson "fought like a tiger and won the boy's praise" as Gillett described the cook's action during the battle.[8]

Menard County Sheriff J. H. Comstock investigated the bloody incident and added important details. His letter, written on the second while the details were fresh in his mind, was printed in Austin's *Statesman*. The report read that Reynolds and a five-man squad had arrived in the area on December 23, a week earlier than the Monthly Return indicates, to "assist the county officers in keeping the peace during the holidays." Comstock found that on New Year's night [*sic*] the cook had gone to Scabtown when he was "attacked" by Miller, Clay, and Saunders who leveled their pistols on him and demanded the pistol he wore. The three were drunk so Stevenson, although not identified by name in Comstock's letter, saw he had no choice but to comply. Here Comstock indicated Reynolds had first sent two Rangers to recover the pistol but as they were unsuccessful they returned and reported to Reynolds. At that point Reynolds gathered four men and surrounded the Miller house, telling him who he was and that the pistol had to be returned because it was the property of the state of Texas. Miller cursed the Rangers while Mrs. Miller tried to return the pistol, but it was grabbed out of her hands. "Here, take your damned old pistol" said Miller who foolishly fired when McCarty stepped forward. McCarty managed to get a shot off, "about the same time." When McCarty uttered "Lieutenant, I am killed" Reynolds demanded the surrender of everyone in the house. "No, we'll die first" someone yelled, and then the shooting commenced. Reynolds then ordered his men to return fire. There are errors in Comstock's letter, but he correctly pointed out that McCarty lived twenty-four hours and was then buried at the post.

A coroner's jury determined that the blacks "came to their death while resisting officers in the discharge of their duty."[9]

Reynolds telegraphed Adjutant General Steele the sad news on January 2, while McCarty was still alive, that during the attempt to arrest Steve Saunders, Charles Miller, and Henry Clay, "charged with appropriating State arms they resisted arrest and all killed. Our loss one man wounded Tim McCarty." The next day he followed up with a second telegram:

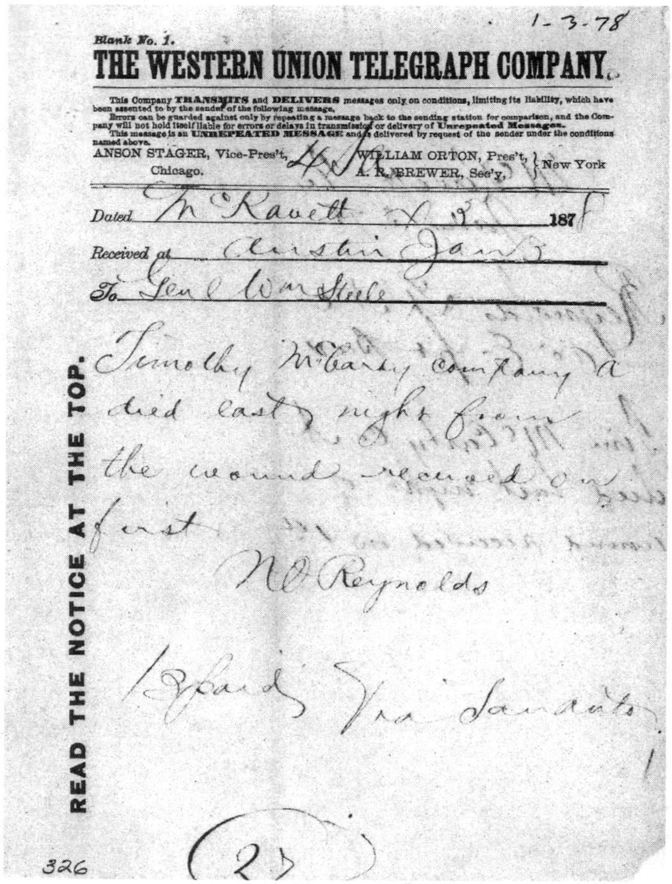

1-3-78

Blank No. 1.

THE WESTERN UNION TELEGRAPH COMPANY.

This Company TRANSMITS and DELIVERS messages only on conditions, limiting its liability, which have been assented to by the sender of the following message.

Errors can be guarded against only by repeating a message back to the sending station for comparison, and the Company will not hold itself liable for errors or delays in transmission or delivery of Unrepeated Messages.

This message is an UNREPEATED MESSAGE and is delivered by request of the sender under the conditions named above.

ANSON STAGER, Vice-Pres't, Chicago. WILLIAM ORTON, Pres't, A. R. BREWER, Sec'y, New York

Dated McKavett Tex 3 1878

Received at Austin Jan 3

To Genl Wm Steele

Timothy McCarty company A died last night from the wound received on first.

N O Reynolds

Repaid Via San Antonio

READ THE NOTICE AT THE TOP.

326

(2)

Lieutenant Reynolds' telegram to Adj. Gen. William Steele informing him of the death of Ranger Tim McCarty. *Adjutant General Correspondence, RG 401-398-1, Courtesy the Archives & Information Services Division, Texas State Library and Archives (ARIS/TSLAC).*

"Timothy McCarty Company A died last night from the wounds received on first."[10] He also took time to write a lengthy letter to Major Jones, adding great detail. The letter, written on Mrs. William Lehne's letterhead, ended with the comment, "The Citizens are Jubilent [*sic*] over the Killing of the Negroes and I think this Place will be quiet for Some time to Come."[11] Reynolds also took the time to write a letter to an unidentified acquaintance in which he expressed "sympathy with the relatives and friends of McCarty."

Ranger Henry McGhee wrote his version of the affair in a letter to his brother John, then residing in Waco, which was printed in the *Waco Weekly Examiner and Patron*. McGhee wrote that the squad had arrived at Fort McKavett on the thirty-first of December, and had "first-rate winter quarters, good tents and everything in good shape." At first he told of how they had expected to be sent out to El Paso to settle the troubles there, and then began his account of how Fort McKavett was "a pretty rough place and the negroes here need killing." McGhee reported that the fight had occurred on the night of January 1 and that four men and a four-year-old Negro boy [*sic*] had been killed, the "boy" killed accidentally. As McGhee wrote:

> There are two negroes with the company, one of whom is the Major's boy and the other a wagoner; both are required to carry revolvers. A crowd of negroes caught these boys last night and disarmed them. They returned to camp and reported the occurrence to our Lieutenant, who accompanied by four Rangers, including myself, started after the negroes for the purpose of arresting them and recovering our arms. We found them in a house and the Lieutenant demanded the pistols and their surrender. They refused to do either, saying that [they] would kill every white man in town first. The Lieutenant insisted, however, and finally they agreed to give up the pistols, but just as a Ranger reached out his hand to receive one of them, the negro shot him, and then the ball opened. We killed all that were in the house except one, who ran and got away, though I think he is wounded. The negroes emptied their six-shooters—it was right lively for a little while. I got in ten shots with

> my Winchester rifle, and I would not be surprised if it did some damage. [Tim McCarty] was seriously wounded. I don't think he will live. He is one of the best men in our command, and is brave as a lion.

In McGhee's postscript he noted that McCarty died at 1:20 o'clock and "died as he fell—true and brave to the last. He was from Virginia to Austin. During the late war he was a member of Pegrams's Virginia battery."[12]

Major Jones discussed the entire incident with Governor Hubbard and Adjutant General Steele who approved Reynolds' action, but at least a few newspapers were critical according to Steele, although he did not identify any by name. In reaction to this Major Jones ordered Reynolds to obtain a certified copy of the coroner's report and forward it to General Steele, so in case there was further criticism it could be published. Major Jones also took the time to write Captain Coldwell, then stationed at Frio Town, that one of his men had been killed in the line of duty.[13] At this point Reynolds, Jones, and Steele no doubt considered the matter closed.

Not surprisingly it is apparent from the remaining documentation that it was a general feeling among the Rangers, as with most every other white man at the time, that the white race was superior to other races. Gillett especially revealed that attitude as he wrote that the former soldiers had been associating with "white gamblers and lewd women" so much that they felt themselves "the equals of white men," which to Gillett certainly was an erroneous attitude on their part. Reynolds found that the local citizenry was jubilant over the killings, but was it because those three dead men were bullies and ruffians and had been troublesome to those in the area, or was it because the three were black? Ranger McGhee in his private letter indicated a belief perhaps common to many of the era, that "the negroes here need killing," an idea that perhaps was intended to remind all that every so often a killing would remind "the negroes" to remain "in their place" of being subservient to the white. One cannot help but wonder: if the men who took the pistols from the cook and teamster (almost white) had themselves been of the same race as the Rangers, would Reynolds and his men been so quick to fire, to empty their weapons inside a building, not caring particularly where their shots landed?

It was Ida Miller, now the widow of Charles Miller, however, who demanded what in her mind was justice; after all she had lost not only her husband but her little girl as well. On January 3—the victims of the tragedy hardly settled in their graves—she wrote a brief note that appeared in the *San Antonio Daily Express,* which in turn was printed in the *Galveston Weekly News.* She stated her husband, the "little child," and two others, naming Stave Saunders and Henry Clay, had also been killed. "My little child's head was shot to pieces and my husband was shot in four places. The other two were shot and fell in the fire."[14]

How long the thirty-four-year-old widow stayed at Fort McKavett is unknown, but by March she was at Fort Concho, Tom Green County, some fifty miles to the northwest, where on March 21 she wrote to Fritz Tegener, a Justice of the Peace in Travis County, who she had formerly known. Ida Miller, now nearly three months after the killing, wrote that "my husband and one of my little girls [were] killed the other day, by the Rangers." She explained that she had been divorced from her former husband, one Wallace,[15] before marrying Miller, and reminded Tegener that she used to wash clothes for him when he was at Fredericksburg. With this explanation as to an earlier acquaintance she felt justified in writing him. "I hope you will assist me by explaining [examining?] this letter when you receive it and help by your in fluence to bring the Murderers of my husband and child to summary Justice." And it was not only that she had lost two of her loved ones, but "Since they Killed my people all Save four little children they have robbed me of my property in Menard County and left me helpless, with one arm broken to pieces to Support myself & little ones, they threatened my life if I should go back to McKavett to look after my effects or to make complaint, as the Lieutenant of the Rangers fears the consequences of his bloody work." Mrs. Miller concluded by asking Tegener if she should appear at District Court and asked him to tell Mrs. Tegener and their "little children Howdy." Tegener no doubt wondered what good would it do for him to get involved and "respectfully referred" the letter to Governor Hubbard, who then referred it to Adjutant General Steele "with instructions as hereafter—to have this completely examined."[16]

The letter is most unusual as it raises more questions than it answers. All that is certain is that her husband and her daughter had both been killed by the Rangers under Lieutenant Reynolds, who she probably held entirely responsible for her loss. Was her arm "broken to pieces" in the gunfight or some other mishap? Who threatened her if she should return to Fort McKavett? What did she know to justify her making the statement that Reynolds *feared* "the consequences of his bloody work"—and what property did she have at Fort McKavett that was taken and by whom could it have been taken? As yet no answers to these questions have been found and all we can do today is speculate. Apparently Fritz Tegener forgot about the matter after shifting her letter elsewhere, and ultimately it was ignored by state officials. Steele did take some action, in that he and Major Jones discussed the incident and then, six days after Mrs. Miller had written the letter, he wrote to Major Jones: "I fear that this company is becoming too much antagonized with many people in that Section to be of much service as formerly." Curiously this sentiment was the opposite of the feelings expressed by Reynolds himself.[17]

Of the many men who served under Reynolds during his nearly five years in various ranks, Tim McCarty was the only one to lose his life in the line of duty. Mustered into the Frontier Battalion by Major Jones on September 10, 1877, his service record shows him as twenty-seven years old, five feet nine-and-one-half-inches tall, having black hair, blue eyes, and dark complexion, and born in Virginia. For his service to Texas and his small contribution to the Frontier Battalion—and giving up his life to recover a pistol belonging to the state—he was to receive $42.66.[18] McCarty's grave has been lost, perhaps originally marked only with a wooden cross. But he has not been forgotten, as on the Lost Lawmen Memorial in Austin his name is alongside hundreds of others, among the names of lawmen who lost their life in the line of duty.[19]

While Reynolds and his men were returning from the Fort McKavett killings, other scouts kept on working to reduce the number of fugitives on the loose. Private John R. Banister and a squad had delivered murderer John Gray to the Burnet County jail. They hoped to capture Caleb

William L. (left) and his brother John Riley Banister when they were cowboys during the early 1870s. *Courtesy Sue K. Porter.*

Hall on the same scout but like so many times before, they failed to do so, having covered a total of three-hundred and sixty miles.[20]

On January 14 Reynolds issued Special Order No. 4, unusual in that it was issued in three parts. First, pursuant to General Order (from Jones?), non commissioned officers and privates in charge of the horse herd were to proceed to a suitable place and instruct men on duty to keep their horses saddled during the day; secondly while on post men were to keep their horses in hand and those not on duty were to keep their horses staked at the guard post; and finally no members of Company E were to be allowed to play at cards. The order to keep a closer watch on the horse herd was made probably due to rumors that Indians were in the area, and nothing could be more damaging or embarrassing to a Texas Ranger than to lose his horse. There is no known incident where Reynolds' men gambling in camp caused problems, but something must have motivated the commander to issue this order. Possibly it was his attempt to elevate the reputation of his men in the aftermath of the Fort McKavett tragedy.[21]

In spite of some scouts that resulted in nothing but tired men and horses, some were very successful. On January 16 Corporal Warren and a detachment returned from delivering prisoners from Mason and Llano Counties to Austin. They had also assisted Sergt. G. W. Arrington at Wortham in arresting the deadly Alf Rushing; on the return the group arrested William McDonald, charged with a murder in Kansas.[22] McDonald, on August 31, 1874, was in charge of a herd of cattle when a man named Michael Pointing led a group attempting to rustle the cattle. McDonald killed Pointing and then fled to Texas with rewards totaling $1,000 of Kansas money offered for his arrest. Two and one-half years later McDonald was arrested by some of Reynolds' men in Mason County, although the details of just how this was accomplished were not recorded. McDonald was turned over to Kansas Sheriff J. M. Lane and was ultimately convicted of manslaughter and sentenced to serve seven years in the state penitentiary. Reynolds must have become concerned about the reward as on March 22, Adjutant General Steele advised him that McDonald's attorneys, Redmond and Jenkins, had informed him that one reward of $500 was offered by Coffey County, Kansas, for his capture, and another $500 was offered by the state of Kansas for his arrest and conviction. Reynolds must have felt cheated, as Steele advised him that if he felt he had been "unfairly dealt with by the parties who came for McDonald" then he should consult with McDonald's attorneys. Had the Rangers received one reward, and Sheriff Lane taken the other, or had the Kansas officers taken the entire amount? Incomplete records do not allow one to determine the exact handling of the reward money, unfortunately.

Sheriff J. M. Lane returned home to Kansas where he told a reporter of the *Burlington Patriot* that when he reached Austin, he found his prisoner in the hands of Major Jones and Ranger J. W. Warren. "He paid over the $500 reward to these gentlemen," reported Lane, "and learned the capture was effected by J. W. Warren, who captured him on Red river, Mason county, where he was employed tending cattle for a dealer named Leight [Zach Light?],with four or five others. Mr. Warren rode into their camp, got the 'drop' on his man with a revolver, and he quietly surrendered and was taken to Austin and lodged in jail." It is doubtful if Warren or Reynolds ever saw a cent of the Kansas reward money.[23]

Richard Dublin was another fugitive who had frequently been the subject of Texas Ranger scouts. Ironically, years before he had been a cowboy with James B. Gillett and the Banister brothers, John and Will, but by the mid-1870s he was on the wrong side of the law. In January of 1873 he and "Ace" Langford killed two men named Payne and Hughes, ending an argument over a horse race in Coryell County; they were charged with the murder in April 1873.[24] On learning that these former friends were now with the Rangers, Dublin declared he would whip them with his quirt like dogs if they ever tried to arrest him.[25] But in spite of all his threats, it was Dublin who had avoided the Rangers, never challenging any of them face to face to back up his braggadocio. Besides the taunts of Dublin, which could only motivate the Rangers to increase their efforts to bring him in, the $700 reward for his arrest and conviction was very much in their minds. Gillett recalled that while in camp the sheriff of Tom Green County, following a trail of stolen cattle, came and requested assistance. Reynolds sent Sergeant Nevill and several others to ride with him, when the cattle were discovered around the South Llano. While scouting around the herd a man rode up who had not noticed the Rangers' presence in the near darkness. His horse almost stepped upon the Rangers when they rose up with a command to halt. "Yes—like hell!" came the reply and Dublin lunged into the cedar brake. Dublin managed to escape in a "shower of bullets" by savagely whipping his horse with his quirt.[26]

It meant little that the Rangers had recovered some stolen cattle. Reynolds, greatly angered upon learning Dublin had managed to get away, belittled their marksmanship and declared that the camp cook could have shot him if he had been in their place. Reynolds' outburst "mortified the boys a great deal" Gillett recalled.

According to Gillett, Reynolds knew that Dublin lived a mere ten miles from their camp, and he was greatly disappointed that he remained a fugitive. "It is a reflection on all of Company E," said Reynolds. "There is one thing sure, if I can't capture him I will make life miserable for him. I will keep a scout in the field after him constantly." Reynolds placed Gillett in charge of the squad and gave him free rein as to where to scout after Dublin. His last words of advice were, "If you come in contact with him don't let him get away."[27]

After being out two days Gillett felt it was perhaps wise to head back to camp and timed their return so as to be near the Tom Potter ranch about dark.[28] It was known that "Old Man" Potter was a friend and neighbor of Dublin's, and it was known that Dublin was frequently there. About sundown, a mile from the Potter ranch, they stopped and prepared camp. Gillett left John R. Banister and David L. Ligon as guards while he took Tom Gillespie, Will Banister, and Ben Carter with him to "round up" the Potter place on foot. About fifty yards from the house the Rangers squatted down in the bed of "Pack Saddle Creek," a shallow stream now called Bailey Creek, to survey the scene before them. They had, so far, advanced without being seen, and now could make out Old Man Potter and one of his sons unloading some hogs from a wagon, and a single horse tied to a wagon. They knew they would be seen as soon as they left the creek bed, so they ran for the house as fast as they could. They believed the horse was one that belonged to Dick Dublin.

As soon as they approached the house—running on foot, certainly not too fast in their heeled-boots—Old Man Potter saw them and yelled, "Run, Dick, run! Here come the rangers!"[29] Dublin was in the house, but he had no time to mount his horse or even get his gun, so he raced for the brush on foot. Gillett ordered him to halt but the warning went unheeded. Gillett fired but missed as Dublin disappeared from view. He hurried on to where Dublin was last seen and "spied him running up a little ravine." He stopped and drew a bead on him, and again ordered him to halt. Running,

Dublin threw his hand back under his coat as if he were attempting to draw a pistol, and Gillett fired. His bullet struck the fugitive in the small of the back just over the right hip bone and passed out near his left collar bone. It killed him instantly. Dublin was bending over as he ran, and this caused the unusual course of the bullet. By then the other Rangers had arrived and strangely Ben F. Carter fired two shots into the body on the ground. Gillett ordered him to stop as the man was dead. On examination Gillett discovered Dublin did not even have a gun, only a belt of cartridges around him. Regretfully Gillett recorded that the $700 reward could never be collected as it was offered for his arrest and conviction. In his copy of *Fugitives from Justice* Gillett penciled in by Dublin's name, "Killed by James B. Gillett 2nd Corpral [*sic*] Co E Texas Rangers on Pack Saddle Creek Kimble Co Texas January 18th 1877 [*sic:* actually the 16th of 1878] While resisting arrest."[30]

Richard "Dick" Dublin had two brothers who swore vengeance on Gillett and the two Banister brothers, but James Richard "Roll" and John Sheldon "Dell" Dublin did not have the nerve to challenge any of the three; nothing ever came of their threats. Reynolds succinctly summed up the entire episode in his Monthly Report: "Jan. 16 Corpl Gillett and five men went in pursuit of Richard Dublin and killed him while resisting arrest[.] distance marched 90 miles."[31]

Corporal Warren provided a report of the killing that differs from Gillett's, although Warren did not witness the action. He referred to Dublin firing back at the Rangers, possibly believing that Dublin would naturally be armed and would of course resist by shooting back. He was at Fort McKavett when he wrote this letter which appeared in the *Lampasas Dispatch,* in part:

> On the evening of the 17th [*sic*] a scout commanded by Corporal Gillett, surrounded Dick in the brush and ordered him to surrender. As usual, he dashed off, firing back at the Rangers as he ran, Several shots were fired over his head as a warning, but as he continued galloping and firing back, careful aim was taken, and the desperado fell pierced through the body and brain by two Winchester balls. Thus has passed away a murderer, bandit and cow thief, who for eight years defied the laws of God and man.[32]

Reynolds heard all the details of the fight and on January 22 wrote a lengthy letter to Major Jones, explaining what he believed to be true about the killing. He explained that he had sent Corporal Gillett with five men out in pursuit of Dublin. After scouting on the head of the South Llano they turned across to the head of the Kiace Creek where they "secreted themselves" close to the ranch of Tom Potter. They waited, and late in the evening of the eighteenth Dublin came riding in and sat down to eat supper. The squad came upon Dublin and demanded he surrender but he jumped up from the table and ran. Corporal Gillett claimed that he ordered him to halt three or four times but he continued to run. Several shots were fired in his direction to intimidate him. Dublin kept running and gaining ground and only then did the Rangers realize that if they wanted to stop him they would have to shoot him, and only then did they fire in earnest, intending to cripple him, not to kill him. Richard Dublin received two "Dead Shots" and died instantly about two hundred yards from the house.

Reynolds concluded his letter stating: "I think this to be the Most quiet Co[unty] on the Frontier at Present[.]" Reynolds received unprecedented praise in the *Galveston Daily News* when it reprinted an item from the *Austin State Gazette*. In reporting news from Menard County the *Gazette* gushed: "Menard is a frontier county. One year ago it was filled with desperadoes. Today it [is] as law-abiding as any shire in England. Major Jones established Lieut. N. O. Reynolds on Bear creek, with orders to settle the county into a peaceful condition. It was done. Dell Dublin is in chains and Dick in his grave. The gang [members] are scattered far and wide, and Menard county, with open arms, invites industry to her bosom, where fortune may be won by every honest wooer."[33]

Was Menard then as "law-abiding as any shire in England" and perhaps Kimble was as well? Either way it was a remarkable statement. But anxiety rode along with Reynolds after the Dublin killing. In a letter from Camp Steele he expressed his concern, fearing that Corporal Gillett and his five men would be indicted and charged with the murder of Richard Dublin. Further, he wrote, "Not Haveing [*sic*] Heard from you for Some Time I thought It Best to Ask Something about What to Doe [*sic*] in the

Event of an Indictment against My Men."[34] As far as known nothing ever came of the threats of indicting the Rangers for having killed a fugitive attempting to evade arrest.

The killing of Richard Dublin is commemorated by a state historical marker some eleven miles southwest of Junction on Highway 377. Erected in 1968, the marker is entitled "Doom of the Outlaws of Pegleg Station" and informs the viewer that Dublin was shot and killed one hundred fifty yards south. Ironically the legend identifies only "the intrepid James B. Gillett" as one of the Rangers who rushed his hideout. The marker explains that ultimately six of the Dublin gang were captured after one member of the gang turned informant. In all five of the outlaws were found guilty of stagecoach robbery and were convicted in August of 1880.[35]

The remaining Dublin brothers were together for some time; when Travis County census enumerator Thomas K. Taylor arrived at the jail he listed some fifty prisoners following the name of as head of household—the jailer—Albert W. Nichols. Among them was Dell Dublin, twenty-two years old and married, and his brother Roll, twenty-three years old and single. Both gave "Stock Raiser" as their profession. Brothers Thomas and William Potter were there, twenty-seven and twenty-three years old respectively, both natives of California. Others who were there thanks to the work of the Rangers included William Allison, Charles Romines, Wesley Johnson (involved in the killing of Rance Moore), and John J. Strickland, former sheriff of Burnet County. Strickland had recently been arrested by Williamson County Deputy Sheriff James Milton Tucker, charged with forging a receipt for a prisoner and collecting the reward for his arrest.[36]

Corporal Warren and his squad returned on January 16, 1878, having delivered prisoners from Mason and Llano Counties to Austin. They then were on detached service with Lieutenant Arrington at Wortham, assisting with the delivery of Alf Rushing to the Freestone County jail. Warren recorded it was a 1200-mile march. Among their accomplishments were the arrest of William Garrett, charged with murder in Dallas County and the arrest of J. P. Wren and one Wilson, charged with assault and battery. They had turned Wren and Wilson over to the Mason County sheriff. Garrett could not be positively identified and had to be released.

On January 17 Reynolds arrested two men believed to be Nick Ware and Robert McIver, both suspected of belonging to the gang of Pegleg Station coach robbers in Menard County. Unable to be positively identified they too had to be released. Private Abram Anglin had searched McIver's house looking for stolen property, but had found nothing. A week later Nevill and five others went on scout and arrested George Tidwell, charged with swindling in Lee County, and Thomas Bailey, charged with theft in Denton County. They also had to be released due to insufficient identification.[37]

Nevill was fortunate, as on this same scout he managed to arrest a noted character, Reuben Hornsby Boyce, who was charged with the murder of Robert Anderson, his brother-in-law. Boyce, born January 8, 1853, in Williamson County, married Adeline Pearl, the daughter of John Pearl Sr. in 1876. Her sister Elizabeth married Robert Anderson, whom Boyce killed not long after. Nevill provided no details in his report, merely writing: "Sergt Nevill and five men went in pursuit of fugitives [and] arrested R. H. Boyce for murder in Kimble Co." Nevill delivered Boyce to the Travis County jail but he later escaped with the aid of his wife on Sunday, January 4, 1880, and never did stand trial for the Anderson killing. Reports frequently appeared in Austin's *Statesman* telling of raids and robberies committed by Boyce and his "armed band of desperadoes." Later, similar reports came from the New Mexico Territory. In June of 1881 he was reported to be in the town of Socorro, but by the time authorities arrived there to take him back to Texas he had disappeared. By December 1881 Boyce was again in the Austin jail where he gave a lengthy interview to a *Statesman* reporter. At the time Boyce had "every reason to believe that I will be acquitted" and if so vowed to settle down to "honest labor and let my life convince the people of Texas that I am not the outlaw the people of Texas have been led to believe I am." At his trial he was, indeed, acquitted. Years later he claimed to have been a Texas Ranger, an Indian fighter, a lawman in El Paso, New Mexico, and Arizona, and a gold miner in Alaska. He may have experienced many different callings in his life but his only activity with the Texas Rangers was when Charles Nevill arrested him. Boyce died on May 23, 1927, in Coahoma, Texas.[38]

Corporal Warren and two others arrested J. C. Stephens in Menard County on February 2. He was "charged with the conniving of the escape of prisoners from the jail at Henrietta, in Clay County." Bringing in Stephens resulted in a $200 reward issued to Reynolds, which he certainly divided with Warren and the two others who were instrumental in the fugitive's capture. Two days later Sergeant McGhee and four others went out in pursuit of James Polk Mason and other fugitives, but Mason again eluded the lawmen. But Robert McIver was arrested along with the noted John Ringo, the pair being picked up in Junction City for disturbing the peace.[39] They were turned over to the Kimble County sheriff and then released on bond. Nevill rounded up a man identified as Nick Ware,[40] then went on to attempt to arrest W. W. Pope, wanted for a Guadalupe County murder. Nevill failed to find Pope but did arrest a Gonzales County man, Andrew Darnell, charged with stealing cattle in neighboring Wilson County.[41]

Darnell had experienced troubles with the law before. On February 2, 1875, he had been indicted on a charge of assault and battery for his involvement in a brawl in the town of Gonzales. He was fined $5 and costs. On February 21 Reynolds and a six-man squad started out to deliver Darnell and Stephens to the Travis County jail.[42] It was to be a rewarding trip.

Stark Reynolds remained elusive, managing to stay out of the clutches of the law in spite of their hunts for him. He was charged with horse theft and murder, making him a very attractive target for Ranger patrols. With Lieutenant Reynolds on this scout were J. B. Gillett, the Banister brothers, Dave L. Ligon, Ben F. Carter, and Richard C. Ware. As the group passed by the Stark Reynolds place, the Rangers saw him at the same time he observed them—an accidental meeting. Stark Reynolds dashed wildly to the Llano River bottoms some three miles away, believing that if he could reach the river he could escape. Ranger Reynolds and his men started in pursuit through the scrubby live oak and mesquite brush, thick and dense enough to slow down a galloping horse. Gillett recalled that this was "the fastest race I ever saw the rangers run."

Lieutenant Reynolds emptied his pistol at the fleeing fugitive but missed, and it looked like he would again escape. Gillett was close enough to his lieutenant to ask if he could ride ahead, obviously having the better horse. Lieutenant Reynolds turned and looked "with the wildest look on his face that I have ever seen. His hat was gone, his face was badly scratched by the brush, and the blood running down over his white shirt bosom." The reply was to stop the man—to kill him if he had to. Ranger Dave Ligon had run on ahead and had caught up with him; when he saw he could not escape, Stark Reynolds wisely surrendered, perhaps recalling the fate of Richard Dublin. The race had covered about three miles. During the mad gallop through the thick brush and uneven terrain Gillett's horse was crippled.[43]

In 1914 John R. Banister recalled that he "was with a scout of 8 Rangers and had a two mile chase after — and captured—Stark Reynolds, a notorious horse thief, more than twenty shots being fired at him during the chase. We took him to Austin in a wagon with several other prisoners and put him in jail there."[44] Banister's brief memoir is as accurate as Gillett's but there is nothing of the drama in his account.

The crime for which the law wanted Stark Reynolds was the theft of a horse in Tarrant County, according to the fugitives list. With him in the theft were John Allen and Marion Trimble. The theft was committed in 1873 but no indictment issued until 1876. He had been last heard of on the Guadalupe River. He was also charged with theft of a gelding in Kimble County.[45]

But there was more in Stark Reynolds' criminal career than the occasional theft of a horse. Back on November 13, 1874, Reynolds was involved in a brutal affair in Milano, Milam County. Someone had robbed an old man, seventy-six years of age and a cripple, known as "Chuck-a-Luck John" Murray. What was stolen was part of the old man's dice game, a shawl used as a "table" on which to throw the dice. The boys jokingly accused Stark Reynolds of having stolen it. Whether he was the actual thief or not was never determined but Stark Reynolds chose to kill the old man and did so in his own camp, shooting him as he lay on his pallet. Reynolds stayed in the area for a time, apparently being ignored by various officials whose duty was to arrest him.[46] With a murder in his past the theft of a horse was not the major concern of the young desperado.

With Stark Reynolds in irons, now confined in the same wagon with Stephens and Darnell, Lieutenant Reynolds could boast that with this "old brier-breaker captured" he had accomplished the task set out for him and he was now ready to go elsewhere.[47]

Although the name of Stark Reynolds as an outlaw is virtually unknown today, his capture did result in considerable newspaper coverage at the time. From Fort Mason someone sent a telegram to the *Galveston Daily News* which headlined the article "Capture of a Desperado of Nine Years Standing" and described Reynolds as a "noted horse thief and desperado" who was captured after an "exciting chase of two miles" in which several shots had been fired before he surrendered. Stark Reynolds acknowledged having led the life of an outlaw for the past nine years.[48] The *Austin Gazette* printed news of the arrest, which was in turn picked up by the *Dallas Weekly Herald*, only with additional details. Stark Reynolds "is a horse thief. His dodging period has lasted for nine years. Andy Darnell is charged with cow stealing in Wilson county." Further, Lieutenant Reynolds was to receive a reward of $200 for the apprehension of J. C. Stephens, charged with "the conniving of the escape of prisoners from the jail at Henrietta, in Clay county."[49]

The Rangers and their trio of prisoners, described as "desperate characters, from the West" arrived in Austin on February 28.[50] Tarrant County authorities came to pick up Stark Reynolds for prosecution in Fort Worth. Sheriff J. M. Henderson was interviewed but had to admit he was unable to learn anything of value as to the particulars of the arrest as prisoner Reynolds "would tell him nothing, that he had had dealing with the reporters before, and that he had no use for them whatsoever. He wouldn't pump worth a cent." Sheriff Henderson did provide some copy to the reporter, however, saying that Stark Reynolds "was a noted horse thief who stood charged with that offense in three different indictments found by the grand jury of Tarrant county about four years ago, at which time he made his escape." The prisoner was described as appearing to be about twenty-four years of age, and "wearing a haughty, impudent look."[51]

In 1967 the state of Texas erected a historical marker commemorating the capture of Stark Reynolds. The marker's title is "Teacup Mountain" named for the unusual formation of a distant mountain and records that "Near here occurred . . . the capture of a wanted man by Lt. N. O. Reynolds, and four fellow Texas Rangers in 1878."[52]

Gillett wrote that before Stark Reynolds stood trial for his crimes he was waylaid and killed but provided no details. One newspaper headlined its version with a flair for alliteration, although misspelling the name: "Runnel's Race Run," and described him as being one "of the most notorious desperadoes and professional horse thieves" of the state. He "passed in his life chips . . . at the county jail, from the effects of pistol-shot wounds, received some time ago while resisting the arrest of officers in Milam county. He escaped from this jail about a year ago, but was recaptured and again incarcerated by Sheriff Henderson about two weeks since."[53] On November 11, 1879, the District Attorney of Milam County requested the court to dismiss the case against Reynolds. There was a May 26, 1875, indictment against him and two others, identified only as Palmer and Brown, all charged with theft of money. Reynolds was the only one who had ever been arrested and further "the said defendant Stark Reynolds is dead and that there is no probability of [fully] identifying the said other defendants."[54]

In spite of Lieutenant Reynolds' boast that he had caught the last of the briar-breakers, there were still plenty of desperate men riding the Texas sky line threatening peaceful Texas citizens. In late February train Number 4 of the Texas Central Road had been robbed at Allen's Station in Collin County. Six robbers were in waiting, and although express agent James Thomas resisted he could not hold them off. They stole between $1,500 and $2,000 and Governor Hubbard now promised that transportation would be provided for Texas Ranger Lee Hall and his men to capture the robbers. Hubbard offered a reward of $500 for each member of the Sam Bass gang.[55]

11

Protecting the Man Killer

"I was carefully guarded by Lieut. N. O. Reynolds. . . . But I knew the power of the mob, the spirit that possessed them, and knew that my life hung on a thread."
—John Wesley Hardin, April 22, 1878

Two events in March of 1878 had to cause some frustration for the commander of Company E, Frontier Battalion. On March 4, in Austin, Reynolds arrested a black man, whom he believed to be Mitch Cotton, wanted for a killing in Limestone County. There had been a gunfight during the elections in Groesbeck, the county seat, on September 30, 1871. At the time contemporary reports issued from Groesbeck indicated that gamblers D. C. Applewhite and Dan Gallagher entered a saloon to have a drink when Cotton observed the former displaying a derringer. As to who fired first after Cotton's initial demand for the weapon—Attorney J. S. Thurmond stated that Cotton fired first—should have been irrelevant. Applewhite wounded Cotton in the left arm before he was shot and then died. Almost immediately a riot erupted, the town of Groesbeck becoming "almost instantly a carnival of raving, debauched and blood-thirsty men." Many white citizens "took possession of the town, threatening to exterminate the negroes and white Republicans." Governor E. J. Davis declared martial law before the crisis was over.[1]

D. C. Applewhite, formerly an auctioneer in various communities along the Texas and Central Railroad, resided in Robertson County in 1870, a twenty-seven-year-old husband and a father of one child.[2] From contemporary accounts it is clear that Applewhite was killed resisting arrest by a lawful demand to surrender a weapon to an authorized policeman.

Nevertheless on June 22, 1872, Cotton, a special policeman and a mulatto, was indicted for murder; on February 24, 1874, Governor Richard Coke offered a reward of $750 for his delivery within the Limestone County jail.[3] As far as known this killing was the only "crime" ever charged against Cotton, at one time a special policeman of the Texas State Police.

Mitchell Cotton was described as being six-feet-tall, "copper colored" with a straight nose, having angular features. He walked very erect, was quick spoken and spoke distinctly. He was thirty-five years of age and bore a wound in his left arm from a pistol ball.[4] Just how Cotton was arrested is unknown, but on March 4 Reynolds held a man in custody who strongly resembled Mitchell Cotton, the fugitive. On the next day Reynolds left for Groesbeck with his prisoner. Any lawmen would have relished the opportunity to deliver this man to jail; for some working men in Texas the reward amounted to more than half a year's salary. After taking the prisoner to Groesbeck, Reynolds had to release him as positive identification could not be made. He had made a round trip of 246 miles and had nothing to show for his efforts.[5] Whether Cotton was ever brought to justice is unknown; he had been captured once in 1877 but later escaped; detective Jack Duncan later claimed the reward for his arrest but he was still a fugitive as late as 1884 when he was reported to be in Mississippi.[6]

About this same time some party or parties unknown fired upon Ranger John R. Banister while he was in camp. On the night of March 16 a number of Indians approached and fired on the man who was guarding the horses. Banister rightly returned fire, waking up the entire camp; a brief skirmish ensued but with no casualties.[7] Reynolds led the chase after the elusive Indians but all got away. He reported the incident to Adjutant General Steele, explaining that he supposed the firing was done by Indians, and that about fifty shots had been fired back by the Rangers.[8] Banister later recalled the incident.

> The night of March 16, '78 I was fired upon from ambush by Indians, just below the mouth of Bear Creek on North Llano. We had been warned by a runner just at dusk that Indians had been seen in the vicinity, and when I went on guard, just after midnight, I was more alert than

John Riley Banister, who with brother Will arrived at Round Rock after the gun battle with Sam Bass. *Courtesy Sue K. Porter.*

usual. I noticed one of our mules pulling back on its rope and looking intently at something over the fence that enclosed our camp. I had my Winchester ready and stood in the shadow of the pile of sacked corn. The flickering of the moonlight and shadow under the trees disguised everything so that I could not be sure whether I was seeing an Indian or not. At last I decided to fire, and did so, with little chance of a direct shot in the half-light, and was surprised to see a gun blaze and bang ahead of me and a man jump and run toward the river. I ran and fired as I ran, heading him along the bluff which was high on one side. The other Rangers all leaped from their cots and came running, yelling and

> shouting. At last the Indian ran down the bank and into the shallow water, our rifles knocking fountains all around him, and in mid-stream he fell, but got to his feet and away into the trees, where several other savages waited for him. . . . We found the bullet lodged in a corn sack about a foot from where my head had been when he shot.[9]

Although the incident did nothing more than produce some high level excitement among the Rangers, they were soon in serious pursuit as a fresh trail was reported found near Kimbleville, heading north. They followed the trail for about ten miles but lost it near Gentry's Creek. Two suspicious looking men were taken into custody, however, identified as George Harper and J. L. Roberts. Nevill wrote that on coming in sight of Walton's ranch the men saw the Rangers and ran into the brush. They gave chase and returned them to camp, but as no charges could be found against them they were released.[10]

Sergeant McGhee was more successful on March 22 when he led a scout of seven men searching for stolen livestock reported to be in the vicinity of the Dublin and Allison ranches. The Rangers found thirteen head of cattle and arrested Mac Potter for theft. Two days later he was delivered to the Menard jail. On the twenty-sixth Reynolds and two others went out in pursuit of Joseph Joy, charged with theft in Tom Green County. They didn't find him but two days later Pvt. William T. Clements arrested him and turned him over to Menard County authorities.[11]

Although Reynolds may have had doubts about the gravity of the Indian menace, there were plenty of citizens who were keenly aware of danger. To calm the settlers' fears Reynolds and his men conducted considerable scouting. But towards the end of March he complained to Adjutant General Steele that they had not been able to strike an Indian trail to produce any real results.[12]

The Rangers had orders to take special pains to avoid offending the honest citizens and to avoid showing any preference to feuding families, but in spite of their best efforts occasionally antagonism was expressed against the men of the Frontier Battalion. Reynolds had experienced this after Corporal Gillett and his squad had killed fugitive Richard Dublin while resisting arrest. On March 27 he wrote Major Jones inquiring what he should do in case his men were indicted for murder.[13]

Major Jones could only reply that if there were indictments against them they should give bond for their court appearance and stand their trial. Jones was prepared to engage an attorney and have the trial moved to Menard County if needed. He expressed doubt there was any danger of their being indicted, but "they need not be uneasy about it, but keep quiet and attend to their duties properly, and they will come out all right in the end." In the same letter Jones stressed to his commander to take particular care to say nothing or make enemies among the people of Kimble County, advising, "our business is to enforce the law and keep the peace, [and] we must have no personal quarrels or feelings in the discharge of our duty, and should carefully guard against strife or ill feelings against either good or bad people." Jones was responding to "some reports" that Reynolds and his men had made enemies there and had become unpopular with the citizenry. Jones did state, showing his confidence in the choice he had made for commander, he could "scarcely believe this report but give you these hints to guard you against anything of the kind."[14]

Adjutant General Steele however did express some doubt as to the continued effectiveness of Company E. He had heard that the Dublins had employed counsel to indict Gillett.[15] Reynolds replied and expressed the opposite viewpoint, and responded that he would be glad to see the adjutant general during court, then he could acquire a better opinion of the conditions of the county. Furthermore, Reynolds had heard some citizens say that they could not control order during court, but he was "of the Opinion that we Can Without Much Trouble[.]"[16]

Reynolds did not hesitate to defend his men to Major Jones or anyone else. He stated clearly in his letter to Major Jones that his men had made no enemies in that county or in the adjoining counties, and did not believe that any of his men had done anything or said anything that could be considered "out of our Regular Duty." But, on the other hand, Reynolds pointed out that he had received many insulting letters but had not given them any consideration and did not expect to. He suspected that any complaints had come from some personal enmity and wanted Jones to investigate the matter thoroughly. He concluded: "I am Satisfied that you will find that All Good Law Abiding Citizens Are Perfectly Satisfied with My Opperations [*sic*] here and Often Express themselves to that Effect [.]"[17]

On April 11 Sergeant Nevill and four others delivered Dell Dublin from the jail in Austin to Kimble County for trial. The next day they arrested James Douglas for a Kimble County murder and delivered him to the sheriff. Besides those arrests and attempts to arrest the Rangers provided an escort for Judge William A. Blackburn. Gillett and two Rangers provided protection for the witnesses in Dublin's trial, as there had been threats from Dublin's family intimidating witnesses. On the twenty-eighth Reynolds moved into Junction to assist the sheriff as needed in guarding the prisoners and preserving order. One of the first things accomplished,

Nelson O. Reynolds and Charles L. Nevill, dressed up for a photographer of the Capital Studio of Austin. *Courtesy Kimble County Historical Commission.*

and no doubt unsuspected, was arresting Sam Williams on May 1, wanted for theft in San Saba County. [18]

John Wesley Hardin had not been forgotten and he had not forgotten the Rangers. He wrote to the editors of Austin's *Weekly State Gazette* on April 22. Typically Hardin began his communication in thanking the editor for his "kindness on other occasions" and requested to be allowed to give his version of the trial at Comanche the previous fall, and reveal the "influence" which resulted in his not being able to receive an "impartial trial."

> When I entered the public square of Comanche City I saw the faces of dozens of the same men who took part in hanging my brother Joe. G. Hardin and my four cousins in 1874. Both my brother and my cousins were in the custody of Capt. Waller's company of Rangers at the time that they were mobbed, and I strongly suspect that the Rangers were direct or indirect parties to the deed of violence. It was alleged at the time that my brother and cousins were parties to the killing of Charles Webb, but at this day none in that county will deny that they were entirely innocent of the charge with the exception, perhaps, of one of the Dixon boys. Thus died five men, four of whom it is granted, even by those who slew them, were entirely innocent of crime. My brothers and the two Dixon boys were hung and Anderson and Borekman [*sic*] were shot to death while asleep on their pallets in the jail. I was carefully guarded by Lieut. N. O. Reynolds, who commanded twenty-five well armed brave men but I knew the power of the mob, the spirit that possessed them, and knew that my life hung on a thread.

Naturally Hardin presents in this self-serving communication his belief that the result of the trial was already determined before it began due to the hostile witnesses against him. In addition he insisted that the Rangers under Waller were actually murderers themselves, claiming that they participated in the lynching of brother Joseph and the two Dixon brothers—his cousins—and then shooting two other cousins while they slept in the Comanche jail. Hardin of course did not see the written report of Captain Waller, explaining how he and his Rangers and some Comanche citizens worked together in pursuing members of Hardin's entourage, finding them far from the jail hidden in the brush, and who fired back when the two cousins fired upon them. Hardin continued:

> Accustomed to scenes of excitement from infancy, I read in the looks of the rangers, in everything that I saw from the grated windows of the prison, and on my trips to and from the jail to the courthouse, that a woeful death awaited me if once the mob obtained the mastery. Indeed it was hinted to me that if I obtained a continuance or a change of venue the beginning would be made of the bloody end. Therefore I went into trial knowing that I was prejudged and already harshly sentenced by the jury appointed to convict me of a crime I never committed.[19]

As a fugitive from Texas justice, John Wesley Hardin appeared more like a successful businessman than the most wanted desperado in Texas. This is from the original tintype made in Florida in 1875. *Courtesy the Robert G. McCubbin Collection.*

Hardin had had experience with Texas Rangers as well as numerous members of the Texas State Police force from the 1870–1873 period. Of all those lawmen, including police captains Jack Helm and Leander H. McNelly as well as Texas Ranger Captain Waller, N. O. Reynolds was the only one for whom Hardin expressed any kind of praise or exhibited respect.

On May 7 Major Jones ordered Reynolds to move Camp Steele to Burnet County, some seventy miles closer to Austin. No reason was given except he was to have the company "convenient to Austin to be used for duty anywhere in the interior of the state."[20] Reynolds soon established camp on the South San Gabriel River in Burnet County. Now among other duties Reynolds was to furnish an escort to Frontier Battalion Surgeon Dr. E. G. Nicholson to Frio City. On his safe arrival there Dr. Nicholson wrote to the adjutant general regarding his experience. He had heard that Reynolds was to be ordered to Burnet and that would offer a new field of "opportunities" to "display his efficiency" as the officers of Fort McKavett were hailing him as "the dashing young Lieutenant." Dr. Nicholson wrote that Kimble County was "thoroughly worked up" and Reynolds' handling of things in the county was "admirable, he stood pat and went for all alike; he was respected but not popular, which from a class of people of Kimball [*sic*] status was the highest compliment."[21] High praise indeed for the lawman!

A deadly disturbance in San Saba placed Reynolds into a new and dangerous adventure. The conflict began on voting on the local option law. Although the election results indicated the city would be "dry" some saloon owners defied the results, claiming that due to certain "irregularities" in the conduct of the election, the declared result was invalid. One saloon owner who continued dispensing liquor in spite of the election results was William A. Brown, a noted trouble maker. Besides his own crowd he had his brother to back him up, and that brother was James Madison Brown, the sheriff of Lee County.[22]

County Attorney S. S. Brooks began legal proceedings against William A. "Billy" Brown. The prosecution process reached the courthouse when Brown, on May 21, allegedly attempted to shoot Brooks. Law partner Thomas G. T. Kendall was present, and in an effort to save his partner's life, he shot and killed Brown. Brooks holed up in the courthouse with about twenty friends when Brown's cronies formed into a mob to lynch him. Two days later County Judge John I. Guion sent an urgent communication "to the commander of any detachment of State Rangers." Guion was desperate, and it is not known how his message of panic reached any Ranger group, but Lieutenant G. W. Arrington of Company C was some sixty miles away and after a forced night march reached the town just as Brown's friends were preparing to mob the courthouse. Kendall requested to be taken to the Travis County jail for safe keeping. Guion wrote that "the lives of the officers of San Saba are now hanging by a thread—Delay would be fatal; and our streets the scene of a bloody conflict between the officers and a mob." Guion begged his communication be kept secret, "for it would be as much as my life is worth to have the contents of this letter made public." He managed to escape in time as just prior to his leaving three unidentified men approached his house. The trio scattered when Guion shot at them.[23]

On the twenty-eighth Major Jones ordered Lieutenant Reynolds to move his company to San Saba "without delay" so as to relieve Arrington who was needed in Taylor County to deal with the troubles there. Reynolds was to bring or send Kendall to Austin under a strong guard and advised him, "In doing this you will be particularly careful to guard against a surprise and will protect the prisoner, at all hazards, against the violence of the mob which I understand threatens to take him from the guard and murder him."

Major Jones, always conscious of the community itself in which there were threats of violence, wanted Reynolds to peacefully prevail upon the "contending parties" and cause them "to drop the difficulty and allow the law to take its course." Major Jones advised him that he would probably have to operate in San Saba County "for some time to come as there is said to be much lawlessness there." Jones hoped to be able to arrive in San Saba within a few days, as he was then detained in Austin as a witness in court. He hoped to be through with court quickly so he could go to San Saba to "look into the troubles there myself" but if he could not then Reynolds was to "use all means in your power to restore peace and quiet to that county." He was authorized to use whatever legal means were necessary "to force them to submit to the law."[24]

Arrington was not forgotten by the people of San Saba as on June 1 a group of citizens signed a petition acknowledging their satisfaction with his conduct there. "[T]heir presence has been sufficient to calm all disturbances" they wrote, but they were fearful that if the Rangers were removed the mob troubles would resume immediately. Forty-nine citizens signed the document, among them Attorney S. S. Brooks and Judge John I. Guion.[25]

On the same day Reynolds and sixteen men moved camp from the San Gabriel to San Saba, arriving there on June second. Then he and thirteen men escorted Kendall along with Wilson Hughes, an escaped convict, to the Travis County jail. Gillett was likely one of the Rangers since he left a detailed version of the affair. "General Jones was notified and ordered Lieutenant Reynolds at Junction City to march to San Saba with his company, take charge of Kendall, and relieve Captain Arrington's men. It was probably two weeks after the killing before Company E reached San Saba, but Mr. Kendall was still holding the fort in the upper story of the courthouse." Gillett related that when Reynolds and the company arrived, Kendall requested a preliminary examination. When court convened, he waived examination and asked to be transferred to Austin. Realizing the feelings against him the court ordered his removal.

Gillett also wrote of a near gunfight between Reynolds and Lee County Sheriff James M. Brown, brother of the late Billy Brown. The sheriff, who had killed a number of men in personal difficulties, had temporarily left his area of jurisdiction and responsibilities to avenge his brother's death. No doubt the arrogant sheriff had contemplated riding into San Saba, killing Kendall, and then riding back to Lee County with no interference and satisfied with his work. He was there when a hack was pulled up to the courthouse door to take Kendall out. "When the time came to remove him a hack was drawn up, where a great crowd had assembled to see the prisoner," wrote Gillett.

> Jim Brown . . . had taken his station, heavily armed, within ten feet of the door. Just before Mr. Kendall descended the courthouse steps Lieutenant Reynolds ordered the crowd to fall back fifty feet from the hack. All immediately obeyed with the exception of Jim Brown, who

> sat perfectly still on his horse. The lieutenant looked at Brown for a minute, then turned to his rangers and ordered them to draw their guns and move everyone fifty yards from the courthouse. Like a flash every ranger drew his gun, dismounted, and waved the crowd back.

At this point, Jim Brown, no doubt awed by this display of firepower and certainly realizing he had no chance to carry out his mission against such overwhelming numbers and survive, still managed to exhibit an air of bravado. He turned to Reynolds and stated, "I am going to Austin with you." Reynolds calmly replied, "If you do, you will go in irons. Move back!"

Brown, realizing his defeat, slowly turned his horse and rode away. "He did not know the man with whom he was dealing," wrote Gillett.[26] There were no further incidents in delivering Kendall to jail where they arrived on June 5, along with San Saba County Sheriff William R. Doran and thirteen Rangers. Sheriff Brown, after some reflection and perhaps realizing how close to death he had been, later apologized to Reynolds for his unprofessional conduct that day in San Saba.[27] This apology must have taken place in Austin.

Sheriff Doran was not the strong enforcer of the law that was Lieutenant Reynolds and he received negative attention in the press. A reporter described how Billy Brown had not only defied the efforts of the local option supporters, but had, while the court was in session, actually got up in the judge's stand, rapped for order, and sent out for liquor or beer. One of his men brought in a bag of bottles and ordered everyone to have a drink. Spencer S. Brooks refused. Kendall also refused, and bravely told Brown that he should stop his actions, that he was doing wrong. It was only moments later that Brown pulled out a pistol and attempted to shoot Brooks, at which point Kendall shot Brown to save his partner's life.

Reportedly Doran had refused to sign the petition for the Rangers to be kept in San Saba, that he had allowed friends of the deceased Brown to go into his cell—armed—and threaten and abuse Kendall and that Doran refused to arrest people on the streets of the town who were openly wearing deadly weapons.[28]

With such accusations of wrong-doing published in the *Galveston Daily News*, Sheriff Doran could not let that go without a response; his long letter of defense appeared in the *News* in July. He pointed out that he had been sheriff of San Saba for five years and that the laws were enforced there as much as in other places. He admitted that many men could be seen wearing six-shooters on the streets but they were people who had a right to wear them, such as soldiers, police, travelers, and peace officers. He claimed that many had been arrested for the offense. Doran also claimed that he was out of town on county business the day of the Brown trial. But he would have been there if he had known the case was to be called for that day. And if Brown's friends had been allowed to enter Kendall's cell, armed, it had been against his orders.

Doran further explained that he had not signed the petition for the Rangers because he felt it was the responsibility of the local officers to enforce the laws and that if the Rangers were kept there then that would leave the frontier open for marauders elsewhere. "The majority of our people do not wish to take from the border, where Indians and Mexicans alike raid, the needed services of the frontier troops. We do not wish to permanently abandon all ideas of home government, and all duties as citizens, and to always look to hired soldiers to perform those duties."[29] Sheriff Doran's defense for his actions at San Saba apparently satisfied his constituents, as he served as sheriff from his first election on December 2, 1873, until November 5, 1878, and then after a term out of office, was elected again to serve one more term from November 2, 1880, until November 7, 1882.[30]

Events of lesser import occurred in June. Private Lowe R. Hughes and a scout assisted Llano County Sheriff J. J. Bozarth while court was in session. Private P. C. Jackson also assisted Bozarth in delivering the Cain brothers—Neal and "Sugar" —to the Travis County jail. On the seventh Richard C. Ware and Chris Connor reported to Cpl. Vernon Coke Wilson for duty at Austin. On the following day Sergeant McGhee and two others were out hunting for Warren Goodin, wanted for a murder committed in Orange County, Texas. Ironically he had been hiding out in Lampasas County during the previous year, and in April of 1878

Young Texas Rangers Charles L. Nevill (standing) and Chris R. Connor in 1877.
Courtesy Pansy Gillett Espy.

had been in custody of Neal Coldwell's Rangers but had managed to escape. He had also been in custody of Lee County officials, but managed to escape from them as well. Sergeant McGhee and his squad failed to capture the man, now in his seventies. But in 1880 he was in Huntsville State Penitentiary, serving time.[31]

It is uncertain how long Reynolds stayed in Austin after delivering Kendall and Hughes safely to the county jail. He was there as late as the twenty-third as on that day Reynolds visited John Wesley Hardin, now comfortably placed in a cell by himself. Hardin wrote to his wife Jane on June 23, complaining of "pains & weakness from my old wounds which at this time Dear are very Servere [*sic*] but Hope they will not last long . . . am treated very Kindly by my Keepers being crowded with company." But most interesting of all is his statement that he had "a nice treat to ice Cream to day by lieutenant Rundels [*sic*] who taken me to Comanche," which reminded him of their visits to the ice cream parlors in New Orleans and Jacksonville, Florida, only a few years before.[32]

Was Hardin the only prisoner who was so kindly treated to ice cream that hot day by the Ranger commander?

The impressive grave markers of Chris R. Conner (April 11, 1850–January 23, 1916) and his wife Belle (September 1, 1861–April 3, 1930) as they appear today in the Madisonville, Texas cemetery. *Photo by Parsons.*

12

Gunsmoke at Round Rock

"Then, mounting his own horse, Jackson and his chief galloped out of the very jaws of Hell itself."

—James B. Gillett

Even with the feud between the Horrell and Higgins factions essentially over, there were still troublesome individuals in Lampasas County who demanded the attention of the law. On the 4th of July Reynolds wrote a hurried note to Major Jones concerning the arrest of W. H. Crabtree "for False Swearing In Navarro Co." Reynolds wasn't positive as to his true name, explaining that his initials might be H. W. but his name appeared on the *Fugitives* list. Reynolds believed he was wanted in other counties but did not identify which ones nor what made him think that. He asked to be informed "At Once" as to what he should do with the man. In reality the man referred to was the fugitive J. W. Crabtree, indicted for "false swearing" committed in 1874.[1]

D. B. Kennedy, editor of the *Daily Times* of Lampasas, which he had founded just over a year previously, provided this glowing report of Reynolds' men's accomplishments.

> A squad of rangers, under command of Lieut. Reynolds, is encamped near the upper spring, where they have been for a week or more. On the Fourth they arrested a man named Wm. Crabtree, and carried him before Justice Brown on a charge of carrying a pistol. He plead guilty

> and was fined $25. We learn that Crabtree is wanted in Navarro County for some offense, and has been sent there.

Kennedy was aware that the arrest could have turned violent as Crabtree "showed a disposition" to resist the arresting officer, but "yielded at the dark end of a six-shooter. Mr. James Gillette [*sic*], one of the bravest men in Texas, assisted by two others, whose names we did not learn, made the arrest."[2] Major Jones investigated the matter and had to inform Reynolds that there were no longer any charges against Crabtree in Navarro County.[3] Crabtree was released after paying the fine for carrying a pistol.[4]

Editor Kennedy may have known what a hard character Crabtree really was and gave Gillett the public praise for good reason. False swearing was among the tamer of his actions: he was considered a close associate of the Horrells back when they were feuding with Pink Higgins; he later was a participant in the robbery and murder of J. T. Vaughn in Bosque County. Later still he turned state's evidence against his fellow murderers, which resulted in Tom and Mart Horrell being arrested and jailed in Meridian, Bosque County, charged with aiding and abetting in the murder. Crabtree could not stay in protective custody forever; on November 28 while walking along the Bosque River someone ended his life with a shotgun blast. Then on December 15 a group of friends and sympathizers of Vaughn mobbed the Meridian jail and shot to death the Horrell brothers in their cell.[5]

Reynolds was a man of action and to him things were getting too peaceful in Lampasas County. He wrote to Major Jones on the thirteenth complaining that there was nothing of interest, other than "the Same Trouble" which certainly suggests that the embers of the Horrell-Higgins feud might flare up at any time. Reynolds admitted that much of the populace of the county feared the troubles would erupt again as the Horrells were accused "of Manny [*sic*] bad things." He was inclined to think it was not without cause, as the Horrells had a "Verry [*sic*] Bad Class of Men With them"—one of whom had been Crabtree. It was suspected by some that Sheriff Albertus Sweet had neglected his duty as he was more concerned with getting re-elected than enforcing the law. Throughout the experience with the feuding factions the Horrells were consistently considered the "Bad Class."

Although admitting that their efforts at eradicating the old feud may have only been temporary, Reynolds did have some good news to relay to Major Jones. His physical problems were gradually improving; he explained that he would be leaving for San Saba and added, "I am a Great Deal better and think will be Entirely well Soon."[6]

Some feelings of failure may have overcome Rangers during that early part of July as they were simply not accomplishing as much as they would have liked. For instance: in spite of their numerous patrols the stage between Mason and Menard was held up near midnight on July 5 near Pegleg Crossing. The robbers cut open the mail sacks and took everything except the receipt showing they were the registered packages mailed at Fort McKavett. Also, John H. Slaughter, charged with theft in Atascosa County, was arrested on July 7 by Corporal Gillett. But when delivered to Austin he had to be released as he could not be positively identified. This is the same John H. Slaughter who would later gain fame as the sheriff of Cochise County, Arizona Territory. Then on July 13 Gillett arrested George Von Cannon for assault in Coryell County. He was turned over to Coryell County Sheriff W. H. Belcher. On the sixteenth Lieutenant Reynolds and two others went out in pursuit of the unknown murderers of John McMasters but failed to accomplish anything. His slayer had shot-gunned McMasters while he slept some seven miles east of Lampasas. His wife found the body. There was no indication if this killing was connected to the feud or merely an isolated murder. On the next day, the seventeenth, Reynolds and part of his company left for San Saba, leaving a portion at Lampasas. While they were gone someone killed McMasters' father-in-law, a man named Slaughter. He was not related to the John H. Slaughter who had been arrested earlier in July by Corporal Gillett, as far as known. These deaths remained a mystery and apparently no one was arrested and convicted for these murders.[7]

Rangers Lowe R. Hughes and Henry Maltimore were sent out to assist the sheriff of Fayette County and returned to camp on the nineteenth. "Nothing accomplished" was the comment in the Monthly

The train robbing quartet well before Round Rock: Sam Bass, standing left next to John E. Gardner; seated Joe Collins (left) and his brother Joel Collins.
Courtesy Robert G. McCubbin Collection.

Return.[8] In spite of the lack of significant success in dealing with fugitives, Gillett recalled this period with fondness. He wrote that Reynolds moved camp on the San Saba "to a beautiful pecan grove, an ideal summer camp, about two miles from the town of San Saba. From this point we scouted all over Llano, Lampasas, Burnet and San Saba counties at our favorite pursuit of rounding up bad men. It was from this camp that we made our sensational ride to Round Rock after Sam Bass, the notorious train robber."[9]

Virtually everyone is somewhat familiar with the brief career of Texas outlaw Sam Bass. The young man became an American legend, a more popular hero-thief in Texas than any other brigand. Many a lawman devoted much time and energy in the pursuit of the gang, but history knows his life and criminal exploits much better than any lawman who pursued him.

Sam Bass was born in Indiana, July 21, 1851, but left home in 1869, taking the railroad to St. Louis, Missouri, and then by 1870 had continued on down the Mississippi—now adept at card playing and handling a pistol. Historian Walter Prescott Webb wrote that Bass overcame the stigma of being from the north "and was perhaps the first Yankee to gain popularity in Texas after the Civil War." He first entered the state in late 1870 and for a while worked for Denton County Sheriff William F. Egan who later was to spend time pursuing him. For the next few years Bass was to spend more and more time away from honest labor and perfecting his skills at gambling and horse racing.

In the mid-1870s Bass met up with Joel Collins, a young man in his early twenties who had killed one man, had been acquitted of murder, and who then trailed longhorn cattle to Kansas until 1874. He and Bass then partnered in racing horses until 1876 when they gathered a herd of cattle, drove them north on the cattle trails, and ended up in the Black Hills of Dakota Territory. Instead of returning with the money from the sale of the cattle they squandered it on gambling and horse racing and perhaps loose women. They needed ready cash and it was not long before Bass and Collins joined up with Jack Davis and Tom Nixon, and perhaps others, and began robbing stage coaches. Not satisfied with the small return from robbing coaches, Collins—then the real leader of the gang—developed a plan to rob a Union Pacific train carrying gold being shipped to the east. The date was September 18, 1877, and the place was Big Springs, Nebraska.

Bass, Collins, and four others successfully robbed the train of $60,000 newly minted twenty-dollar gold pieces, each marked 1877. After the robbery the gang of six separated into three pairs, each with their share, but they did not live long to enjoy their stolen wealth. Collins and Bill Heffridge were killed resisting law officers and soldiers a week later. James Berry returned home but foolishly showed off his newly acquired wealth; while resisting arrest he was shot and captured near Mexico, Missouri, dying from the effects of the shotgun blast in the hands of Audrain

County Sheriff Harry Glasscock on October 16. Tom Nixon escaped the country and disappeared forever in Canada.

Only Bass and Jack Davis made it back to Texas. Davis disappeared in Denton County leaving Bass alone of the six who had accomplished one of the biggest train robberies in United States history. Other than eluding the law, Bass' main concern now was probably figuring out a way to duplicate the Nebraska robbery, and to gather trustworthy gang members.[10]

The first Texas strike was on December 22, 1877, when the Concho stage was held up by three men only nine miles from Fort Worth. The mail was not disturbed but two passengers lost a total of $40, one of them having successfully hidden $300 and a gold watch in his clothing. On January 26, 1878, the Weatherford–Fort Worth stage was robbed by two men. This holdup was slightly more successful as the five passengers gave up $400 in cash and gold watches. On February 22 the gang moved up from stage coaches to trains. Number 4 of the Houston & Texas Central at Allen Station in Collin County was robbed, eight miles from McKinney. Here the gang met with resistance for the first time. Express messenger James L. A. Thomas fought back until he had but one bullet; with the robbers threatening to burn the car he surrendered. Their take this time was between $1,200 and $1,500, certainly a significant haul, but it resulted in Governor Hubbard issuing a reward of $500 each for the six robbers. He also called in Texas Ranger Lee Hall of the Special State Troops to develop a plan to destroy the Bass gang. The railroad, the stage coach line and individuals who had lost money to the robbers were now anxious to see the gang broken up; as yet no individual had been physically harmed during their robberies.

The gang struck the Texas Central again on March 18, 1878. The train was stopped at Hutchins and this time James Thomas' cousin, Henry Andrew "Heck" Thomas, was the messenger. He managed to hide $4,000 in the stove, which was carelessly overlooked by the bandits. This time the gang was enriched by about $600. During the night of April 4 they struck at Eagle Ford, and then six days later at Mesquite. Up until this time the identity of the gang had not been released, but on April 10 the *Galveston Daily News* identified three of the robbers as Sam

Bass, Henry Underwood, and Frank Jackson. These robberies proved to be reckless acts and captured the imagination of the public, but the frequency also brought greater attention from the authorities. It was not long before the daring group was dubbed "Sam Bass & Company." Soon other gang members, known or suspected, were identified, including Seaborn Barnes, Tom Spotswood, Sam Pipes, Albert G. Herndon, and "Arkansas" Johnson, whose real name is unknown.

Other than Lee Hall, the Rangers did not become actively involved in the Bass pursuit until Adjutant General Steele ordered Major Jones to take charge. Jones quickly went to Dallas and organized a detachment of Company B to be commanded by experienced lawman Junius "June" Peak. Besides these thirty Rangers, many professional detectives and law officers as well as amateur bounty hunters took up the chase. The eagerness of the pursuit was not because the public had been outraged by the robberies, but because of the inducement of large rewards offered by the express companies and the railroad.[11]

Major Jones developed a plan to destroy the Bass gang from within rather than engaging them in deadly gunfights. He had as many people arrested as possible, on suspicion or being an accessory or for having harbored fugitives. On April 22 Captain Peak arrested Pipes and Herndon, both charged with the robbery at Mesquite. The next day Scott Mayes was arrested, charged with harboring and abetting train robbers. By the end of April the Rangers had warrants for the arrest of Sam Bass, Seaborn "Sebe" Barnes, Frank Jackson, Henry Underwood, and "Arkansas" Johnson. On June 12 Peak and a posse gave battle to the gang in Wise County. Two of the gang's horses were killed but more significantly the gang lost "Arkansas" Johnson, shot dead by Ranger Sergeant Thomas Floyd.

James W. Murphy and his father Henderson were both indicted for harboring Bass. Knowing his father innocent, twenty-five-year-old Jim Murphy offered to betray Bass in exchange for his and his father's freedom. Several times he attempted to "set-up" the gang but he was not successful until the attempted robbery of the bank in Round Rock, Williamson County, to take place on the nineteenth or twentieth of July. Perhaps it was the way Sam Bass wanted to celebrate his twenty-seventh birthday.

Traitor Murphy had managed to get a message to Major Jones, then in Austin attending the trial of Pipes and Herndon, telling him of the plan to rob the Williamson County Bank at Round Rock. There were Rangers in Austin but Jones did not want to leave the capital unguarded as there were rumors that the Bass gang planned to raid the Travis County jail, release Pipes and Herndon and John Wesley Hardin as well, then raid the state treasury and escape to Mexico. The nearest Ranger group of any size was that of N. O. Reynolds, stationed at Camp San Saba, some 115 miles away. Four of Reynolds' men were on detached service as part of Major Jones' escort: Vernon Coke Wilson, Richard C. Ware, George Herold, and Chris R. Connor. In the absence of the telegraph, a rider had to notify Reynolds. Wilson, a nephew of former Governor Coke, was ordered to deliver the message to Reynolds. Wilson's horse was not in shape for the

Texas Ranger Vernon Coke Wilson, the Paul Revere to end the Bass gang rider.
Courtesy the Robert G. McCubbin Collection.

long hard ride but he did get to Lampasas before the horse collapsed and died from lockjaw. Wilson caught a stage and then delivered the orders to Reynolds at Camp San Saba. Gillett recalled:

> I well remember the hot July evening when Corporal Wilson arrived in our camp with his orders. The company had just had supper, and the horses had been fed and tied up for the night. We knew the sudden appearance of the corporal meant something of unusual importance. Soon Sergeant Nevill came hurrying to us with orders to detail a party for an immediate scout. Lieutenant Reynolds' orders had been brief, but to the point. "Bass is in Round Rock. We must be there as early as possible tomorrow. Make a detail of eight men and select those that have the horses best able to make a fast trot."[12]

In thirty minutes all was ready with 1st Sergeant Charles Nevill, 2nd Sergeant Henry McGhee, 2nd Corporal Gillett, Pvts. Abram Anglin, David L. Ligon, William T. Derrick, and the two Banister brothers eager to ride. Reynolds was again too ill to ride horseback so two pack-mules were hitched up to a light spring wagon. He grabbed some blankets and crawled in. Wilson, not having slept for thirty-six hours, also lay down, hoping to get some much needed rest. It is doubtful if either got much rest that night. Gillett wrote that they left camp on the San Saba River just at sunset and traveled in a fast trot and sometimes in a lope the entire night.[13]

The Rangers crossed the North San Gabriel fifteen miles south of Lampasas just as the sun rose, thirty miles from Round Rock. Reynolds allowed a thirty-minute break for rest and breakfast—the men hurriedly devouring bread, broiled bacon, and coffee, while the horses were given a bundle of oats each. They did not halt again until reaching Old Round Rock in the early afternoon of July 19.[14] Reynolds immediately established camp on Brushy Creek and went into town to report to Major Jones. Whereas Gillett made the all-night ride into an adventure, Reynolds merely reported: "July 18th Lieut. Reynolds and Nine men left camp to go to Round Rock to meet Maj Jones and assist in effecting the capture of Sam Bass and party who [were] expected there to rob a bank."[15]

Gillett recalled the names of the eight men who made the ride with Reynolds, but Reynolds' report indicated the number was nine, the difference possibly being the driver of the spring wagon. Nevill however recorded that Reynolds and "ten men left camp" to go to Round Rock on July 18 "to meet Sam Bass & others who were expected there to Rob a bank" but did not provide any names. If one counts Wilson, the wagon driver, and those named by Gillett the count is ten, plus Reynolds. The *Galveston Daily News* also reported that ten men and Reynolds made the ride to Round Rock.[16]

For all their hard effort the Rangers were unable to get to Round Rock in time. Bass, Murphy, Barnes, and Jackson had been there to look over the bank one last time before the next morning's raid. Jim Murphy left the gang to go into town to get tobacco, he told them, but in reality to somehow get word to Major Jones. As Bass, Barnes, and Jackson got off their horses, "Sam's coat tail blew up and exposed his pistol. Frank and Sebe had their pistols in their saddle-pockets, and if Sam had had his in his saddle-pockets he might be living yet." But his pistol was exposed and by chance Deputy Sheriff Alijah "Hi" Grimes and Travis County Deputy Sheriff Maurice Moore both observed the trio and the exposed pistol. Bass and Jackson went into Henry Koppel's store followed by the lawmen, intending to arrest Bass for violating the ordinance against openly wearing weapons. They did not know it was Bass they were going to arrest, and did not expect any resistance. But resist they did. Grimes was killed and Moore wounded. This action, Bass knew, ruined their plans to rob the bank. Their intention to look over the bank one last time had now turned into a desperate fight to save their lives.[17]

Murphy was not aware of what was transpiring. He was separated from the others and did not see the gunfight at Koppel's store. Major Jones had arrived in town earlier and alerted the deputies of the probable invasion of the bank robbers. Grimes and Moore, to their harm, ignored Jones' information. Murphy also could not have realized that within moments after the first shots that Rangers would appear in the street ready to do battle. Ranger Richard C. "Dick" Ware was posted in the barber shop; although some have written he was getting a shave or waiting his turn for a shave, this seems unlikely. Probably he was in that particular

Richard C. Ware, the man whose bullet helped end the career of Sam Bass.
Courtesy the Roland Graham Collection.

building because it gave him a good view of the street. When he heard the first shot he rushed into the street, pistol in hand, and saw Bass, Barnes, and Jackson. One of them fired at Ware, the bullet hitting the hitching post only inches away, knocking splinters in his face. Ware "was as brave as courage itself" Gillett wrote, " and never hesitated to take the most desperate chances when the occasion demanded it. For a few minutes Dick fought the robbers single handed."

Major Jones was at the telegraph office and arrived on the street moments later, armed only with a small Colt revolver. Chris Connor and George Herold quickly joined in the fray. The bandit trio managed to reach their horses "with the energy of despair," fighting every step of the way. Richard Ware fired a shot that hit Barnes in the head, killing him immediately. Jackson now held the Rangers back and at the same time mounted his horse. He would not leave his wounded companion, and now helped Bass. With his pistol in his right hand Jackson managed to unhitch Bass' mount and push him up into the saddle. Then "Jackson and his chief galloped out of the very jaws of hell itself. . . . Jackson was holding Bass, pale and bleeding, in the saddle," as Gillett described their escape years later. Citizens and Rangers pursued the outlaws as they galloped out of town. Two hours later Reynolds and his exhausted group rode in, having missed the big street fight. They were all bitter over missing the action, and Gillett expressed it best: "The battle was now over, and the play spoiled by two overzealous deputies bringing on a premature fight, after they had been warned to be careful. Naturally, Moore and Grimes should have known that the three strangers were the Sam Bass gang."[18]

Alley in Round Rock where the Sam Bass gang was shot to pieces as it appears today. *Photo Courtesy Rick Miller.*

Reynolds did not express this belief in his brief report, merely pointing out that previous to his arrival Grimes and Moore attempted to arrest the men wearing pistols. After Grimes was killed and Moore wounded, Major Jones, Connor, Ware, and Herold followed in pursuit. Reynolds identified Ware as the man who killed Barnes, and Herold as the man who gave Bass the wound that would cause his death. The trail of Bass and Jackson was lost and it was not until the next morning, the twentieth, when Sergeant Nevill and a squad of eight men from Company E renewed the pursuit.

At daybreak Sergeant Nevill and eight Rangers with Williamson County Deputy Sheriff James Milton Tucker left camp after Bass and Jackson, following the trail by the drops of blood left on the ground. The trail led to a man lying under a large oak tree. When Nevill approached, the man held up his arm and said, "Don't shoot; I am unarmed and helpless. I am the man you are looking for. I am Sam Bass." The dying man explained to Nevill and Tucker that he "was out of money and was after a raise." Wounded mortally—one bullet had entered to the left of the spine, ranged upward near the kidney, then exitted about three inches to the left of the navel and the other bullet had shot off the ring and middle finger of the right hand—Bass had lost a lot of blood the previous evening and could go no further. He had convinced Jackson to leave him to save himself.[19]

Nevill recalled, years later, what he did the morning after the street fight.

> When I learned upon my arrival of what had happened, I immediately started after Bass. I knew from the bloody trail he had left he was badly wounded. After Jackson left, Bass had started back in the hope of finding someone who would dress his wound and give him shelter. He left his horse and managed to walk about a mile. When I came upon him he was sitting against a tree. I didn't know how badly he was hurt, and taking no chances, covered him and ordered him to throw up his hands. He obeyed, and I walked up to him [and he] told me how badly hurt he was and I sent back for an ambulance, and a doctor. When the doctor

arrived, he told Bass he couldn't live more than a few hours. Bass ridiculed the idea.[20]

Sam Bass had achieved such notoriety that the *New York Times* considered his passing worthy of page one news. Headlined "Capture of a Texas Desperado" the *Times* reported: "A special dispatch to the [Galveston] *News* from Round Rock says a squad of State Troops, under the command of Lieut. Reynolds, captured the desperado Sam Bass, who yesterday killed Deputy Sheriff Grimes, about seven miles from here this morning. Bass was fatally wounded."[21] This was the second time the name of N. O. Reynolds appeared in the *New York Times*.

John R. Banister was one of the Rangers who received a memento from Bass. He must have performed some favor for the dying man, as Bass gave him his revolver. On the day after Bass died, Banister wrote his mother that he and his brother Will were both well, adding that "the notorious Sam Bass died yesterday at 4 20 Pm." Bass had made no request, but "2 minutes before his death he Said the world is but A bubble [with] Troubles wherever you goe [*sic*], & after Saying this in 2 minutes his Soule [*sic*] was Launched into eternity. I have a Relic which he gave me his Sixshooter, Belt & Scabert [*sic*]." Banister explained that the bullet that would be fatal to Bass had passed through the scabbard and through the belt. He further noted that Dick Ware had killed Barnes and George Herold killed Bass and that "an awful excitement prevails over the Little town" of Round Rock."[22]

The wagon carrying the dead outlaw started to the small cemetery by the time Banister finished his communication. The corpse was buried just to the right of the newly dug grave of Seaborn Barnes. Just when the grave of Sam Bass was marked, or Barnes' either, is uncertain. It was given some type of marker shortly after as in May 1879, ten months later, someone placed flowers on the grave. The Belton newspaper remarked that it was a "Romantic" notion.[23] A headstone was placed there by his sister not long after, and soon the short and tragic life of Sam Bass became one of the Texas legends. As early as July 29, 1880, a newspaper noted the placement of a stone over "the last resting place of the unfortunate

The early monument placed at the grave of Sam Bass, rural Round Rock.
Courtesy Former Texas Rangers Foundation.

and daring desperado, Sam Bass." The writer stated the stone was "a kind and heartfelt momento [*sic*] from his sister, a resident in the native state of her brother [Indiana]." The inscription, the article stated, was "sculptured appropriately."[24] It is not certain if this marking of the grave's location noted by the Belton newspaper was the first or the second stone placed on Bass' grave. Either way, the inscription raised the eternal question of why some follow an evil path and others do not. Visiting Bass' grave was (and remains so today) a popular activity but souvenir hunters broke off bits and pieces until it was necessary to replace it with a new stone. The present Bass headstone, along with a new stone for Seaborn Barnes as well as a new one for deputy Grimes, although his original stone still stands, were installed in 1990. The inscription merely records Bass' birth date of July 21, 1851, and his death date, July 21, 1878, and asks the question: "A brave man reposes in death here/ why was he not true?" To the left is the stone of Barnes who died in the last gunfight of Sam Bass, merely recording that he died July 19, and that "He was right bower to Sam Bass."

Elsewhere in the small Round Rock cemetery is the grave of "Hi" Grimes who died in the same gun battle. The inscription on the original grave marker informs the viewer that he was the son of R. H. and E. Grimes, and was born on July 5, 1850, in Bastrop County, Texas, and that he died on July 19, ending with the time honored phrase "Gone But Not Forgotten." Today the second grave marker for Grimes includes additional information, that he was a deputy sheriff of Williamson County and a former Texas Ranger, that he left a wife and three children, and that Mrs. Grimes received $200 and the horse of one of the gang as indemnity for the death of her husband.[25] Major Jones made the decision as to the division of the spoils. Besides the horse given to Mrs. Grimes, Sam Bass' Winchester, hidden in the brush near Round Rock, was recovered and turned over to Corporal Wilson. Bass' compass was given to Charles Nevill.[26] Just why Bass gave John R. Banister his pistol, belt, and holster is unknown. Presumably this was done before Jones decided who was to receive what. The whereabouts of these priceless relics is today unknown.

The grave of Sam Bass as it appears today in the Round Rock Cemetery. To the left is the grave of Seaborn Barnes, killed by Richard C. Ware. *Photo by Parsons.*

The question as to who rightfully deserves the credit for killing Bass continues to be debated. Lee Hall was interviewed at the time of the death of John Wesley Hardin in August 1895, although his involvement with outlaws had taken place years before. His interview appeared in the *San Antonio Daily Express* entitled, "How Sam Bass Was Killed." Hall explained that he had been ordered to go to Round Rock to communicate with traitor Jim Murphy about the planned bank robbery. He claimed he took with him, from Austin, Rangers T. N. Devine, James E. Lucy and his brother Richard M. Hall. Arriving at Round Rock he left the others some miles from town (although no reason was given) and proceeded and remained out of sight as—or so he claimed—Barnes and Jackson knew him by sight. Hall felt the trap could be sprung while the robbery was in progress. Grimes and Moore had been instructed to just keep the Rangers informed, not to initiate any action of their own. Hall repeated the fact that the gang was in town to finalize their plans when the deputies challenged them for their weapons.

Hall claimed that after the street fight he followed the trail of Bass for six miles into the country, accompanied by Dick Ware and George Herold. Evidently the group lost the trail as during the night "an old negro" came into town and told of a man lying in front of his cabin, wounded. Major Jones then sent out a detachment to investigate and it was determined the man was Bass. "The next morning we went out," Hall recalled, "taking a doctor and some others. We found him lying in front of a negro cabin under a live oak tree."[27] What is perplexing is that Hall did not even mention the presence of Reynolds nor his men, either being involved in the gun fight or in the pursuit, or the presence of Sergeant Nevill and his squad who made the actual arrest of the mortally wounded Bass. Curiously Hall failed to mention the role of his brother and the others in the capture. Much of what Hall gave in this interview in 1895 is contradicted by the records of men who were actually involved in the affray when it happened, not almost two decades later.

Gillett wrote in his *Six Years With the Texas Rangers*, self-published in 1921, that Bass' death wound was from the pistol of Richard Ware. In 1902, some nineteen years prior to the book's publication, he wrote that the statement of the doctors that the fatal wound was in the back, together with Bass' statement that he was shot in the back, "led every member of Company E to think that Dick Ware had fired the fatal shot, because he was known to be a fine pistol shot, cool and steady under fire, and for a while after leaving the store he was fighting them alone. Yet no man ever heard Dick Ware say that he killed Sam Bass. Of all the rangers I ever knew he was the least boastful, and cared less for notoriety than anybody." Gillett recorded that at the inquest Ware was asked if he had shot Bass, to which Ware replied, "No sir, not that I know of." Then George Herold "was put on the stand and swore that he had killed Bass, so it is written in history."[28] John R. Banister who was there as well, wrote that Richard Ware killed Barnes and it was George Herold's bullet which caused Bass' death. Reynolds recorded in his monthly return: "Ware killed Barnes and Heorold [*sic*] wounded Bass but he made his escape with Frank Jackson."[29] Major Jones stated that he was "quite sure that Ware killed Seaborn Barnes, as he was very near him and looking at both of them at the time. The coroner's jury decides [*sic*] that George Harrell [*sic*], another ranger, fired the shot which proved fatal to Sam Bass."[30] The actual coroner's report has not surfaced but the men making up the jury were there at the time and certainly talked with others who were witnesses or participants in the street fight. Thus it is reasonable to believe that George Herold's bullet ended the life of outlaw Sam Bass, although the controversy will probably continue as to whether it was Ware or Herold who deserves the credit.

Unfortunately Richard C. Ware did not make a personal statement as to his actions in Round Rock that day. Ware later lived in Colorado City, Mitchell County, Texas, and became the county's first sheriff. He never admitted or denied the killing but in 1967 the State of Texas placed a historical marker at Ware's grave in Colorado City, on which it is recorded that Ware's bullet gave Bass the wound from which he died.[31]

Born December 23, 1867, James Bradley Warden was a young boy when the Bass gang was shot up and he later related what he had seen that day as he and his father had stopped on their way home from Austin. His version of the street battle is essentially the same as other reports.

His version does reflect, however, the frustration of the men of Reynolds' command at arriving too late for the fight. "My daddy and me had met the Rangers four miles out of town. When they found that they had missed the fight after riding for two days and two nights, they were mad and cussed and stamped their feet. I thought daddy and me might be in as much danger from the Rangers as we were from the outlaws." Warden also had comments about the gravestones. "Sometime later, Bass's sister came to Round Rock to place a monument on Sam's grave, but people kept chipping off pieces and would carry it off for souvenirs." Also, as to who shot Bass, Warden had this to say: "Now and then someone will claim that his uncle or a relative shot and killed Sam Bass. Heck, nobody knows who shot Sam Bass! I was there. The ones who done the shooting were out of sight. Bass never had much of a chance to fight back."[32] Young Warden and his father, Benjamin, a farmer residing in Burnet County, were there by chance, but the action that day remained with him the rest of his life, certainly the most memorable event of his youth.[33]

As there was disagreement among men who were in a position to know, there will never be absolute certainty as to whose bullet proved to be the fatal one. But as far as Reynolds and at least some of his men were concerned, it was Ware who killed Barnes, and Herold's bullet that killed Bass. Although terribly disappointed they had missed the big fight there were more problems demanding their attention. While at Round Rock, Reynolds learned that one Hargraves, who had shot a man named Cook some weeks before, had himself been killed a day or two before at Lampasas by parties unknown. By July 26 Reynolds and his men were back in San Saba ready for more work hunting down outlaws.[34] Reynolds and his squad had covered 227 miles riding from San Saba to Round Rock and back in camp.[35]

13

A Sheriff vs A Ranger

"[T]hey are a different set of rangers to what Waller's men were. Besides I believe they would of stood by me until the last hour in the day."
—John Wesley Hardin to Jane Hardin, October 1878

Certainly any action following the defeat of the notorious Sam Bass gang, even if Reynolds had missed the big street fight, would be anticlimactic. He had fought against Indians, had delivered John Wesley Hardin safely to and from jail during his trial, had captured the Horrell party, had safely delivered Thomas G. T. Kendall to Austin, rescuing him from the hands of the San Saba mob, and now his men had captured Sam Bass. By July 26 he and his command were back in San Saba. George Herold requested a discharge on July 31, stating a need to visit his sick father in San Antonio. Herold later worked in far West Texas fighting Apaches, and then joined the El Paso police force.[1]

The month of August 1878 was occupied with scouting, dealing with problems in San Saba County, and guarding the Lampasas County jail. Sergeant Nevill and a squad of four men were there as well to assist the sheriff as needed due to the crowds swelling the population during the county fair. Nevill made numerous arrests between August 5 and 11, three of them for indecent exposure: James and Henry Fry and John Blackwell. He also arrested John Z. Bean and an unidentified man for assault and battery. Curiously some five years later Bean would be a candidate for the position of Lampasas City Marshal, running against N. O. Reynolds.

Bean received only eleven votes. Two fugitives not found were Joe Henry and George Hoy, both accused of stealing cattle and horses.[2]

An incident occurred on Sunday, August 11, which revealed Reynolds' ability to fight with his fists, his first known encounter using anything other than a six-shooter or Winchester. It involved, oddly enough, one of his own men who challenged his authority. In such a situation Lieutenant Reynolds had but one option: take out the challenger or face possible resignation, or at best lose face. John Binford, Reynolds' teamster, had mustered in only four months before on April 19, 1878. Now on that Sunday morning Binford had gone into San Saba and spent the day drinking, returning to camp late and in a drunken condition—and wanting to fight. Reynolds spoke to him about his neglecting his camp duty but Binford responded in an "insolent manner." To compound his problem Binford then ordered some of the boys out, telling them that he "was running this end of camp."

Reynolds then ordered Binford to go and turn the mules loose, which Binford started to do but stopped at the tent of Dave Ligon and asked him for a drink of whiskey. Ligon either didn't have any or else refused to give him any. When Binford "showed fight," Ligon threw a rock at him. At this point Reynolds had reached the scene and he and Binford started to fight, a bare-knuckled fist fight in which Binford received "a complete thrashing" from Reynolds. The defeated Binford was then dismissed from the service to be replaced by D. H. Bowen, a twenty-seven-year-old white man from South Carolina.[3]

Lieutenant Reynolds wrote to Major Jones the following Saturday to explain what had happened, suspecting that he may have heard "some false reports in regard to the affair." He wrote that Binford was the only one who had been drinking, and that he expected to pay his fine and "attend to my own business" and see that others did the same. No record is available to indicate if Jones did impose a fine on his commander for action in this case; it is doubtful if he was fined, as what else could Reynolds do as the man had challenged his authority? If he had allowed Binford to continue his drunken behavior he would have lost the respect of his men. Reynolds expressed to Major Jones his belief that there was "great prejudice here against Rangers" but would nevertheless "act with discretion."[4]

Additional irritation came the following week when a large crowd fired into the courthouse and other dwellings in San Saba. Apparently Reynolds' old antagonist, Sheriff William R. Doran, did nothing to determine who the guilty parties were and circulated a report that men of Company E had done the shooting. Reynolds explained to Major Jones that none of his men could have done the shooting as none of them were in town that night. "I have been holding off to see if the sheriff or deputies would not call on us for assistance or maybe some of the citizens but as yet none have said a word." Reynolds explained to Major Jones: "If you will allow me to stop this riotous conduct here I can do it. There is one way to stop it and until that way is put into effect there will be disturbance[s] here. There are just a few who do this mischief and the law cannot convict. Here citizens are intimidated." Reynolds did not further explain what that "one way" to stop such activity was, but apparently Jones knew what he meant.[5]

Sheriff Doran or a deputy finally did call for assistance from the Rangers, as on August 24 Sergeant McGhee and five men went with Doran to capture unknown parties for shooting and disturbing public peace. James Moore was arrested for carrying a concealed weapon and shooting in the street and was then turned over to Sheriff Doran. During the next several days Rangers were sent out to provide further assistance to the sheriff but no additional arrests were made.[6]

Major Jones responded in a supportive manner to Reynolds' concerns, expressing his belief that Reynolds had done right in both instances, but adding his own concern about showing any favoritism to either side in local troubles, urging again, "as I have here to fore done, the imperative necessity of avoiding and guarding your men against any undue sympathy with, or predjudice [*sic*] against any of the parties in the troubles in localities where you are operating, or the expression of any opinion as to the guilt or innocence of parties against whom there are charges in Court." And Jones continued with reminding Reynolds what the primary duties of the Rangers were: "Always bearing in mind that it is our duty to put down strife, preserve the peace, assist in the enforcement of the law and give protection alike to all citizens good or bad, and that we must not allow our personal feelings to interfere with our official duty." One cannot help but wonder if Jones pondered the events back in Mason County when Reynolds resigned in the midst of those troubles because he could not in good conscience pursue fugitive William Scott Cooley.

In the same communication Major Jones gave Reynolds orders to take half of the company to Austin to deliver John Wesley Hardin back to Comanche for his sentencing, scheduled to take place on September 23. The other half was to stay in San Saba to provide an escort for T. G. T. Kendall if needed and preserve the peace generally during district court. Jones also shared with Reynolds a letter he had recently received regarding a plan to take Hardin from the Rangers and mob him while on the road, somewhere between Austin and Comanche. Jones again showed his confidence in his commander's ability: "I . . . shall be much surprised to hear that Hardin or any other prisoner has been taken from you either by force or strategy." Sergeant McGhee also learned that a mob had been organized and was ready "to make Shure [*sic*] of Killing Wess Hardin this time at Court."[7]

The threats of mob action against Hardin were commonly known and given attention in the national press, not only increasing Hardin's reputation as a man-killer, but at the same time giving Texas a bad name. The *National Police Gazette*, the most popular sporting journal of the time but also a frequent vehicle to provide news of scandals and gruesome murders, carried an item from Houston reporting that "the notorious Hardin" was soon to go to Comanche "to receive his ridiculous sentence of twenty-five years. A heavy guard of state troops will accompany him to prevent lynching." Obviously the *Gazette* would have preferred Hardin to be the victim of a lynch mob, as that would make much better copy than merely being delivered to a prison.[8]

On September 11 Reynolds and fourteen men arrived in Austin to take Hardin from the Travis County jail and deliver him to Comanche. Although there was great apprehension that the Ranger escort would be attacked and Hardin taken and mobbed, there was also an expression of confidence that the guard would prevent any such attempts. Further, although Hardin had killed many men, he still deserved the law's full protection. "Whatever may be the history and character of this unfortunate man," stated a San Antonio newspaper, "he is entitled to the shield of law from mob violence."[9]

Hardin, handcuffed and shackled, was taken from his cell and placed in a two-horse wagon. Before departure, his wife Jane was allowed to see him. She seemed "much affected at first, but as she conversed aside with her husband she became more composed." She was a "prepossessing lady of rather slight figure, and above the medium height, showing traces of care and sorrow upon her face" as the *Express* described her. Hardin himself "appeared in good health, was unusually cheerful and laughed and talked with those around him. He seemed perfectly resigned to his fate."[10]

At Liberty Hill, in Williamson County, on the eighteenth, a newspaper correspondent identified only as "Yours Truly" wrote how the entire town was thrown into momentary excitement by Hardin with his Ranger escort passing through. "It is a shame that the boasted murderer of over a score of men should get but 25 years in the penitentiary," he wrote, "with a good possibility for escape. Hardin looked considerably bleached by his long confinement, but seemed to be in good spirits."[11] In camp near San Saba Hardin was allowed to write to his beloved Jane, reassuring her that he was well and "under the Circumstances" had "Had a good time as yet for I have Been in camps with the rangers ever Since I left Austin and Have fared as they have in other words have had a good time." Hardin estimated he would arrive in Comanche within a few days but would remain there only long enough for his sentence to be passed. Hardin apprehended "no danger as I wil[l] have a true & good guard."[12]

Thomas Ripley, in his study of the better known Texas gunfighters, wrote that after sentence had been passed and preparations made to start the trip to Huntsville, Reynolds, given the rank of *Captain*, placed four of Sheriff Wilson's deputies in the wagon along with Hardin, "locked to the seat." With four deputies, Hardin, and the other prisoners, it must have been very crowded in that wagon. Once in Comanche, according to Ripley, after Hardin had told Reynolds how to arrange the guard, Reynolds gave out a public statement that if any effort was made to lynch Hardin he would "personally place pistols in his hands and turn him free to rough it for himself."[13] Certainly Reynolds had his own idea as to how best to arrange the guard, but may have listened to what Hardin had to say nevertheless. Unfortunately Ripley did not indicate his source for these remarkable statements.

At Comanche Judge J. R. Fleming passed sentence on Hardin, but added that he might in the event of his profiting by the moral instruction that he would receive in the penitentiary, at some future time use his influence in procuring him a pardon, which "greatly elated the prisoner."[14]

After sentencing, Reynolds and the guard headed on to Fort Worth where they arrived on October 3. A reporter of the *Fort Worth Democrat* was allowed to interview the prisoner. If we believe what the reporter wrote, then the entire city of Fort Worth was "thrown into a state of curious excitement" on learning that John Wesley Hardin was arriving. Hardin's life, supposedly, had "been written up and compiled in book pamphlets, whose picture has been paraded time and again in the *Police Gazette*, and the mention of whose name is calculated to inspire one with a feeling of awe." This is assuredly creative reporting; as yet there is no "book pamphlet" known to exist about Hardin's life in 1878, in contrast to that of Sam Bass about whom one had been published while he was still alive. Incomplete files of the *National Police Gazette* are problematic for searching for an image of Hardin. Again, in contrast to another Texas desperado, "Bloody Bill" Longley was the object of several illustrations in the *Gazette* at the time of his legal execution in Giddings, Lee County, in October of 1878.[15] The reporter then reviewed briefly what crime Hardin had committed, his trial, and the sentencing, and that he was to be delivered to Huntsville to begin his sentence. Due to many threats upon his life while in custody, Hardin "demanded of the state sufficient protection to insure a safe overland trip to this city, on his way to Huntsville. In answer to this demand, Lieut. Reynolds, captain of the company of the state rangers stationed at San Saba, was assigned to guard and protect the prisoner. . . . The company numbered twenty well-armed men, armed to the teeth with breech-loading Winchesters, six-shooters, etc."

The Rangers, "took possession of a small frame house in which Hardin was placed with three other prisoners, accompanying him to Huntsville, a strong guard was stationed outside and in during the day and night, and none was permitted to hold intercourse with the prisoners but a few officers of the law and several newspaper men."

The *Democrat* reporter was ushered in and introduced to Hardin, "with whose general appearance he was most favorably impressed." When Hardin learned of the reporter's "mission" he "courteously invited him to a seat on a pallet of old coats and pants." The reporter and Hardin shook hands; this made the reporter "feel as comfortable and easy as though he had been sent to interview a minister of the gospel, instead of a man who rumors and reports have it, has killed a regiment." The reporter was extremely impressed with Hardin, not only in their conversation but by Hardin's physical appearance. For those readers who could not possibly get to see him, the reporter wrote:

> Wesley is what any lady would describe as being a fine-looking fellow. His worn and shabby clothes did not detract a jot or tittle from his rather handsome face. He has a fine well developed forehead, and a large, piercing, dove-colored eye, which shows not only determination, but a world of bravery and daring recklessness, coupled with an equal amount of shrewdness and intelligence. His complexion has been tanned from his long journey in the sun, but is naturally inclined to the brunette type, so to speak. Dark brown hair and mustache and chin whiskers beneath which are a pretty set of white teeth, complete the pen picture of our hero's face. He stands about five feet, nine inches, and weighs about one hundred and sixty pounds.[16]

The several photographs of Hardin perhaps confirm he was a good looking man, although one wishes that a photographer had been able to visit this "small frame house" and photograph the prisoners together and individually, so the public could actually judge the accuracy of the description by the *Democrat* reporter. Obviously, he was impressed with every aspect of the prisoner, actually calling him a hero. If a photograph of Hardin and Reynolds together had been made, which would the reporter call the hero?

After Fort Worth the group continued via the railroad, allowing a portion of the guard to return to camp. Hardin wrote his wife a letter from Tyler on October 4, in which he mentioned the Fort Worth reporter. Hardin's original misspellings have been retained.

> Dear Wife. This leave me well at present & hope it may find you injoying the same . . . I think the comanchie People are changing in my favor more than ever was expected[.] all looks favorable for a better future [.] Lieut. Renols with 6 of his men are Still with me[.] Frank Wilson allso I saw many Friends at ft Worth Yesterday. . . . Jane Dearest I hope and believe that I can Manage So You can come to See me once an ocasionley So keep in Cheer I Send you a piece out of the ft Worth Democrat Let me Know if you receive it Dearest Good by.[17]

Hardin was safely delivered to Huntsville, where he was assigned # 7109. He was able to write again to Jane, and mentioned the good treatment, as well as alluding to the possibility of violence and the trust he had placed in Reynolds to prevent mob action. His letter read in part:

> Dear I Had a Splended time with the rangers for we went by Sansaba where they were camped and Staid 7 days in camps with the rangers [.] there treatment to me was the very best for they done all in their power for my convenience and tried to make me as comfortable as possible [.] you can tell ma that they are a different Set of rangers to what Wallers men were besides I believe that they would of Stood by me untill the last hour in the day[.] So Did the mobb [*sic*] [.][18]

So did the mobb . . .

Those men from Comanche or Brown County who wanted to lynch Hardin because he had killed deputy Charles M. Webb believed the lieutenant would stand by Hardin until the last hour of the day. And he would have.

As Hardin had carried this belief about Captain Waller for four years, he no doubt believed that all Rangers were like him—willing to give up prisoners to lynch mobs, as Hardin believed Waller had done. Finally Hardin was experiencing first-hand the quality of a Ranger totally different, one in whom he could find no wrong. This was high praise indeed for N. O. Reynolds, praise coming from the deadliest gunfighter Texas had produced.

Reynolds and his squad returned from delivering Hardin on October 12, having covered a distance of 1,150 miles by horse-drawn wagon and train. Sergeant C. L. Nevill had been in charge of the company in Reynolds' absence.[19]

It had been in June that Reynolds had had the confrontation with Lee County Sheriff James Madison Brown, a lawman who disregarded his oath when it came to a personal matter, intending to kill the man who had killed his brother. Reynolds had given him no special treatment just because he was a sheriff, and Sheriff Brown had backed down. It may be true that Brown later did apologize for his behavior that day in San Saba, but the Brown troubles were not yet over.

On September 17 San Saba County Attorney Spencer S. Brooks was shot down while riding along the road leading to his home. Brooks struggled to continue but was again fired upon, this time the bullet taking effect in his back. Before dying, Brooks was able to identify his assailant as "a man by the name of Brown," thus identifying the man who killed him as James Madison Brown, the sheriff of Lee County.[20]

Immediately Sergeant Nevill and four others went to San Saba County to assist the sheriff in capturing the murderer of Brooks. On the nineteenth Sheriff Brown himself came in and surrendered to the sheriff. The October Monthly Return told of these actions, but in the "Remarks" section appears the simple notation that Private W. L. Banister had been discharged on September 21 and then had "Joined by enlistment" on the twenty-fourth.[21] Reynolds' Special Order No. 9, dated September 21, discharged Private Banister for "Neglecting to Discharge His Duty."[22] Reynolds' explanation was that on the evening after S. S. Brooks was killed, Banister, on scouting detail under Sergeant Nevill, halted Brown, who refused to stop and then was allowed to get away. Reynolds didn't feel that Banister was cowardly or a friend of Brown, but acted in very poor judgment in allowing Brown to pass. When leading citizens learned that Banister had been discharged, they implored Reynolds to reinstate him, as his testimony was very important in an upcoming case. In addition to this concern, Reynolds reported

William L. Banister, one of the Rangers who made the desperate ride to Round Rock. *Courtesy Sue K. Porter.*

that the sheriff had "acted Verry Imprudent" and ordered Sergeant Nevill "Not to Arrest or attempt to [arrest] anny [*sic*] of the Brown Party as He Had Made Evry thing all right and J. M. Brown Would Come In and Surrender In the Morning." Reynolds also explained his feelings toward the San Saba County Sheriff, W. R. Doran. "The Sheriff of this Co[unty] Is a Blank as far as His duty Is Concerned[.] There are 4 Indictments against Him for embesilment [*sic*] Receiving Bribes &c."[23]

Additional details on the Banister question were shared with Major Jones in Reynolds' report. Written on October 14, two days after Reynolds' return from delivering Hardin to Huntsville, Banister had been left in charge of the horses while the men went on scout after Brown. His orders were to halt all persons passing near him. Two men did come in: James Brown and his brother Asa. James Brown said, "don't Shoot you know us." Banister had a weapon but Asa Brown came near enough to tell him "If you Shoot Him I will Shoot you." Banister didn't shoot and the Browns made good their escape to the house of their father who lived close by.

Sergeant Nevill was prepared to round up the house but Sheriff Doran had come up by then and informed him to let the Browns alone as they would come in the next morning and surrender to the authorities. Reynolds added: "At first I thought Sergt Nevill did Not doe [*sic*] as He Should Have done but Civil Officers [out] Rank Military I believe (The Sheriff Here Is a Sweet Scented young Man)." Reynolds explained that he took Banister back more to get his testimony than for any other reason. He had little hope for the San Saba situation, stating that no charges would occur until a sheriff could discharge his duties properly. There were six candidates running for office but none of them was fit for the job, thought Reynolds.[24] Although he would have preferred chasing fugitives or trailing Indians Reynolds may have suspected he would have to stay in the San Saba area for some time due to the Brown troubles.

Lee County Sheriff James Madison Brown and his brother did remain for a while, and citizens had been sufficiently intimidated by them so their cooperation with the Rangers was virtually nonexistent. Reynolds was quite aware that there were fears more murders would be committed, and by Sheriff Brown himself. He was watching the Browns as best he could, but he could learn nothing of their plans, as everybody was afraid to talk.[25]

Then Reynolds had to devote his energies to solving another killing. On October 2 William H. Lipsey was killed near San Saba. Three men were suspected: Robert and Ben W. "Dock" Thornton and Elijah Estep Jr. Sergeant Nevill and a three-man squad went in pursuit of the trio. No details of the scout were provided except that Nevill caught up with them and Robert Thornton was seriously wounded in his attempt to get away. Estep and Ben Thornton chose to surrender, and were delivered to Sheriff Doran. Nevill believed Thornton's wounds would prove to be fatal, but left Ranger Henry Maltimore and one other man with him, suspecting he would die soon. But Thornton improved in health and on October 16 Pvt. L. R. Hughes and others were able to move him to jail where other Rangers continued to guard him from mob action.

Reynolds learned that the killing of Lipsey was the result of an old feud between several families. What was so frustrating was that after the killing the county officers had neglected to make any kind of investigation or to arrest the killers. The dead Lipsey had been buried without an inquest being held; then the body had to be disinterred—probably by Reynolds' order—and then it was difficult to find a jury of inquest. The verdict was that Lipsey came to his death from a shotgun fired in the hands of Jim Thornton, presumably a relative of Robert and Ben Thornton. Nothing came of the result of the inquest.

Of all the various communities in which Reynolds served during his Ranger days, certainly San Saba was the most vexing. He found serious fault with the elected sheriff; he found the behavior of the citizens strange due to their handling of the Lipsey murder; the Browns—one of whom was a county sheriff—intimidated the citizenry to their detriment. The opportunity to go elsewhere came with a rumor there was an outlaw camp two days away near Fort Concho. Reynolds learned from Ranger Dick Ware that John Parks, living at Williams Ranch in Mills County, knew where a large band of outlaws were headquartered. Parks was supposedly tired of the bad company he was keeping and wanted to get his life turned around. Parks identified such hard characters as Joe Olney, Tom and Sam Redding, Caleb Hall, and Joe Henry as being there. Reynolds expressed enthusiasm for making the scout after these fugitives in spite of his concerns that the Browns would go on a killing spree during his absence.

But Lieutenant Reynolds was unable to get to Fort Concho to make a raid on the outlaw camp, if indeed the report from Parks was accurate. Instead Major Jones ordered him to move the company to the headwaters of Johnson's Fork of the Llano River and "to look out for Indians . . . to use all means in your power to prevent a repetition of the outrage recently committed by them."[26]

The outrage was the slaughter of the Dowdy children in Kerr County.

The photographer's name is often lost to history but McArthur Cullen Ragsdale's name is preserved due to a number of images of Capt. Dan Roberts' Company D. The series of six was made in 1878, after Reynolds' service in Company D but it was no different from other camps of the period. This image shows Roberts (left) with Sergt. L. P. Sieker at the hack. Mrs. Roberts is shown to the left of tent opening. *Courtesy Former Texas Rangers Foundation.*

M. C. Ragsdale's image of Captain Roberts' camp near Fort McKavett, Menard County, in 1878. Note tents in background. *Courtesy Former Texas Rangers Foundation.*

"Dinner in Camp" as identified by Mrs. Lou Roberts who included this series of Ragsdale images in her book *A Woman's Reminiscences of Six Years with the Texas Rangers*. Note Rangers wear their side arms even during a meal.

Courtesy Former Texas Rangers Foundation.

Lou Roberts captioned this image as "Waiting for Orders" and is apparent there is no excitement present. Sergt. L. P. Sieker is the tall man standing at left by tree.

Courtesy Former Texas Rangers Foundation.

This image shows the Rangers preparing to leave on a scout. By 1878 the scouts for recent Comanche or Kiowa "sign" were rare; this image shows the men preparing to go after a fugitive from justice. *Courtesy Former Texas Rangers Foundation.*

The Rangers have returned from the scout and now may relax in camp. It is believed Ragsdale made the images in a series and later Mrs. Roberts created the captions; it is unknown how long Ragsdale visited the camp. Presumably the standing figure at right in suit is Captain Roberts. *Courtesy Former Texas Rangers Foundation.*

14

An Outrage Upon Children

"Wixon would be the first man killed."
—Corporal J. W. Warren, November 3, 1879

Even though it had been some time since the citizens of Kerr County had suffered from Indian raiding parties, the menace was far from a distant memory. It is not known why the James Dowdy family had left their home in Goliad County, Texas, but in the fall of 1878 they had located in Kerr County and continued to raise sheep. No one suspected there was any real danger from Indian raiding parties, but on the fifth of October something happened to bring back all the old fears. On that day the four youngest children of James and Susan Dowdy were watching the sheep, their chores to perform in the morning. That day also, Richard, the eldest son, and a young man engaged to a Dowdy daughter, were to have their meal first, then go and relieve the other children watching the sheep. After their meal the two young men went out and discovered the sheep scattered and the four others nowhere in sight. They returned to the house to spread the alarm; after a brief search all four of the children's bodies were discovered. Although some citizens were firm in their belief that a band of Indians returning from a horse-stealing raid chanced upon the children away from their home and killed them, others believed that it was a combination of Indians and Mexicans, while others believed there were renegade Anglos involved. This last Indian raid in Kerr County, as the state historical marker put it, took the lives of four of the Dowdy children: James C., eleven years old; Susan V., fourteen; Martha, sixteen; and Alice C., eighteen.[1]

San Antonio newspaper correspondent "Adobe" reported that the slaughter had taken place on Johnson's Fork of the Guadalupe, only eighteen miles from Kerrville, the county seat of Kerr County. He wrote that arrows and spears as well as rifle balls had inflicted the killing wounds, and although bruised and mangled, the bodies had not been scalped. The bodies of the four children were scattered over several hundred yards, indicating each had run some distance attempting to escape.[2]

Neighbors Samuel Fessenden and Louis Nelson gathered up the remains and hauled them to the Dowdy home. Here Mrs. Fessenden helped prepare the bodies for burial, which took place the next day, October 6. When the family lived back in Goliad County there had been seven children, and now there were but three, Thomas, Richard, and Mary.[3]

The graves of the four Dowdy children, victims of a raiding party, believed by many to be the last Indian raid of Kerr County. *Photograph by Parsons.*

The tragedy was widely reported throughout the nation as the idea of Indian raids were now considered a thing of the past, at least in this "settled" area of Texas. The *Post* of Washington, D.C. placed the story on page one, citing information from General John S. Mason and other sources confirming the slaughter. This communication differed from that of Adobe in that Mason reported that "the young girls were first outraged and then had their scalps removed and were left with their skulls bare and bleeding." Then, according to General Mason, the "human devils . . . butchered the three innocents in a most horrible manner, leaving their bloody corpses on the prairie near their dwelling. The little boy's scalp was sheared."[4] A special report from San Antonio cited "additional particulars" provided by a Major Bates. He reported that the bodies had been "somewhat mutilated" and the outer garments of the girls and the pants of the boy had been taken. In contrast to General Mason's claim, Bates denied the girls had been raped and there had been no scalping.[5] Obviously there were conflicting reports regarding the degree of savagery inflicted upon them. All that was consistent was that the four Dowdy children had been killed. Another source indicated that Mrs. Dowdy was able to get to Alice while she was still alive, and she whispered a name—the name of a white man who was with the raiders before she expired. A posse of citizens did go out in pursuit of the raiders, whoever or wherever they were, with a two-fold purpose: to recover the stolen horses, if indeed there were stolen horses with this group; but more importantly avenge the deaths of the children. They failed in both their purposes. In the Sunset Cemetery, a few miles west of present-day Ingram, the four children were buried.[6]

The orders came for Lieutenant Reynolds to move camp to the headwaters of Johnson's Fork and to establish camp on John Joy's ranch. His principal work would be to scout for Indian sign and to send out patrols to warn settlers and to advise them of the company's location so they could report sightings. By November 1 Reynolds had established his camp at the mouth of Contrary Creek, ready—and no doubt eager—to find and fight savages and perhaps as much to fight white desperadoes.[7]

Major Jones returned to Austin from the frontier on October 29. He reported that Indians had made another raid, that horses had been stolen, "from within a stone's throw" of Fort McKavett in Menard County. He also expressed his belief that the party who had murdered the Dowdy children were not Indians but in reality Mexicans disguised as Indians. This came at a time when the legislature was seriously considering reducing the size of the Frontier Battalion. "The frontier generally," stated Jones, was much "excited and discouraged over the prospect of reducing the State troops. In portions of the country where they have been temporarily removed the settlers have been obliged to fall back."[8]

Adobe was present in Kerrville and learned of Major Jones' concern and also the fears of the average citizen who now thought the Indian menace was still a reality, in particular the fears of any settler living a few miles outside of Kerrville or other smaller settlement. His writing not only provided news but also ridiculed the action of the legislature wanting to reduce frontier protection, no longer convinced there was a reason to continue such a force. He wrote that the Frontier Battalion was "westward bound" and that Reynolds would be stationed on the head of Contrary Branch, a tributary of Johnson's Creek, some two miles from where "the spot [was] made memorable by the butchery" of the Dowdy children. "This company will remain in Kerr county until our next Legislature can be informed that this agitation as to frontier protection is only the work of little brainless demagogues, etc., and, acting out the hint, disband the rangers." Adobe explained that Lieutenant Roberts was stationed in Kimble County, near the mouth of Bear Creek, and Lieutenant Dolan was in Edwards County, immediately south. Citizens were encouraged to communicate with these lieutenants any information as to the sightings of Indians or their trails.[9] Gillett recalled that they were stationed on the Dowdy ranch and that the raid that took the children's lives was "perhaps the most heartrending." They herded their horses on the very ground where the children had been killed. At the time of the killings the ground was soft and muddy from recent rains, and for months afterward the children's tracks where they had run to escape could be seen. Gillett estimated that one of the girls had run at least four hundred yards before being overtaken. While guarding their horses during their stay in this area the Rangers gathered rocks and piled them in the form of monuments, each one eight or ten feet high, where the children had finally been taken. Today these are but modest mounds of rocks, three close together and the fourth some hundred yards distant. Although they may indeed have been "eight or ten feet high" in 1878, as Gillett recalled, he may have actually meant eight or ten hands high, using the common measurement for determining the height of a horse.[10]

Major Jones had earlier explored the area for the best site of the commander's camp. Reynolds followed up on Jones' recommendation but

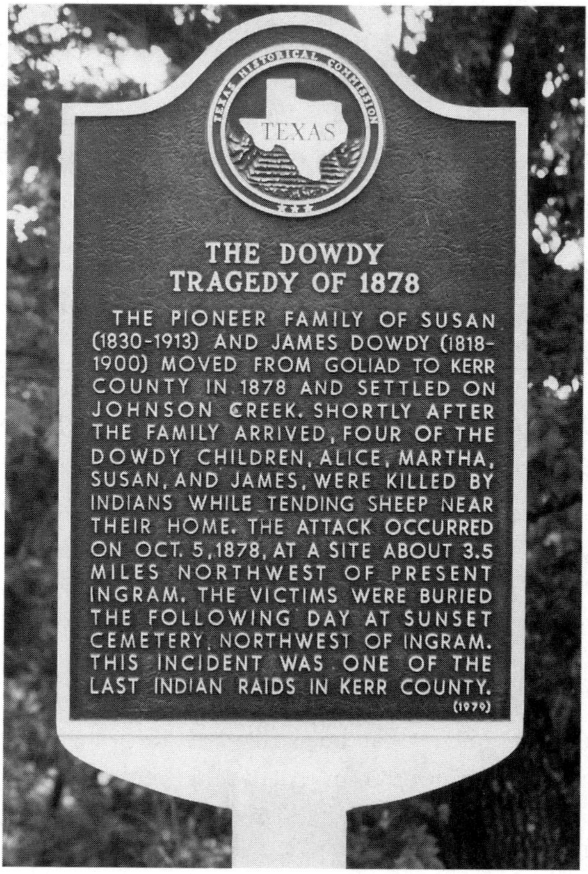

The historical marker not far from the Sunset Cemetery where the Dowdy children are buried. *Photograph by Parsons.*

found the head spring of Contrary Creek so rough that he concluded to make camp on its mouth. He tactfully explained that unless Jones "Insisted" on moving he would remain there; he had already notified "all the citizens here" where they would be. Reynolds planned to make a scout soon to the head of the Guadalupe River to "Get My Men familiar with this Country." Jones later supported Reynolds' decision but advised that he had felt his first choice was preferred as it was more convenient to grass. "Make your men as comfortable as possible," he wrote, "as you will probably have to remain there during the entire winter."[11]

Strangely one of Reynolds' men during this period proved to be unacceptable for continual duty. Reynolds had "Overheard Some talk" among the men that Sergeant McGhee, while at Lampasas during court, had seen Bob Mitchell of the Higgins party draw his pistol on "Old Man Fox" and threaten to kill him. Instead of arresting Mitchell, McGhee simply ordered him and his friends to get on their horses and leave town. They did so, riding towards Meridian in Bosque County, "at a Verry lively Gait." Reynolds had not yet had the time to investigate the report fully, but let Jones know he did not approve of such conduct, and wanted to know what Jones thought. He suggested that perhaps Corporal Warren would be more deserving of the rank McGhee currently held.[12]

Major Jones, by November 13, had also heard of Sergeant McGhee's conduct, but not from anyone who was actually present and witnessed the exchange. Jones thus wanted Reynolds himself to "investigate it *thoroughly & report the fact*" to him. Jones promised that if the unacceptable conduct was true then McGhee would be discharged from the service. "I will allow no man and more especially an officer to remain in the Service who does not come fully up to his duty under all circumstances. I wish the matter attended to at once." No written record of the investigation has been found but on November 26 Major Jones provided an honorable discharge to Sergeant Henry W. McGhee "on account of his aged father requiring his presence at home to attend to his wants."

In the same communication to Reynolds, Major Jones explained he was developing a plan to deal with the Indian raiders, if the reports of their presence and the numbers proved sufficient. If news came to

Reynolds of Indian sightings he was to send couriers to Roberts and Dolan and Jones, the unexpressed idea being to strike the Indians from different directions.[13]

The presence of the Rangers had a very quieting effect in the area as the winter of 1878–1879 was very calm. In spite of their yearning for action there were no confrontations with Indians. The Rangers did make contact with "but one real bad man," Eli "Wixon," as identified by Gillett, although the name was properly spelled Wickson. Reynolds reported that on November 3 Corporal Warren and four men had gone to the head of the Guadalupe River, then to the mouth of Johnson's Creek, and then arrested Eli Wickson, who was charged with murder in Milam County.[14] The arrest was not quite that simple.

It was election day and Wickson, now a highly respected citizen of the community, was at the Eller school house precinct, some sixteen miles west of Kerrville. Corporal J. W. Warren, Privates Will Banister, Abram Anglin, Charles L. Ware (younger brother of Richard C. Ware), and an unidentified fourth private made up the patrol. When ordered to drop his gun belt and pistol and surrender Wickson appealed to his friends to protect him from the Rangers! The crowd started to come to his relief, as Gillett recalled, and for a time it looked like there would be gunplay. Wickson verbally abused the Rangers, calling them a set of dirty dogs and dared them to shoot him. What could have become a bloody confrontation was prevented due to Corporal Warren's bravery and resolve. He told Wickson "his abuse did not amount to anything, that the rangers were there to arrest him and were going to do it." Corporal Warren warned the citizens to be careful how they broke the law and if they started anything he declared Wickson would be the first man killed. The four privates held the crowd back with their Winchesters while Warren disarmed Wickson. The prisoner was handcuffed and shackled. This treatment "usually took the slack out of so called bad men and it worked like a charm with our new prisoner."[15] Gillett only identified three privates making up Warren's patrol, but Reynolds and Nevill both recorded that the squad was made up of Corporal Warren and four men, that they had left camp and arrested Wickson for murder on the third, and then on the sixth he and three others escorted Wickson to Kerrville where he was turned over to the sheriff.[16] Perhaps the unidentified Ranger was Gillett or Nevill.

Hans Mickle, a wandering reporter for San Antonio's *Daily Express*, was at Kerrville at the time of the arrest and witnessed some of the election day's events. Although he would have preferred dramatic news to report, such was not the case. He attempted to add drama to his story through the use of war imagery: "The agony is over; and as the battle-clouds clear away, you see happy and sad faces, the latter in the majority because there were so many candidates for the same office." Mickle wrote there were no sensational news items to chronicle as all was quiet on the streets, "no riding about brandishing of weapons, or no bragadocia [*sic*] that would make fine material for a sensational article for some eastern newspaper." He did not witness the actual arrest, but he did see Wickson in custody. Mickle recorded that it was a little after noon when

> The rangers belonging to Capt. Reynolds' Company E arrested Mr. Eli Wixon, who for some eight or nine years has been living in the western portion of this county and was at the time acting as a judge of election in the Eller schoolhouse precinct, sixteen miles west of Kerrville. The charge was the alleged murder of his step-father in Wilson [*sic*, Milam] county. It is said that the killing was done in self-defense while protecting his mother from the brutality of her second husband. Mr. Wixon is favorably known as a good, law-abiding citizen, and public sympathy is in his favor. He has never evaded arrest, and much surprise was expressed at the time and place taken to make it. He arrived in Kerrville just as I left, under escort of some rangers, and I do not know what disposition has been made of the case, although I understand that an effort would be made to obtain a writ of habeas corpus.[17]

Wickson was the second son of Dyrun and Charity Francis "Fannie" Wickson; the family resided in Milam County as early as 1850, when the family was composed of Eli, older brother John, younger brothers Robert and James and sister Emeline. A decade later, after six more children were born to their union, including a set of twins, the name of Dyrun had disappeared and Lemuel Bess appeared as head of household. Besides the new Wickson children, there were three additional children named Bess, presumably from Lemuel Bess' first marriage. Dyrun Wickson died presumably the latter part of 1859, as the twins were seven months old in that year. [18] When the Rangers arrested Eli Wickson in late October 1878 it was reported that he had killed his stepfather Lemuel Bess some eight or nine years earlier, suggesting the year 1869 or 1870.[19] If indeed this was true then Charity Wickson-Bess and her second husband had allowed their union to slowly deteriorate during the 1860s.

The Milam County courthouse burned in mid-1874 and on May 21 of that year it was ordered that "in all Cases now pending on the Criminal Docket of this Court it is ordered that both parties have leave to substitute lost or destroyed papers." Later the name of Eli Wickson appeared in a group of 158 whose cases were dismissed. Then the destroyed cases were substituted, as on May 3, 1880, cause # 1915 was entered into the record, the one pertaining to Wickson. Beside it a court clerk noted, "Alias capias and continued." Through November 1883 the cause was called again, at which point the name disappears from the record.[20] As Wickson was indicted and arrested in 1878, then listed as a fugitive as late as 1886, he probably had escaped from the Milam County authorities before his trial.[21] The balance of Eli Wickson's life remains a blank, although there is a record of an Eli Wickson dying in Bee County, Texas on July 29, 1924.[22] This could be the same man but nothing was discovered about him in the available Bee County newspapers or court records.

Reynolds had time for reflection during this time of relative inactivity. With his health occasionally troubling him he considered something other than the Ranger service for a career. Gillett, who claimed he knew Reynolds better than anyone else, wrote that as the winter wore on, Lieutenant Reynolds, "with but little to do, became restless. He once said of himself that he never had the patience to sit down in camp and wait for a band of Indians to raid the county so he might get a race. Action was what he wanted all the time, and when compelled to sit idly in camp, he chafed like a chained bear."[23]

Reynolds may indeed have been restless during that winter of 1878–1879, since the only news the *Express* correspondent "Texan" reported from Kerrville was that the new sheriff was F. J. Hamer, that Lieutenant (Guy B.) Broadwater with Company A had passed through that very day going to Frio City, and that Reynolds "now situated in this county, is constantly on the lookout for evil doers."[24]

During this time of little activity several changes were made in the ranks. On November 24 Gillett was promoted to the rank of 1st Corporal "for good and meritorious conduct." Private L. R. Hughes was then promoted to the rank of 2nd Corporal, replacing Gillett.[25] Two days later, at Camp Dowdy, Private R. L. Moore was discharged for being absent from the command without leave. Sergeant Henry McGhee received his honorable discharge, as mentioned earlier, to take care of his aged father. Ironically Private C. R. Connor was honorably discharged as well to take care of his aged mother. Private Thomas R. Johnson was discharged to give personal care to his brother's children.[26] The McGhee, Connor, and Johnson trio went immediately to Austin for their presence was noted in the *Statesman* in the "Personal and Local Dots" column as being in the city.[27] Then on December 1 Richard C. Ware was promoted to the rank of 2nd Corporal "For good and Meritorious Conduct" and J. B. Gillett promoted to the rank of 2nd Sergeant.[28] Three days later Reynolds wrote to Major Jones advising him that his pistol had been found, but could only add that there was "No news of importance Here."[29] News did reach the Rangers that two of their former prisoners, Mart and Tom Horrell, had been killed while in jail at Meridian, Bosque County for the murder of John T. Vaughn.

The murders of the Horrell brothers would have provided Reynolds with food for thought. Jailed without bail, the Horrells could only wait until the opening of district court. According to a witness to the affair, Dr. S.A. Owens of Belton, Bell County, rumors had circulated that the friends of the Horrells were planning to break them out of jail. On the night of December 16, a Sunday evening while many of the citizens were presumably attending church services, four men tricked the jailer—a *ruse de guerre*—into opening the jail door and entered with cocked six-shooters. They forced their way to the cell on the second floor and while another prisoner was forced to hold a candle, the mob did its deadly work. "The affrighted wretch did as he was bid," reported Dr. Owens, "squeezing into one corner with the flickering candle in his hand, and the lynchers took position at the door of the cell." Tom and Mart Horrell were trapped inside their cell, helpless as the mob continued to fire. They were "literally riddled with bullets and fell dead on the floor of their cell." The mob then rode off yelling and firing their pistols. The doctor's report concluded with the statement that the general supposition at Meridian was that the mob was composed of friends of Vaughn and were determined to avenge his death. Of course the good people of Meridian "regret the forcing of their jail and murder of men who have not yet been proven guilty, but the general comment is the Horrells were guilty."[30]

Certainly N. O. Reynolds paused to reflect on the manner of the Horrells' death. A little over a year before when they were feuding with the Higgins clan he had arrested them and had earned their respect, and now they had been mobbed while in the custody of county officers. Mobs had operated in Mason County while Reynolds was there, and mobs had operated in Comanche County after Hardin had killed deputy sheriff Webb. He must have contemplated the fact that he had never allowed a prisoner to be taken and mobbed while in his custody. That would not change during the years to come as he continued his career as a lawman.

The lack of any activity of importance was reflected during the remaining Monthly Reports of 1878. Daily patrols were sent out regularly to look for Indian sign, but nothing substantial resulted from these scouts. On December 17 newly promoted Charles L. Ware and a squad of three men went in pursuit of horse thieves in Williamson County, the Hardin brothers. They did arrest a man identified by Reynolds as A. W. Pickens, alias J. W. Johnson, who, along with John Hardin, alias Tom Thomas, and William Hardin, alias "Shug" Hardin, had broken into John Mays' store in Fort Bend County, about November 20. Prior to that they had stolen two horses in Guadalupe County and one in neighboring Caldwell County. Before Reynolds had made a decision as to what to do with the prisoner identified as Pickens, Corporal Hughes rode into camp with William Hardin in custody along with some of the merchandise stolen from the Mays store. Prisoner Hardin then informed Reynolds that John

Hardin was hunting somewhere between Houston and Galveston, and had the balance of the stolen goods in his possession. The prisoners were ready to admit what their future plans included, in hope of being treated lightly by the authorities. In spite of their names, Reynolds certainly knew that these Hardins were not related to the notorious John Wesley Hardin, then in Huntsville penitentiary, or if they were the relationship was distant. Among their plans, which would never reach fruition, was robbing the bank in Luling, Caldwell County. With two prisoners in his custody, both wanting easy treatment, Reynolds was not sure what to do, having first promised to assist Pickens if he would betray his pals. "Now what Shall be done[?]" he asked. Reynolds anticipated that Major Jones would receive letters soon, probably from others who had been victims of thievery, and requested that Jones "open all letters and Dispatches addressed to me at Austin."[31]

Although Corporal Ware must have made the actual arrest, credit was not given to him in the report in the *Express,* which stated that Pickens and Hardin had been arrested a few days earlier "by the efficient officer N. O. Reynolds and lodged in the Austin jail."[32] The *Statesman* of Austin did give them credit for their good work, however: "On Thursday evening [January 9] a squad of Lieut. Reynold's [*sic*] company of rangers arrived from Kerr county, bringing two men, Hardin and Pickens, charged with 'mistakin' the brands on cattle. Hardin is a cousin of John Wesley Hardin."[33]

In answer to Reynolds' question as to what to do with Pickens and the Hardins, Major Jones explained that no agreement could be made at Reynolds' level, not with thieves, that such agreements could only be made by the governor. Jones did indicate he was supportive of the idea, adding, "If I can make an agreement with one thief by which he will enable me to catch and convict a sufficient number of other thieves, whom I could not catch without his assistance, I would have no hesitation in asking the Governor to pardon him." Major Jones continued his communication indicating his high regard for Reynolds' good judgment: "You will have to exercise your own discretion in regard to what you had better do with Pickens." Pickens did betray his companions and gave a "full acc't of their rascalities from which I think he is the greatest rascal of the three" as Jones expressed his thought.[34]

The Hardins and Pickens had left Guadalupe County in October, having tired of picking cotton for Frank Staples. The trio stole horses from various individuals to sell as well as for transportation. By the beginning of December they were making fence rails near Richmond in Fort Bend County, but then robbed Mays' store not far from where they were employed. After hiding out for several days they went to Houston where they sold a horse. Then William Hardin and Pickens went to Kerr County where they were arrested. Pickens described his brutal partner John Hardin, the only one of the group still at large, as nearly six feet tall, rather "raw-boned, red complected [*sic*], about 23 years old, very small blue eyes and squints." He further described Hardin's wife Cinthia, as a "low heavy set woman [of] light complexion, blue eyes, hair cut short and bushy, has scar on left eye where he [had] struck her with a spade." The loving couple had two sons.[35]

The inactivity of the winter was again reflected in the last return for 1878. On December 21 a Kerr County citizen reported that someone fired upon him, supposedly Indians, near the head of Johnson's Fork of the Llano River. Lieutenant Reynolds sent out Gillett and five men to investigate but returned the same day having determined it was a false report.[36]

15

Dealing with Fence Cutters

"Hands up or we will shoot!"

—Sheriff Reynolds to the fence cutters, summer 1886.

The Sixteenth Legislature met in early 1879 and perhaps to no one's surprise determined that it was again necessary to reduce the number of Rangers, due to financial uncertainty. Gillett recalled those sad days, especially how his commander, Lieutenant Reynolds, "was compelled to sit idly by and see his experienced rangers dwindle away before his eyes, and what he said about those shortsighted law-makers would not look well in print."[1]

The oath prepared at Camp Contrary on January 1, 1879, to which all solemnly swore to "bear true faith and allegiance to the State of Texas" and to "serve her Honestly and faithfully, and defend her against all her enemies or opposers whatsoever" as well as to "observe and obey the orders of the Governor . . . and the orders of the Officers appointed over me" carried the names of only twenty-two men, a drastic reduction from the seventy-one men enrolled in Captain C. R. Perry's Company D back in May of 1874.[2]

One of the matters left unresolved from the preceding year was that of the Hardins and Amos W. Pickens. Officials believed that the fugitive Hardin was in the Buffalo Bayou area south of Houston. Corporal Charles Ware and William Clements were sent to Fort Bend County to locate and arrest the fugitive.

At the same time John M. Parks was mustered in to act as an undercover agent. There was considerable doubt in the minds of both Reynolds and Major Jones as to his capabilities, but Reynolds was willing to take a chance. After all, if he did not work out it would not cost the state anything. Major Jones wrote to Reynolds that he had enlisted Parks, with the understanding that he could go wherever he pleased under Reynolds' direction from that date until the last of March, a "probation period" of two months. He was to search for criminals of course, but in particular he was to look specifically for members of the Baird and Olney clan. If Parks provided Reynolds or any other officer of the command information that would result in the conviction "of a notorious character," or if it was apparent that he was working in the interests of the State in good faith, then he was to receive the same pay as any of the other men. If he did not produce—not "accomplish anything"—to the satisfaction of Reynolds, then he was to be discharged without pay.[3]

If Parks actually did accomplish anything for the Rangers the record does not indicate what it could have been. The incomplete Ranger service records show that he was mustered in as a private in Company E on January 1 and was provided with a state pistol valued at thirteen dollars. He served for two months and earned eighty dollars, less the pistol price. An additional document shows he served from February 28 through March 31, 1879, per the record signed by C. L. Nevill at Camp Contrary at the end of March. Parks may have had the best of intentions but not long after, he left the service and headed further west to New Mexico Territory where for a while he was in close association with two men who had earlier been the object of Ranger patrols: John Ringo and Joe Olney, both associates of the Baird-Olney crowd. So far as known John Parks did nothing to search in particular for members of this gang in order to bring them to justice.[4]

Promotions in Reynolds' Company E were not the only changes taking place within the Frontier Battalion. Major John B. Jones now was elevated to the position of Adjutant General of the State of Texas, replacing William Steele. Reynolds read of the promotion and proved to be capable of diplomacy in sending congratulations to him. "I Notice in the Papers," he wrote, "that you Have Been Appointed Adt. Gen. I Can Only Say That It Meets with the Approval of Manny [*sic*] People on the

Frontier." Reynolds further stated that he felt if there was anyone worthy of the position, Jones was the man.[5]

But as Reynolds wrote this letter to the new adjutant general, he himself was contemplating leaving the service. According to Gillett, inactivity caused Reynolds to consider such a decision, but in reality his health was a more pressing concern. It had occasionally bothered him, most noticeably in July 1878 when he was unable to ride a horse in the haste to get to Round Rock to fight the Sam Bass gang. On February 14, at Camp Contrary in Kerr County, Reynolds wrote another letter to Adjutant General Jones. He first reminded him that he had been in the service for the past four years, and he desired to change his occupation on account of ill health; thus he was turning in his written resignation to be effective February 29, 1879. At first he was vague about the condition of his health, but in a second letter written the same day (still using capital letters usually) he was more candid. "The facts are that I Have Not been Really Able for duty Since last April But Have been Patched Up By first One Dr. and Another Untill [*sic*] I have Concluded that I Had better quit the Service and then Probably it Might be that I Could Keep from Riding on Horse back [.] This Is What Keeps Me from Getting Well." But it was more than just his health that caused Reynolds to consider a career change. He continued by explaining that he had no one to recommend for his replacement. He had been so disappointed in the conduct of some of the men he had recommended that "it Has Made Me Think that to recom[m]end a Man Is to Publish Him as a Rascal."[6] Although he said that he had no one to recommend, a statement of February 28 indicated his preference was for Sergeant C. L. Nevill. Sixteen men of the company signed a statement giving their preference for Nevill. He "is held in high esteem by his comrades [and is] Known to have all the qualifications [for the position] and having sustained an honest sober soldiers conduct since his enlistment we think (aside from his rank being next in order) he merits the promotion." This document, no doubt prepared by Reynolds but written by P. C. Jackson, was first signed by Reynolds, followed by sixteen others, all who were in camp at the time.[7]

Gillett was one of those out on scout, and when he returned to camp and was told what had happened, he thought it was a bad joke. But when convinced the lieutenant had indeed resigned he was "shocked beyond measure. The blow was too strong and sudden for me, and I am not ashamed now at sixty-eight years of age to admit that I slipped out of camp, sat down on the bank of the Guadalupe River, and cried like a baby. It seemed as if my best friend on earth had gone forever." Gillett was able to articulate why Reynolds had meant so much, not only for him but for every man in the company. Reynolds had transferred him from Coldwell's company to Company E when he "was just a stripling." When old enough to be trusted in charge of a scout, and vacancies occurred, he was promoted to the rank of sergeant. Reynolds had trusted him to go up against the most noted outlaws and criminals in the state. The confidence that Reynolds showed in the young man certainly was repaid years later when Gillett wrote his memoirs.[8]

P. C. Jackson and the members of Company E, Frontier Battalion, did not let N. O. Reynolds ride off into the sunset, as on March 6 they prepared a testimonial to show how much they appreciated him. It resulted in a document with which perhaps no other Ranger commander was ever so honored. Jackson was "called to the chair" and C. L. Nevill was chosen secretary. L. W. Rogers, J. H. North and T. P. Gillespie were appointed to draft "suitable resolutions expressive of the sentiments of the Company." After a "short time" the committee returned, expressing with "profound regret that personal interest has demanded the resignation of our highly esteemed and much loved friend and officer Lieut. N. O. Reynolds from further service" and resolving the following: First, that in the person of Reynolds "we recognize every qualification that characterizes the true type of gentleman"; second, that throughout all the "meandering scenes and vicissitudes of camp life for the past three years" Reynolds was ever the same, "good, noble . . . just and impartial." He has been "Brave and true as steel." Third, as an officer Reynolds has "discharged the onerous duties that have devolved upon him with a zeal; with a fearlessness with a fidelity" that merits "not only the commendation of the men he has commanded but the government he has so faithfully served." Fourth, while the boys "grievously lament the loss of service" and companionship of Reynolds, they "tender him" best wishes for his future success in whatever avocation or profession he may continue in; resolution fifth, the signatories "desire to express our heartfelt Sympathy for the loss of so able and efficient an officer"; and six, a copy of the resolutions be given to Lieutenant Reynolds, and a copy sent to the newspapers in San Antonio, Galveston, Austin and Mason and request that the resolutions be printed in full.[9]

The several newspapers did publish the resolutions of respect, although with slight alterations. The *San Antonio Daily Express* printed it in full in the March 11 issue; and on March 16 it appeared again in the "State News" column as state news from Mason County. The additional comment of the editor of the *Mason News Item* was also reprinted: "It is with sincere regret that we chronicle the resignation of Lieut. N. O. Reynolds as commander of company E, Frontier battalion. This competent officer has commanded company E (one of the very best and most efficient companies in the service) for three years past and has won hosts of friends among the frontier people."[10] No doubt he considered himself to be a personal friend.

Reynolds' departure from the service "practically broke up the company" as Gillett recalled. Nevill was promoted to the rank of lieutenant and later to captain and he, too, left an enviable record. At Austin Richard C. Ware and both Banister brothers received a transfer to Company B, commanded by Bryan Marsh; brothers Ben F. and P. S. Carter, Chris R. Connor, and William Clements resigned and returned to private life. Abram Anglin also resigned and became—according to Gillett—a policeman in Austin. Gillett and Henry Maltimore, at their own request, transferred to George W. Baylor's Company C for duty in El Paso County.[11]

As Reynolds' life changed, he contemplated where to go and what to do after leaving the responsibilities of leading a company of strong young men eager to fight Indians and track down fugitives from justice. He had been a Texas Ranger since mid-1874 and was extremely successful. Continuing in law enforcement would not be out of character; after all, numerous

N. O. Reynolds and a group of friends; Reynolds is seated right.
Courtesy the Stephen Reynolds Davis and Bernard Davis Collection.

Rangers, after leaving the hard outdoor life, became a county sheriff or city marshal. In time Reynolds would serve in both these capacities.

Little has been found of Reynolds' activities in the remainder of 1879. Even having resigned from the Ranger service, he was not through hunting fugitives from justice. A two-line item originating in Blanco County provides only a clue as to his activities: "Lieut. Reynolds, formerly of the rangers, returned this week after a fruitless pursuit of the murderers of the stranger on little Blanco [Creek]. His discoveries remain secret but it is highly probable that he found sufficient [information] to give the detectives good clues to work upon."[12] No further information has been found regarding this curious case.

Reynolds may have stayed in Austin for a while contemplating exactly what his next endeavors would be. He may have considered residing in Austin. He did for a while own a dog, which wandered away and for which Reynolds placed a notice in Austin's *Daily Democratic Statesman*: "Lost, Dog—A spotted setter is lost, had on a chain locked round her neck. N. O. Reynolds scratched on it. A reward will be paid by leaving her at this office." No follow-up item appeared about the lost dog being found.[13] Another reason for his presence in Austin may have been for strictly business purposes. Within a short time he would become a retail liquor dealer; thus making appropriate contacts in Austin would be necessary. But perhaps the real reason to be in Austin was Irene Temperance Nevill, the younger sister of Sergeant C. L. Nevill. Exactly when the two met or under what circumstances is not known, although it is logical that her brother Charles may have introduced them. After all, N. O. Reynolds was considered a very handsome man in his day and it may have been Irene who induced her brother to introduce her to his commanding officer. Born September 10, 1862, the daughter of Zachariah L. and Ann Lewis Nevill, she was just three days past her twentieth birthday when on September 13, 1882, she and the thirty-five-year-old Nelson O. Reynolds were married at the residence of her parents on Mesquite Street in Austin. Reverend Allen J. Adkisson officiated. The *Statesman* identified the groom simply as *Lieutenant Reynolds of Lampasas*.[14]

But in 1879 the marriage was still in the future. By early 1880 Reynolds had made his decision to enter into the liquor business. The now-former Ranger chose the town of San Marcos, located on the headwaters of the San Marcos River in central southeast Hays County, where years before he had assisted Sheriff Z. P. Bugg in guarding prisoners, as the location of beginning his new career. San Marcos was designated the county seat in 1848 but remained a small settlement for some years. By 1870 the population was less than 750, but during the next three decades the town tripled in population to over 2,000.[15]

The father of Charles L. and Irene Temperance Nevill, Zachariah T. Nevill, shown here with his second wife, Sarah T. Townsend Nevill.
Courtesy the Bernice Lear Collection.

The Texas Exchange of San Marcos, formerly the Travis House, was the "People's Favorite Hotel." It offered to travelers "all the advantages of metropolitan luxury, and the quiet of a home . . . centrally located, and is supplied with every convenience for the comfort of guests." Thus read the advertisement from S. L. Townsend, hotel proprietor in the *San Marcos Free Press*.[16] Reynolds chose to make the Texas Exchange Hotel his home, at least for a while, as well as "home" to an assortment of men closely associated with the liquor business. He also bought the nearby Sample Room for his business.

In mid-June census enumerator Calvert Watkins visited the Texas Exchange Hotel, which was located on the southwest corner of the courthouse square in San Marcos. Thirty-six-year-old Samuel L. Townsend managed the hotel with the help of his wife Mary. Six sons and daughters ranging in age from a newborn to a ten-year-old were enumerated along with the guests. In addition to the eight Townsends there were eleven boarders: Townsend's brother-in-law, two civil engineers, a tin smith, a laborer, a physician, a gambler, a bartender, and a man identified not by his full name or initials but by what one might consider an honorific title: *Major Reynolds*. The nickname given to him in the last days of the Civil War had remained with him; perhaps census taker Watkins knew Reynolds and naturally wrote down the name that everyone knew him best by rather than his actual name or initials. True to his task Watkins recorded the basic information the census form required: race, sex, age, marital status, and "Profession, Occupation or Trade of each person, male or female." He was white, male, thirty-one years old, single, a "Retail Liquor Dealer." "Major Reynolds" gave as his state of birth as Missouri. He gave Kentucky and Pennsylvania as the birth place of his father and mother.

Other San Marcos residents included William Moore, a twenty-three-year-old gambler and Claiborne Kyle, a bartender. In the next dwelling Watkins enumerated another bartender, George Miller, and adjacent to Miller's dwelling resided William H. Creech, a "Boot and Shoe Mftr." One can't help but wonder if Reynolds and Creech ever discussed the intricacies of working with leather as Reynolds had once told Gillett he was a boot and shoe maker by trade. Another bartender in the Creech residence was Thomas Elliott, as well as another man named George Miller, a fifty-three-year-old boarder from Wurstenburg, Germany.[17]

By now Major Reynolds had established his own place of business and it is tempting to speculate that more than one of those bartenders worked for him in the Sample Room. This was a large two-story building located on the south side of the square, boasting an elegant bar, a billiard room, and store rooms. Bartender Claiborne Kyle was designated as the "attendant" who "renders himself indispensible in all departments."[18] Seemingly Reynolds, by mid-1880 and now in his mid-thirties, settled himself in a business, ready to take life much easier than what those years of being a horseback Ranger had provided. He was now ready to become a pillar of the San Marcos community. He had acquired property on the east one-third of lot 7, Block 13 in San Marcos, from Augustus M. and Amanda M. White of Bell County. In April 1881 Reynolds sold a two-foot section of the east side of this property to Charles and William A. Book, and in October of that year he sold his remaining property to Curran and Claiborne Kyle.[19]

Strangely, Reynolds had resigned from the Rangers partly because of health reasons and in part because of his disappointment in the quality of so many men. When an opportunity came to take command of Company D, Frontier Battalion, however, he expressed interest in the position. Apparently during the hiatus between early 1879 and mid-1880 his health had improved; or was it a matter of tending bar in quiet San Marcos lacked the excitement of running down Dick Dublin or arresting the Horrells? But if he had had problems in riding long distances on horseback it would not be logical for him now to even consider becoming a horseback Ranger again. Unfortunately, the correspondence between Major Jones and "Major" Reynolds is not complete; hence one is forced to speculate about this opportunity for N. O. Reynolds to become a captain of Company D.

This is what we do know: On August 23, 1880, John B. Jones, the new Adjutant General, addressed a letter to N. O. Reynolds, Esq., and explained that Dan W. Roberts had sent in his resignation to take effect on October 15. Jones, in "casting about for some one to take his place," thought of Reynolds as "the one whom I would prefer to anyone else." Jones did not know what engagements Reynolds had, or even if he was interested in entering the service again, but if Reynolds wanted to become commander of Company D the position was his—with the rank of captain, higher than when he was commander of Company E.[20]

Five days later Jones received a telegram from Reynolds accepting the offer, stating that he was willing to become the new commander "at the time you wish me to."[21] On September 13 Jones wrote to Roberts that Reynolds would be his replacement.[22] Other Rangers were satisfied with Jones' decision. L. B. Caruthers, Sergeant of Company E at Fort Davis, wrote Neal Coldwell: "I am glad to hear of Lieut. Reynolds promotion and think Co. 'D' will make a better police record."[23] The commission was prepared and orders ready when Jones requested that Reynolds be in Menard County a few days before October 15.[24]

But Reynolds was a businessman now and could no longer simply mount a horse and ride off to deal with a new assignment as he could when a Ranger. He had believed he could easily dispose of those business interests, but on October 4, only eleven days before he would take command of Company D, Jones had to write to Roberts that Reynolds "has been disappointed in disposing of his business in San Marcos as he thought he had done and I have agreed to give him longer time."[25] Naturally Roberts would remain on duty until the end of the month.

The last letter of 1880 is dated October 15 when Jones advised Reynolds that if he was successful in closing out the business he was to go directly to the camp of Company D.[26] No additional correspondence has been located until the letter dated *October 9, 1881*, almost a full year later. Herein Lamar P. Sieker wrote to the new Adjutant General, Wilburn Hill King, acknowledging receipt of Special Order No. 11 appointing him (Sieker) to the command of Company D with the rank of captain.[27] Lamar Pemberton "Lam" Sieker had joined Captain C. R. Perry's Company D back on May 25, 1874, in Blanco County, the same day that N. O. Reynolds had joined. Then, Sieker was a private with Reynolds a sergeant. Sieker had finally found his entry into Texas Ranger greatness. He would continue long years in the service, taking command of Company D on September 1, 1882; then, on October 15, 1885, he was appointed to the position of Quartermaster and then in 1889 appointed Assistant Adjutant General.[28]

Was N. O. Reynolds serious about taking the command of Company D? It seems curious that if he was, and if he was having difficulty in selling his business by the time he wanted, he could not have made some kind of arrangements with one or more of his bartenders to act as managers, at least for a few months, until Reynolds had a buyer. Did he simply not have the patience to wait out the possible buyers for his establishment? Or did he realize that, deep down, he simply did not want to return to the life of a horseback Ranger? Ironically the only other document in the correspondence relative to his possibly taking command of Company D is a telegram Reynolds sent from San Marcos dated October 11, 1881, just two days after Sieker had written to General King. The telegram read: "I am out of business. Can Come most any time."[29] As Reynolds had arrived too late to participate in the Sam Bass battle on the streets of Round Rock, he now was too late to take command of Company D. Business affairs held him back from the position of becoming captain of a Ranger company.

Reynolds however had not simply worked at the Sample Room but become involved with community concerns, just as he had years before when the matter of San Marcos incorporating arose. On Monday, January 17, 1881, the San Marcos Hook and Ladder Company was permanently organized. Officers elected were Thomas H. Franklin, President; Ed R. Kone, vice president and N. O. Reynolds as Foreman. He had two assistants: S. L. Townsend and N. R. Faris.[30] With wooden buildings making up most business districts in typical communities a primary concern was fire prevention.

On July 19 of that year Reynolds' first commander, Major John B. Jones, died at the age of forty-seven. One report stated that his death was the closing event "in the history of one of the most picturesque and romantic characters in Texas. General Jones . . . was during his career the hero of wild adventures, desperate enterprises and bloody forays among the hostile Indians and more savage outlaws of the Texas frontier, enough to have furnished material for a carload of blood-curdling fiction of the most sensational sort." The article, entitled "A Border Chief," provided a brief sketch of Jones' life but failed to mention Reynolds or any of his other commanders.[31] The *Statesman* stated that the "desperadoes of the frontier feared him as they feared no other man. They looked upon him as the embodiment of bravery, honor and truthfulness, and the promises he made to them were relied upon with an unfaltering faith."[32]

Reynolds now made a decision to make another move, this time back to Lampasas. No indication was given as to why he left San Marcos, and no solid evidence is known for the reasons he returned to Lampasas, rather than, say, to Mason or San Saba or Kimble County. His stay in San

Marcos had been brief, and perhaps it was the beauty of the Hill Country which attracted him, or possibly the mineral springs proved beneficial to his health. Failing to settle his business affairs in time to take command of Company D certainly must have caused him some frustration. Did the death of Jones bring back fond memories and now San Marcos seemed too "civilized," which Lampasas was not? Just when he left San Marcos is undetermined, but it was in early 1882. By May of that year bartender Claiborne Kyle had also left San Marcos, and had "gone to Lampasas again to go into business with Maj. Reynolds."[33]

Advertisement for N. O. Reynolds' Brunswick Saloon in Lampasas, from the *Lampasas Dispatch*, September 1889. *Courtesy Jeff Jackson.*

Being a businessman now instead of a lawman allowed Reynolds to spend time with former Rangers to relax and discuss the wilder days they had experienced. On one such occasion he and J. W. "Society Jack" Martin dined together and had "a long talk about the boys and old times." Frontier Battalion Quartermaster Neal Coldwell had inquired of Martin if he could recommend some good men for the service. Martin responded on March 3, 1882, from his home in Senterfitt in Lampasas County. It is of value as it confirms that Reynolds was known as Major even after he left the service. "You wrote to me about a year ago asking me to recommend some young men for service in [the] Front[ier] Batt[alion]", Martin wrote. "I was busy at the time . . . hence never replyed [*sic*] to your letter." Martin continued, "Lieut Reynolds ("Maj") dined with me to-day, we had a long talk about the boys and the old days." Martin learned from Major Reynolds that Captain G. W. Arrington was going to resign soon and he, Reynolds, was offered command of the company, but "he was so situated at present he could not accept of the offer." Thus on two occasions Reynolds had the opportunity to serve as a Frontier Battalion captain, but could not accept. Martin did recommend P. C. Jackson, a former Reynolds Ranger, a man who had served three years in the Confederate Army and two years with Reynolds, "who will speak of him as the soul of honor."[34] Jackson was not chosen to command a Ranger company.

Reynolds was in Lampasas when a fire broke out in a building owned by one Myer Crown. Myer and his brother Morris Crown and Max Speer, who owned a shooting gallery next door, were arrested on suspicion of arson. N. O. Reynolds filed an affidavit on April 26 identifying those three as arsonists. A jury of "six good and lawful men" after being sworn in by law went to the burned out building to investigate. After examining the premises they returned to court and concluded that the fire had been started in a pile of boxes and other combustibles in a store house owned by the Crown brothers and the fire was started by Max Speer. Further, the jury determined that Myer Crown was either an accessory or a principal. Myer Crown and Max Speer were placed on bond, and Morris Crown was released from custody. Ultimately the three men were found not guilty. Reynolds, having been foreman of the San Marcos fire department, certainly could appreciate the need for an effective fire department in a frontier community.[35]

Reynolds again was in the liquor business in Lampasas, now operating the Lampasas Saloon. Ironically Reynolds had learned from experience the inherent dangers when rowdy men and liquor got together, especially when six-shooters were also present. Sometimes the saloon operator himself was directly involved in the affray. On May 12, 1882, a difficulty occurred between Reynolds and one J. C. "Doak" Bradley. Reynolds was charged with committing assault and battery, specifically by striking Bradley on the head with his fist and kicking him. The alleged assault had taken place in Reynolds' saloon. How this case was ultimately settled is unknown due to missing court records and newspaper accounts. Bradley was quite a hard character and that same year was charged with exhibiting a "fortune bank used for gaming purposes" in the back of Stilwell's Saloon. Among the witnesses were Claiborne Kyle and former feudist Pink Higgins.[36]

Later that year Reynolds' name appeared again in the court record. On November 21, J. D. Grizzell swore that "in the last six months" he had seen drinks issued out to customers in Estep's Saloon as well as N. O. Reynolds' saloon. At the time saloons were not allowed to sell bottles of alcohol for consumption off-premises on Sundays. Grizzell had been a longtime resident of Lampasas County, having been there at least since 1870. He and his brother were both from Alabama, and during the "terrible seventies" the Grizzells had been close associates of the Horrells, as well as close neighbors. In 1873 James Grizzell had been identified as one of the Horrell party involved in the killing of Capt. Thomas Williams and several state policemen in Lampasas. Now, nearly a decade later, Grizzell acted as a witness against Reynolds for violating the liquor sales law.[37]

Reynolds had been involved in local concerns in San Marcos, and now he became interested in the concerns of Lampasas, but this time his interest was directed at law enforcement, namely the position of City Marshal. No details on how the contestants campaigned have survived, but on April 17, 1883, municipal elections were held and N. O. Reynolds emerged victorious as the new city marshal. Reynolds received 184 votes, a solid result as his nearest competitor, John Z. Bean, received but eleven votes; the other two candidates, John Bishop and Joseph Horthorn, received one vote each. The race for city marshal was clearly no contest. J. D. Grizzell lost in his race for alderman, to A. G. Walker. Tillman Weaver was elected mayor. Trouble may have been expected, as in reporting the results, one newspaper noted that the election had passed off quietly, perhaps hiding the wish for some type of disturbance for the sake of better headlines.[38] Reynolds, who had resigned from the Frontier Battalion for health reasons and had twice missed the opportunity to become a captain of a Ranger company, was a lawman once again, still in the era of the "horse-back ranger." Perhaps Reynolds believed that the position of city marshal would not require so much horseback riding.

Reynolds had earned the respect and trust of Lampasas citizens—certainly the results of the recent election had proved that—but there were some anxious to discredit him, and once again that had involved the liquor business. H. G. Christian swore that he had seen Major Reynolds selling whiskey on a Sunday afternoon in mid-April. He also swore that he had seen whiskey being sold at George Scott's saloon and a game of *monte* being played at the Commercial Saloon on March 1. A. M. McFarland swore that he had seen Reynolds selling liquor on a Sunday, and that he had bought some himself on May 13 in clear violation of the law. Sam Mellon swore he had seen drinks being sold on a Sunday and Paul B. Taylor as well swore he had seen drinks being sold at Reynolds' saloon and also George Scott's saloon on a Sunday. C. M. Ross swore he had bought "spirituous liquors" from Reynolds' Saloon on Sunday May 13. As a result of these complaints, Reynolds was charged with selling whiskey to A. M. McFarland on Sunday, May 13, "and several times prior."[39] Again missing records prevent leaning the final results of these charges. Most likely Reynolds had to pay a small fine.

Occasionally news of Lampasas dealt not just with lawlessness in the area but much more peaceful pursuits such as shooting contests. Neither Reynolds nor any other Ranger claimed to be "dead-shots" even though handling revolvers and Winchesters may have become second nature to them. Nevertheless attempts to prove their marksmanship were popular.

During the 1883 county fair Reynolds participated in such a competition, the results showing that perhaps he was only an above-average shooter. A Lampasas reporter boasted of how the ball at the Grand Park Hotel had "passed off quietly" on the night of the seventeenth of July, and then provided his readers the results of the shooting contest. A. Erickson and J. J. Johnson killed five birds each, then shot off for first place money "which was won and divided." A list of eight names of those who killed only three birds each included that of N.O. Reynolds. The county fair had attracted individual shootists as well as gun clubs from Houston, Austin, Gainesville, Waco, Dallas, and Fort Worth, as well as Lampasas and smaller communities.

Horse races were also popular during the county fair, and one of the most respected turfmen of the period was Lee County Sheriff James Madison Brown, now in Lampasas with Leroy Lee of Bastrop County. Possibly it was on this occasion that Brown apologized to Reynolds for his behavior back in San Saba during the troubles there. Brown and Lee were there with a number of fine horses, preparing for the races to be held in August.

Work was progressing on the new courthouse, one which would be much stronger than the edifice destroyed back in the days of the Horrell-Higgins troubles. When ground-breaking ceremonies were ready a photographer was hired to record the scene, providing history with one of the few street scenes of early Lampasas. Architect W. C. Dodson of Waco had been employed as designer and contractor to supervise the construction of the new building. By September 6 the cornerstone was placed under the auspices of the Masonic Order. In the cornerstone niche were placed coins, badges, Confederate bills, a Holy Bible, a copy of the *Galveston Daily News* dated September 6, a copy of the *Houston Age*, the *Lampasas Dispatch* and the first and latest issue of the *Lampasas Globe,* among other items.[40]

As if the normal activities of the county fair and the anticipation of the horse races were not enough, Lampasas was plagued by arsonists, or so it was believed. About 9:00 on the night of July 26 citizens discovered the lumber yard of E. W. Thorp in flames; both the house and lumber yard were destroyed with a loss estimated at $9,000. There was no insurance. Arson was suspected. The very next night a building owned by J. Q. Manly went up in flames. The loss was placed at $500 and again there was no insurance. With two fires in two nights there was much talk on the streets that it was time for Lampasas to organize a volunteer fire department.[41]

Occasionally shooting erupted on the streets of Lampasas, reminiscent of the days when the Horrells and the Higgins parties took shots at each other on the public square, in spite of the ordinance prohibiting the firing of weapons within the city limits. On the evening of July 30 George W. Scott, proprietor of the Sunny South Saloon, and Lampasas County Sheriff George Wolf, fought each other with their fists, "clinching and falling" but resolving nothing. What must have been a most humorous situation for the onlookers, the fighting pair then continued by throwing rocks at each other, Scott "receiving two ugly wounds on the head" and Scott being "bruised some." Someone managed to separate the pair, but they were still not satisfied and then drew their revolvers. Their aim with throwing rocks was better than their aim with revolvers, as they each fired and both missed the other. With fists and rocks and then bullets flying on the streets of Lampasas it was a miracle that nobody was seriously injured. Either City Marshal Reynolds or friends of the pair separated and quieted them down before serious injury or damage occurred to anyone or anything. The telegram to the *Galveston Daily News* stated—perhaps with unintentional irony—that Sheriff Wolf "was not acting in his official capacity at the time." A report appearing in the *San Antonio Daily Express* provided fewer details but in spite of the row had good things to say about the city, reporting the city was "improving rapidly, and visitors continue to pour in. Business never better."[42]

While Lampasas residents still talked of organizing a volunteer fire company, on the morning of Tuesday, July 31 a third blaze within the week was discovered. This time it was the wholesale grocery store of J. E. Tumey. The contents as well as the building were destroyed; the loss was placed at $20,000. Before the ashes had cooled the city fathers had organized the hook and ladder company.[43]

To add further problems to the overworked city fathers, the recent "Sunday laws" prohibiting the selling of alcohol on Sunday were to be enforced during this time when the streets were filled with strange faces. At the same time the hook and ladder company was organized, the residents were expected to alter their Sunday drinking habits. Not all did, as some forty cases were reported for violating the Sunday law, "mostly soda water and confectionary houses, a few druggists and merchants" were the guilty parties.[44]

It must have been a considerable task to enforce the Sunday laws in Lampasas at this time, as there were at least a dozen establishments considered a saloon, and also numerous other places that could circumvent the law if the owner so desired. One saloon was operated by N. O. Reynolds. But in spite of the numerous saloons, Lampasas could also boast of numerous churches: Methodist, Baptist, Presbyterian, and Catholic faiths were represented there. In addition there were two schools, a planing mill and flour mill, two ice factories, a courthouse, three private water works, a fire department, specialty and general stores, blacksmith shops, and other facilities. The stagecoach left daily to San Saba and to Burnet at a cost of $4.00 and $2.50 respectively. There was even a telephone exchange, street railways and gas lighting. William E. Beall was the County Judge, N. O. Reynolds the City Marshal, and George Wolf was the County Sheriff.[45]

Presumably Lee County Sheriff James M. Brown had by now made his peace with City Marshal N. O. Reynolds. We know he apologized from Gillett, but Gillett failed to indicate when or where this newsworthy event occurred. The races drew hundreds of onlookers and there were many men who were willing to wager great sums of money on the outcome. The Park Hotel was surrounded with an "anxious multitude" long before the races were to begin on Saturday, August 18. At the center judge's stand ready to declare the winners were Judge A. Carmichael, J. C. Morgan, and no less a notorious individual than Mannen Clements, first cousin of John Wesley Hardin. One race for a purse of $500 set J. J. Hale's seven-year-old "Grey John" against Leroy Lee's two-year-old, "Bill Fleming" and Jim Brown's "Big Emma," a five-year-old. "With cheers and hurrahs from the excited crowd they came down the track beautifully," the *Galveston*

Daily News reporter telegraphed to his newspaper. Black colt Bill Fleming won by a neck with Brown's Big Emma coming in second and Grey John finishing third. Pools sold were three to one on Big Emma. The reporter estimated that about $800 had changed hands on that one race.[46]

Although Lampasas was once on the frontier line, and now could boast a city marshal with extensive experience in handling law breakers and many modern conveniences, vestiges of the violent days of the 1870s still occurred. No better example serves than the lynching of the Bailey brothers in nearby Comanche County in mid-November of 1883. Reynolds had ridden many hours on scouts after this pair after they had shot down and left for dead Deputy United States Marshal Mastin Reynolds "Boss" Greene on May 12, 1877, in Comanche County. On November 11, an hour or so before midnight, the Comanche jail was surrounded by an armed mob of forty or fifty men, only some of whom wore masks. They overpowered the guard and took the two men about a mile north of town and hanged them to a tree near the southeast corner of the graveyard. Reportedly the guard put up a "hard struggle" to protect their prisoners but they were quickly overpowered. No details of the arrest of the brothers have been unearthed, but once they were in jail Dee Bailey's wife was alerted to come to Comanche from Coryell County to take him home, she being led to believe that the brothers would be released on bond. Only after she had arrived in Comanche with her small son did she learn she had become a widow. The bodies were taken to Coryell County for burial. According to the *Galveston Daily News* reporter, who may have witnessed much of the tragedy, it was "to the credit of the people of Comanche that the Bailey brothers . . . were kindly cared for after they were cut down. The bodies were dressed nicely and put in neat coffins, ready for interment." It was reported that the mob came from Coryell County. Certainly City Marshal Reynolds learned of this mob action, taking place only some seventy miles north of his own jurisdiction. Nearly everyone could remember back in 1874 when a mob of citizens took Joseph G. Hardin and two Dixon brothers—cousins of John Wesley Hardin—out of the Comanche jail and strung them up to a tree limb and left them. Were the Bailey brothers taken to the same tree? The men from Coryell County, or more likely men from Comanche and some from Coryell County, were only continuing a grisly tradition for dealing quickly with men considered worthy of frontier justice.[47]

Another fire broke out at about eleven o'clock at night on August 14, 1884, and this time the damage was staggering. The wind was blowing briskly from the southwest, causing the flames to feed quickly onto adjacent buildings. Preliminary reports indicated that half of the business portion of Lampasas had been destroyed. Within two hours a livery stable and eleven wooden and five rock stores were in ashes. The initial estimate of the loss was placed at $200,000 with very little of the destroyed property insured. It had originated in Eckles & Solloman's ice cream parlor on Western Avenue then burned rapidly across the block north and then across Third Street. The major losses were Wolfson & Kritzer's Saloon, the S. D. Crittenden General Merchandise store, the Greer Saddlery, Billy and Joe's Saloon, the Pickwick Saloon, the Brunswick Saloon, the Blue Front Restaurant, the Malone & Co. dry goods and bank building, F. W. Caruthers hardware store, Meyer's restaurant, the White Elephant Saloon, the general merchandise store of Noble & Son, and the Rasberry & Townsend livery stable. There were several other meat markets and small grocery dealers, barber shops, and fruit dealers who were among the forty business dealers burned out. Almost immediately an affidavit was sworn out: Frank and Richard Eckles, Frank Sollomon/(Solloman) (also spelled Zollomon and Zollman) and Will Scott were arrested and charged with arson.

The central portion of Lampasas was a mass of ruins. Five of the buildings were two-story and the remaining were small wooden structures, now in ashes. The shock from the fire almost paralyzed the city. A preliminary trial was rapidly held for the quartet charged with arson. The jury's verdict was that Solloman had set fire to the ice cream parlor of Eckles & Sollomon and Eckles and Scott were charged with being accessories. The accused waived examination and their bonds were set at amounts ranging from $1,000 to $2,000.[48]

Dealing with the problems and criminal acts of Lampasas city citizens apparently was too confining for N. O. Reynolds who had served for years covering matters in numerous counties. He had been chosen to be the town's leading law enforcing officer, but now he had his eyes on the county position: Lampasas County sheriff. Since what could be termed personal papers of Marshal Reynolds seemingly no longer exist, if he ever had any, one can only speculate as to why he chose to surrender the position of Lampasas *City* Marshal to become a candidate for the position of Lampasas *County* sheriff. Was it to increase his salary to support his new wife, or was it due to an inner need for greater responsibility or power? Unless such personal items may be found revealing his intentions, one is left to wonder. Prior to his election there are bits and pieces about his activities, one such being a report that he was in Brenham, Washington County—and adjacent to Lee County—staying at the Exchange Hotel, in late November 1884. He and G. M. Snodgrass of Lampasas were there, although of course no reason was given for their presence in Brenham.[49]

Reynolds was the eighteenth sheriff of Lampasas County. Wolf, elected on November 4, 1878, served until November 2, 1886, when Reynolds was elected with 788 votes over Wolf's 693 and 36 votes for the unknown J. H. Fox.[50] He would be returned to the office on November 6, 1888, and then serve until November 4, 1890. Ironically, following Reynolds' last term in 1890 William R. Wren, a man who had figured prominently in the Horrell-Higgins feud of the 1870s, was elected to fill the office. Albertus J. McFarland was elected county attorney at the same time. A. D. Kent was elected Justice of the Peace of Precinct No. 1, which included the town of Lampasas. The county judge was W. P. Beall, but he died in office. Martin V. B. Sparks replaced him.[51]

As sheriff, Reynolds would be responsible for the collection of taxes and one of his main concerns was to bring men to justice who were wanted for crimes committed before he took over as sheriff. The state now printed a list of fugitives from justice in booklet form. It was a listing of those indicted for felonies based on reports from sheriffs throughout the state. This was not the first time this was done as such a list of fugitives had been published as early as 1878 in booklet form. A descriptive list of escaped convicts was also included in this publication. The Lampasas County section, sent in by Sheriff Reynolds, contained the names of fifty-four men wanted for all types of offenses, ranging from horse theft to murder. Felonies listed were theft (thirty-four); murder (seven); assault to murder (four); embezzlement (three); forgery (two); and one each for perjury, sodomy, jail breaking, and bigamy. One of those listed was Sam Horrell, wanted for murder from the old days of the Horrell-Higgins feud.[52] Another name from Reynolds' old days as a Ranger was William Z. Redding, wanted for jail breaking. George Washington "Wash" Short was still wanted for having shot then-Lampasas County Sheriff Shadrick T. Denson while resisting arrest back in 1876.

Two others were Lorenzo and Isaac Clawson, both wanted for murder. They were brothers from Coryell County and had only recently moved to the Senterfitt area in eastern Lampasas County. D. B. Taylor had sent cattle from Coryell County to San Saba; one of his cowboys was James J. Smith. The Senterfitt citizens were curious about the Clawsons and spoke to Smith about them, perhaps out of friendliness or perhaps out of idle curiosity. Smith foolishly informed the curious neighbors that the Clawsons were no good and that they had left Coryell County under a cloud, suspected of cattle theft. Naturally these statements got back to the Clawsons and they challenged young Smith, demanding that he retract what he had said, regardless if it was the truth or not. Smith happened to be with his father-in-law when he met up with the Clawsons, still angry over the accusations. Young Smith admitted that he would have to take it back—uttered with a pistol held by one of the Clawsons aimed at his direction—when one of the Clawsons fired, the bullet going through his arm and entering his side. Smith managed to call the Clawsons "damned cowards," begged his father-in-law to take care of his family, then sat down, and waited for the end to come. J. H. Hubbard, Smith's father-in-law, tried to make him comfortable, but Lorenzo Clawson ordered him not to interfere, that he didn't mind watching a man die. They stayed around for nearly ten minutes until Smith was nearly dead, then left the scene. With Reynolds now the sheriff, two of the most wanted fugitives were Isaac and Lorenzo Clawson.[53]

In January of 1887 Sheriff Reynolds had found where the two men were, or believed he did. How Reynolds worked the matter up is unknown but he suspected the fugitives were in Kerr County, where former Ranger Frank M. Moore was sheriff. Reynolds wanted to know where the nearest Rangers were and contacted his former Ranger companion, L. P. Sieker. "My reason for this is that I think I have Some Parties Spotted," he wrote, "and I notice F. M. Moor[e] is Sheriff there and Am afraid to trust it to him if he is the Same man that used to Command Co 'D.' . . . My Idea is to Get the Men and not make a blunder[.]" Sheriff Frank Moore was also aware of the Clawsons and wrote to Adjutant General W. H. King for help in locating them. One man was sent but the Clawsons evaded arrest. Further details on this manhunt have not surfaced. As late as 1898 their names were listed in a report to the adjutant general as still being at large. Besides a brief description of them, a description which would have fit many a man of the time, law officers only suspected they had gone to New Mexico Territory. It is doubtful if the Clawsons ever were brought back to Texas to pay for their crime.[54]

Although not listed as a felony in 1886, one of the major problems facing Texas ranchers and lawmen in this period was that of fence cutting. In the early seventies such a problem did not exist, but now with the days of the open range in the past some men were willing to cut fences, ignoring the realities of farmers who fenced their property legally. These illegal actions of cutting have been called the "Fence-Cutters War." The violence never gained the attention of historians that other feuds, such as the Mason County War or the Horrell-Higgins feud, did, perhaps because relatively few lives were lost; there was, however, a great deal of financial loss to ranchers and farmers. According to Oran M. Roberts, Texas governor from 1878 to 1883, fence cutting occurred extensively on or near the frontier line. It happened generally where large tracts of land were enclosed with wire fences in or near the neighborhood of farmers whose cattle had formerly grazed upon the now fenced range. Long use of other people's land for grazing resulted in the common belief that they had a right to the open range. "However strange such an illegal view of right may seem to those persons who reside in a well-settled section of the country," Roberts wrote, "it has been a sort of common law established by custom on the frontier that those who have undergone the hardships and

Texas Ranger Capt. Frank M. Moore after his Ranger service.
Courtesy Former Texas Rangers Foundation.

privations of frontier life have a right to appropriate to their own use the grass and timber on large tracts of land owned by people at a distance." Fencing tracts of land for the use of stock was considered by many "only as a public nuisance."[55]

Lampasas County was to see its share of fence cutting. On July 28, 1886, while still the city marshal, but obviously concerned with problems people face outside the city limits, Reynolds penned a letter to Adjutant General Wilburn H. King telling how P. H. Huling's pasture fence had been cut during the night of July 19. Not only did the fence cutters destroy two miles of fence but they had also cut down a number of posts. Huling had gone to Reynolds for help. "Our present [county] Officers," Reynolds wrote," are not doing Anything to Stop this nefarious work." Huling had asked Reynolds to contact King to "Send a man Out here."

Reynolds wanted action in a hurry, as on the next day he wrote to former Ranger companion Captain L. P. Sieker. Now Reynolds asked Sieker to send "a Good man" to him or if he could not do that to recommend the name of a private detective. On the reverse of this letter King made a notation that he would send Ranger Ira Aten.[56]

Ira Aten at the time was twenty-three years old and serving in Company D of the Frontier Battalion. Whereas Reynolds left history with no reminiscences of his service as a Texas Ranger or lawman, Aten authored a number of articles and contributed significantly to several biographies.[57] He had proved early on that he was dependable and self-reliant. During much of the spring of 1886 (from March 6 to June 24) he was away from camp on special assignment. During March he had been searching for two men: C. W. "Wesley" Collier and Jackson "Jack" Beam; on March 24 he arrested Beam and then from March 25 to April 29 he searched for Collier. On the twenty-ninth he caught up with Collier and "exchanged shots" but Collier escaped. Aten continued the pursuit: on May 25 he had him tracked down, having a deputy to assist in making the arrest named John Reynolds Hughes.[58] The two men tracked the fugitive down but instead of responding to Aten's demand to surrender Collier resisted; he was not able to return fire when Aten's single bullet ended his criminal career. He reported he had "met & Killed Collier while resisting arrest."[59] During the summer of 1886 he was ordered to report to General King's office for special duty. After the conference King ordered him to proceed to Lampasas County "to catch the fence cutters who had been destroying wire fences on a large ranch there."

Aten did not identify whose ranch this was, nor did he explain how he ingratiated himself with the young men who were cutting fences. He did explain that on one moonlit night he and two young fence-cutters were out doing their illegal acts of cutting wires, when they heard a voice order: "Hands up or we will shoot!" Aten immediately dropped his nippers but his two companions wanted to run. Aten warned them if they did run they would be shot. All three wisely surrendered. At this point, Sheriff Reynolds, as Aten later wrote: "walked out of the brush with his deputies, put us under arrest, handcuffed us and took us to jail."

When the case came to court naturally Aten was called in to testify. On the witness stand the defense attorney asked if had not told "a lot of lies" while trying to catch the fence-cutters. Aten had to admit that he had. The attorney then asked if he was not still telling lies. This slur on his character so angered young Aten that he nearly jumped over the table. He shook his fist at the attorney, yelling: "I want you to understand there is a great deal of difference between swearing to a lie and telling a lie to catch a damned rascal." Short-tempered Ira Aten tried to apologize to the court, but Judge W. A. Blackburn fined him fifty dollars for his outburst. This was the same judge who had requested an escort from the Rangers in order to hold court safely back in Kimble County in 1877. Aten certainly had had earlier communication with Reynolds, who was not yet sheriff during the summer of 1886 but could have been working with General King to catch fence-cutters, and the arrest had been carefully staged between the lawmen. Aten recalled that the two fence-cutters were boys, "still in their teens" and that they were doing it more for notoriety than for any other reason. Fence cutting was rampant in some of the adjoining counties, and they thought they would start it in Lampasas County, although it had been declared a felony. The identity of the two boys cutting fences "for notoriety" was not disclosed.[60]

The entire Hill Country suffered from the fence cutters. The drought in the western counties caused some ranchers to simply ignore the law. Henry M. Holmes, attorney at Mason who had become very familiar with lawless acts during the Mason County War, knew the importance of the Rangers. Holmes feared "serious trouble" and shared his concerns with Adjutant General King via letters. Cattle owners, due to the drought, were forced "to look in other places for grass—they have taken Menard County and turned loose thousands of cattle—it is intimated by reliable authorities that they intend to have grass and water —if they have to cut every fence in the country." Holmes stated "this means war" and feared it could only be prevented by having a body of men who would do their duty regardless of the parties involved. Holmes believed ten or twenty Rangers stationed near Pegleg Crossing for a few months would prevent fence cutting and bloodshed. Holmes reassured King that he was "not an alarmist" but was certain trouble would come.[61]

On Christmas Eve, when Reynolds was sheriff, W. A. Patterson, Cotton and Wool Dealer of Lampasas and owner of 4,500 acres of land in the upper portion of Lampasas County and 500 head of cattle, wrote to Governor John Ireland telling him how the fence cutters had given him notice that his fences would be destroyed and his employees murdered if he did not open his land for public use. Notices of the threats had been posted on his pasture gates. Patterson had already hired a detective to guard the fence lines, which Reynolds had recommended be done, at a cost of $50 per month plus room and board. On the same day Reynolds wrote to Governor Ireland to request the state to find means to assist Patterson in protecting his own property against fence cutters. Reynolds had detailed deputy Joe Stillwell to guard over the property, a man who had had experience as a deputy marshal and a deputy sheriff, who Reynolds believed to be "fully capable and trustworthy." In addition to Stillwell, Reynolds sent out one of his regular deputies. Reynolds had to admit that it would be impossible to have enough deputies to guard all fences, and suggested that one or two residents of the county be hired by the state to perform the protection service or to detail men from the state troops to protect the fences. Governor Ireland recommended to General King to send a squad of troops to assist Patterson.[62] No squad of state troops was sent but the order to send help resulted in Capt. William Scott of Company F sending two privates—T. S. Crowder and Dee Caldwell—to Patterson's ranch "to look after fence cutting troubles."[63] The two Rangers left camp on December 31. No details were recorded but the pair did return to camp on January 4 and reported that Patterson "did not want the Service of the Rangers." Possibly Patterson felt that with Joe Stillwell and one other of Reynolds' deputies—all aware of the fence cutters' threats—the Ranger privates would just be in the way. Nevertheless, in spite of the rejection on the fifth of January Captain Scott sent Sergeant James A. Brooks with four men and a wagon to make "a general scout" in Lampasas, San Saba, and McCulloch Counties to investigate. Brooks reported that "no recent depredations of that nature" in any of those counties had occurred. The squad returned to camp on January 11.[64]

Another case Reynolds worked on was the murder of sixty-four-year-old Alexander Brown, a longtime Lampasas resident. Brown had been in Texas since at least the 1840s, as William Banta who served on the jury of inquest over Brown's body recalled meeting him in Austin in 1849 when Brown was a wagon-master for the government. Banta recalled that Brown had been "in most of the Indian fights in Burnet, Lampasas, and San Saba counties as a volunteer." As testimony to his patriotism Brown had lost his brother John to Indians and had lost another brother, Oliver, at the massacre at Goliad in 1836.[65]

Old Alexander Brown's body was found in his home on Lynch's Creek on New Year's Day, 1887. It was sprawled on a mattress on the floor, tied hand and foot, badly bruised and his scull broken. Justice H. Wallace of Precinct No. 2 was one of the first on the scene and telephoned Sheriff Reynolds. Soon he and Squire A. D. Kent with two deputies were also there to investigate. Wallace wrote to the *Galveston Daily News* about the tragedy, saying that the jury of inquest had been hard at work investigating and that "spies" had been sent out in different parts of the county. Although no arrests had been made, they "still have some hope of capturing the demons."[66]

It would be many months before anyone would be called to account for the murder of Alexander Brown, but ultimately several men were charged with the crime: Jack Renfro, John Dugger, Jerry Dugger,[67] Van Reeves, Will Thompson, and Raider Thompson. They were indicted, having "with malice aforethought [did] kill and murder Ellick [*sic*] Brown by Striking beating bruising and wounding him with a blunt instrument or instruments . . . against the peace and dignity of the state."[68] Today Alexander Brown rests peacefully in the Nix Cemetery, some fourteen miles west of the Lampasas County courthouse, beneath an obelisk nearly ten feet tall. The impressive stone was placed there by Banta and other friends. The inscription reads: "My heart was well cleansed. God was the Potter; I was the clay. Thy will, not mine, be done."[69]

Occasional items of interest appeared in the press throughout the state regarding N. O. Reynolds. In January 1887 the *Galveston Daily News* reported he had been elected to the post of Past Chancellor of the Knights of Pythias Lodge. In February he attended the Sheriffs Association Convention, allowing him to renew acquaintance with other former Rangers who had also become county sheriffs.[70]

Later that year Reynolds was working to recover a stolen horse. Typically county sheriffs advertised lost or stolen property in the columns of the *Galveston Daily News*, as that was then the most widely read newspaper in the state. This notice, appearing in May in the *News*, read as follows: "Look out for one sorrel horse, about 14 ½ hands high, one white hind foot, branded half-circle D lying down on shoulder, 7 years old, harness and saddle marks. Will pay a liberal reward for the horse and thief. Address S. T. Denson or N. O. Reynolds, sheriff."[71]

Presumably the horse belonged to Denson, a former Lampasas County sheriff, who reported it stolen to Sheriff Reynolds. They discussed what would be the "liberal reward" and Reynolds placed the advertisement in the newspaper.

16

The Cornett-Whitley Gang Emerges

"The fire was returned with interest."
—Lampasas Leader, October 6, 1888

The typical felonies of the late nineteenth century were those of a century before and the same as the century following: arsonists deliberately set fires; burglars invaded homes and stores; women were raped; men and sometimes women murdered others; cattle and horses were stolen. The cutting of fences now became a new felony, adding to the range problems of the 1880s. One can learn of the frequency of such felonies by reading the Texas attorney general's reports, a publication that apparently did not appear with any regularity until 1885. It is nigh impossible to make comparisons between the terms of Sheriff Reynolds and his predecessors not only because of missing records but also because the character of the frontier had changed. Men no longer concerned themselves—at least in Lampasas County—with Indian raiding parties stealing or killing livestock, taking women and children captives or simply killing settlers attempting to establish a home on the frontier. Now fears were more concerned with the doings of white men, stealing horses or cattle, fence cutting, or robbery. However, the 1885–1886 report can be compared with the available 1887–1888 and the 1889–1890 reports. The felonies reported were arson, burglary, embezzlement, forgery, murder, perjury, rape, robbery, theft, and others.

There are striking numbers: in 1885–1886 there were five cases of arson in Lampasas County. In the two subsequent reports no arson was reported. The number of burglaries was also reduced: ten cases in 1885–1886 to six and then in 1889–1890 only one case of burglary. The number of cases of embezzlement and forgery was also reduced, but the number of murders in 1885–1886—one—doubled in the following years, two murders in each year. There were no rapes or robberies reported in those years. The number of reported horse or cattle thefts was reduced from thirty-two in 1885–1886 to nineteen the following year and only eleven in 1889–1890.[1]

With such small numbers overall it is needless to determine percentages of increase or decrease in the number of felonies reported. However, the number of felonies committed during Reynolds' years as sheriff decreased significantly, with the exception of murder. Certainly his reputation alone had much to do with the decrease in the number of felonies.

On October 6, 1888, the premier issue of the *Lampasas Leader* appeared under the editorship of W. T. Campbell. An editorial, "About Lampasas," compared the old and the new Lampasas and contained the following vignette referring to the new dispensation brought about by N. O. Reynolds:

> Where once the rowdy variety shows and the noisy dance halls thrust their disgusting presence on you there are now large stores. And instead of some roystering [*sic*] tough parading the streets discharging his six-shooter an officer of the law moves quietly along.[2]

Reynolds' work as sheriff obviously impressed editor Campbell, who probably was unaware of those statistics presented in the official reports of the attorney-general. He may have been well aware of the previous decade when the Horrell party shot it out with members of the Texas State Police, and the shootout on the town square of not too many years before.

Virtually no record has survived showing how Sheriff Reynolds could be characterized. Was he a "horseback sheriff" making his presence felt throughout the county by constant patrolling, or, due to his occasional physical ills did he allow his deputies to do most of the work requiring horseback travel? Reynolds could have done the more mundane work of delivering papers and serving court documents, relying on his reputation to keep ruffians and hard cases in line. He participated in the Texas Sheriffs Association meetings, as it is so recorded in February 1887 and again in December of that year. The ninth annual meeting was held in San Antonio in December, and among the former Rangers who were now sheriffs present were Bryan Marsh, now sheriff of Smith County; L. L. Wright of Captain McNelly's old company, vice president of the association, now serving as sheriff of Duval County; Pat Whelan of Nueces County; Buck Hamilton of Bandera County; Frank Moore of Kerr County; and N. O. Reynolds of Lampasas County.[3]

Although maintaining order in Lampasas town and in the county brought little recognition beyond the county lines, Reynolds did gain considerable acclaim when challenging members of the becoming-notorious Cornett-Whitley gang of train robbers. During the latter part of the 1880s the men riding with Braxton "Brack" Cornett and William Henry Whitley created a great amount of work for lawmen over a large portion of Texas. The gang never caught the attention of the public as John Wesley Hardin or the Sam Bass gang did, but they gained considerable notoriety for robbing trains and banks. In early 1887 Brack Cornett, also known as "Captain Dick," a native of Goliad County, Texas, Will Whitley, Ed Reeves, James "Bud" Powell, John W. Barber, Samuel Dawson "Kep" Queen, John Bybee, and a few other lesser known toughs gathered in force.[4]

The gang struck close to the capital itself on May 17 by robbing the northbound Missouri-Pacific passenger train at McNeil Junction, some fifteen miles north of Austin yet still in Travis County. Initial reports suggested there were fifteen in the gang, certainly an exaggeration. They robbed both the express and passengers. Two men were shot and slightly wounded by the thieves. Lawmen who gathered to form posses included former Texas Ranger and now Travis County Deputy Sheriff Samuel M. Platt and United States Marshal John T. Rankin. The posse hoped to obtain Winchesters from Quartermaster Lamar P. Sieker, one-time Ranger companion of Reynolds, but he had to decline the request because the state had loaned guns to lawmen so many times previously without their return that he now had none to loan. Two hours after the news had reached Austin the posses were under way. Not surprisingly the posses returned empty handed.[5]

One month later the gang struck again. This time the target was a Southern Pacific train at Flatonia in Fayette County. El Paso County Sheriff James H. White was a passenger and it was he who identified the leader as "Captain Dick" Cornett (no known relationship with desperado Alf Cornett). The number of gang members now was reduced to a dozen and, judging from the manner in which their work was performed they were old hands in the business, at least according to White. Estimates as to the amount of plunder taken ranged from $1,500 to $10,000.[6]

The gang, now consisting of only six men, split into pairs comprising three groups: Cornett rode off with Milton Day, a newly acquired gang member from DeWitt County; Barber and Whitley chose to remain in Texas. The third pair, Ed Reeves and James "Bud" Powell left the state, going to Hot Springs, Arkansas. Instead of remaining quiet and avoiding potential trouble they were arrested for carrying pistols. Released on bail they quickly returned to Texas before Arkansas authorities discovered their true identities.

Ed Reeves learned nothing from his close call in Hot Springs. In early October Johnson County Sheriff John H. Boyd learned that Reeves was hiding out at his brother-in-law's home in Grandview, Texas. After several nights watching the house the fugitive and lawmen confronted each other. Much ammunition was expended by the two parties but Reeves avoided capture in spite of being wounded in the head and legs. The following day—after thoroughly scouring the countryside—Boyd and his posse found the wounded Reeves, asleep with his pistol in his hand. After having the balls extracted and the wounds dressed, he was placed on a train to be delivered to San Antonio for safe keeping.[7] Authorities learned that a rescue attempt was planned at a point where the train would stop for water. Seeing an opportunity for capturing at least some of the gang the law purposely passed the word out that Reeves would be transported via a certain route, hoping the gang would attempt a rescue. Not released however, was the fact that one car would be filled with special deputies, or the "bravest thief-hunters of Texas" as correspondent Walter Barlow Stevens described the group. Reeves had been informed of the rescue attempt but his comrades failed to show. Their rescue plans were spoiled due to a confrontation with Sheriff Reynolds and a posse from Lampasas County. "The Major," unaware of the plan to trap the outlaws, "had attacked them with a posse on his own hook and had run them out of their course." Reeves felt betrayed by his pals and out of spite made a detailed confession of the gang's activities.[8] Unfortunately Sheriff Reynolds made no report of his action of attacking the gang members; if he had still been a Ranger he would have written up some type of report describing this action.

Well-known gunfighter-lawman Alfred Y. Allee now appeared on the scene. On February 12, 1888, Allee caught up with Brack Cornett and shot him to death in a Frio County pasture. [9] The death of their leader and the capture of Reeves did not diminish the gang's enthusiasm for recklessness however, as four days later they attacked the bank at Cisco in Eastland County. Four unmasked men, a "rough-looking set" as cashier and treasurer L. G. Leveaux described them, robbed the bank of a sum between five and six thousand dollars. The thieves, later identified as Will Whitley, John Barber, Samuel "Kep" Queen, and E. C. Foster, alias Stephens, headed into the Indian Territory where lawmen trailed them so closely they felt compelled to return to Texas.[10]

Two of the gang—Whitley and Barber—now decided to lie low and foolishly selected Lampasas County for their peaceful hiatus between crimes. Not surprisingly Sheriff Reynolds quickly learned of their presence and resolved to bring them to justice, or else drive them so mercilessly they would flee his territory. Fortunately Sergeant Ira Aten was on detached service in Lampasas County and wrote to Quartermaster L. P. Sieker concerning plans to capture the train robbers. Whitley and Barber had been seen on July 25 in Lampasas County and the next day in Williamson County. Aten started following them on the twenty-sixth when in Florence, a small community in Williamson County, he conferred with

A young Ira Aten, armed and ready for action as he appeared in 1885.
Courtesy Former Texas Rangers Foundation.

Sheriff John Thomas Olive.[11] From his discussion with Sheriff Olive, Aten believed he was closing in on them. One of the Cox boys had joined the gang, although he was acting more in the role of an informant than anything else. Whitley had married Cordelia Cox and Aten suspected her brother Tom was informing the gang of the lawmen's activities. When Aten temporarily lost trace of Whitley he returned to spy on the Cox place, hoping to learn something of their whereabouts. With her husband on the run Mrs. Whitley was now staying with her brother Tom Cox. "I see her from the brush Very near every morning *when she first gets up,*" wrote Aten. "They have never caught me watching the house yet. Sheriff Reynolds send[s] a deputy sheriff with me when ever I ask for one, or goes himself." Aten was confident that if Barber and Whitley ever returned they would visit the Cox house and he intended to capture them. On August 6, Aten wrote to Sieker

> They have went below now to do some rascality from what we can learn. I have notified the officers in the lower country to be on the lookout for them. I think my best place is to remain in Williamson Burnet & Lampasas counties & adjoining counties, principally the three above named. The Sheriff of the three named co's I can rely upon [Reynolds, John T. Olive of Williamson and John W. Wolf of Burnet]. It is only a question of time until we will pick them up if they remain in Texas. They are very badly scared, but determand [*sic*] men. Not necessary to write more. I will watch Coxes house to night. Don't know when I will be down [to Austin].[12]

The very next day Aten wrote again to Sieker, indicating that he had received a phone call from William Stanley, deputy sheriff of Williamson County, that the Barber outfit was definitely "making for Lampasas County" and at the time Aten was writing were perhaps within the county lines already. He explained that he could not go watch the Cox house as planned because the "Anti Prohibitors" had held a meeting and trouble was expected, but all went off quietly. Aten concluded his letter: "We will certainly search the rough for [the] Barber outfit. I Knew they were below but now they are on their way back." Ironically, the night William Stanley informed Aten that the Barber outfit was headed for Lampasas, the sixth, he was lured into an ambush. On the night of August 6 three men awakened part-time deputy and part-time farmer Stanley, informing him that his fence had been cut. While investigating, he was ambushed and shot down, eight to ten shots taking effect, killing him instantly. Sheriff John T. Olive conferred with Governor L. S. Ross, who then offered a reward of $500 for the murderers. Sheriff Olive also offered a reward of $500 each for the murderers, dead or alive. At the time of his death Stanley was fifty-four years old with a large family to care for. The news of her husband's murder prostrated the widow, at the time "ill" in bed with a one-day-old baby.[13]

Final resting place of William Stanley, a victim of the Cornett-Whitley gang's revenge. *Photograph by Parsons.*

Stanley, according to the *Galveston Daily News*, had been "very active in hunting up criminals," which marked him to be killed. No names were given by the *News*, but it did state the "murderers are supposed to be two men at present under indictment." Readers of the *News* presumably would know the identity of the killers.[14] Walter Barlow Stevens' lengthy article in the *St. Louis Globe-Democrat* recorded that the outlaws had tried to find a hiding place in Lampasas County. But Sheriff Reynolds had been warned,

> and took the field with a posse. For two or three weeks it was run and fight and run. Whitley became tired. He wanted Barbour [*sic*, Barber]

> to stand with him and have it out with the posse. Barbour preferred his Indian tactics. The two outlaws quarreled over their plans. One morning it was understood they were to give the Sheriff a fight, but Barbour ran as usual. After that the two parted company. Barbour made his way to East Texas, but by this time every part of the State was aroused. In Tyler County he stopped to rest, but the Sheriff was soon on his track, and he was chased into the Louisiana swamps, where he is now hiding.[15]

Presumably it was Sheriff N. O. Reynolds who chased Barber "into the Louisiana swamps" but Stevens may have intended his readers to understand it was the Tyler County sheriff who did, or perhaps they combined forces, but neither was successful. Barber had managed to elude the law yet again.

Although no other specific details have been learned about Reynolds' unsuccessful pursuit of Barber and Whitley in August, one newspaper account placed him in a gunfight with *three* members of the gang during the next April, 1888. In the new *Lampasas Leader* newspaper of October 6, in reporting the death of Will Whitley, editor Campbell wrote that on April 26, about sundown, Reynolds and two deputies "were riding along when they were suddenly fired upon from ambush. The fire was returned with interest. A bold charge was made." Three men who were afterwards identified as Whitley, Barber, and newcomer John Bybee broke from their hiding place and a desperate running fight ensued. With night descending, darkness forced an end to the fight; of the trio only Bybee was captured along with horses, some weapons, and other equipment. Although Whitley and Barber managed to escape in the darkness Barber was badly wounded. Bybee was ultimately sent to Huntsville penitentiary.[16]

Things were especially rough for the gang as earlier that same day deputy sheriff John Jamison and special deputy William Patton of Burnet County had exchanged shots with Barber and Whitley. The deputies had been lying in wait for several days hoping to catch them; with a $1,500 reward for each of them, they were prime targets. The deputies, watching the home of Bryce Smart, suspected of harboring the fugitives, were ready when Whitley and Barber emerged about 1:00 a.m. Barber sensed something was wrong and, spurring his horse, plunged into the thick brush. Jamison shot Barber's horse, which managed to run two hundred yards before collapsing. Patton shot at Whitley and wounded him. Although the country was extremely wooded and rough Whitley managed to get another horse from the Smart pasture and escaped.[17]

With the outlaws barely escaping capture and eluding officers after two gunfights on the same day, they must have felt extremely confident in their ability to evade the law's grasp. They had engaged Jamison and Patton in a gunfight and then later on the same day barely escaped from the gunfire of Sheriff Reynolds and his posse, although one of their number was captured.

On September 22, 1888, Will Whitley, Samuel H. Neff, brothers Will and Eli Harrell, and perhaps others attempted to rob the Southern Pacific at Harwood in Gonzales County, some seventy-five miles east of San Antonio. John T. Rankin, United States Marshal for the Western District of Texas, and other lawmen were on the train hoping to capture the gang. Not only did they fail to capture the outlaws but the robbers failed as well.[18] Three days later, on September 25, 1888, lawmen were more successful. Marshal Rankin shot and killed William Henry Whitley near Floresville in Wilson County, south of San Antonio. Whitley was "one of the most desperate characters ever known in southwest Texas" according to one report. He had said on more than one occasion that he would never be taken alive. Whitley had "outlived his day, and, like others who preceded and men who are to follow him, he went over the divide with his boots on."[19]

Whitley, born September 7, 1864, in Smithville, Mississippi, had moved to Texas with his parents as a young boy. As a young man he had driven a stage coach in South Texas and then on December 16, 1883, had married Cordelia L. Cox in Williamson County. Two children were born to this union. Whitley is buried in the Mahomet Cemetery in Williamson County, his grave marker standing tall and strong against the elements, alongside other family members. The marker gives his birth and death dates and memorializes him: "He was a kind and affectionate husband, a fond father, and a friend to all." Like many gravestones, this one does not necessarily reflect the feelings of everyone who knew the deceased.[20]

Final resting place of outlaw Will Whitley, shot to death by lawmen in 1888, in Mahomet Cemetery in rural Burnet County. *Photograph by Parsons.*

Although Sheriff Reynolds had not ended the life of any member of the gang, nor brought any into custody, people still praised him for the work he had done. They realized that with Whitley dead and the remainder of the gang in flight, his efforts had contributed to the gang's destruction. Editor Campbell found reason again to praise the man, writing, "They were outlaws of the most desperate character and were thoroughly bad. The world is well rid of them," he proclaimed, almost daring someone to challenge his prose. Campbell then focused on the lawman himself: "Sheriff Reynolds has spent a great deal of time and money hunting them, but they were very careful to keep a good ways from him. They knew there was no show for them with the best sheriff in West Texas on their trail."[21] Reynolds, whether he realized it or not, did have a good press agent on his side.

John Barber had not long to live. Along with his half-brother Stanley "Kep" Queen, he returned to the Indian Territory, relocating in the Creek Nation. They managed to avoid Texas lawmen but on November 15, 1888, Sheriff Ed Sanders and a posse caught up with the pair near Claremore, Indian Territory. Queen was killed resisting arrest, but Barber again escaped, although again wounded. A year later on Saturday morning, December 7, 1889, U.S. Deputy Marshals Connelley and White brought down Barber. Called to surrender, he "wheeled his horse and opened [fire] on them." Another report identified deputies J. A. Petty and Rutherford among the officers in addition to White and Connelley. Barber grabbed his Winchester and fired on the posse, "Indian fashion," crouching behind his pony after each shot, but was shot through the heart after fifty shots had been exchanged. Besides his involvement in numerous robberies he had killed "three sheriffs of as many counties in Texas" as well as other individuals. The rewards offered for his capture were estimated to be in excess of $4,000. His body was delivered to Fort Smith, Arkansas.[22] Judge Isaac C. Parker, of "Hanging Judge" notoriety certainly praised the work of deputies White and Connelley, although he may have preferred to have the outlaw swing from his gallows.

Reynolds' primary concern remained Lampasas County, no matter how great the reward may have been for fugitives who could roam at will across the southern states. And Lampasas County did occasionally provide his job with excitement. On October 6, 1888, twenty-four-year-old prisoner Whitfield "Witt" Chalk Jr., jailed for horse theft in Lampasas County and wanted elsewhere for theft and burglary, made a break for liberty.[23] For several days previous to his escape attempt he had gathered bits of cement and other hard substances from around the jail. When he had collected a sufficient amount he secured it in a towel, which made an effective and dangerous bludgeon.

On that Saturday morning when jailer William A. "Billie" Brown carried dinner to the prisoners Chalk struck him twice on the head with the homemade weapon. Brown managed to take the weapon from the prisoner and struck him over the head with it as his wife, "with commendable

The frontier-era jail of Lampasas, preserved today as a historic building.
Courtesy Jeff Jackson.

courage and bearing that should be rewarded," grabbed a revolver and guarded the only opening through which the prisoner could escape. Even if Chalk had overpowered Brown he probably would have been shot by Brown's wife. There were five other prisoners in jail at the time, two for murder and three for theft. Brown had been jailer for four years, and in that time had handled 380 prisoners. "This is the first, and we trust the last, trouble he has had with any of them," commended the *Leader*.[24]

The county elected Reynolds for a second term as sheriff on November 6, 1888 against George Wolf. It must have been an exciting campaign as the *Leader* reported that the "bids on Shrievealty [*sic*] were spirited. Bets were even." The candidates for the various offices were compared to horses, but in the excitement of creating equine imagery George Wolf's name was incorrectly given. He wrote in to correct the editor, pointing out that he was George Wolf, not "L. Wolf."[25]

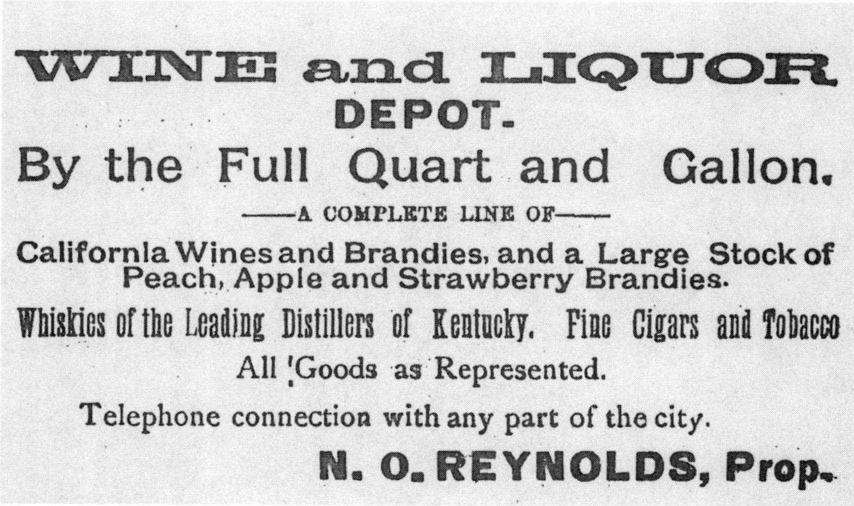

An advertisement for N.O. Reynolds' "wine and liquor depot" in Lampasas, from the *Lampasas Dispatch* of December 10, 1890. *Courtesy Jeff Jackson.*

When the votes were tallied Reynolds had received 722 while Wolf had received only 588. The election had passed quietly, with the main interest being in the races for sheriff, county judge, and county attorney. Reynolds now entered his second term, and would be working with County Judge D. C. Thomas and County Attorney S. D. Foote. Commented the *Leader*, "This being a law abiding community not even the back doors of the saloons were opened and there was no sign of even a private bottle."[26] The *Leader* later provided a sketch of the newly elected officers including a paragraph about Reynolds. It is worthy of preserving in spite of the several errors.

> The newly re-elected sheriff Major N.O. Reynolds, was born in Clark county, Missouri, and is now 41 years old. He was educated in his native county and since coming to Texas has held the following offices. He was deputy sheriff of Hays county, Texas. Then commencing as 4th sergeant in the State troops, by his bravery and his ability he was promoted step by step until he occupied the position of captain of Company E, Frontier Battalion and commanded this company 2 years. He was elected Sheriff

> of Lampasas County in 1886 and the people have shown their appreciation of his services as an officer by re-electing him to the office over one of the most popular men and efficient officers in this county.[27]

On Saturday, November 3, Lampasas County resident Sam H. Neff, one-time member of the Cornett-Whitley train-robbing gang, was arrested by Mills County Sheriff J. W. Cunningham, and charged with carrying a pistol. Reynolds went to county seat Goldthwaite to take charge of the prisoner and now brought against him the more serious charge of attempting to rob the train at Harwood on October 22. Neff was well connected in Lampasas County, having married into "one of the best families" when he became the husband of sixteen-year-old Margaret L. Hamilton in September of 1886. Groom Neff was twenty-eight. He also owned a large amount of livestock. But in spite of his efforts to become a respected member of the community Neff had developed "an unenviable reputation." Indicted for horse theft in Lampasas County and for carrying a pistol in Mills County, Neff was now taken to Belton, in Bell County for safe keeping and then to San Antonio to be placed in the more secure Bexar County jail. Neff stood trial for robbing the U.S. mail during the robbery at Flatonia. He was found guilty and received a sentence of five years' imprisonment at Columbus, Ohio. With his conviction on a federal charge the lesser charges of carrying a pistol and stealing a horse were dropped.[28]

The proceedings of the Commissioners Court were reported occasionally in the Lampasas press, which offers an insight into the workings of a county sheriff in Texas in the 1880s. For the final quarter of 1888 Reynolds received $95 for attending court and acting as a court officer. He received $7.50 for guarding prisoners.[29] No doubt Sheriff Reynolds himself had to go and collect the wood for the stove, or perhaps that job was delegated to a deputy. The *Leader* also provided information concerning Reynolds' work as a sheriff. A letter dated December 15 from Townsen Mill from "L. Carol"—no doubt a *nom de plume* inspired by the Christmas season—stated that Major Reynolds, and his deputy Tom Denny had been out in that neighborhood during the previous week. "Don't think they were after any one for the Townsen Mill people are all

An advertisement for N. O. Reynolds' Brunswick Saloon in Lampasas, from the *Lampasas Dispatch* of December 10, 1890. *Courtesy Jeff Jackson.*

quiet, peaceable, law abiding citizens" assured editor Campbell. In the same issue Reynolds posted an official notice: "Persons holding a commission as Deputy Sheriff, will return the same to this office and have them renewed where it is considered necessary."[30] Obviously receiving a commission as a deputy once did not guarantee a renewal of that position.

Only scraps of information remain of a case involving W. G. Baird and Reynolds, the only surviving record preserved in the Civil Minutes Book, cause number 1207 dated November 11, 1889. On first call plaintiff Baird had "leave to file 1st amended original petition and the case continued under rule for costs." A year later, on November 5, 1890, the entry read simply: "Plaintiff will no longer prosecute." Plaintiff Baird's sureties were J. A. Baggett and R. E. Baird. The defendants were Reynolds, D. F. Vorhes, T. J. Largen and H. T. Hill. The court ordered that the defendants would "recover of said plaintiff and his said sureties all costs by them expended in this behalf for which let execution issue."[31] Nothing else has been discovered about this matter due to missing court records.

Sheriff Reynolds patrolled the town and the county, as well as his deputies, checking that doors were locked after hours and investigating any unusual sounds or suspicious matters. During his term no one attempted to rob the bank, and about the time of his resignation or shortly thereafter, the First National Bank paid him a bonus "for his services in so carefully protecting our bank against robbery during his term of office."[32]

On July 2, 1889, a man named Jones was in the saloon of C. B. Marsh mishandling his pistol when it discharged. Jones "carelessly lodged the contents in the wall above the door" rather than in the body of an unsuspecting customer. Sheriff Reynolds arrested Jones at once and lodged him in jail. This was probably Reynolds' last official act as sheriff as he chose to resign prior to the end of his elected term. "With deep regret" noted the *Leader*, "we learn that Major Reynolds, sheriff of this county, has tendered his resignation to take effect the 1st of July [*sic*, August?]." Reynolds was "a courteous gentleman, painstaking, efficient and watchful" as well as being "a terror to evil-doers." The reason given for his resignation was that the fees of the office were too small to justify him keeping it. Joseph M. Stillwell, a deputy who had gained much experience under Reynolds, was chosen to complete the term. Stillwell served until November 4, 1890 when J. S. Clark was elected to carry on the duties as sheriff.[33]

N.O. Reynolds now returned to his former trade and on August 20 purchased the Brunswick Saloon in Lampasas from C. B. Marsh, whose customer Jones had carelessly put a hole in the wall which Reynolds now owned. The *Leader* again took the opportunity to praise the man, "[Reynolds] has hosts of friends here, to whom he is well known and who have watched with pleasure the admirable manner in which he has filled various positions of trust." Reynolds placed the following advertisement in the same issue:

> After presenting my compliments to the public, have to say that it is no pleasure to me to be engaged in the liquor traffic, only a matter of business. In carrying on this I expect to comply strictly with the law and to those who have relatives who bemay [*sic*] prohibited by notice from

> drinking, I will take it as a favor to receive same in writing, also students of any college and habitual drunkards, I don't want your trade and ask that you do not annoy me. I wish to do a strict legitimate business and ask for a share of respectable patronage.[34]

It not only amounted to an announcement of his new business but a strong statement that he wanted to avoid problems so common in the liquor trade. His firm statement that he expected to comply "strictly" with the law was a veiled reference to the earlier days when he was charged with breaking the Sunday liquor laws. In the collection of the Lampasas County Historical Commission are notes dealing with Reynolds and how he was remembered. According to Jack Townsen, he knew Reynolds and his saloon was known as a "quart and gallon house." In the rear of the building was a café where Clint Washington prepared meals. As an unusual curiosity piece Reynolds kept a *panther* near the cafe and on one occasion it snapped at Townsen, who then acquired the nickname of "Panther Jack." Mrs. W. H. Moses related how Reynolds lived west of the Baptist Church in the old Greenwood House. "His wife had afternoon parties & pitchers of beer were sent up to the house."[35] There was no indication of how often she held these parties, however.

N.O. Reynolds was extremely successful as a businessman. A letterhead displayed in the Lampasas Museum carries the imprint: "N. O. Reynolds & Co." a business which dealt in Kentucky whiskey, California wines, tobacco, and cigars. Reynolds' Brunswick Bar was one of three business houses identified on the letterhead, the others being the Cotton Exchange at 212 Third Street, and the Quart and Gallon House on West Third. Reynolds' business, typically, was on the courthouse square.[36] With such a location his business was convenient for all who had dealings at the courthouse, such as lawyers, clerks, and lawmen.

On February 22, 1890, trees were planted on the courthouse yard to beautify the town square. N. O. Reynolds provided a blooming willow on the northeast corner of the square while Deputy J. M. Stillwell, Moses Hughes, and County Attorney S. D. Foote provided poplars. The *Dispatch* and the *Leader* both provided an evergreen and J. W. Townsen provided a mulberry.[37] Reynolds had truly become a pillar of the community.

17

A Loss and a Final Guard

"Night Foreman Paper Mill."
—N. O. Reynolds

Following his 1889 resignation as sheriff of Lampasas County, N. O. Reynolds, now nearing his mid-forties, left the Hill Country of Texas to live in the Gulf Coast at Angleton, Brazoria County. It was here that he again worked in the shoe business. He spent at least four years there, 1889–1893, prior to relocating in Lockhart, the county seat of Caldwell County.

Information is not available about what Reynolds did in the intervening years, but ten years after leaving the saloon business in Lampasas, Reynolds again became a saloon operator in Lockhart. In June of 1899 the *Lockhart Post* announced the transfer of two saloons in the city: Louis Halfin purchased the Iron Front Saloon, proprietor T. A. Reed having retired. Reynolds, "formerly in the shoe business at Angleton," purchased the stock of liquors and unnamed business from George S. Moon. "Mr. Reynolds," reported the *Post*, "says he has traveled over Texas since last December seeking a location and to his mind Lockhart is the best town in the State."[1] Lockhart was the "best" town in the state apparently due to its rapid growth, not to mention its proximity to Austin, only some thirty-five miles northwest. After Caldwell County had been established in 1848, Lockhart was named the county seat, attaining incorporation in 1852. With the beginning of the cattle industry in the late sixties Lockhart became a starting point for the Chisholm Trail

A view of Angleton, Texas, where Reynolds lived and lost property during the 1900 Galveston hurricane. *Courtesy the Brazoria County Historical*

and developed into an important trading center. As early as 1890 there was electricity, waterworks, streetcars, four schools, seven churches, and a national bank to serve the population of approximately twelve hundred residents. Three railroads added to the economic growth of the area. Ten years later, or roughly when Reynolds had made his decision to settle there, the population had almost doubled, now numbering more than 2,300.[2]

Reynolds applied for a liquor dealer's bond on June 1, which four days later was approved with himself as principal and Ed Friedrich and J. E. Mugge as sureties. The bond set was $5,000. Reynolds was allowed "to engage in the sale of spirituous, vinous and malt liquors, and mediated bitters capable of producing intoxication, to be drunk on the premises, in quantities of one gallon or less, on the S[outh] side of the Public Square, in the city of Lockhart." No one under the age of twenty-one nor a student of an institution of learning, nor a habitual drunkard, could be served. Nor could anyone be served if the sheriff had served the license holder in writing that the individual was not to be served. Those under the age of twenty-one years were not allowed to enter and remain, nor were games allowed which were prohibited by the state to be played, dealt or exhibited, nor could adulterated liquors be sold.[3]

Reynolds announced through the columns of the *Lockhart Post* that all was ready for business, stating that he had purchased "the entire stock of wines, liquors, cigars, etc. of Mr. Geo. S. Moon" and to reduce the inventory he would reduce the prices. His notice indicated he would stock "light wines which are first class in quality, ripe with age, and suitable for the family table, medicinal and sacramental wine. . . . I hope by fair and impartial treatment to merit the patronage of the public."[4]

In Lockhart Reynolds operated a saloon facing the south side of the court house square. The front has been totally remodeled, but the rear has not. This is the rear of his saloon as it appeared in 1987. *Photo by Parsons.*

On June 10 Reynolds returned to Angleton where he spent two days packing the family possessions for the move. By the thirteenth he was back in Lockhart, ready to establish a new home with Irene and the two daughters, Emma Elizabeth and Lula Jenkins.[5] That home was located in the southern portion of Lockhart, a "certain tract of land" being all of lot 12 and the southern half of lot 11 in the W. R. Smith Addition. This land was purchased from A. B. and his wife M. A. Jeffrey for $600 with 10 percent interest per annum on January 2, 1900.The note was held by James G. Burleson and was paid in full on November 23, 1900.[6]

A view of Lockhart's courthouse, designed by famed architect Alfred Giles. Many of the buildings in this 1893 image still stand. Reynolds' Saloon was on the south side of the square facing this edifice, within easy walking distance to the front door of his drinking establishment. *Photograph No. 351, Caldwell County Courthouse, from the photographic collection of the Caldwell County Genealogical and Historical Society.*

During the move, Louis Halfin was remodeling the old Iron Front Saloon. By September he and Reynolds had formed a corporation consolidating the Iron Front and Reynolds' Brunswick Saloon into a new business to be known as Halfin & Reynolds. The two adjoining "houses" had been joined by cutting an archway in the partition wall between them. The new owners assured the public that the "same force will be employed and no extra charge [will] be made in the business."[7]

Even while the changes were taking place and Reynolds could anticipate becoming a respected businessman, his old ailments returned to bother him. For some relief he and his family visited Burdette Wells (variously named Burditt, Burdett, and Burdette Wells, accoring to the Handbook of Texas online), an early-day health resort located between the two major towns in Caldwell County, Lockhart and Luling. The waters contained large quantities of magnesia and sulfuric acid and were capable of curing virtually any ailment, or at least that was what Dr. Burditt of Luling claimed. Although we can't be sure, the similarity of names suggests that Dr. Burditt may have been personally interested in the success of the wells. The water's curative powers proved to be so popular that a large two-story hotel and bathhouse were constructed, and a railroad spur and even a post office were established. One early traveler visited the watering place and by "personal test" boasted that he was "convinced that the various diseases attendant on torpid liver, impure blood and indigestion are vigorously and successfully assailed by these waters, and for those complaints particularly may be recommended."[8] Nothing remains of the site today and it is unknown if Reynolds really benefited from the waters of Burdette Wells.[9]

Perhaps as relaxation from the stress of the business Reynolds also engaged in horse racing during this time. He posted a $5.00 reward for the return of a "fine blooded Hamilton," which he suspected was on the San Marcos River near the Staples Store, a small community in northeastern Guadalupe County.[10]

In spite of his ailments, his business in Angleton, Brazoria County and other activities N. O. Reynolds concentrated on his saloon business. In early February 1900 the firm was dissolved by mutual consent. Halfin had decided to retire leaving Reynolds sole proprietor. He now consolidated the two saloons, using the fixtures for one bar.[11]

The 1900 census enumerating the N. O. Reynolds family listed the head of household as a forty-five-year-old saloon keeper, *a native of Missouri*, and his parents as natives of Kentucky. He, or someone in the family, told the census taker Reynolds was born in November 1845 and had been married eighteen years. Wife Irene Reynolds is shown to be thirty-nine years of age, married eighteen years and the mother of two children, both living. Emma was born in August of 1883 and Lula was born in December of 1885. Mrs. Reynolds was keeping house and the daughters were both attending school, which lasted four months of the year.[12]

Three months following the peaceful enumeration of the Reynolds family the island of Galveston was hit by the most destructive hurricane of the century. The winds, clocked in excess of 120 miles per hour, damaged a huge amount of property and took thousands of lives. Property losses were estimated at forty million dollars; between six and eight thousand people lost their lives. The damage covered much of the Texas coast, including the city of Angleton some fifty miles from Galveston and twenty miles from the coast. The specific property Reynolds held is not known, but the monetary loss to the property was set at $300. On September 17, a week after the destructive storm, Reynolds left Lockhart to personally inspect the damage in Angleton.[13]

Occasional items of interest appeared in the Lockhart newspaper concerning N. O. Reynolds. Fully aware of the dangers of fire in May of 1901 Reynolds donated $15 to the local fire department. The secretary was instructed to tender him thanks from the department. A motion was made to make Reynolds an honorary member of the fire department, a motion which carried unanimously.[14]

T. P. Baker bought into Reynolds' firm in early 1902. Reynolds completed the form for the liquor license on March 1, indicating he would be the proprietor of the firm to be known as Reynolds & Baker, although patrons continued to refer to it as the Kentucky Saloon, perhaps because that was the name when it was owned by Mr. Moon. Sureties were Otto Wahrmund and Otto Koehler.[15] Later, on September 12, another license was applied for but the location was now specifically at Clear Fork, a small community four miles west of Lockhart.[16] Yet another license, dated September 29, was to sell liquor near the railroad depot.[17] Less than a year later, in March 1903, readers of the *Lockhart Post* learned that Major N. O. Reynolds of the firm of Reynolds & Baker had sold his interest in the Kentucky Saloon to James G. Stagner.[18]

Yet Reynolds experienced another change when in September 1903 he and Ed Kalies of Marion, Guadalupe County, opened a saloon in the Walter Pieper house on the west side of the "Plaza," or the courthouse square. Reynolds and Kalies had applied for the license on August 25, the principals being both Reynolds and Kalies and sureties represented by the Fidelity & Deposit Company of Maryland. Reynolds and Kalies intended "to conduct a first class business in every possible manner. Our goods will always be found to be standard and the best that can be bought, and our service thorough in every particular."[19] During that move in August Reynolds collapsed, an incident found to be newsworthy by the *Post*, the reporter expressing the belief that he had been weakened by the strenuous effort of packing furniture in a hot room.[20] The new firm of Reynolds & Kalies lasted only several months, as by mid-December the partnership ended. Kalies intended to re-open in nearby New Braunfels, Comal County, while Reynolds intended to remain in Lockhart.[21]

Major Reynolds again proved newsworthy as on Saturday, January 30, 1904, he presented *Lockhart Post* editor William B. Smith with a twenty-shot repeating rifle. Smith, a Kentucky lawyer who had purchased the newspaper in 1879, described the .22 caliber Winchester as "perhaps the finest gun of its kind ever brought to the city." Why Reynolds gave the gun to the editor is not stated. Smith explained the gun "does not go into our museum as its modern make and usefulness bars it from forming a part of that interesting feature of our office."[22] Later, to prove Reynolds was an important businessman in the city, editor Smith noted he had left on the evening of February 3 to go to Houston on business. He was consistently referred to as *Major* Reynolds.[23]

Perhaps the "business in Houston" failed to materialize but resulted in an opportunity opening in Orange, the seat of Orange County, some

100 miles east of Houston on the Texas-Louisiana border. A lengthy and early description of Orange, which Reynolds may have read, appearing in the *Galveston Daily News*, may have been the reason he was attracted to the city. The town was "situated on the bank of the Sabine river, extending about one mile and a quarter around a most beautiful and fascinating bend, four miles from Sabine Pass, where we have the full benefit of a fresh and invigorating breeze from the gulf. . . . The state of society is the best—churches of various denominations, schools, and everything indicative of an intelligent, law-abiding, prosperous and happy people."[24] By 1910 Major and Mrs. Reynolds were residents of Orange, the "Gateway City." Neither of their daughters was living with them, and now, when the census enumerator visited the house, the old Ranger and saloon keeper gave his occupation as "Night Foreman Paper Mill." Orange was enjoying the benefits of being the center of the lumber industry, but during Reynolds' years there the city became the center of considerable racial conflict, including Ku Klux Klan activity.[25]

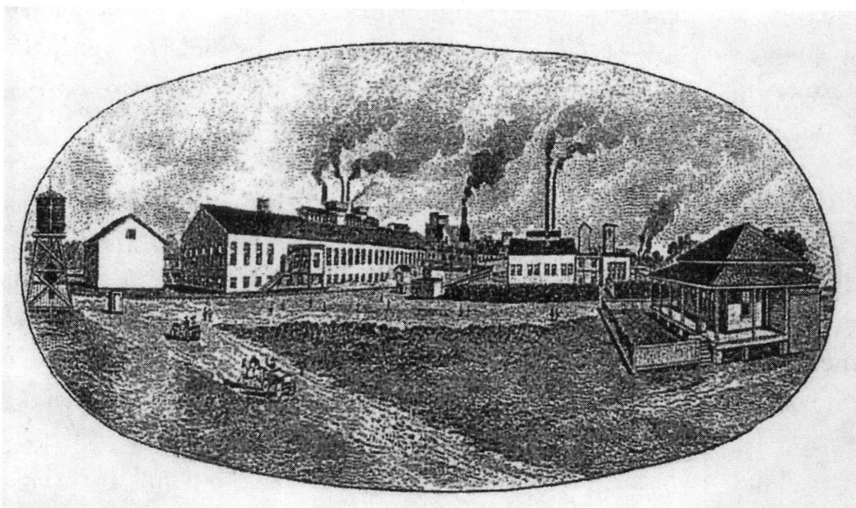

N.O. Reynolds' final employment was as night watchman at the Yellow Pine Paper Mill, shown here. This engraving appeared on Reynolds' personal correspondence.
Courtesy Kris Mize.

On March 26, 1912, Reynolds' mother died at the home of her daughter Edla, now Mrs. E. A. Rockwell in Troy, Bradford County, Pennsylvania, where she had resided following the death of her husband Hiram G. Reynolds shortly after the end of the Civil War and where she had started a new life. The one newspaper obituary noted that she was survived (incorrectly) by four daughters and one brother, Volney.[26] No mention was made of her son, although her only son did return home for the funeral. Upon his return he must have felt like a stranger among his own family members. The mother's grave in the Granville Cemetery is marked with a simple stone, the inscription reading "Betsy D. Reynolds/ 1827–1912."[27]

Reynolds worked at the Yellow Pine Paper Mill in Orange. Among the very few documents preserved in the family archive is a letter of recommendation for him written by George S. Holmes, the mill's general manager, dated April 22, 1914. The letter, addressed simply: "To Whom It May Concern" is as follows.

> This is to certify that Mr. N.O. Reynolds has been [in] the employ of this Company for the past seven years as watchman, etc., and during this entire period has given absolutely the best of satisfaction in service.
>
> Mr. Reynolds is leaving us because he wishes a change in climate and with extreme regret on our part.
>
> We recommend him unconditionally as absolutely dependable, with a high sense of honor, responsibility and loyalty.[28]

With a letter of recommendation such as that it would seem N. O. Reynolds could have had any position he was qualified for. The qualities which Reynolds exhibited to his superiors in 1914 were the same as those qualities that resulted in advancements back in the 1870s when fighting raiders and white outlaws and renegades. Those were the qualities which caused his men to think of him as "The Intrepid" when recalling their experiences with him.

Whereas previously the official census records showed Reynolds as a family man living with his wife and children, the census of 1920 shows him still residing in Orange, but now living as a boarder, alone. Mr. and Mrs. Reynolds had not separated due to marital difficulties, Irene having relocated to their home in Center Point in eastern Kerr County. On May 1, 1918, N. O. had purchased eight acres from Zula Crotty of Bisbee, Arizona, paying $2,300 for the land. On that acreage on the edge of Center Point was a rock house, which became their home; it still stands and until recently was occupied by a great-granddaughter and her family. The century-plus-old house was made from hand-cut blocks of limestone from Verde Creek in Bandera County, Texas, the

After his days as Texas Ranger, city marshal, and county sheriff, N. O. Reynolds relaxes on the porch of his Center Point home. *Courtesy Stephen Reynolds Davis and Bernard Davis.*

rocks providing natural insulation as they are approximately eighteen inches thick. After her husband's death Irene continued to live in this house until her own death.[29]

Although the coast had attracted Reynolds for employment in the teens, it was in the Hill Country where he chose to live out his final days. The Hill Country is noted for its natural beauty, and he certainly thought of it often while working in Orange County. It was this natural beauty which attracted him to the small community of Center Point in eastern Kerr County. He had first become acquainted with it back in the seventies as a Ranger commander. A description of the village had appeared in the *Galveston Daily News* back in 1877. In addition to the springs of fine clear water, which were plentiful, the running streams made Kerr County among the best watered counties in the state. In Kerrville and Center Point "all requisite commodities may be purchased, and the shops of the blacksmith, carpenters, etc. be found." Then the two communities were about the same population. Center Point had saw and corn mills and cotton gins and "one of the best flouring mills in all the west." In addition Center Point had a school and two churches. If Reynolds had not read the newspaper's laudatory write-up of these towns in the Hill Country when it first appeared, he remembered the beauty of the land decades later, when outlaws and the threat of Indian raids were a distant memory.

Certainly the greatest tragedy of Reynolds' life came on April 16, 1921, when daughter Lula Jenkins Reynolds Blunt died at her home in San Antonio, apparently from an appendicitis attack. Born in Lampasas on December 18, 1885, she had grown up in Lockhart. She had moved to Orange with the family where, on November 10, 1905, she married Charles H. Blunt in the family home. The couple moved to San Antonio in 1918 and resided at 114 Woodlief Avenue. Charles Blunt worked as an assistant manager of the Southern Products Company. Mr. Blunt was left to care for their four children: Dorene, Florence, Reynolds, and Carlos. Lula Blunt was buried in the Lockhart Cemetery, less than a mile from where the Reynolds home had been located.[30]

Reynolds' daughter Lula Jenkins Reynolds Blunt. *Courtesy the Stephen Reynolds Davis and Bernard Davis Collection.*

Although personal items of Reynolds', such as letters to family members or a journal providing him with notes for later memoirs, are virtually nonexistent, one special item that Reynolds cherished impresses one with its sincerity. Among the personal possessions preserved by the family is a first edition of J. B. Gillett's *Six Years with the Texas Rangers*, first published in 1921. On the inside cover of this copy Reynolds wrote: "This little book is the property of Mrs. R. C. Bean, Center Point, Tex[.] Don't Borrow it with the intention of never RETURNING. N. O. Reynolds, January 27, 1922."[31]

Shortly thereafter, on March 1, 1922, death claimed the old Texas Ranger. According to attending physician Dr. Charles Clinton Jones Sr. of Comfort, death was caused by pneumonia, contracted at Orange. Dr. Jones had attended his patient from February 26 until February 28, and indicated that death had claimed his life on March 1.[32] Whereas during his life he was often identified as a native of Missouri, and his birth given with a variety of years, his death certificate, based on information

The last known photograph of the old lawman, standing on the porch of the Center Point home. *Courtesy Stephen Reynolds Davis and Bernard Davis Collection.*

Mamie Elizabeth Bean and her sister Roberta, granddaughters of N. O. Reynolds. *Courtesy the Stephen Reynolds Davis and Bernard Davis Collection.*

Four generations of the Reynolds family. From left: Mrs. N. O. Reynolds; daughter Emma E. R. Bean; granddaughter Mamie Elizabeth (Mrs. James J. Davis Sr.); holding James J. Davis Jr. *Courtesy the Stephen Reynolds Davis and Bernard Davis Collection.*

provided by widow Irene, states he was born on November 21, 1846, in Pennsylvania, the son of H. G. and B. D. Taylor Reynolds. His occupation was given as "assistant manager Paper Mill" although he had retired from that occupation. Mrs. Reynolds could just as easily have stated he was "Texas Ranger Commander." Undertaker Wade Richardson of Center Point was in charge of the interment at Center Point, which was merely across the road from the home. Reynolds was survived by his widow and one daughter, Emma Elizabeth, born August 1, 1883, now Mrs. Robert C. Bean, and four grandchildren.[33]

Reynolds' last will and testament, dated February 28, 1922, only one day before his death, provided that all his property, both real and personal, should go to Irene. Also, he requested that she be made sole administrator and executrix of his estate. James Crotty, who had known Reynolds for about eight years, and S. J. Watters were witnesses. At the time of his death Reynolds had in the bank $333.76, owned eight acres of land valued at $1,500 and fifteen shares of stock in the Southern Pacific Railway Company (certificates #F180160 and #G101889). These shares were valued at $1,500. The household furniture was valued at $100, for a total value of $3,433.76. There were no claims against the estate.[34]

The *Kerrville Mountain Sun* gave considerable space to Reynolds, headlining its notice "Capt. N.O. Reynolds Died," noting his passing and also his adventurous life. The native of Pennsylvania, born there in "1849 [*sic*]," had served under Rangers Caldwell, Roberts, and Jones and had been known as "Reynolds the Intrepid." The obituary pointed out that he had received the rank of 1st Lieutenant after capturing the Horrells, had scouted after Sam Bass and had escorted and guarded John Wesley Hardin. Incorrectly the obituary stated he had been elected sheriff of Lampasas County three successive terms. For the past eighteen years he had been with the Yellow Pine Paper Mills of Orange County.[35]

Daughter Emma Elizabeth Reynolds (standing center) with two unidentified friends. *Courtesy the Stephen Reynolds Davis and Bernard Davis Collection.*

The last years of Mrs. Reynolds, at least financially, were not kind. In August of 1922 she wrote to "Widow Division" U.S. Pension officer, Washington Gardner (as part of her application for a pension as the widow of a Union soldier) that she would not have "appealed to you had it not been that I am crippled with rheymatism [*sic*]. I am a professional nurse & could manage were it not that I can not walk without cruthes [*sic*, and] any assistance would be greatly ap[p]reciated."[36] On March 21, 1923, still working on the application and unable to hire an attorney, she again wrote Gardner and admitted her "friend Lawyer" did the work gratis. "We come out here in the hills," she explained, "thinking it [would] benefit us both[.] I was in hopes I would be able to get a little something planted in order to raise chickens, to help out a little financially: my funeral expenses were very heavy having lost a daughter & then a husband very soon after."[37] In spite of her financial difficulties, Mrs. Reynolds remained a beloved member of the Center Point Community; whereas some women in her situation would easily have fallen into despair and self-pity, she did not. She had her own style of intrepidity. With her knowledge of nursing, residents often came to her first when they were ailing, wanting and trusting her to remedy their problem.

Irene Temperance Nevill Reynolds lived over two decades after her husband's death, passing away on April 27, 1947, in a San Antonio hospital. Her death certificate incorrectly shows she was born on September 11, 1862, in Fayette County, Texas. Her actual birthdate was September 10. This daughter of Z. L. and Ann M. Lewis Nevill died of coronary thrombosis due to sclerotic heart disease. She was eighty-four years, seven months and sixteen days of age. Funeral services were held on Tuesday, April 28 at the Memorial Funeral Home in Kerrville. Irene Reynolds was interred in the Center Point Cemetery beside her husband. She was survived by her daughter Emma Elizabeth who had married Robert Carr Bean; granddaughters Mamie Elizabeth (Bean) Davis and Roberta Reynolds (Bean) Andrews; and four great-grandchildren. Apparently some grandchildren had died after her husband's death in 1922, when he was survived by four grandchildren, but no records have been discovered. [38]

Grave markers of N. O. Reynolds and Irene Temperance Nevill Reynolds in the Center Point Cemetery. *Photo by Parsons.*

Reynolds' remains lie today in the peaceful and well-kept cemetery at Center Point, his grave marked with a simple stone with only the name "N.O. REYNOLDS" engraved at the base. No dates or any other inscription appear on his or the matching stone of his lifelong spouse. At the foot of these graves is that of a descendant, James Jackson "Jimmy" Davis Jr. (May 25, 1934–June 19, 1973) and Reynolds' other daughter Emma Elizabeth, her grave marked "Elizabeth R. Bean, 1883–1964."

On August 22, 1987, the graves of the thirty-two Texas Rangers buried in the Center Point Cemetery were marked with small Texas flags, part of the ceremony when a state historical marker was unveiled at the cemetery on that date.[39] More than 400 people, many of whom were descendants of these early Texas Rangers, attended the ceremony. Several of the Rangers buried there had worked with Reynolds during the 1870s, including Neal Coldwell, Frank M. Moore, and William H. Rishworth. The Kerr County Historical Commission, with the Center Point Sesquicentennial Committee, sponsored the marker dedication.

On October 23, 1999, a Texas Ranger Memorial Service was held at the Center Point Cemetery, sponsored by the Former Texas Ranger Association of San Antonio. Rust-red Texas Ranger crosses bearing the traditional Ranger badge were unveiled at the grave of each ranger as his name was read to the hundreds of interested people in attendance. A small Texas flag, faded but standing proud next to a permanent marker, today marks the final resting place of Nelson Orcelus Reynolds, the Texas Ranger known as "The Intrepid."

Elbert and Ella Alvira Reynolds Santee, sister of N. O. Reynolds. Between them is Floy Leonard, daughter of a neighbor, who later married Thomas Parsons. Image from the original tintype. *Courtesy Kris Mize.*

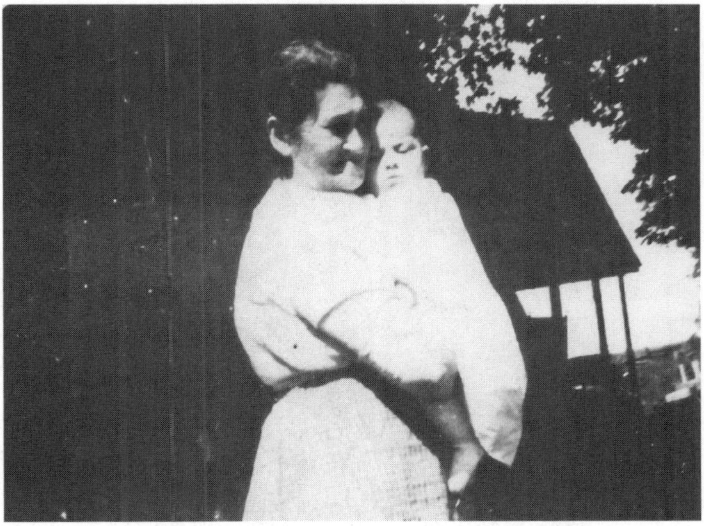

Ella Alvira Reynolds Santee, sister of N. O. Reynolds, holding granddaughter Etheleen Savage. *Courtesy Kris Mize.*

Ella Alvira Reynolds, sister of N. O. Reynolds. *Courtesy Kris Mize.*

Elbert Irvin Santee, who married Ella Alvira Reynolds. *Courtesy Kris Mize.*

Santee group. From left: unidentified neighbor; Efner Santee; Ella A. Reynolds Santee; Gladys Santee Savage, niece of N. O. Reynolds. In foreground is Elbert Santee, Ella's husband, with children Doris and Gerald Savage. *Courtesy Kris Mize*

Stephen Reynolds Davis and wife Polly Gayle Davis, standing at rear of the "N.O. Reynolds Saloon" in Lockhart, Texas, 2004. The front of the building has been totally remodeled. *Photo by Parsons.*

AFTERWORD

By Stephen Reynolds Davis, Great-Grandson of N. O. Reynolds

I was fortunate as in my growing up days I was able to spend lots of time in the N. O. Reynolds home in Center Point, purchased by Major Reynolds in 1918. That is where I spent lots of time, either living or visiting. The "Old Rock House" as it was called by all the kids, was where my grandmother Mrs. Robert C. Bean (Emma Elizabeth Reynolds) lived. She was the daughter of N. O. Reynolds, born in 1882, and where the widow Irene T. Reynolds lived after her husband's death in 1922.

My father, James J. Bean Sr. moved our family to the Hill Country to establish a law firm in Kerrville, Texas. He moved in with my grandmother—Mrs. R. C. Bean—until our house was ready. Grandmother's home was located about a hundred and seventy-five steps from the Center Point Cemetery, the "Ranger Cemetery," as there are thirty-two known Texas Rangers laid to rest there, one of them being my great-grandfather and my namesake, N. O. Reynolds.

I was fascinated—perhaps it was only natural—for a small boy of five years of age and very curious about the graveyard across the road and the man who dug the graves—Mr. Brock Storms. I spent lots of time listening to Mr. Storms' stories and pestering him with questions about death and whose grave "we" were digging. Mr. Brock was my sitter, you might say, and the graveyard was my playground. Little did I know that someday there would be a book written about my great-grandfather who is one of the Rangers buried there. It seems only natural for me today to relate that Mr. Brock Storms, who dug so many graves there, is also buried in the Center Point Cemetery. His "lost" headstone was only found recently.

My mother (Mamie Elizabeth Bean Davis) and grandmother had told me the story about Reynolds going after Sam Bass and this was really all I knew about him until the present day.

I was completely unaware of what an "honorable" man he was—"intrepid"—and how well respected he was by his fellow Rangers and prisoners alike. If you were taken into custody by Reynolds, you had a damn sight better chance of surviving a lynch mob than under anyone else. N. O. Reynolds never gave up a prisoner to a mob or let a prisoner escape.

To research someone's life can become an addiction. I wonder what Reynolds the man was like. Was he quiet? Was he talkative? Did he have a sense of humor? I know he was not a braggart. My brother Bernard tells me of stories told by my mother about her grandfather, one story being the one about a panther.

Mamie, Roberta (her sister) and "Mama Bean" (Mrs. R. C. Bean) were living with Mr. and Mrs. N. O. Reynolds in Lampasas, Texas, where Reynolds ran a saloon/general store there, and was also sheriff. One warm evening Mamie was sitting by the back porch of the house when she got a feeling something or someone was watching her from the edge of the yard. She sat still for a while; then she walked to the other end of the porch. The feeling stayed with her. Becoming scared she hurried inside to tell her mother Mama Bean. Mama Bean immediately went to the porch and into the yard. Seeing nothing, but hearing a rustle in the brush, she went inside to tell her mother Mama O (Mrs. Reynolds), what was happening. Mama O went to a neighbor's house for help. The neighbor's husband went to Reynolds' saloon to report the situation. According to Mamie, Sheriff Reynolds dispatched three customers to their homes to get their weapons and a dog one of them owned.

Reynolds arrived home and began looking around the yard and outbuildings. He was carrying his pistol and a kerosene lantern. Shortly he returned, laughing, to the house, where he told his family he had found his pet panther in the barn looking around. Then the three armed customers and the dog showed up. Everyone, except Mama Bean and Mama O, had a good laugh.

According to Mamie, Reynolds at one time had some animals caged up at his house but had moved them to the rear yard of the saloon when his daughter Mama Bean and his granddaughter came to stay with them. The panther, probably a mountain lion, just got homesick and went back "home."

At the story's end, Mama's eyes would sparkle and she would extend her right hand above her head and say, "N. O. Reynolds, Texas Ranger, my hero."

And yes, my heroes have always been Texas Rangers—and they still are today.

Final resting place of Reynolds' brother-in-law, Charles L. Nevill. The grave is near the opening of City Cemetery # 4, San Antonio. *Photo by Parsons.*

APPENDIX A

The Gentlemen in White Hats

The Men of Company E, Frontier Battalion

Claude Leroy Douglas authored three books dealing with Texas history, two of which dealt with the Texas Rangers and Texas feuds. The first was *The Gentlemen in White Hats, Dramatic Episodes in the History of the Texas Rangers*, published in 1934, and we acknowledge borrowing that title for this section. *Famous Texas Feuds*, published in 1936, ushered in the Texas Rangers during such dramatic incidents as the Mason County War and the Horrell-Higgins Feud. Although the men of Reynolds' day had no official uniform and wore whatever headgear they chose, they did at times ride fast and fight hard; the mystique of the Texas Ranger almost demanded that he wear a white hat as the symbol of his being the "good guy." The outlaw and desperado wore the black hat in the collective mind of those of us who grew up with Saturday afternoon western "oaters" and black and white television. The Texas Ranger invariably rode the white horse as well.

When N. O. Reynolds was given command of Company E he also had the responsibility of selecting good, dependable men. His first muster roll, dated September 1, 1877, at Burnet, Burnet County, covered the period from that date until August 31, 1878. Enlistment was for one year, but due to the legislature's reduction in the force and other reasons, the company was not together nearly that long. James B. Gillett wrote that Major Jones was authorized to pick which men he wanted from other companies. "No other officer in the battalion," Gillett believed, "was ever accorded this privilege."

Reynolds was given a week or so to make his selection. When he had the company nearly complete he asked for James B. Gillett to round out the command. Gillett, then stationed on the Rio Grande, received orders to report to the adjutant general's office in Austin but was "nonplussed" as he did not know the meaning of the order. "Out on the frontier where we then were operating we seldom read newspapers or heard what the other companies were doing, so I did not even know Reynolds had captured the Horrell boys and had been commissioned to command Company E."

Reynolds' initial muster roll recorded the name of his two sergeants, his two corporals and initially nineteen men. Although not shown on the roll Reynolds received $75 per month; sergeants received $50; corporals and privates received $40. per month. Teamster Ben Johnson received but $20 per month. The pay roll also recorded reasons for stoppages of pay (loss of cuffs, or pistol for example) and of course the final balance due. The first document Reynolds prepared was a muster roll, listing twenty-four names beside his and minimal information, a "descriptive list" showing age, height, complexion, color of hair and eyes, occupation and place of nativity.

Reynolds' first muster roll carried the names of twenty privates, but at that time the company was not at full complement. Those twenty were:

Abram Anglin, A. H. Arnett, J. H. Bates, J. M. Braden, William Clements, C. R Connor, M. B. Davis, W. T. Derrick, J. H. Gibbs, J. B. Gillett, T. P. Gillespie, J. H. Grizzell, W. P. Hughes, D. L. Ligon, Henry Maltimore, M. S. Moreland, L. W. Rogers, H. J. Thomas, R. C. Ware, and J. R. Banister. Within a few months Company E was at full strength, with the following names added: B. F. Carter, W. L. Banister, Ben Johnson (teamster), L. R. Hughes, George M. Hughes, P. C. Jackson, R. L. Moore, George Herold, T. R. Johnson and C. L. Ware.

The following gentlemen made up Company E and were selected by Reynolds as good and dependable men. He left no memoranda book making note of the particular qualities to explain to later historians why he selected each of them, so one must assume he believed each could ride hard, could shoot accurately, would follow orders and would not bring disrepute upon the company. These qualities, indeed, were basically the job requirements for any Texas Ranger in the 1870s. And they, indeed, may have on occasion worn a white hat.

Abram Anglin

"A. Anglin" as he consistently signed his name, was the fourth son of Abram and Rebecca Anglin. The 1850 Limestone County census shows the family with little Abram eight months old. His Kentucky born father is listed as a farmer with $3,000 worth of personal estate. Mrs. Anglin was born in Tennessee and neither parent could read nor write. A decade later the Anglins were still living in Limestone County but the family's financial situation had improved considerably. Mr. Anglin claimed $9,400 worth of real estate and $15,700 worth of personal estate. Prior to joining Company E Anglin had served from July 11 to August 31, 1877, in Frio County under Captain Coldwell. On September 1 he was mustered into Reynolds' Company E as a private and served until he was honorably discharged on February 3, 1880. He then served under Reynolds' successor, Charles L. Nevill. Anglin was five-feet and six inches tall and gave his occupation as a farmer. Gillett later wrote that Anglin became a policeman in Austin but his name has not been found in any of the Austin city directories in that capacity. On May 6, 1880, he and Miss Jane Pierce were married in Austin by Christian Church minister W. E. Hall. On the following day the *Daily Democratic Statesman* reported their marriage with considerable humor, pointing out there was "certainly a revival in the matrimonial market" as two other couples were married in the same evening. The Anglins and one other couple were employed in the Lunatic Asylum but—smirked the *Statesman*—neither that couple nor the Anglins were inmates. Later, in the 1885–1886 Austin city directory the Anglins are shown to be still employed there. Anglin was listed as an "outside steward or head farmer state Lunatic Asylum" and "Janie" Anglin as "supervisoress" in the asylum. While Anglin was acting as supervisor A. J. Garrett escaped, but Anglin pursued him and located him in Robertson County and returned him to the asylum without difficulty. Perhaps Gillett was aware of this incident and considered this to be a policeman's duty as part of Anglin's regular work.

According to his obituary, after his Ranger service Anglin spent "more than twenty years of his life" in Mexico, although it does not say in what capacity. His obituary also states he was an Austin policeman, and a policeman at Groesbeck, Limestone County, as well. Anglin, called "Goach" by his friends, was at his place of business when death took him on February 3, 1916. He had been an Odd Fellow for more than thirty years, affiliated with the Groesbeck Lodge No. 499. He is buried in the Faulkenberry Cemetery of Groesbeck, beside his wife Janie (November 23, 1854-November 1, 1920) and the nickname "Goach" is on his headstone.

Sources: 1850 Limestone County census, 369 and 1860 census, 352; 1880 Travis County census, 100; Ranger Service Records; *Daily Democratic Statesman,* May 7, 1880, April 23, and June 26, 1884; *Morrison & Fourmy's General Directory of the City of Austin, 1885–86*, 63; the *Groesbeck Journal*, February 10, 1916.

Albert Henry Arnett

Arnett was born in Burnet County on August 5, 1856. Apparently his father, Colin C. Arnett, died early, perhaps in the war, as in the 1870 census his mother, Elizabeth (Warren) Arnett is shown to be head of household. She was born in Tennessee and in that year she claimed $2,000 worth of real estate and $200 worth of personal estate. Albert Henry Arnett had five siblings listed in that census, ranging in age from David, the oldest at twenty-three, to Joseph, eight years, and all born in Texas. Albert Henry was listed as working on the family farm. The next family and dwelling enumerated was that of George C. Arnett, probably the oldest son of Elizabeth Arnett. Curiously the next family shown is that of S. W. Moreland, whose son Millard S. also became a Reynolds Ranger. No books or articles have been written about Arnett's contributions to the establishment of law and order to Texas and his name is essentially forgotten, only a name appearing on Reynolds' muster roll.

Arnett first joined the Ranger service on May 30, 1874, and served under Capt. William J. Maltby in Company E through December 12, 1874. He then served under Capt. Berch S. Foster, then commander of Company E, from September 1, 1875, through August 31, 1876. He was then mustered into Reynolds' company on September 1, 1877, and served until his resignation. Major Jones issued Special Order No. 117 on January 7, 1878, allowing Arnett to be honorably discharged at his own request, "on account of having important business at home which requires his personal attention."

Following his service to Texas, Arnett relocated to Dickinson, Stark County, North Dakota, where he lived for twenty-seven years. He married Caroline "Carrie" Louise Dobson on February 17, 1887, in Dickinson. The bride was born in June 1862 in New York. The 1900 federal census shows the Arnetts having been married for thirteen years and having five children, all living. They were Lucy, Albert, James, Warren, and Olive, all North Dakota born. Arnett was listed as a "Stockman." A decade later, still in Stark County, Arnett is listed as president of a bank. The children now have a younger sibling, Catherine L., five years old. Sometime during the next decade the family moved to Wyoming, as his pension, filed on July 20, 1917, shows him residing in Big Horn County. In the 1920 census he is no longer shown to be a bank president but now is an "Oil man." When he left Wyoming is not known but he died August 4, 1943, in San Leandro, California, and is buried there in Mountain View Cemetery.

Sources: 1870 Burnet County census, 251; 1900 Stark County, North Dakota census, E.D. # 163, Sheet 134; 1910 Stark County census, E.D. # 162, sheet 9; 1920 Big Horn County census, E.D. # 1, sheet 16; Declaration for Survivor's Pension—Indian Wars, *Index to Pension Applications for Indian Wars Service between 1817 and 1898*, transcribed by Virgil D. White (Waynesboro, Tennessee: The National Historical Publishing Company, 1997), 23; Declaration for Survivor's Pension, Texas State Archives.

John Riley Banister

John R. Banister was born in Camden County, Missouri, May 24, 1854, the eldest son of William Lawrence and Mary Ellen (Buchanan) Banister. In 1867 John and his younger brother William Lawrence ran away from home and first "settled" in Texas. As cowboys they made several trips up the trail to Kansas cattle markets. John served in Company E from October 9, 1877, until February 29, 1880. He was a Railroad Officer for the Santa Fe Railroad and a Special Officer for the U.S. Treasury Department from 1890 to 1898. John then became Chief Inspector for the Texas Cattle Raiser's Association, becoming their first field inspector from 1898 until 1914. Banister's first wife was Mary Ellen Walker, the couple being joined together in November 1892. Mrs. Banister died ten years later on September 14, 1892, leaving him with four small children. He then married Emma Susan Daugherty on September 21, 1894. He was elected sheriff of Coleman County and was in office when he died. Upon his death, his wife Emma was appointed to the position on August 5, 1918. She served until November 5, 1918, having been the first woman sheriff in the history of the State of Texas.

In the Santa Anna City Cemetery in Coleman County is a state historical marker at the grave of John R. Banister, installed in 1964 and which reads as follows:

John R. Banister
(May 24, 1854–Aug, 2, 1918)

John Banister left home in 1867 and came to Texas. He received training as a cowboy and participated in several cattle drives to Northern Markets. Banister served with his brother, Will, as a Texas Ranger and participated in the Capture of outlaw Sam Bass. Other contributions to the state included his service as a railway officer, inspector for the cattle raisers' association, and Coleman County sheriff.

Sources: Ranger Service Records; "The John R. Banister Family" by Leona Bruce in *A History of Coleman County and its People,* vol. 1 (San Angelo, Texas: Anchor Publishing Company, 1986), 398–99; White: *Index to Pension Applications*, 36; Declaration for Survivor's Pension, Texas State Archives; Leona Bruce, *Banister Was There* (Fort Worth: Branch-Smith, Inc.,) 1968. The late Leona Bruce was the daughter of John Riley Banister.

William L. Banister

William Lawrence Banister, John R.'s younger brother, was born on September 12, 1856, in Camden County, Missouri. In their early years both boys ran away from home "to satisfy a long standing desire to go to Texas." Upon reaching Texas both boys stayed with a rancher and his family in Menard County. They both went up the trail several times. Will enlisted in the Rangers at Bear Creek, Kimble County, in Company E on November 20, 1877, and served under Reynolds until transferring to Capt. Ira Long's Company B on May 13, 1880. Curiously, alongside Banister's name on the muster roll for occupation is written "Loafer." He resigned from the service on November 30, 1880, at Camp Hackberry in Mitchell County. While on duty at San Saba he met Virginia Rebecca Daniels whom he married on February 24, 1881, in San Saba. Following his Ranger service Banister ranched in the Texas Panhandle but lost his herd in a severe winter, which forced him to retire from the cattle industry. He then moved to Coleman County. He died in Temple, Bell County, on January 4, 1921. His wife preceded him in death on February 9, 1913. Both are buried in San Saba.

Sources: See John R. Banister; Declaration for Survivor's Pension; Obituary, "Man in Last Fight with Sam Bass Died Recently in Temple," *Santa Anna News* (Santa Anna, Texas), January 14, 1921.

J. H. Bates

Bates was from Dade County, Georgia, and first gained experience as a Ranger under Berch S. Foster, joining at Coleman City on May 31 and serving through August 31, 1877. He was twenty-five years old when he mustered in at Burnet in "Major" Reynolds' company. He gave his previous occupation as farmer. Bates served under Reynolds continually until March 31, 1879.

Sources: Texas Ranger Service records.

J. M. Braden

Braden was born on March 8, 1851, in Giles County, Tennessee. In the 1860 Giles County census there is a nine-year-old James W. Braden who is perhaps the future Ranger, the "W" and "M" easily mistaken due to the penmanship of the census enumerator. If so Braden was the son of Washington and Mary E. Braden, parents of a large farming family. Existing Ranger records reveal Braden was mustered in at Coleman City in Berch S. Foster's Company B on January 15 and served until August 31, 1877. He then was mustered into Reynolds' Company E as a private on September 1 and served until October 10 by Special Order No. 103. His pension application was completed on May 25, 1917, but it was rejected as there was "no evidence that service was rendered in defense of the frontier of Texas against Indian depredations." Following his Ranger service Braden lived in Austin and gave his occupation as "automobile service industry."

Sources: 1860 Giles County, Tennessee census, 23; White, *Index to Pension Applications*, 85; Ranger Service Records; Declaration for Survivor's Pension, Texas State Archives.

Benjamin Franklin Carter

B. F. Carter was born near Salina, Jackson County, Tennessee, on May 11, 1848, the second son of Jesse and Mary Sims Carter. A younger brother, Parish Sims Carter, also served under Reynolds and then under C. L. Nevill, joining Lieutenant Reynolds on September 1, 1878. B. F. Carter married Louise Parilee Perry on December 17, 1884, at Baby Head, Llano County. The couple lived on a farm north of Lone Grove, Llano County and had four children: Josie, Willie, Vollie, and Ida. One record shows Carter first served in Company C under Captain J. C. Sparks from January 18 to August 31, 1877, before joining Reynolds' company. Reynolds' first muster roll shows he was not mustered in until October 21, serving until November 30, 1877. Carter died at Llano on May 6, 1918. His wife survived him until February 21, 1940. B. F. and his wife L. P. Carter are both buried in Board Branch Cemetery near Lone Grove.

Sources: Ranger Service records; Pension Application # 14124; *Llano County Family Album: A History* (NP: Taylor Publishing Company, 1989), 84–85. *Cemeteries of Llano County, Texas* (Llano: Wade-Smith Genealogy Service, 1990), 41.

Parish Sims Carter

P. S. "Dock" Carter was born in Jackson County, Tennessee, on June 24, 1854, and died in Gorman, Eastland County, Texas, on December 30, 1933. Carter joined Reynolds' Company E on September 1, 1878, and served until August 31, 1880, then served under Capt. Charles L. Nevill. He retired from the Ranger service on August 31, 1880 at Fort Davis, Texas. P. S. Carter married Rebecca Annie Havens on February 27, 1881, in Llano County and farmed north of Lone Grove until 1907 when they moved to Gorman. P.S. Carter is probably buried in the Baby Head Cemetery in Llano County, as his parents are buried there in marked graves. No marked grave for P. S. Carter nor for his wife has been discovered.

Sources: See Benjamin Franklin Carter; Ranger Service Records.

William T. Clements

Clements' origins are obscure. Gillett wrote that Clements was born and raised in Brown County, Texas, but his initial enlistment records shows he was from Rusk County, Texas. He was described as five-feet, nine-inches tall with fair complexion, blue eyes, and light-colored hair. Gillett recalled him as "a perfect blonde," nearly six feet tall, "of a quiet disposition, not inclined to talk much, but friendly and sociable." He was first mustered into Ranger service on June 1, 1875, by Captain D. W. Roberts in Menard County for a period of three months. He was then nineteen years of age. Gillett considered him the best marksman in the company, having been raised in frontier conditions in which people "were compelled to almost sleep with their guns and pistols in their hands." If this is true, then Brown County was much more of a frontier county than Rusk. He did attract attention by using a Smith & Wesson pistol instead of a Colt 45, "which nearly all Rangers used." In 1880 he was serving with Captain Roberts and is enumerated on the Menard County census as a "soldier" with the "State Military." He is shown to be twenty-four years of age, suggesting a birth year of 1856. In 1885 Clements operated a saloon in Junction, Kimble County. One of his bartenders, W. W. Baker, became involved in an argument with freighter-gambler George Graves. Clements found Graves in the Star Saloon; the confrontation ended when hot words turned to violence. Clements killed Graves and was later tried and acquitted. Clements married Amanda Clements (no relation), the daughter of Joseph Hardin Clements, who was a first cousin of John Wesley Hardin. Gillett recalled in 1924 that William T. Clements was a very healthy individual "never sick until some twenty years ago [when] he was stricken with pneumonia and died within twenty-four hours."

Sources: J. B. Gillett, "'Slick' Clements Was a Good Marksman," *Frontier Times*, February 1924, 17–18; Muster Roll of Company D, Frontier Battalion, Camp Saline, Captain D. W. Roberts; Bill C. James and Mary Kay Shannon, *Sheriff A. J. Royal: Fort Stockton, Texas* (Wolfe City, Texas: Henington Publishing Company, 1984, 1987), 2–3. Correspondence from Robert W. Stephens, March 23, 2000.

Christian Rasor Connor

Christian Rasor Connor was born in Alabama on April 11, 1850, the fourth of six children born to Merriwether Lewis and Sarah Ann Jane Rasor Connor. Six years later the family was living in Madison County, Texas. In 1870 Connor was living with the Robert Westmoreland family, a farming family of Madison County. Connor was then nineteen years of age with no specific occupation shown but he certainly helped out on the farm. On July 11, 1876, he joined Capt. Neal Coldwell's Company A in Frio County, then transferred to Reynolds' Company E on August 31, 1877. He served with Reynolds until his resignation at Camp Contrary in Kerr County on November 30, 1878. By 1880 he was married and farming in Madison County, living with his wife and three children: Rube W., Hope C., and Travis Steele. Connor died at Madisonville on January 23, 1916, survived by his wife Belle and children. His grave is marked.

Sources: Robert W. Stephens, *Texas Ranger Sketches*, 39–43; White, *Index to Pension Applications*, 168; Josephine Connor Wills, "The Connors," *A History of Madison County, Texas* (Madisonville, Texas: Madison County Historical Commission, 1994), 192–93; Patsy Westmoreland Strawther, "Merriwether Lewis Connor," *A History of Madison County, Texas*, vol. 2 (Madisonville, Texas: Madison County Historical Commission, 1997), 73; 1860 Madison County census, 447; 1870 census, 319; 1880 census, 307 and 1900 census, E.D. # 29, Sheet 17; interview with Patsy W. Strawther, May 24, 2002. Connor's proper name, Christian Rasor, has proven to be problematic with numerous authors. The pages of the family Bible, an 1885 edition from the American Bible Society, read: "*Christian Rasor Connor* son of Merriwether L. Connor and Sarah A. J. his wife was born on the 11th day of April 1850." Copies provided by Patsy W. Strawther and correspondence from her to Parsons, May 29, 2002.

M. B. Davis

At the age of thirty-three, when mustered in on September 1, 1877, by Major Jones, Mervyn Bathurst Davis was the oldest man in the company.

He was from Virginia, born there on October 14, 1844. During the Civil War he served in Company E, 59th Infantry and was then transferred to Company G, 10th Virginia Cavalry, "serving under Gen. Lee." Davis began his Texas career in journalism, serving as a newspaper reporter on the staff of the *Waco Daily Reporter* in 1873. He then left for Austin, where he determined to join the Ranger force, and at Camp Bear Creek on September 1, 1877, joined Reynolds' command and served until November 30, 1877. Davis was discharged on that date by Special Order No. 111, due to the Texas State Legislature's reduction in force. He later served under Captain Roberts from January 31 through March 31, 1878, and was honorably discharged on that date. During his service he provided several lengthy letters, which were published in the *Galveston Daily News*. The content of the letters focused on his experiences with the Rangers, each letter signed simply "Mervyn." Following his brief career as a Texas Ranger he found further success in the newspaper field with Dallas and Fort Worth journals, and then finally became a leading force in McLennan County, with Waco the county seat. During his successful journalism career he was "aided materially in organizing the Texas Humane Society" and was made a representative in Texas of the National Audubon Society. Captain M. B. Davis died June 18, 1912, in Waco, survived by his wife, children, and grandchildren. On Saturday, May 21, 2005, a Confederate marker was unveiled at his grave in Waco's Oakwood Cemetery. The ceremony included presentation of the colors by Boy Scout Troop # 497, Baylor University; opening and closing prayers by Bro. Joel Densman of Prairie Lea, Texas; opening remarks by Byron Johnson, Director of the Texas Ranger Hall of Fame and Museum; and additional remarks courtesy John A. Stovall of Tarleton State University; Rick Miller of Harker Heights, Texas, Nada Wareham, Regional Representative of the Audubon Texas Board. Unveiling was done by Byron Johnson and John A. Stovall.

Sources: White, *Index to Pension Applications*, 204; Ranger Service Record; *Dallas Morning News*, June 19, 1912; Application for Widow's Pension # 23364; *Waco Daily Times Herald*, June 18–20, 1912; 1880 Bexar County census, 77; 1900 McLennan County census, E.D. # 75, Sheet 14. Program of M. B. Davis marker unveiling.

William T. Derrick

Derrick was among the tallest men in the company, if not the Frontier Battalion, at six-foot, two inches. From Mississippi, he gave his age as twenty-eight when mustered in on September 1, 1877. Prior to serving under Reynolds he was a private in Company C under John C. Sparks, mustered in December 15, 1876, and discharged August 31, 1877. After Reynolds' resignation he continued serving under C. L. Nevill. His record shows he served continually from December 15, 1876, until his honorable discharge on November 30, 1879. Major Jones wrote out Special Order No. 37 on November 29, 1879, that he be discharged at his own request "for the purpose of getting married" to take effect on November 30, 1879. When the 1880 census was conducted W. T. Derrick was shown to be married to a Texas-born woman, Melissa ("Malissy"), twenty-one. They were farming in Llano County. William T. Derrick died on May 7, 1893, at La Luz, New Mexico Territory and was survived by his widow Melissa Jarrell Derrick.

Sources: White, *Index to Pension Applications*, 214; 1880 Llano County Census, 527; Ranger Service Record.

John H. Gibbs

Gibbs gave Erath County, Texas, as his origin when he was mustered in as a private. He was twenty-four years of age. This may not be quite correct as when the Erath County census was conducted in July of 1860 four states were given as birthplaces for the four family members: father John H. Gibbs, a thirty-one-year-old grocer in Stephenville, born in South Carolina; his wife, "Philo" also thirty-one but from Tennessee; son John H. Gibbs, nine years old and born in Mississippi, and younger sister Nancy Jane, seven, born in Alabama.

Sources: Ranger Service Record; 1860 Erath County census, 124.

Thomas P. Gillespie

Gillespie was twenty-three years of age when he was mustered in on September 1, 1877, as a private in Company E. He had first joined Company

D on May 25, 1874, under the command of Lieutenant D. W. Roberts and was honorably discharged on May 25, 1875. His additional service was extensive, serving again under Roberts, then under Lieutenant J. M. Denton, then under Capt. Neal Coldwell. He served continually until his resignation April 30, 1879, under Reynolds.

Following his Ranger service Gillespie ranched near San Angelo in Tom Green County. Gillespie died at the age of seventy-two at the Fort Worth home of his nephew, Edward E. Bradley, on Friday June 11, 1926; he is buried in Fairmount Cemetery in San Angelo.

Sources: *Fort Worth Star-Telegram*, June 11, 1926; *Fort Worth Record Telegram*, June 12, 1926; *Dailey Standard*, San Angelo, June 11 and 13, 1926; White, *Index to Pension Applications*, 305.

James Buchanan Gillett

J. B. Gillett was mustered into Reynolds' command on September 1, 1877, with the rank of 2nd Corporal. He remains among the best known Texas Rangers due to his popular autobiography, *Six Years With the Texas Rangers,* first published in 1921. He was born in Austin on November 4, 1856, the son of James S. and Elizabeth Harper Gillett, and died on June 11, 1937, in a hospital in Temple, Texas. He is buried at Marfa, Presidio County. The *El Paso Times* described him as "one of the most famous of the early Texas Rangers, the bulwark of law and order in the bloody days of the early Texas Rangers." Following his Ranger career he was City Marshal of El Paso from the spring of 1882 until April 1, 1885. He was elected sheriff of Brewster County on November 4, 1890, and served until November 8, 1892. He then managed the G-4 Ranch in Brewster County, then operated his own ranch, becoming a successful cattleman near Marfa.

During the administration of Governor Ross S. Sterling (1931–1933) and of Adjutant General W. W. Sterling Gillett was honored with an appointment as Captain of all Texas Rangers for life "the only person ever to receive that honor." Besides the autobiography he contributed numerous articles to the popular *Frontier Times* magazine of J. Marvin

Hunter. At his death Gillett was survived by his widow, two sons, Milton and Harper, and three daughters, Mrs. G. W. Evans Jr., Mrs. Lee Evans, and Mrs. Lou Wilson.

Sources: J. Marvin Hunter, "Captain James B. Gillett Passes On," *Frontier Times*, August 1937, 489–94; Sammy Tise, *Texas County Sheriffs*, 67; *El Paso Times*, June 13, 1937; *Big Bend Sentinel* (Marfa) June 18, 1937.

J. H. Grizzell

John Henry Grizzell was born January 22, 1856, at Idabel (Mt. Ida?), Arkansas, the son of James and Nancy Grizzell. By 1858 the family had located in Lampasas County, as younger sister Josephine, born in 1858, was Texas born. Twenty-one years of age when mustered into the command, he had already worked with the Horrells. His service with the Rangers was brief: mustering in at Camp Bear Creek on September 1 and receiving his honorable discharge by Special Order No. 111 on November 30, 1877. He had earned $120 for his service, but owed the state $28 for his Winchester, $13.50 for his Colt pistol, $2.10 for sidelines, "hopples" (what we'd call "hobbles" today) and horse shoeing and nails and $5.50 to John R. Banister, thus leaving the service with $49.10. On October 21, 1879, he married Martha E. Horrell, the widow of Merritt Horrell, at Palestine, Texas. John's sisters, Sarah A., Artemisa, and Martha V. married Horrell brothers: John W., James Martin, and Benjamin F., respectively. John's brother, James Daniel, married Nancy J. Horrell, an aunt to the Horrell brothers; another brother, Samuel Hicks Grizzell, married Louisa Bates, another aunt to the Horrells. In 1880 he and his wife and two step-children, Merritt and Lula Horrell, were residing in Taylor County, Texas, farming and keeping house. This census shows his birthplace as Texas, contrary to the muster roll showing his birthplace as Arkansas. Grizzell died on February 21, 1941 in Wilson, Oklahoma; his wife had earlier died there on January 25, 1935, as the result of a household fire. John and Martha Grizzell are buried in the Hewitt Cemetery near Wilson. Their graves are marked.

Sources: Correspondence from Jeff Jackson, June 15, 1999; Ranger Service Records; *Daily Ardmoreite*, Ardmore, Oklahoma, January 27, 1935, and February 27, 1941; *Wilson Post-Dispatch Democrat*, February 27, 1941; 1870 Lampasas County Census, 406; 1880 Taylor County, Texas census, 272.

George Herold

George Herold listed "Blacksmith" as his occupation when he transferred from Company B on May 11, 1878, to Company E. His name appears as "Heorold" on the muster rolls but his children used the "Herold" spelling. He was illiterate, which no doubt caused some confusion as to the name's proper spelling. He was born May 9, 1840, near Richmond, Virginia, but was in Texas prior to the Civil War. He enlisted in Captain T. T. Teel's Company of Texas State Troops in 1861; following the war he resided in San Antonio. In 1879 he enlisted in a "Frontier Force" unit and soon thereafter was City Marshal of Laredo. When enlisting in Dan W. Roberts' Company D on October 16, 1877, he resided in San Antonio and gave his occupation as a blacksmith. He served under Reynolds from May 11 to August 1, 1878, then served under Lt. George W. Baylor in Detachment C from September 12 to December 26, 1879. He married Virginia Garcia about 1867 and next Ojina Garza in 1873, both in San Antonio. His third marriage was to Jesusita Saiz in 1884 and last to Mrs. Manuela Larroque Gallardo in El Paso in 1899. Herold served as a scout in the U.S. Army but details are lacking as to the exact nature of that service. One obituary stated he was involved in the capture of Geronimo while serving under General Nelson A. Miles. At the time of his death Herold "had six bullet wounds in his body as evidence of his activity in the Civil War and in helping to put Texas horsethieves out of business in the early days when he was a ranger." Herold died in El Paso on December 12, 1917, and is buried in the Confederate plot of the Evergreen Cemetery.

Sources: Robert W. Stephens, *Texas Ranger Sketches*, 59–61; White, *Index to Pension Applications*, 373; *El Paso Morning Times*, December 13, 1917.

George Madison Hughes

Hughes gave his occupation as a carpenter and claimed Ashe County, North Carolina, as his birthplace. The 1860 Ashe County census shows the Thomas and Rachel "Hughs" family, the head of household a shoemaker, with between five and eight children, impossible to determine as the names of two are blurred and one crossed out by enumerator W. H. Gentrey, suggesting he erred and attempted to correct his mistakes. There is a twelve-year-old [?] George listed, who is the future Ranger. Hughes, nicknamed "Hog" according to Gillett, was twenty-six when mustered in by Lieutenant Reynolds at Camp Steele in Kimble County on March 17, 1878. In 1879–1880 he was serving in Company D under D. W. Roberts. Hughes married Sarah "Sallie" Evelyn on October 22, 1882, in Junction, Kimble County. The 1900 Kimble County census shows Hughes, born in October 1853, and his wife Sallie, age forty-three, and their ten children ranging in age from sixteen years down to one-year-old. He owned his own farm, free of mortgage. The family removed to New Mexico in 1902, settling on the Rio Bonito. In 1907 they moved to Carrizozo in Lincoln County. George M. Hughes died suddenly in his home from a heart attack on November 7, 1916. The funeral service was held in his home followed by interment in the Evergreen Cemetery in Carrizozo. His grave is marked. His widow, born January 22, 1855, survived until November 1, 1939, passing away at the age of eighty-five.

Sources: White, *Index to Pension Applications*, 402; 1860 Ashe County, North Carolina census, 802–03 (hand written number) and 491–492 stamped numbers; Gillett, 119; 1900 Kimble County census, E.D. #45, sheet 11; *Carrizozo Outlook*, November 10, 1916 and November 3, 1939.

Lowe R. Hughes

Lowe R. Hughes was from Etowah County, Alabama, born about 1853. He gave his occupation as farmer when mustered in by Reynolds in Kimble County on March 13, 1878. In 1880 he was one of several "State Rangers" when enumerated by Richard A. Boyce on June 3 for the Travis

County census, giving his age as twenty-seven and from Alabama. Since they were enumerated as a group perhaps they were in Austin delivering prisoners or guarding the jail. He resigned from the service on August 31, 1880. He married Elizabeth Belle Mason of Bagdad, Williamson County; but shortly thereafter Hughes died on January 26, 1881. On May 31, 2010, a Texas Ranger Memorial Cross was dedicated at his grave in the Bagdad Cemetery near Leander, Texas, Williamson County. This was sponsored by the Martin Wells Chapter of the DRT and the Former Texas Rangers Association.

Sources: 1880 Travis County census, 30; Ranger Service Records; Gillett, 119; program for the dedication of the Texas Ranger Cross.

William Parker Hughes

William P. Hughes was one of two brothers who joined the Rangers, the most famous being John R. Hughes who served from 1887 to 1915. William Hughes was mustered into Company E on September 1, 1877, as a private and served until November 30, 1877. Hughes was born in Salem, Illinois, on October 14, 1857. While still a youngster he moved with his family to Mound City, Kansas, and thirteen years later to Independence, Kansas. After receiving a good education he entered a newspaper office to learn the printer's trade. He applied himself so diligently that at the age of fifteen he was granted membership in the Typographical Union. To gain further knowledge of the trade he traveled extensively in the United States and Canada and worked for various newspapers. Only nineteen when he joined Company E under N. O. Reynolds, he later wrote he was "only a kid, having spent the night of my 20th birthday patrolling the corridors of the old State Capitol building, it being understood there was danger of robbery of valuable papers in the Attorney General's office." He was in the service only three months when a reduction in force was required and he was honorably discharged by Special Order No. 111, the reason being his youth and lack of experience. He received his honorable discharge at Camp Bear Creek. Following his brief career in the Rangers he returned to the printer's trade, holding a position with the

Rocky Mountain News in Denver, and the *Laramie Times* in Wyoming. In June 1882 he married Miss Alice Murphy in Denver, and to their union three children were born. Soon afterwards he became assistant foreman of the *Morning Sentinel* in Eureka, Nevada. Then he purchased the *Los Gatos Mail* of Los Gatos, California, which he operated for eight years. Hughes also established the *Saratoga Sentinel* and the *Los Pinos Tribune*. In 1892 he went to the Spokane, Washington, area and was employed by the Spokane Falls & Northern Railway Company to start a newspaper in Northport. When the railroad was built only to Little Dalles, five miles from Northport, he moved his newspaper by ox cart and on July 4, 1892, printed the first issue of the *Northport News*. While at Northport he was named first postmaster, was elected mayor and appointed police judge. William Parker Hughes died on April 5, 1940, in Northport.

Sources: Ranger Service Records; *Northport News*, January 30, 1925, an autobiographical sketch by Hughes; obituary appearing in the same newspaper April 12, 1940; "Was a Texas Ranger Fifty Years Ago," a reminiscent letter written to *Frontier Times* editor J. Marvin Hunter in issue November 1927, 88; correspondence to author Parsons from Margaret Evans, Northport, January 14 and 29, 1977; *An Illustrated History of Stevens, Ferry, Okanogan and Chelan Counties, State of Washington* (Spokane: Western Historical Publishing Company, 1904), 236–34; *History of the City of Spokane and Spokane County Washington From Its Earliest Settlement to the Present Time,* vol. 3 (Spokane: The S. J. Clarke Publishing Company, 1912)., 559–60.

P. C. Jackson

From Alberfoll, Alabama, Peter C. Jackson, born on March 14, 1848, came to Texas "as a young man." An obituary stated he had enlisted in the Confederate Army "when just a boy to fight for the Southern cause." He was thirty-one when mustered into the Ranger service by Lieutenant Reynolds on April 9, 1878, at Camp Steele, Kimble County. He died February 24, 1930, in Lometa, Lampasas County, survived by his widow Florence E. Senterfitt Jackson. Married on November 23, 1879, they were the parents of nine children, three of whom died in their early years. Jackson was active in civic affairs and was a successful businessman, building the first cotton gin in Lampasas County, located at Senterfitt. In 1880 he was acting assistant marshal enumerating the Lampasas County census. He was also involved in the building of the first school in western Lampasas County. When the town of Senterfitt was moved to the railroad it was renamed Lometa. There Jackson and his wife established a hotel. While living at Lometa Jackson worked at railroad construction, ranching, and operating the hotel. He was a member of the Church of Christ and "is said to have lived faithful to the teachings of the Bible. He was honest in his dealings, and during his long life in and around Lometa had found many lasting and admiring friends."

Sources: White, *Index to Pension Applications*, 429; Jonnie Elzner, *Lamplights of Lampasas County, Texas* (Austin: Firm Foundation Publishing House, 1951), 58–59; "Prominent Lometa Citizen Died Monday" obituary in the *Lampasas Record*, February 27, 1930; 1880 Lampasas County census, enumerated by Jackson, 329.

Thomas R. Johnson

Johnson was another Georgia native, mustered in on September 1, 1878, at Camp Contrary, Kerr County, and served through November 30, 1878. He was described as thirty years of age when taking his oath, was five-feet, eleven inches tall with light hair, gray eyes, and fair complexion. His occupation is shown as "Ranger" suggesting he had seen prior service. He also served under Capt. Thomas Oglesby from September 1 to November 30, 1881.

Source: Ranger Service Records.

David L. Ligon

Another six-foot, two-inch-tall Texas Ranger, from Weekly County, Tennessee, Dave Ligon was twenty-nine when mustered in on September 1, 1877. The 1880 Howard County, Texas, census enumerated by Henry C.

Foster spells his name Lygon but Ranger service records show he spelled it "Ligon." At the time of the census he was a 2nd Corporal under Capt. Ira Long. Others then in the company who had earlier served under Reynolds included Richard C. Ware and both Banister brothers, John and Will. With Captain Long the muster roll carried the names of twenty-eight Rangers and two cooks.

Sources: Ranger Service Records; 1880 Howard County census, 404.

Henry Maltimore

Henry Maltimore was born in 1848 in Silver Creek Township, Greene County, Ohio, the sixth child and third son of Henry and Mary A. Maltimore. The family resided there in 1850 but it is unknown when Henry Maltimore moved to Texas. He was among the oldest of Company E, twenty-nine when mustered in as a private, the same age as given for Commander Reynolds. Maltimore gave "Ranger" as his occupation, as he had earlier served under Captain Roberts. He served until February 28, 1878.

Sources: Ranger Service Records; 1850 Greene County, Ohio, Census, 403.

R. L. Moore

Ransom L. Moore was mustered into Company E on May 2, 1878, in Austin by Major Jones. He was one of the few men in the command who was a native Texan, born in McLennan County and twenty-three years of age when joining. He served only briefly with the Rangers, his pay records showing service from May 30 through October 17, 1878. Less than a year later on September 4, 1879, he married Miss Fannie C. Neill in McLennan County. In 1880, he and his wife, then eighteen years old, were living in Waco; he was clerking in a store while she was keeping house. She died April 19, 1883, of heart disease at their home. Ransom L. Moore died June 8, 1890, and both are buried in Waco cemeteries.

Sources: Ranger Service Records; 1880 McLennan County census, 66; John M. Usry (compiler and editor) *Early Waco Obituaries and*

Various Related Items 1874–1908 (Waco Central Texas Genealogical Society), 88; *McLennan County, Texas Marriage Records,* vol. 2 (Waco: Central Texas Genealogical Society),44.

Millard S. Moreland

In 1870, Burnet County census enumerator W. W. Brooks first visited the home of Elizabeth Arnett, whose son Albert H. served under Reynolds, and then two dwellings later visited the dwelling of Samuel W. Moreland. In the latter family was thirteen-year-old Millard, the future Texas Ranger, working on the farm. This indicates he was born in 1856 in Tennessee. Samuel W., his father, was an early-day circuit riding Methodist preacher who also practiced medicine, was sixty years of age; his wife Mary P., was forty-eight. The eight children listed ranged in age from the first son, M. B., twenty-two, to six-year-old Samuel. All family members were born in Tennessee except the last two, Samuel and Mary, who were born in Texas. This would suggest the family had moved to Texas at least by 1858.

Millard S. Moreland first served in the Rangers under Captain W. J. Maltby, mustered in on May 30, 1874, and received an honorable discharge on December 12, 1874. Lieutenant Reynolds then mustered Moreland into Company E on September 1, 1877 as a private. During those three years out of the Ranger service Moreland probably returned to the farm. Surviving pay records show Moreland served continually from September 1, 1877, through May 31, 1878, and then again from September 1, 1878, through December 31, 1878. Rather than being out of service during those three months of June-August, it is more likely the particular pay record has been lost; in all likelihood he served continually from September 1, 1877, until discharged December 31, 1878. Moreland died in 1890 and is buried in the Bear Creek Cemetery at Bertram, Burnet County.

Sources: Ranger Service Records; 1870 Burnet County census, 251; "Moreland" by Kate Wolf and Mrs. Lewis Alexander in *Burnet County History, Family Histories*, vol. 2 (Burnet: Eakin Press, 1979), 216–17.

Henry W. McGhee

Henry McGhee was mustered on September 1, 1877, with the rank of 2nd Sergeant, twenty-four years of age, and height given as six-feet two inches tall. He was born in Lawrence County, Alabama, on January 1, 1854; the family moved to Texas shortly after the Civil War. Service records show he was appointed a 2nd Corporal in Company A, Major Jones's escort, on June 30, 1877. Presumably he served with Major Jones until transferred to Company E, mustered in on September 1, 1877, rising to the rank of sergeant. He received an honorable discharge from Major Jones on November 26, 1878, after Jones learned that instead of arresting Bob Mitchell in Lampasas for threatening another man's life, McGhee merely told Mitchell to get out of town. In 1880 a Henry McGhee, born in Alabama, was operating a saloon in Mason and it is believed this is the same man. Although his service record shows his age at twenty-four at the time of muster in 1877, suggesting a birth year of 1853, the Mason County census shows his age as twenty-five, suggesting a birth year of 1855. Henry Warren McGhee died in Brownwood, Brown County, on May 31, 1919 after "a long period of suffering with dropsy" and was survived by his widow Emma D. McGhee.

Sources: Texas Certificate of Death # 15074; 1880 Mason County census, 490; White, *Index to Pension Applications*, 529; Ranger Service Records; *Brownwood Bulletin*, June 2, 1919.

Charles L. Nevill

Charles Lilburn Nevill was the son of Zachariah L. and Ann Lewis Nevill, born at Carthage, Alabama, on April 6, 1855. Three years later the family moved to Fayette County, Texas. Nevill joined Captain C. R. Perry's Company D on May 25, 1874, and served until March 31, 1875. The "1875 Schedule of Inhabitants in the City of Austin" shows Nevill at home with his parents and nine younger siblings. He is listed as being twenty years old with no occupation given, although he probably helped in his father's mercantile store. His sister Irene Temperance married Nelson O. Reynolds on September 13, 1882, at the residence of her parents. Born September 10, 1862, she had just turned twenty. The marriage date may have been selected close to her birthday for the special occasion.

Nevill served under John M. Denton and Neal Coldwell in Company A from September 1, 1876, until December 15, 1876, and then under Reynolds from September 1, 1877, until August 31, 1879. He entered Company E with the rank of 1st Sergeant. He was one of the men arriving too late for the street fight at Round Rock, but on the following day it was to Nevill that the dying Bass surrendered. On September 1, 1879, he assumed command of Company E and became captain in the summer of 1881. Earlier that year he and George W. Baylor and other Rangers destroyed a band of Apaches in the Diablo Mountains of West Texas. On December 19, 1881, Nevill, rancher-surveyor John T. Gano, four Rangers, and two others made the first successful trip by boat down the Rio Grande through the canyons now incorporated in the Big Bend National Park. He resigned as captain on November 25, 1882, having been elected sheriff of Presidio County on November 7, 1882. He was re-elected November 4, 1884, and again on November 2, 1886, and served until November 6, 1888, having served six years. On June 4, 1883, he married Miss Sallie E. Crosson at Fort Davis, Texas. In 1889 they moved to San Antonio and for four years he was chief deputy sheriff, besides holding other offices. At the time of his death he was district clerk of Bexar County. The Nevills lived in San Antonio until his death on June 14, 1906, and he is buried in City Cemetery No. 6. He was survived by his parents, his wife, and eight children.

Sources: *San Antonio Daily Express*, June 13 and 15, 1906; *San Antonio Daily Light*, June 14, 1906; copy of Nevill Family Bible family birth, marriage, and death pages and genealogical material provided to authors courtesy the late Mrs. Bernice Lear; *A Twentieth Century History of Southern Texas*, vol. 1 (Chicago: The Lewis Publishing Company, 1907), 434–37; Ranger Service Records; 1875 City of Austin Census, archived in the Austin History Center.

Lowe W. Rogers

From Perry County, Alabama, Lowe W. Rogers was twenty-three when mustered into Company E. After his service with Reynolds he served under Captain D. W. Roberts. On June 14, 1880, he was with Roberts when the company was enumerated for the Menard County census by N. Q. Patterson. He is listed simply as L. W. Rogers, twenty-eight years old and a native of Alabama. Gillett referred to him as "Shape" Rogers with no explanation as to how he received that nickname.

Sources: 1880 Menard County census, 131. Rogers is one of twelve Rangers in the company; others who had served under Reynolds were William Clements and L. P. Sieker. Ranger Service Records.

Henry J. Thomas

Thomas first joined the Frontier Battalion under Capt. Ira Long on September 1, 1875, then nineteen years old. He was still with Company A one year later, serving under Lieut. John M. Denton. George W. Arrington and Nelson O. Reynolds were 1st and 2nd sergeants, respectively. Thomas must have been a good judge of horse flesh as when the Rangers' mounts were evaluated Thomas' was valued at $154, the highest in the company. Gillett recalled that when the Rangers moved John Wesley Hardin from the Travis County jail in 1877 there were between one and two thousand people watching. The Rangers were stationed outside the jail, and Gillett and Thomas were ordered to go in and bring Hardin out. "Heavily shackled and handcuffed, the prisoner walked very slowly between us. The boy who had sold fish and game on the streets of Austin was now guarding the most desperate criminal in Texas; it was glory enough for me."

A disastrous fire destroyed many businesses of Burnet on May 4, 1893, including the saddlery firm of H. J. Thomas, a $2,300 loss with insurance of only $1,000. In the Odd Fellows Cemetery at Burnet is found the grave of one H. J. Thomas, presumably Henry J. Thomas the Texas Ranger (April 2, 1856-April 17, 1897) and Sallie Thomas his wife, and other Thomas family members. If indeed this is the Texas Ranger then his parents were

John Preston and Amanda Melvina (Payne) Thomas. Unfortunately Henry Thomas left no known memoir of his service as a Texas Ranger during the frontier period. Ironically older brother Marshall Braxton Thomas was one of the key players in the Mason County War.

Sources: Ranger Service Records; Gillett, 125–26; *Burnet County Cemetery Records, 1852–1982*; Burnet County Historical Commission & Burnet County Heritage Society, comp. (Austin: Eakin Publications, Inc., 1988). Correspondence from Dave Johnson to Parsons, April 10, 2000; Personal notes from visit to Odd Fellow Cemetery, Burnet.

George F. Walker

The single document in George F. Walker's service record file shows he was mustered into Company E with the rank of 2nd Corporal on September 1 and served through October 15, 1877. At the time of muster he was twenty-one, six foot two, and from Jefferson County, Mississippi. In contrast Special Order No. 104 lists him to be discharged November 30, 1877.

Sources: Ranger Service Record and Muster Roll.

Charles L. Ware

C. L. Ware was the younger brother of more noted Richard C. Ware, son of Benjamin F. L. and Mary J. Ware, born July 9, 1859 in Floyd County, Georgia. He was mustered into Company E on August 14, 1878 at San Saba by Lieutenant Reynolds. When the first officials for the Fort Worth and Denver City Railroad were chosen Ware was named as livestock agent. He later repurchased the C Bar Ranch in Mills County, the ranch on which his parents had settled when they first came to Texas from Georgia. He once owned ranches in Dallam and Mitchell Counties but by the time of his death had disposed of all save the C Bar Ranch. An obituary states that at the time of his death he had in his possession a pistol used by brother Richard C. Ware in the fight with Sam Bass, as well as a pistol carried by Bass when he was killed. In 1900 he was a Live Stock Commissioner in Tarrant

County, living in Fort Worth with his wife Mamie, born in Texas in February 1868, and son Bryan, born in February 1892. They had been married for thirteen years. Ware died on August 11, 1925 (according to his head stone, but August 12 according to his official death certificate # 30804). He is buried alongside his wife Mamie B. Ware (February 6, 1868–November 2, 1925); his parents and his brother Richard, as well as numerous other Wares, rest in the Colorado City Cemetery in Mitchell County.

Sources: 1860 Campbell County, Georgia, census, 246; 1900 Tarrant County, Texas census, E.D. # 105 sheet no. 1; showing Ware's birth year as 1860; *Dallas Morning News*, August 13, 1925; *Fort Worth Star-Telegram*, August 12, 1925; *Colorado Record*, August 14, 1925; *Colorado City A.D. Cemetery, Mitchell County, Colorado City, Texas*, compiled by Jimmy and Pat Gifford (no date); see also Richard C. Ware.

Richard Clayton Ware

R. C. Ware, the son of Benjamin F. L. and Mary Jane Ware, was born in Rome, Georgia, on November 11, 1851. By June of 1860 the family resided in Campbell County, Georgia, and by 1870 the family had moved on to Texas. Ware first joined Berch S. Foster's Company E on April 1, 1876, and then served under Reynolds and Nevill in Company E until March 4, 1880. He then transferred to Capt. Ira Long's Company B. On June 24, 1880, the company was in Howard County and enumerated by census taker Henry C. Foster. Long was "Captain Ranger Company" and each man was "Texas Ranger." Ware held the rank of 2nd Sergeant. With Long as captain, there were two sergeants, two corporals, and twenty-three privates. In addition there were two black men listed as "servant" and "Company Cook." Both Banister brothers were in this company at this time.

On January 10, 1881, Ware became the first sheriff of Mitchell County, county seat Colorado City. He was re-elected five times, serving until November January 26, 1892. From May 11, 1893, until January 26, 1898, Ware served as United States Marshal for the Western District of Texas. R. C. Ware died in Fort Worth on June 25, 1902, and was survived by his father and brother Benjamin T. who lived in Amarillo, brother

Charles L. of Dallas, and a sister who lived in Colorado City. An obituary appearing in the *Dallas Morning News* of June 27, 1902, identified Ware as "a gallant and fearless officer in his efforts to capture the notorious train robber and desperado, Sam Bass, who operated in Texas in the early days and who was finally killed by Capt. Ware at Round Rock in 1878 in a desperate battle." Ware is buried in the Colorado City Cemetery in Mitchell County alongside several family members, his father Benjamin F. L. Ware (February 21, 1827–August 27, 1908), his mother Mary Jane (July 20, 1831–December 23, 1904), brother Charles L. (July 9, 1859–August 11, 1925), brother James A. (July 27, 1856–January 1, 1888) brother William (September 24, 1849–January 29, 1886) and other family members. The state historical marker at Richard C. Ware's grave, erected in 1967, gives the date of his joining the Rangers incorrectly as 1878. The marker includes the statement that it was Ware's bullet that gave Bass the wound from which he died although that statement remains controversial.

Sources: *Dallas Morning News*, June 27, 1902 (obituary); 1860 Campbell County, Georgia, census, 246; 1880 Howard County, Texas, census, 404; Jimmy and Pat Gifford, comp., *City A.D. Cemetery, Mitchell County* (no date, no place); Robert W. Stephens, *Texas Ranger Sketches*, 159–62; correspondence to Stephens from U.S. Marshal's Service, December 16, 1970.

J. W. Warren

J. W. Warren, from Jefferson County, Mississippi, entered Company E with the rank of 1st Corporal. He was thirty years old. The *Proceedings of the First Annual Reunion of the Texas Rangers Association and Organization of the Texas Ranger Battalion, held in Austin on October 4, 1897*, included this paragraph: "Warren, J. W., Austin, Travis County, Co. E, Frontier Battalion, entered service at 31, now 51; four years in the service, during which time was on many scouts and Indian chases, and took part in several 'shooting scrapes' with white fugitives."

Sources: Ranger Service Records, *Proceedings . . . October 4, 1897*, copy provided courtesy Dan Lengefeld, Johnson City, Texas.

Texas State historical marker at the entrance of the Center Point Cemetery, listing the names of the 32 Texas Rangers buried there, including that of N. O Reynolds and his wife and other family members. *Photo by Parsons.*

APPENDIX B

Texas State Historical markers Relevant to N.O. Reynolds' Career

Texas is famous for its pride in the state's history, as revealed in the high number of historical markers stretched along the highways of the state. N. O. Reynolds' name appears on several, and there are others that refer to his command. The following is the text from those markers which mention either Reynolds by name or his work. There may be others. Our thanks to Claude Dooley and Betty Dooley for their outstanding reference work, *Why Stop? A Guide to Texas Historical Roadside Markers*. Each of the below have easily been found and visited thanks to their directions.

Edwards County
Stopping Place on
Ft. Clark–Ft. McKavett
Military Road

One of many roads connecting U.S. Cavalry's frontier posts. This route led south to Ft. Clark and north to Ft. McKavett, 1852–1883.

This spot, Paint Rock Springs, at head of South Llano River, was a natural midway rest stop, as it had abundant water.

Here too, Maj. John B. Jones, Frontier Battalion assembled in 1877 to begin the famous outlaw roundup, to make this area safe for settlement by ranchers.

Besides its army uses, this road was open to immigrants, cattle drovers, pioneer ranchers, mail carriers and freighters.

This marker was erected in 1967 and is located in U.S. Highway 377 at Paint Rock Springs, twenty-one miles northeast of Rocksprings.

Jack County
This is Lost Valley
(area about 20 sq. mi., Surrounding This Park)

Marked by "seven blue hills" in distance. To right is Spy Knob—a lookout during pioneer days.

Noted atrocity site: in 1857, the Cambren and Mason families, settlers, were victims of white renegades and Indians. On May 18, 1871, on western rim, teamsters of Warren Wagon Train were killed soon after Gen. W. T. Sherman of the U.S. Army had traveled safely through this valley. On July 12, 1874, the escort party of Maj. John B. Jones, Commander of the Frontier Battalion, Texas Rangers, was ambushed here, with two men killed. In later years, this has been peaceful farm-ranch area.

This marker was erected in 1970 and is located on U.S. Highway 281, twelve miles northwest in Carter Park.

Kerr County
The Dowdy Tragedy of 1878

The pioneer Dowdy family of Susan (1830–1913) and James Dowdy (1818–1900) moved from Goliad to Kerr County in 1878 and settled on Johnson Creek. Shortly after the family arrived, four of the Dowdy children, Alice, Martha, Susan, and James, were killed by Indians while tending sheep near their home. The attack occurred on Oct. 5, 1878, at a site about 3.5 miles northwest of present Ingram. The victims were buried the following day at Sunset Cemetery, northwest of Ingram. This incident was one of the last Indian raids in Kerr County.

This marker was erected in 1979 and is located on State Highway 27, seventeen miles northwest of Kerrville.

Kerr County
Center Point Cemetery

The earliest known settlers in the area were Mrs. Elizabeth Denton and her children and slaves, who arrived in 1852. They were joined in 1858 by the family of Dr. Charles Ganahl, who named the new community Zanzenburg, after his hometown in Austria. The town became known as Center Point in 1872, and settlers continued to move into the area.

In 1872 land was purchased for a church and cemetery on this site, and in 1881 two acres were added to the property to enlarge the cemetery. The church was moved off the property, and another land acquisition in 1901 increased the cemetery property to 5.3 acres.

Approximately 1,452 graves have been located here. The oldest marker is that of Lydia Burney (1795–1875). Many early pioneers and community leaders are buried here, as well as 32 Texas Rangers, whose names are: W. D. C. Burney; N. Coldwell; J. A. Gibbens; H. T. Hill; F.

L. Holloway; R. J. Irving, Sr.; R. J. Lange; J. H. Lane; S. T. Lane, Jr.; T. Lane; M. A. Lowrance; J. L. McElroy; S. G. McElroy; A. S. Moore; F. M. Moore; G. K. Moore; G. R. Moore; G. W. Moore; H. C. Moore; James Moore; J. T. Moore; M. F. Moore; D. C. Nowlin; J. C. Nowlin; R. W. Nowlin, P. Alonzo Rees; N. O. Reynolds; W. H. Wishworth; J. L. Sellers; A. J.Sowell; W. H.Witt; S. G. Wray.

This marker was erected in1986 and is located at the entrance to the Center Point Cemetery.

Kimble County
Old Bear Creek
Texas Ranger Camp
(300 yds S)

Established October 1877 as patrol base for Co. E, Frontier Battalion, Texas Rangers, on the lookout for Indians and outlaws along the Llano River. Area was popular refuge for cattle and horse thieves, murderers, mail robbers—and within a few weeks many were captured by the unit of 30 men commanded by Lt. N. O. Reynolds. The Rangers in 1878 helped fight off one of the last Indian raids in the area.

Ranger protection given from this camp (used until mid-1880s) opened the way for peaceful settlements in Kimble and nearby counties.

This marker was erected in 1966 and is located on U.S. 290/I-10, 4.3 miles northwest.

Kimble County
Teacup Mountain

Named for its peculiar formation. Probably used as a lookout post by both whites and Indians in pioneer days. Near here occurred the Indian killing of pioneer James Bradberry, Sr., in 1872, and the capture of a wanted man by Lt. N. O. Reynolds and four fellow Texas Rangers in 1878.

This marker was erected in 1967 and is located on U.S. 377, eight miles east of Junction.

Kimble County
Doom of the
Outlaws of Pegleg Station

Here the climax of a western track-down occurred on Jan. 18, 1878, when Texas Rangers killed suspected murderer Dick Dublin, member of a gang of outlaws.

Although a friend yelled for him to run, Dublin was shot (150 yds. S) as the intrepid James B. Gillett and 3 other Rangers rushed his hideout (60 yds. E).

Dick's brothers (Role and Dell), Mack Potter and Rube Boyce were captured after a partner of the gang turned informer.

Three of them (plus two others) were convicted Aug. 23–24, 1880, of the 1877 robbery of the U.S. mail at Pegleg Station.

This marker was erected in 1968 and is located on U.S. 377, 10.8 miles SW of Junction.

Lampasas
Horrell-Higgins Feud

The Horrell and Higgins families were among the early settlers of Lampasas County. Tom, Mart, Merritt, and Sam Horrell were accused of many crimes, including cattle rustling and murder. Pink Higgins was a cattleman and trail driver who, in1876, began accusing the Horrell brothers of stealing his cattle. On January 22, 1877, Pink Higgins shot and killed Merritt Horrell in the Gem Saloon. This was the beginning of s six-month battle between the Horrell brothers and Pink Higgins, Bob Mitchell, Bill Wren and their followers.

On March 26, Tom and Mart Horrell were ambushed on their way into Lampasas. Captain John C. Sparks of the Texas Rangers went in pursuit, but no one was captured. Higgins remained a fugitive, but eventually surrendered and was ordered to appear in court. On June 4, the Lampasas District Clerk's office was burglarized and District Court records were destroyed. Three days later, the biggest battle of the feud took place on the public square in Lampasas; one man from each side was killed.

Major John B. Jones, commander of the Texas Ranger Frontier Battalion, came to Lampasas and sent Sergeant N. O. Reynolds and a company of rangers out to capture the Horrells. The brothers were arrested and agreed to make peace by sending a letter of reconciliation to the Higgins party. The treaty was the formal end to one of the worst feuds in Texas history. What was perhaps the true termination of the feud came in 1878 in the town of Meridian, when Tom and Mart Horrell were murdered in their jail cell by a vigilante mob. Sam Horrell left Texas, resettled in Oregon and died of old age. Pink Higgins eventually settled near Spur in West Texas and went to work as a range detective.

This marker was erected on the courthouse lawn and was dedicated on Saturday, October 14, 2000.

Mason County
The Whorlie Well

Named for a victim in famous "Hoodoo War," provoked by cattle rustling in Mason County. John Whorlie (or Worley), a deputy sheriff, on May 13, 1875, lost a prisoner to a lynch mob. On Aug. 10, 1875, Whorlie was killed and scalped while working on this well. His killer was identified as Scott Cooley, a friend of the lynched man. Masonic burial for Whorlie was conducted by the McCulloch Lodge No. 273, A.F. & A.M. of which he was a member.

No one in Mason County was ever convicted for wrongdoing in the "Hoodoo War," but after 1876 law, order and peace were restored.

This marker was erected in 1971 and is located close to the downtown area of Mason. We might note here that in David Johnson's *Mason County "Hoo Doo" War, 1874–1902* the spelling is given as Wohrle, which is generally accepted as correct.

N. O. Reynolds

Lieutenant Nelson Orcelus Reynolds was a noted Texas Ranger, born in 1846 in Pennsylvania. Reynolds served in the Union Army during the Civil War. In 1874 he enlisted as a Texas Ranger in Blanco County. Reynolds captured the Horrell brothers and forced them to sign a peace treaty to end the feud with the Higgins faction. As a result, he was given command of the newly formed Company "E." Reynolds was later responsible for jailing, transporting, and guarding John Wesley Hardin for his trial in Comanche County. He retired from Ranger service in 1879 and later served as Lampasas County sheriff. He married Irene T. Reynolds in 1882. The couple had two children and lived in Center Point, where Reynolds was buried after his 1922 death.

This marker was erected in 2010 and is located at 106 Cane Lane across the road from the Center Point Cemetery. Marker is property of the state of Texas.

NOTES

Chapter 1: Continuing the Warrior Tradition

1. Standard Certificate of Death, # 8901, Bureau of Vital Statistics, Austin, Texas. The "warrior tradition" background can be traced to Eli Holcomb who was a corporal in Capt. Isaac Colton's company, David Brewer's Regiment in 1775 during the War for American Independence. His son, Sterling Holcomb, became the father of Louisa Holcomb who married Levi Taylor. Their daughter Betsy D. Taylor married Hiram Gillett Reynolds in 1846 (or 1849, date is uncertain) who were the parents of N. O. Reynolds. N. O. Reynolds' sister Edla Reynolds Rickwell, (#83528) provided lineage for the National Society of the Daughters of the American Revolution, *Lineage Book*, Editor Historian General Mary H. DeBolt., Vol. 84, 1910 , 200. Genealogical research courtesy Jean Shroyer and Donaly E. Brice.
2. U.S. Census: Hays County, Texas, 1880, 30–31; Caldwell County, 1900, Enumerator District (E. D.) # 1218, Sheet 9; Orange County, Texas, 1910, E.D. # 117, Sheet 18; Orange County, Texas, 1920, E.D. # 148, Sheet 18.
3. James B. Gillett, *Six Years With the Texas Rangers, 1875–1881*, 123, hereafter cited as "Gillett." There are numerous editions of this work, considered by many to be a Ranger classic. It was first printed by von Boeckmann-Jones in Austin in 1921, then reprinted by the Yale University Press in 1925, edited by Milo M. Quaife. This edition was then reprinted by the Lakeside Press of Chicago, Illinois, in 1943. In 1927, in collaboration with Howard Driggs, the World Book Company, Yonkers-on-Hudson, New York, printed an edition under the title *The Texas Rangers*. There have been later editions as well. Page references in this biography refer to the Lakeside Press edition of 1943.
4. U.S. Census, Bradford County, Pennsylvania, 1850, 74. Genealogist Pat Buck of Endicott, New York, suggests that Franklin Reynolds was the second son born to Hiram and Betsy Reynolds, born in February 1850, but did not survive past infancy. "Descendants of Hiram G. Reynolds" with correspondence, June 1993.
5. *Bradford Star* (Towanda, Pennsylvania), March 28, 1912. Obituary and photograph of the grave marker, courtesy Ms Pat Buck, Endicott, New York.

6. Kris Mize to Donaly E. Brice, July 13, 1994.
7. Information received from Gladys Savage regarding her uncle, N.O. Reynolds with correspondence from Kris Mize to Donaly E. Brice, July 13, 1994.
8. Charles Bent, ed., *History of Whiteside County, Illinois From Its First Settlement to the Present Time* (Facsimile edition, Morrison, IL: Sterling-Rock Falls Historical Society, 1877), 230–31.
9. Deed records: Grantor, Whiteside County, Illinois, Book 10, 303. Although the record shows the spelling as *Orcelus*, later Reynolds spelled his name as *Orselus*. See also Chuck Parsons' "Texas Ranger N. O. Reynolds' Lost Years" in the *Quarterly* of the National Association for Outlaw and Lawman History (NOLA) 26, no. 3 (July-September 2002): 34–38.
10. U.S. Census: Bradford County, Pennsylvania, 1870, 197; Whiteside County, Illinois, 1870, 144; Clement F. Heverly, *Pioneer and Patriot Families in Bradford County, Pennsylvania 1770–1800* (Towanda, PA: Bradford Star Printing, 1913), 325–26; H. C. Bradshaw, *History of Bradford County, Pennsylvania, With Biographical Sketches* (Chicago: S.B. Nelson & Company, 1891); data regarding Emma Reynolds' deafness from information received from Gladys Savage regarding her uncle N.O. Reynolds, courtesy Ms. Kris Mize. Emma Reynolds married Marble Benninger, who was also deaf. They had five girls, none of whom was hearing impaired. Gladys Savage was the daughter of Ella Alvira Reynolds and married Elbert Irvin Santee. Correspondence to Brice from Kris Mize, July 13, 1994.
11. Texas Centennial Historical Society, *The Texas Centennial Roster, 1836–1936* (San Antonio: Stationers Exchange, 1936), 16. Copy courtesy Candice DuCoin, Round Rock, Texas.
12. Gillett, 122.
13. Declaration for Pension, #1,168, 355, subscribed and sworn July 2, 1912, in Orange County, Texas. Charles Bent, who had been a lieutenant during the war in the 147th Illinois Infantry, wrote that the regiment was mustered out on January 20, 1866, and returned to Springfield where it was discharged in February, "being one of the last Illinois regiments to be discharged." Bent, 52.
14. Company Muster and Descriptive Roll: Orcelus Reynolds, National Archives, Washington, D.C. This record shows the date of Reynolds' enlistment as February 8, 1865.
15. *The War of the Rebellion: A Compilation of the Official Records of the Union and Confederate Armies* (Washington, D.C.: Government Printing Office, 1897), Series 1, Vol. 49, Part 1, 86. Colonel H. F. Sickles to Major S. B. Moe,

Assistant Adjutant-General, March 13, 1865, from Dalton, Georgia. Hereafter cited as *O.R.*

16. *O.R.,* 86. Sickles to Moe, March 14, 1865, from Dalton, Georgia.
17. *O.R.*, Series 1, Vol. 39, Part 3, 382. Maj. Benton D. Fox to Maj.-Gen. James B. Steedman, from Dalton, Georgia, October 20, 1864.
18. Company Muster Roll and Regimental Return of Thomas Polk Edmondson, National Archives, Washington, D.C. "Thomas Polk Edmondson" on Ancestry.com, no author cited but possibly Conway Gregory who is credited on this site as being the author of the accompanying poem, "North Georgia Scouts."
19. "Thomas Polk Edmondson"; *O.R.*, Series 1, Vol. 49, Part 2, 240; Brigadier-General H. M. Judah to Major S. B. Moe, April 5, 1865 from Dalton, Georgia.
20. Brigadier General J. N. Reece, *Report of the Adjutant General of the State of Illinois,* Vol. 7 (Springfield, IL: NP, 1900), 290.
21. Ibid., 275, 281.
22. Gillett, 122–23.
23. Although Edmondson has been forgotten, one admirer did compose a poem about him and his "scouts" entitled "North Georgia Scouts" apparently by Maurice Thompson, although this has been questioned. Conway Gregory is also cited as the author. The poem is comprised of fifteen quatrains. It concludes with these lines: "So, now you know just how it was/ We had our little fun,/ Speeding our horses to keep up/ With Tom Polk Edmondson." This was first published in *Century Magazine*, 1905. See *www.murraycountymuseum.com* website for complete poem.

Chapter 2: Joining the Frontier Battalion

1. Gladys Savage, niece of N. O. Reynolds, correspondence to Donaly E. Brice, July 13,1994; Declaration for Pension, #1,168, 355.
2. *Galveston Daily News,* June 25, 1886; *Bastrop Advertiser,* July 3, 1886.
3. Nelson O. Reynolds' Application for Pension. Curiously, Texas Ranger George W. Arrington also spent some time in Central America, but as a fugitive. On June 13, 1867, in Greensboro, Alabama, he killed Alex Webb following an argument; he then fled to Honduras where he remained a little over a year. Arrington, whose real name was John C. Orrick Jr., worked in various places in Texas, then drove a cattle herd to Brown County but quit to enlist in the Frontier Battalion, Company E, on September 1, 1875. Jerry Sinise, *George*

Washington Arrington: Civil War Spy, Texas Ranger, Sheriff and Rancher (Burnet, Texas: Eakin Press, 1979), 11–15.

4. Barry A. Crouch and Donaly E. Brice, *The Governor's Hounds: The Texas State Police, 1870–1873* (Austin: University of Texas Press, 2011), 1.
5. Petition to the Honorable Senators and Representatives. . . . Adjutant General Papers, Texas State Library, Austin, *San Marcos Times*, November 1, 8 and 22, 1873. San Marcos was not incorporated until June 30, 1877, by a majority of twenty-five out of a vote of 115. *West Texas Free Press*, San Marcos, July 7, 1877.
6. Alabama-born H. Alonzo McMeans became Hays County Treasurer. By 1880, only thirty-two years old, he had a wife, Texas-born D. Alice, and four daughters, ranging in age from seven years old to one year, all Texas born. Hays County census, enumerated June 12, 1880 by Calvin Wilkins, 31. Reynolds was enumerated on the same page as McMeans.
7. George H. Ward later entered the liquor business as did Reynolds. He was a young man to have the responsibility of a jail guard in 1873, as when the 1880 census was enumerated he was but twenty-six years old. He then was listed as a retail liquor dealer. Hays County, Texas, census, 31.
8. Arkansas-born John D. Hill remained in Hays County as by 1880 he was farming, had a wife, Annie, and three daughters ranging in age from six to two years. Hays County, Texas, census, 80.
9. James Jennings also remained in Hays County. In 1880 he is shown to be farming, thirty-eight years old, and having a wife, Sarah, and a daughter and a son. Hays County, Texas, census, 80.
10. Hays County Police Court Record, Book B, 157. Original in Hays County Court Archives, San Marcos, Texas.
11. *West Texas Free Press*, San Marcos, March 21, 1874. George T. McGehee was the foreman of the Grand Jury. Tennessee-born Zachariah P. Bugg, son of Robert Malone and Martha Laird McErwin Bugg, farmed when not acting as Hays County sheriff. His wife, Emma Jane Davis Bugg, died on May 14, 1874, and he remained a widower until his own death on April 20, 1887. He left two children to the world: Mattie and Ward Robert Bugg. Zach and Emma Bugg are both buried in the historic Pitts Cemetery four miles west of San Marcos. Their graves are marked. Z. P. Bugg's headstone relates he served as 2nd Lieutenant Company H, 23rd Regiment Texas Cavalry, C.S.A. 1880 Hays County Census, 24; Leslie P. Camp. "Edwin J. L. Green" in the *Quarterly* of the Hays County Historical and Genealogical Society, vol. 8, no. 1 (March 1974): 9–10. The *San Marcos Free Press* gave the briefest—but highly complimentary—notice

of his death: "Ex-Sheriff Z. P. Bugg died yesterday evening, after a lingering illness. The moral of his life is too well known to need repetition." See *San Marcos Free Press*, April 21, 1887.

12. *West Texas Free Press*, September 12, 1874 and April 10, 1875. Francis Stovall, et al., *Clear Springs and Limestone Ledges, A History of San Marcos and Hays County* (Austin: The Nortex Press, Eakin Publications, Hays County Historical Commission, 1985), 554.
13. *Lampasas Leader*, November 10, 1888.
14. *San Marcos Times*, September 27, 1873.
15. *Troy Gazette-Register*, Troy, Bradford County, Pennsylvania, June 20, 1913. The brief item identified the Ranger simply as "Orcelus Reynolds of Orange, Texas." He was visiting his sisters, Mrs. Burt Santee of Rushville, New York, and Mrs. E. A. Rockwell of Troy. They all visited their sister Mrs. M. Benninger.
16. The amount of state funds missing was $37, 434.67. In spite of State Police Capt. Leander H. McNelly pursuing him, Davidson escaped from Canada and ultimately settled in New Zealand. For a complete history of the creation and existence of the police force, see *The Governor's Hounds: The Texas State Police, 1870–1873* by Barry A. Crouch and Donaly E. Brice (Austin: The University of Texas Press, 2011).
17. Rick Miller, *Texas Ranger John B. Jones and the Frontier Battalion, 1874–1881* (Denton: University of North Texas Press, 2012).
18. *Daily Democratic Statesman* (Austin), May 9, 1874. Jones died July 19, 1881, and his remains were buried in Austin's historic Oakwood Cemetery. A huge angel monument marks his grave site.
19. Major John B. Jones, Major Commanding, May 1, 1874, Texas State Archives, Austin.
20. Ibid. In 1870 Ledbetter was thirty-five years old with a wife and five children. See 1870 Fayette County Census, 509. In 1897 he resided in San Saba County and attended the first Annual Reunion of the Texas Rangers Association. The proceedings of this meeting provided brief biographical sketches of some of those in attendance, having this to say, in part, about Ledbetter: "[F]irst lieutenant, Co. D, Frontier Battalion, previously commanded 'minute men'; entered service at age 30, now 54; never in a pitched battle with Indians, but took part in numerous 'little bruises' with them, and was once struck with an arrow." *Proceedings of the First Annual Reunion of the Texas Rangers Association and Organization of the Texas Ranger Battalion at Austin, Texas, October 4th, 1897*, 38. Copy provided by Dan Lengefeld, Johnson City, Texas.

21. "William Steele" in *The New Handbook of Texas*, Vol. 6, 79, no author given. Steele died on January 12, 1885, and is buried in Oakwood Cemetery in Austin.
22. Adj. Gen. William Steele, General Order No. 2, May 6, 1874.
23. For an extensive study of Newton H. Murray's career see "Plunk Murray: The Quantrill Guerrilla Who Became a Texas Ranger" by Duncan Hansen and Chuck Parsons in *A Reunion in Death: Gravesites of the Men Who Rode With William Clarke Quantrill*, Vol. 2 by Duncan E. Hansen (Independence, Missouri: Two Trails Publishing, [2003]), 129–42.
24. C. R. Perry Muster Roll, May 25, 1874. Perry was forty-six years old in 1870, with a wife and four children. 1870 Blanco County Census, 360.
25. Thomas Cutrer, "Cicero Rufus Perry" in *New Handbook*, Vol. 5, 157. Perry died in Johnson City, Texas, on October 7, 1898. Minnie Cox. "Rufus Perry, Texas Ranger" in *Heritage of Blanco County, Texas* (1987; repr., Dallas: Curtis Media, 1996), 194–97.
26. *Daily Democratic Statesman* (Austin), May 30, 1874.
27. Ibid.
28. Frank L. Britton, *Report of the Adjutant General of the State of Texas, for the Year 1872* (Austin: James P. Newcomb & Co., 1873), 200. "Roster of Officers and Men of Companies for Frontier Protection Organized in 1870."

Chapter 3: Removal of Cattle from their Accustomed Range

1. George Freeman to Adj. Gen. William Steele, May 18, 1874. Freeman's letter gave no clue as to why he chose to leave the service, writing simply: "I have the honor to inform you that I decline accepting the appointment [as 2nd lieutenant]." Written from Fredericksburg, Gillespie County, Adjutant General Papers, General Correspondence. Hereafter cited as A.G.P.
2. Captain C. R. Perry Monthly Return, June 25, 1874, written at Celery Springs, Menard County. A.G.P.
3. Wilson Hey to Gov. Richard Coke, June 25, 1874, Governor's Correspondence.
4. Sammy Tise, *Texas County Sheriffs* (Hallettsville, Texas: Tise Genealogical Research, 1989), 357. Hereafter cited as Tise. Clark served until October 1875.
5. Wilson Hey to Gov. Richard Coke, June 25, 1874, Governor's Correspondence.
6. *Dallas Weekly Herald*, July 18, 1874, citing a report from correspondent "Jack" at Jacksboro.

7. Major Jones to Adj. Gen. William Steele, July 14, 1874, written from "Headquarters Frontier Battalion Camp at Flat Top Mt. Young County Texas," in A.G.P.
8. Ibid.
9. Rick Miller, *Texas Ranger John B. Jones and the Frontier Battalion, 1874–1881*, 53 and 60.
10. Robert M. Utley, *Lone Star Justice: The First Century of the Texas Rangers* (New York: Oxford University Press, 2002), 150. Charles M. Robinson III wrote a one-volume history of the rangers, *The Men Who Wear the Star: The Story of the Texas Rangers*, but provided no clear analysis of the Lost Valley engagement, even giving the date of the engagement as June when it was clearly in July. Pages 174–75.
11. At least two members of the Frontier Battalion later recorded their recollections of this important engagement, both published by J. Marvin Hunter in his monthly publication *Frontier Times*. "Reminiscences of a Frontier Ranger" by Ed Carnal appeared in the December 1923 volume (Vol. 1, No. 3, 20–24). "The Loss [*sic*] Valley Fight" by Walter M. Robertson appeared in the issue of December 1929 (Vol. 7, No. 3, 100–105). Of interest accompanying this article appears a photograph of eight former rangers: S. P. Elkins, H. E. Conn, W. W. Lewis, J. M. Harkey, J. L. Bomer, Walter M. Robertson, D. W. Roberts, James B. Hawkins, then a resident of Montana (101). Carnal wrote that Major Jones' escort was composed of six men from each company, which would total thirty-six, whereas Robertson wrote that the escort was composed of seven men from each company. Z. T. Wattles—on August 22, 1874 in "Camp Near Fredericksburg" – wrote a lengthy account which was printed in the *Corsicana Observer* on September 2. Presumably Wattles sent this first-hand account to Corsicana as that was the home of Major Jones as well as several other men in the battalion who he referred to as "the boys." After describing the engagement, Wattles concluded his letter, "Boys from home all well, and send love to friends. We are resting for a few days on the Perdinallis [*sic*] river, having fine sport fishing. Ranging is a glorious thing when you learn to like it." This clipping is preserved in Record Group 401, Box 1158, Folder 17, Texas State Archives. Two other accounts of the Lost Valley Fight appear in James L. Haley's *The Buffalo War: The History of the Red River Uprising of 1874* (Austin: State House Press reprint, first published by Doubleday, 1976) and Rick Miller's *Texas Ranger John B. Jones and the Frontier Battalion, 1874–1881* (Denton: University of North Texas Press, 2012).
12. S. P. Elkins, providing a chapter in *Into the Setting Sun: A History of Coleman County* by Beatrice Grady Gay (No place, 1936?), 109. The same contribution

by Elkins appears in *Pioneer Days in the Southwest from 1850 to 1879: Thrilling Descriptions of Buffalo Hunting, Indian Fighting and Massacres, Cowboy Life and Home Building. Contributions by Charles Goodnight, Emanuel Dubbs, John A. Hart and others* (Guthrie, Oklahoma: The State Capital Company, 1909), 278. After leaving the Frontier Battalion, Elkins located in McLennan County, Texas where he farmed. In 1880 he was twenty-eight years old with a wife, Margaret, and two children. 1880 McLennan County Census, 128.

13. Details on the death of Cooley's parents appear in *John Ringo* by Dave Johnson (Stillwater, Oklahoma: Barbed Wire Press, 1996), 71 and revised edition *John Ringo: King of the Cowboys, His Life and Times from the Hoo Doo War to Tombstone* (Denton: University of North Texas Press, 2008), 74.
14. Captain Perry to Adj. Gen. William Steele, written from Menardville, July 24, A.G.P.
15. *Austin Daily Democratic Statesman*, July 12 and 28, 1874.
16. Ibid., August 16, 1874.
17. Monthly Return prepared by Daniel W. Roberts, prepared at Elm Creek, August 31, 1874, A.G.P.
18. Beatrice Grady Gay, *"Into the Setting Sun" A History of Coleman County*, 108.
19. Bob Alexander, *Winchester Warriors: Texas Rangers of Company D, 1874–1901* (Denton: University of North Texas Press, 2009), 56.
20. *Dallas Morning News*, October 15, 1925 (obituary) and research notes courtesy Norman Wayne Brown, Scurry County historian. Mann was born Robert Felix Mann on October 23, 1847, although his headstone in the Fairmount Cemetery in San Angelo indicates he was born in 1846. The official death certificate gives his cause of death as nephritis and his occupation as "Livestock Broker." Certificate #36125. As a teenager Mann had gone to New Mexico Territory, served with the California Volunteers during the Civil War, then went to Ellsworth, Kansas as part of a cattle drive. In the early 1870s he was ranching on Bear Creek in Kimble County on the land belonging to Rance Moore. He later worked in Menard County and became eminently successful in the cattle business. In 1880 when the Federal census was taken he was identified as a thirty-two-year-old farmer with a wife and three children. Mann died in San Angelo on October 14, 1925, nearly eighty years of age, having become a leading member of the community, making up for whatever youthful difficulties he committed in his wilder days. The Menard County Historical Society: *Menard County History: An Anthology* (San Angelo: Anchor Publishing Co., 1982), 426–27; *Historical and Biographical Record of the Cattle Industry and the Cattlemen of Texas* (New York: Antiquarian Press, Ltd., 1959 edition), 452.

21. Thomas Hopper appears in the 1880 Menard County census as a fifty-eight-year-old native of Alabama with his wife Lelitha, living in Precinct No. 1. 1880 Menard County census, 481.
22. Major Jones to Captain Perry, August 17, 1874, written on letterhead of David Doole, "Dealer in General Merchandise" in Mason, A.G.P.
23. Major Jones to Captain Perry, Special Order No. 15, September 15, 1874, written at Elm Creek, Menard County; and Paul Durham to Captain Perry, September 15, 1874. A.G.P.
24. 1860 Clay County Census, 102. The Sublettes were close neighbors to Greenup Bird, cashier of the local bank. On February 13, 1866, Bird was at the mercy of the James-Younger Gang when they robbed the Clay County Savings Association in Liberty, Missouri. With their take of $58,000 the gang was off to a spectacular beginning to their outlaw career.
25. Besides Perry, Reynolds, and Cooley, the men signing were: N. H. Murray, Charles Nevill, J. A. Bryan, Paul Durham, C. L. Deggs, James Scott, Thomas Gillespie, Harry Wishworth, J. A. Creel, A. Colbath, F. G. McGrew, James Hawkins, J. W. Vanhauser, F. M. Hotchkis, Joseph E. Harkey, Edward A. Sieker, Lamar P. Sieker, Eugene Campbell, J. B. Brown, Thomas Griffin, Michael Lynch, J. W. Wynn, Nick Donelly, Orange Hamilton, J. V. Wheeler, E. P. Holt, F. H. Dunn, Nick Ware, William B. Traweek, Michael Hill, D. R. Jones, J. L. Bomar, John O. Allen, J. D. Capp, Hugh E. Conn and Andrew Wilson.
26. Undated petition from members of Company D. A.G.P.
27. D. W. Roberts' "Reorganization Muster and Pay Roll of Company D, Frontier Batt. December 9, 1874," A.G.P.
28. Captain C. R. Perry communication written by Newton H. Murray to Major Jones, October 28, 1874 at Camp Elm, A.G.P.
29. Captain C. R. Perry Monthly Return, prepared October 31, 1874, at Elm Creek, A.G.P. The service record of Nick Ware is confusing as there were at least two men of that name. The Nick Ware of this company was mustered into the service on May 25, 1874, and served consistently until honorably discharged on May 31, 1875. He was again mustered into the service on April 1, 1876 and served at least until August 31.The service record document in this case records that he owed L. P. Sieker $20.50, N. O. Reynolds $10, H. W. Merrill $20, T. P. Gillespie $2.88, W. W. Lewis $4.20, C. L. Nevill $1.35, and D. W. Roberts, $5.25.
30. Ibid., November 30, 1874, attachment, no place, A.G.P.
31. Ibid., November 30, 1874, attachment, no place, A.G.P. Austin's *Daily Democratic Statesman*, November 28, 1874. Roberts' action of saving the warrior's

life is also recounted in his wife's memoirs: "A number of people came to camp to see the Indian prisoner. It was contrary to take prisoners, but [Captain Roberts] could not kill a man even if an Indian when he was begging for his life. The prisoner suffered agony from fear while in camp, and his expression showed that he expected momentarily to be killed. At Austin the prisoner was given a ride in a city carriage. He expressed his pleasure by repeating the word, 'bonito, bonito.' Within two years he died in the penitentiary of tuberculosis." Lou Conway Roberts, *A Woman's Reminiscences of Six Years in Camp With the Texas Rangers* (Austin: Von Boeckmann-Jones Company, 1928; reprint by State House Press of Austin, 1987), 17.

32. *Daily Democratic Statesman*, November 28, 1874.
33. *Dallas Daily Herald*, February 10, 1872
34. *Daily Democratic Statesman*, November 28 and December 1, 1874.
35. Capt. Dan W. Roberts. *Rangers and Sovereignty*, 54–55. Just when Little Bull died is not known definitely; according to one report, "Little Bull, the young Indian chief, kept in the penitentiary as a prisoner of war, died recently of consumption." This appeared in the "State News" column of the *Fort Worth Telegram* of January 12, 1878. Roberts provides an earlier date, perhaps within two years after his capture, or 1876.
36. Ranger Service Record of William Scot Cooley, Texas State Archives.
37. Captain C. R. Perry communication written by Sergeant N. H. Murray to Major Jones, November 21, 1874, A.G.P.
38. D. W. Roberts Monthly Return, December 31, 1874, prepared on the Little Saline, Menard County, and Roberts to Jones, December 18, 1874. Roberts' statement that the chase was of forty miles' distance seems extraordinarily high, but the handwriting is clear: "From the point from where they struck the trail . . . was about forty miles."
39. *Daily Democratic Statesman*, November 28 and 29, 1874.
40. The *Houston Daily Telegraph*, December 6, 1874. "Letters from Austin" of December 2, reports not only the arrival of So-no-ya-na (whose name is not present in the *Statesman* accounts), but added considerable satire as well.
41. Roberts, *Rangers and Sovereignty*, 58–59.
42. "Return of Property" [Captured from Indians by Company D] during December 1874, Ranger Correspondence, A.G.P.
43. D. W. Roberts. Reorganization Muster Roll, December 9, 1874, no place, A.G.P.
44. Monthly Return of D. W. Roberts, January 31, 1875, prepared on the Little Saline, Menard County.

Chapter 4: A White Man Takes a Scalp

1. Julius E. DuVos, "Fort Mason," *New Handbook*, Vol. 2, 1110–1111.
2. Daniel W. Roberts, *Rangers and Sovereignty*, 87–93. See also Dave Johnson, *John Ringo*, chapters 7–11.
3. [Lucia Holmes], *The Lucia Holmes Diary 1875–1876. The Hoo Doo War Years*, Entry for February 15, 1875 (Mason, Texas: Mason County Historical Commission, 1985), 3.
4. Johnson, 66.
5. *Lucia Holmes Diary*, Entry for February 25, 1875, 6.
6. *San Antonio Daily Herald*, August 30, 1875, printing a letter from Henry M. Holmes dated August 17, from Mason. Hereafter cited as Holmes, *San Antonio Daily Herald.*
7. Johnson, 65; Roberts, 89. Roberts had arrived on the scene after Clark had cut down the three hanging men. He examined Turley and found that his neck had not been broken and that he was still "warm." From a nearby creek Roberts filled his hat with water, poured it on Turley and rubbed him until he "showed signs of returning to life."
8. *Lucia Holmes Diary*, Entry for March 7, 8. She erred in identifying the man as Tom Gurley, rather than Turley.
9. Holmes; *San Antonio Daily Herald*, August 30, 1875.
10. Ibid., Entry for February 17, 1875, 5. The unidentified man was probably Allen Bolt. Johnson, *John Ringo;* see also Johnson's *The Mason County "Hoo Doo" War, 1874–1902*, 62. Of the death of Bolt, Johnson wrote: "There is also an ominous silence in the official reports filed by Lieutenant Roberts during this time regarding both the Baccus lynching and the killing of Allen Bolt," 64. Indeed, one suspects that Roberts was enthusiastic about pursuing Indian raiding parties, but sympathized with the mob in its vigilante justice with alleged cattle thieves.
11. Henry M. Holmes' "Attorney's Business Book," 4. Ledger in the Bierschwale Collection, Texas State Archives. There was no date provided but probably in December 1874. Wages' attorney was George W. Todd.
12. D. W. Roberts to Major Jones, March 1, 1875, written at Camp Saline, A.G.P.
13. Ibid. In *Rangers and Sovereignty*, Roberts tells of one "Wash" DeLong, an old-timer, who had been shot and maimed by Indians and who may be the same man. Roberts, 69.
14. D. W. Roberts' Monthly Return, March 31, 1875, prepared on the Little Saline.

15. Muster and Pay Roll for Capt. C. R. Perry, May 25, 1874, prepared at Blanco City, Blanco County; John Stribling Moursund, *Blanco County Families for One Hundred Years*, Edited by Mabel Stribling, revised edition (Burnet, Texas: Nortex Press, 1981), 325. After his Ranger days Murray settled in Blanco County where he married Miss Virginia F. Odiorne, daughter of Dr. James Odiorne.
16. Sgt. N. H. Murray to Major Jones, March 15, 1875.
17. D. W. Roberts' Monthly Return, March 31, 1875.
18. D. W. Roberts to Major Jones, April 1, 1875.
19. Johnson, 65.
20. D. W. Roberts' Monthly Return for April, prepared May 1, 1875, at Camp Saline.
21. D. W. Roberts to Major Jones, April 15, 1875.
22. Major Jones to Capt. D. W. Roberts, April 16, 1875.
23. Holmes, *San Antonio Daily Herald*, August 30, 1875.
24. *Daily Democratic Statesman*, May 18, 1875, printing an item from the *Fredericksburg Sentinel* of May 15, "A Man Killed in Mason County."
25. Johnson, 68. *The Life of Thomas W. Gamel As Narrated to Glenn James and Henry Rupe Capps*. Annotated by Dave Johnson (Mason, Texas: Mason County Historical Society, 1994), 19; 1870 Burnet County Census; Tim Williamson is shown to be twenty-three years of age, a "Stock Raiser" from North Carolina, 231. See also Dave Johnson's "Scott Cooley—A Byword for Terror," NOLA *Quarterly* 27, no. 3 (April-June, 2003), 1, 5–20.
26. Holmes, *San Antonio Daily Herald*, August 30, 1875.
27. D. W. Roberts' Monthly Return, July 1, 1875; letter of Roberts to Major Jones, July 1, 1875, from Camp Las Moras, Menard County.
28. Major Jones to Adj. Gen. Steele, July 9, 1875, from Camp Las Moras.
29. Lieutenant Roberts to Major Jones, "Report of Operations for July 75," written August 1, 1876, from Camp Las Moras.
30. Holmes, *San Antonio Daily Herald*, August 30, 1875.
31. Lieutenant Roberts to Major Jones, August 1, 1875.
32. Holmes, *San Antonio Daily Herald*, August 30, 1875.
33. Pay and Service Record for William Scott Cooley, Adjutant General Papers.
34. *Life of Thomas Gamel*, 19–20. In a letter to Roberts written on October 16, 1875, Major Jones wrote that Cooley and George Gladden were then in Menardville threatening certain citizens; he further wrote that some people believed that Cooley was "about old man [John "Humpy"] Jackson's place" and suggested that Roberts scout for him there. Roberts responded that he

didn't think any of the fugitives were at Jackson's, explaining "they don't like him [Cooley] very well & If he should make his appearance there they would Inform on him immediately, but I shall try to find out If he's been there." Lieutenant Roberts to Major Jones, October 17, 1875, written at Camp Las Moras.

35. Gillett, 71–73.

36. *San Antonio Daily Herald*, August 18, 1875, translating an article from the *Fredericksburg Freie Presse* of August 17, "Horrible Affair at Mason."

37. Holmes, *San Antonio Daily Herald*, August 30, 1875.

38. "Executive Record Book (Govs Coke, Hubbard), July 1875–June 1877," 56. The date of the reward was September 6, 1875.

39. D. W. Roberts to Major Jones, August 1, 1875, A.G.P.

40. Major Jones to D. W. Roberts, August 27, 1875, A.G.P.

41. D. W. Roberts' Monthly Return, September 30, 1875.

42. W. M. Holmes to Governor Coke, September 8, 1875, Governor's Papers.

43. [William Steele] *A List of Fugitives from Justice*, Facsimile edition of *Fugitives from Justice: The Notebook of Texas Ranger Sergeant James B. Gillett* (Austin: State House Press, 1997), 77. Hereafter cited as *Fugitives from Justice*. Also Holmes, *San Antonio Daily Herald*, August 30, 1875.

44. W. M. Holmes to Governor Coke, September 8, 1875.

45. William Steele to Major Jones, September 23, 1875.

46. Major Jones to Adj. Gen. Steele, from Cold Springs, Mason County, September 28; and Jones to Steele, September 30, 1875, from Mason.

47. Major Jones to Adj. Gen. Steele, September 30, 1875, from Mason; Johnson, 82.

48. L.M.P. to the *San Antonio Daily Herald*, October 11, written at Llano, September 30, 1875.

49. Major Jones to Adjutant General Steele, September 30, 1875; *Report of Maj. J. B. Jones, Commanding the Frontier Battalion, Texas State Troops, March, 1876* (Houston: A. C. Gray, State Printer, 1876), 5. *Report of the Adjutant General of the State of Texas for the Year Ending August 31st, 1876* (Galveston: Shaw & Blalock, State Printers, 1876), 5.

50. Lieutenant Ira Long Monthly Return, September 30 and October 31, 1875, prepared at Mason.

51. Gillett, 74–75. See also Dave Johnson, "about fifteen men stepped to the front." In the NOLA *Newsletter* 10, no. 1 (January-March 1985): 3–4.

52. Major Jones to Adj. Gen. William Steele, October 28, 1875.

53. Major Jones, Special Order No. 47, October 7, 1875.

54. Curiously a historian will still insist that only two men resigned from the company due to their inability to fulfill their duty of pursuing Scott Cooley. Allen G. Hatley identified only Reynolds and Jason [*sic*] P. Day—totally ignoring the fact that Paul Durham resigned for the same reason. Allen G. Hatley, *Bringing the Law to Texas: Crime and Violence in Nineteenth Century Texas* (La Grange, Texas: Centex Press, 2002), 145.
55. Major Jones, Special Order No. 48, October 11, 1875; 1870 Travis County census, 459; Pardon # 2219, Executive Office, Gov. Richard B. Hubbard. Durham's earlier service was under Capt. James M. Swisher in Company P, Frontier Forces, serving as a private from September 6 to October 21, 1870, and then as a corporal from October 22, 1870, to February 5, 1871. He was mustered into the Frontier Battalion on May 25, 1874, honorably discharged on December 9, 1874, mustered in again on September 1, 1875, and honorably discharged on October 11, 1875. James P. Day was also mustered in on May 25, 1874.
56. Lieutenant Roberts' Monthly Return, October 30, 1875, prepared "near Menardville."
57. Major Jones to Adj. Gen. William Steele, October 28, 1875.
58. Adj. Gen. William Steele to Major Jones, October 27, 1875.
59. Gillett, 76–77. Curiously, in the first edition of Gillett's memoir, self published in 1921, Cooley pulled from his pockets not the *scalp* of Wohrle but his *ears*, 79. In the 1943 Lakeside Classic edition it was the scalp alone. Since Gillett was not in Mason County during that time it is curious why he wrote that Cooley took the ears and then changed his account. The contemporary press reported that Cooley had scalped his victim, but said nothing about the ears. Norman N. Rodgers was born October 14, 1855, in Paris County, Louisiana, according to his own statement. His Ranger Service Record shows he mustered into D. W. Roberts' Company D on September 1, 1875, and served until February 29, 1876. By 1880 he was living in Coleman County with his wife and two children. Norman Nathaniel Rodgers died on September 24, 1928, and is buried in Terrace Cemetery in Garza County. 1900 Kent County census, post office Clairemont; Ranger Service Records; Charles Didway, ed., *Wagon Wheels: A History of Garza County*, the "Nonnie Rodgers Family" (Seagraves, Texas: Pioneer Book Publishers, 1973), 96–98. *Terrace Cemetery, Garza County, Texas*, Typescript copy, Texas State Library, No author, No date, 68. Jeanette Bell, Post Public Library, Post, Texas, correspondence to Parsons, September 1994.
60. Jerry Ponder, "Captain John E. Clark," NOLA *Quarterly* 28, no. 3 (July-September 2004): 37–46. The *Prospect News*, published in Doniphan, Missouri, of

May 4, 1888, reported the death of Clark. It merely said his death occurred the previous Sunday, which was April 29, 1888. A visit to the Wohrle Cemetery a few miles outside of Doniphan revealed there was no marker for the former Mason County sheriff.

Chapter 5: Death of the Avenger

1. Major Jones to Capt. Neal Coldwell, October 25, 1875.
2. D. W. Roberts to Major Jones, November 15, 1875. Roberts used the pronoun "I" indicating he was possibly alone in the pursuit of Cooley.
3. George W. Todd to Major Jones, December 12, 1875. Todd was the first county clerk of Mason County.
4. This cemetery is located on the Mason–Brady State Highway 87 near Mason.
5. *San Antonio Daily Herald*, December 8, 1870, citing a report contributed by "X" from Mason dated December 5.
6. Frederica Burt Wyatt, "James H. Sewell," *Families of Kimble County,* vol. 2 (Junction, Texas: South Llano River Printing Company, 1998), 325–26.
7. *San Antonio Daily Herald*, May 12, 1872. The "Indian News" report was from Kimble County, April 20, contributed by Charles S. Jones.
8. 1870 Kimble County census. Their post office was at Mason.
9. 1880 Travis County, Texas, census. The records of Huntsville penitentiary show that Johnson was thirty-two years old when he was received there on June 17, 1880. He was of average build with blue eyes and light colored hair and had three scars on his right arm and a scar on his upper lip. Sentenced to a five-year term for second-degree murder, his sentence would expire on May 12, 1885. However, the record also shows that on August 21, 1880, barely two months after he entered prison, Johnson escaped from "John King's force," presumably a farm work detail. There is nothing in the Huntsville records to show that prisoner 8804 was ever recaptured. *Convict Record Ledger*, 63. Original and microfilm version available in the Texas State Archives.
10. George W. Todd to Major Jones, December 14, 1875.
11. Todd, born in Virginia on January 15, 1827, later settled in Grayson County, Texas, but by 1860 was in Mason County with his wife, children, father-in-law, and two slaves. On New Year's Day 1865 Mrs. Todd and a slave child were killed and his daughter taken in what has become known as the Todd Mountain Massacre. Todd helped organize Mason County and he was chosen to be the first county clerk. He later helped organize Menard County. During the Mason

County troubles he once shot a man named Foley for having insulted his wife. Foley survived and Todd was cleared of the charge. Besides his ranching interests he was a leading merchant and later became a county judge. He died in Mason on April 1, 1901. Dave Johnson to Parsons, June 27, 1999. Today a Texas State Historical Marker—"Todd Mountain"—on FM 2389, about three miles south of Mason, commemorates the tragedy.

12. *Daily Democratic Statesman*, January 4, 1876. John Clymer was elected Burnet County sheriff on September 20, 1875, and served until February 15, 1876. His successor, John J. Strickland, was elected on February 15, 1876, and served until December 25, 1877. Tise, 76. John Ringo, born on May 3, 1850, was five years older than Cooley.
13. Major Jones to William Steele, April 15, 1876, from Cave Spring, Menard County.
14. *Daily Democratic Statesman*, July 15, 1877, citing a report from the *Lampasas Dispatch*. The report of William S. Gilliam being charged with "negligence of duty" in allowing the prisoners to escape is from the *Lampasas Dispatch* of February 14, 1878, citing an unnamed report from the *Waco Examiner*; Gillett, *Fugitives from Justice*, 178.
15. The "buckskin set of officials" is from correspondence from Roberts to Major Jones, February 16, 1876.
16. D. W. Roberts' Monthly Return, dated April 30, 1876, prepared at Camp Jones, Menard County.
17. Ibid., May 31, 1876, prepared at Camp Jones, Menard County.
18. The *Dallas Weekly Herald* and the *Galveston Daily News* are both of June 27, the *Daily Democratic Statesman*, of June 13 and August 18, 1876. The *Statesman* reported that a man named Rudolph Meyer had brought the news of Cooley's death to Austin, that he had been buried a day or so before near Miller's Creek in Blanco County and death was caused by "fits."
19. Gillett, 77.
20. John W. Bell to Chuck Parsons, January 31, 1994. Mr. Bell is a great-great nephew of Cooley. Further, J. Marvin Hunter and Noah H. Rose repeated a belief that Cooley, in the early 1930s, was "reported to be living quietly on a ranch near Lordsburg, New Mexico." *The Album of Gunfighters* (Privately printed, 1951), 171.
21. Lucille White to J. Marvin Hunter, ed., "Frontier Post," *Frontier Times*, February-March 1976, 3–5. Marvin McNutt and Max Gipson were the gentlemen who placed the new headstone, preventing Cooley's grave from being lost. No

trace has been found of the original stone and one cannot help but wonder if perhaps members of Company D placed the original stone to mark his grave.

22. D. W. Roberts to Major Jones, June 18, attachment to Monthly Return, June 30, 1876, prepared at Camp Jones, "near Menardville."
23. D. W. Roberts to Major Jones, August 16, 1876. A brief biographical sketch of Roberts appeared in *Frontier Times* 4, no. 11 (August 1927): 4. Although no author is given it was probably penned by J. Marvin Hunter, based on a recent visit of Hunter with Roberts in his Austin home.
24. *Galveston Daily News*, October 5, 1876, citing news from Menard County. The report stated that Lloyd had been arrested in Austin, "a few days since, charged with stealing horses in Bosque county." Lieutenant F. M. Moore was also frustrated in his search for the pair. "I have consumed a great deal of my time in trying to get hold of Lloyd and McDowell. They have left this area. Lloyd from the best information I can get is in Comanche Co[.] McDowell I am not able to learn. Supposed to be on the Llano by some that I have talked with. I have a scout in that region now to see if such be the case." F. M. Moore to Major Jones, October 1, 1876, from "near McKavett."
25. D. W. Roberts' Monthly Return, August 31, 1876, prepared in Menard County.
26. Major Jones to "Commanders of Companies," General Order No. 10, August 25, 1876.
27. D. W. Roberts to Major Jones, June 18, 1876; Chuck Parsons and Gary P. Fitterer, *Captain C. B. McKinney: The Law in South Texas* (Wolfe City, Texas: Henington Publishing Company, 1993), 105–7.
28. Major Jones to Adj. Gen. William Steele, August 29, 1876, written at Camp Merritt, Kerr County.
29. The eight others were Sergeant J. B. Hawkins, Samuel Long, Thomas H. Mead, William Clements, William W. Lewis, Nick Ware, Samuel Lloyd, and John W. Martin.
30. Major Jones to D. W. Roberts, August 29, 1876.
31. Major Jones Special Order No. 10, August 25, 1876, and Jones to J. M. Denton, September 25, 1876.
32. Lieutenant J. M. Denton, Muster Roll of Company A, September 1, 1876, prepared in Bexar County.
33. J. M. Denton Monthly Return, October 31, 1876, prepared on the Nueces River in Edwards County.
34. Ibid., November 30, 1876.
35. Gillett, 93–94.

36. William Steele, Special Order No. 35, December 6, 1876, in Special Orders, Ledger 401-1012, 92, Texas State Archives. On Neal Coldwell's Monthly Return he noted that Denton's resignation was accepted by Special Order No. 79. Gillett wrote of Denton's end of service, "He was in bad health and rode most of the way back in one of the wagons. On arriving at the end of the line he tendered his resignation and was succeeded by Captain Neal Coldwell." Gillett mistakenly identified him as *Benton*, 99.

37. Special Order No. 36, "By command of Gov. R. B. Hubbard C in C." dated at Austin, December 8, 1876, in Special Order, Ledger 401-1012, 92. Coldwell's Monthly Return indicated he assumed command per Special Order No. 80. Coldwell Monthly Return, December 31, 1876 at Camp Hubbard, Frio County.

38. J. M. Denton Pay Roll, December 1, 1876. Captain Neal Coldwell Monthly Return, December 1, 1876, prepared at Camp Hubbard, Frio County.

39. Dr. Nicholson was appointed surgeon of the Frontier Battalion by Special Order No. 28, dated March 15, 1876, the position to take effect as of April 1. He was to report to duty to Major Jones. Special Orders, Ledger 401-1012, 88. His resignation was Special Order No. 37, Special Orders, 93, to take effect November 30, 1876. Dr. Nicholson was born about 1840 in Maryland. According to a letter of recommendation written by A. H. Snead of Belton, Texas, to Governor Coke on May 27, 1874, Nicholson had graduated from a medical school in New Orleans. He was commended as "a gentleman & is thoroughly competent for the post." After earning $100 per month as surgeon of the Frontier Battalion he settled in Frio County where he resided in Friotown boarding in the home of Annie McGehee. He then owned two town lots valued at $225 and $75. His other possessions included a carriage, tools and implements, and three horses. He was still listed on the tax rolls in 1881 but not in subsequent years. By 1885 if not earlier he resided in Val Verde County, where he owned four acres in county seat Del Rio. Dr. Nicholson suffered from Bright's disease. After a stay in the Santa Rosa Hospital in San Antonio he went to Mineral Wells, Texas, where he died on February 3, 1893. He was described as "the most prominent physician" in the Del Rio area. Tax Rolls, Frio County, Texas 1880–1881 and Val Verde County 1885–1893; U.S. Census, 1880 Frio County, 623; the *San Antonio Daily Express*, February 4, 1893 and the *Galveston Daily News*, February 8, 1893.

Chapter 6: Rangers Against the Confederacy

1. Captain Neal Coldwell Monthly Return, Company A, January 31, 1877, prepared at Camp Hubbard, Frio County. Caldwell to Jones, January 3, 1877.
2. Neal Coldwell: "Statement of Arrests and Attempts to Arrest . . . ending January 31, 1877." James Gatlin is listed in the *Fugitives from Justice*, wanted in Atascosa County for theft, indicted on September 9, 1876. He was described as having a "dark complexion, medium height dark hair and eyes." *Fugitives from Justice*, 4.
3. Neal Coldwell Monthly Return, January 31, 1877.
4. "Decrease of Public Property" in Coldwell's Monthly Return, January 31, 1877.
5. Neal Coldwell to Major Jones, January 3, 1877.
6. Ibid., January 7, 1877.
7. Private Walter P. Callaway to Major Jones, February 1, 1877. Callaway was discharged by Special Order No. 85, February 4, 1877.
8. Neal Coldwell to Major Jones, February 4, 1877.
9. Private R. H. Eanes to Major Jones, February 23, 1877. Eanes' service record shows he was mustered into Capt. Ira Long's Company A on March 4, 1876, and served until August 31, 1876, then served under Lieutenant J.M. Denton from September 1, 1876 through November 30, 1876. Another document shows he served in Captain Coldwell's Company A from September 1, 1876, through March 12, 1877, at which time he received an honorable discharge by Special Order No. 86.
10. Neal Coldwell to Major Jones, February 24, 1877.
11. Ibid., February 11, 1877.
12. *Fugitives*, 38, 162.
13. Lieutenant Dolan to Major Jones, February 28, 1877, prepared at Camp Wood. F. M. Moore stated in a letter to Major Jones on March 22, 1877, that Brunson was a partner of Caleb Hall. There is a John Brunson listed in *Fugitives*, a man wanted for theft of cattle, indicted in May 1877, from Kinney County, Texas.
14. Neal Coldwell to Major Jones, February 28, 1877, from Camp Hubbard, Frio County.
15. Neal Coldwell Monthly Return, March 31, 1877, prepared at Camp Hubbard, Frio County.
16. "Statement of Arrests and Attempts to Arrest" in Neal Coldwell's Monthly Return, February 28, 1877.

17. *Communication from Governor Pease of Texas, Relative to the Troubles in that State*, House Miscellaneous Document, No. 127, 40th Congress, 2nd Session, May 11, 1868, 11.
18. Neal Coldwell to Major Jones, March 15, 1877; Coldwell Monthly Return, March 31, 1877.
19. Ezekiel Keyser Kountz was born February 3, 1828, in Russell County, Virginia. He married Harriett Shaffer Lindamood on February 10, 1848, and ten children were born to their union. Dr. Kountz died on December 6, 1881, in Brackettville. The Kountz family had located in Kimble County in the early 1870s. "History of the Ezekiel Keyser Kountz Family" by Minnie Laura Kountz Riley in *Families in Kimble County*, vol. 2, by Kimble County Historical Commission, Frederica Burt Wyatt, chair (Junction: South Llano Printing Company, 1998), 231–33.
20. "Executive Record Book, Richard Coke to R. H. Hubbard, July 10, 1875–June 20, 1877," 195. The election for the permanent county seat was to be held on March 21, 1876. Nolan Thompson, "Kimble County" in *New Handbook of Texas*, Vol. 3, 1100–101. Tise, *Texas County Sheriffs*, 307.
21. Tise, 307.
22. "J. M. Reynolds Bond to Kimble County and State of Texas." On the original bond is this notation: "N.Q. Patterson Enters protest April 30 at 8 a.m. 1877."
23. An excellent treatment of the outlaw confederacy, the Roundup, the Rangers and the destruction of the outlaws see Peter R. Rose, *The Reckoning: The Triumph of Order on the Texas Outlaw Frontier* (Lubbock: Texas Tech University Press, 2012). Strangely Charles M. Robinson III in *The Men Who Wear the Star: The Story of the Texas Rangers*, made no mention of the Kimble County Roundup.
24. Margaret V. Pendergrass. "William Franklin Gilliland Family" in *Families of Kimble County*, vol. 1 (Junction: South Llano Printing Company, 1985), 158.
25. Lenore Riley Mudge, "Ezekial Keyser Kountz and Harriet (Lindawood) Kountz" in *Families of Kimble County,* vol. 1, 224–25.
26. Raymond Lewis Temple, "John E. Temple Family" in *Families of Kimble County*, vol. 1, 365.
27. Mariellen Pepper Lee, "Benjamin Franklin Pepper" in *Families of Kimble County*, vol. 2, 294–95.
28. H. B. Waddill to Major Jones, February 27, 1877.
29. Muster Roll, Captain J. C. Sparks, October 1, 1876. Waddill appears twice on the Navarro County census of 1880. On June 10 he was enumerated as a single white male, twenty-six years old, employed by the railroad and boarding in the Mark M.

Bird residence on Dallas Street, 508. On June 11 he was again enumerated but now he was listed as being twenty-four years old, 511. As the muster roll provides his birth year as 1854 he was perhaps twenty-six years of age at the time of the census. Although Waddill may have done superior work for the Rangers, he was unable to avoid personal difficulties. In Milam County, an H. B. Waddill, believed to be the same man, killed one Sam Watson. At his trial on November 26, 1888, he was found not guilty due to insanity. He was temporarily placed in the Milam County jail prior to his being sent to the state asylum in Austin. "Records of Cameron County District Court," Book C, 190, indictment # 4686 and "Register of Prisoners Confined in the County Jail," jail records of Milam County, Texas, 27; Navarro County census, June 10–11, 1880, 508 and 511, post office Corsicana.

30. Neal Coldwell Monthly Return, April 1, 1877 prepared at Camp Hubbard, Frio County.

31. "To His Excellency R. B. Hubbard," petition from citizens of Frio County, April 8, 1877. Reports from Frio County initially indicated that the entire town had been reduced to ashes as a result of incendiaries. County Clerk McMahon easily determined such was not the case. In reality some unauthorized person or persons unknown had gained access and removed county records; in the fire which did destroy the courthouse, some court records were also destroyed.

32. Notation from Major Jones on the Frio County petition, April 12, 1877.

33. Major Jones to Judge W. S. Hiler, et al., April 15, 1877.

34. Judge William A. Blackburn to Major Jones, April 6, 1877, written from Burnet.

35. Major Jones to Adj. Gen. William Steele, April 12, 1877, written at Frio City.

36. Ben Anderson to Lt. Frank M. Moore, Company D, "Names of Parties . . . as given by Ben Anderson," (no date but 1877). Ben Anderson's complete list included C. M. Little, Bill and Haygon Allison, S.M. Monroe, Bill, Corbon and Butler Hedgepeth, three Dublins, two Garland boys, James McNeece, Bill Taylor, Marvin Midleton, Louis Cost, two Calahan boys, Joe Armstrong, Zack Rundals, who may have been Stark Reynolds, Lon White, Bill Deal, Sam Walker, C. Oberchin, C. Edwards, J. C. Cathy, Thomas Griffin, J. B. Franks, Paul Durham, James Deaton and Porter Lancaster.

37. Neal Coldwell, Monthly Return, April 30, 1877, prepared in Kimble County. William Steele to D. M. Young, deputy sheriff of Atascosa County, dated April 14, 1877. Letterpress Book 401-624, Texas State Archives.

38. Neal Coldwell, "Record of Scouts—Supplement," April 30, 1877.

39. Ponton and Walton, along with one Harrison, had escaped from the Lavaca County jail in early November 1876. The pair had been convicted and

sentenced to ten years of confinement in the penitentiary. Harrison was charged with the murder of a Mr. Griffin. *Galveston Daily News*, December 12, 1876, citing news from Lavaca County. Major Jones wrote to the Lavaca County sheriff regarding these two: "I have arrested Jno Walton and James Ponton and will send them to jail in Austin to be held there subject to your order. I arrested Luther Walton also but released him on learning that he had given bond for his appearance at court." Major Jones to Lavaca County Sheriff J. W. Bennett, April 25, 1877, at Junction. The Huntsville "Convict Register—Texas State Penitentiary" shows Ponton as a twenty-four-year-old man with no significant marks, intemperate, with a common education and occupation shown as a laborer. This was based on an August 10, 1877, conviction of theft of a gelding. He was received in Huntsville as prisoner number # 6177 on August 18 and his sentence was commuted to expire on January 1, 1879. Walton was twenty-one years old with "gunshot scars on rump [and] gunshot scars left shoulder from buckshot—scar on back." He was married, used tobacco, intemperate, and like Ponton was a laborer with a common education. He was sentenced subsequently on August 10 and received in Huntsville as convict # 6178 on August 18, 1877. His sentence was likewise commuted so as to expire on January 1, 1879. "Convict Register—Texas State Penitentiary," 1656–66.

40. Record of Scouts (Supplement), April 30, 1877. The April 30 Monthly Return lists H. McMichael and C. (Columbus) Rowley arrested in Menard County, the former for theft and the latter for murder. Both were "Not identified," suggesting the men arrested were not who the Rangers thought they were. Although it is possible Columbus was in Texas, it is more likely that he was in Missouri with his father J. F. Rowley and his brother Napoleon. Columbus Rowley had been charged with the murder of Walter Black in Hays County several years earlier and was rumored to have gone to South America. J. F. and Napoleon were charged with the murder of William Hunter on August 6, 1873. Both these murder victims were black. Columbus Rowley was killed in a gunfight with Barry County Sheriff Hopkins on June 23, 1877. J. F. and his son Napoleon were arrested by Hays County Sheriff James A. Wren in mid-August 1877 and returned to county seat San Marcos. The 1870 Hays County census shows the Rowley family; J. F. the father, a forty-four-year-old farmer born in Virginia, his fifty-year-old wife Susan, born in New York, keeping house. Napoleon, then seventeen, was also farming and was born in Illinois. 1870 Hays County, Texas, census, *West Texas Free Press* (San Marcos), July 7 and 14, August 25, 1877. Nathan A. McFadden, by 1880, was a thirty-six-year-old stock raiser with a family consisting of wife Leonora J., only twenty-four, his mother Eliza, seventy, and three children, daughter

Corney N., six; Joseph O., four, and Liza D., two years of age. All were Texas born and living in Precinct No. 3. 1880 Kimble County census, 281. In the same census N. Q. Patterson was enumerated, a fifty-three-year-old farmer with wife Levania M., fifty, and four children, Franklin G., twenty, working on the farm; Synthia, fourteen, Nancy S., fourteen, and Ellen T., eight years old. All were born in Tennessee except Ellen T. who was born in Texas. They resided in Precinct No. 2, 270.

41. Major Jones to William Steele, May 6, 1877, from Fort McKavett; Peter R. Rose, *The Reckoning,* 66–68.
42. *Fugitives*, 162. Cathey managed to elude the law for about a year. A report from Fort Worth stated that Luke Cathery [*sic*] described as "one of the Johnson county robbers, who made his escape last week" had been captured in Denton County and passed through town the night of June 10 "heavily ironed." Fears were "entertained of his safety en route to Cleburne." The *Galveston Daily News*, June 12, citing a special telegram to the *News* from Fort Worth dated June 11. Cathey's final fate is unknown.
43. Major Jones to William Steele, May 6, 1877, telegram from Fort McKavett.
44. *Galveston Weekly News*, April 30, 1877, citing news from Kimble County.
45. Lt. Frank M. Moore's Monthly Return and Supplement, April 30, 1877.
46. Major Jones to Steele, May 6, 1877; *Galveston Daily News* , May 15, 1877.
47. Major Jones to Steele, Telegram of May 6, 1877.
48. This originally appeared in the *San Saba News* and was reprinted in the *Lampasas Dispatch*, May 31, 1877.
49. Major Jones to Steele, May 6, 1877.
50. Betty Dooley Aubrey and Claude Dooley, *Why Stop? A Guide to Texas Historical Roadside Markers,* 4th ed. (Houston: Gulf Publishing Company, 1999), 369.
51. *Austin Daily Democratic Statesman,* June 7, 1877.
52. *Galveston Daily News*, September 7, 1877.
53. Gillett, 101–2.
54. *Galveston Daily News*, reporting from Travis County via the *Statesman.*
55. Major Jones to Steele, May 6, 1877; Rose, *The Reckoning,* 66.

Chapter 7: Rangers Against the Confederacy

1. Neal Coldwell Monthly Return, May 31, 1877, prepared at Coleman, Coleman County.

2. Ibid. Executive Record Ledger of Governors Richard Coke and R. H. Hubbard, 357.
3. Major Jones to Sheriff R. B. Willson, May 15, 1877. Willson's name is frequently spelled *Wilson* but his signature clearly shows it as *Willson*.
4. Neal Coldwell Monthly Return, May 31, 1877. Reynolds receiving the reward is from the "Executive Record Ledger," microfilm in the Texas State Archives, reel # 3482. The proclamation appears on page 387 and in the margin appears this notation "approved as to J. N. Curtis, in favor of N. O. Reynolds, June 29, 1877."
5. Apparently Luke Cathey eluded pursuit until mid-June 1878. *Galveston Daily News* of June 12 printed an item from a Fort Worth newspaper of June 11 that he had been captured.
6. John B. Jones Special Order No. 92 dated June 7, 1877. Berch S. Foster was born in Ohio County, Kentucky, circa 1849–1850. His Ranger career began as a fifth corporal under Captain W. J. Maltby, Company E, May 30, 1874, in Burnet County.
7. Sergeant N. O. Reynolds, "Report of Operations Detachments of Co's 'A' and 'C,' June 30, 1877," prepared at Lampasas; *Galveston Daily News*, June 30, 1877.
8. *Galveston Daily News*, July 19, 1877. Caleb Hall eventually relocated to New Mexico Territory and continued with his desperate ways. He reportedly died in Cripple Creek, Colorado, on March 12, 1935. Johnson, 229.
9. Reynolds' "Report of Operations . . . June 30, 1877."
10. Major Jones to Reynolds, June 25, 1877. Reynolds' "Report of Operations . . . June 30, 1877."
11. Major Jones to William Steele, June 14, 1877; *Galveston Daily News*, June 15, 1877; Jeff Jackson, *Historical Guide to the Shootout on the Public Square* (1900) and *Law and Order Frontier Lampasas* (2003). Brochures by Lampasas historian Jeff Jackson printed by the *Lampasas Dispatch Record*.
12. *Lampasas Dispatch*, June 30, 1877; *Galveston Daily News*, July 4, 1877; Reynolds' "Report of Operations . . . June 30, 1877." Reynolds wrote that Fowler was also charged with the same crime in Travis and Williamson Counties.
13. Reynolds' "Report of Operations . . . June 30, 1877" and the *Galveston Daily News*, July 4, 1877, summarizing Lampasas news from the *Lampasas Dispatch*.
14. Reynolds' "Statement of Arrests . . . June 30, 1877" Executive Record Ledger, 175. The description of Buchanan is from an unidentified newspaper

clipping in the Adjutant General's Correspondence announcing not only the governor's reward but A. W. Perry's as well. Illinois native A. W. Perry was a well-known farmer in Dallas by 1870 living with his wife and family of eight children. The young son who was killed was Samuel Commodore Perry, the second-born son of A. W. Perry. The family was quite capable of offering the reward of $500 for the murderer of their son. In 1870 their real estate was valued at $8500 and in 1870 was valued at $6000. The Dudley Buchanan who killed Perry is probably the John D. Buchanan found in the Dallas County census of 1870, living not far from the Perry residence. M. E. Buchanan, a fifty-six-year-old white female was listed as head of household with her four children: Joshua A., age twenty-two; Nancy, age eighteen; John D., age sixteen—probably Dudley—and William Z., age thirteen. 1860 Dallas County Census, 331; 1870 census, 398.

15. *Galveston Daily News*, July 4, 1877. Attorney Silas C. Buck to Governor R. B. Hubbard, June 26, 1877. Buck informed the governor of what had happened and asked if there could be a reward. Hubbard offered a reward of $500 on June 29. Napoleon "Bone" Wilson has not been found on the census, but he was the son of Mary A. Wilson, who was enumerated in Jasper County in 1860 as twenty-four and a Louisiana native. She was listed as keeping house, and with two sons, Napoleon, then age four years and Samuel H., two years old. This Napoleon Wilson was born in Texas but younger brother Samuel was born in Louisiana. Possibly this four-year-old is the son of Napoleon "Bone" Wilson. A brief description of the gunfight which cost Sheriff Martin his life appears in the *Daily Democratic Statesman* of Austin, September 27, 1877 and the *Weatherford Exponent* of September 29, 1877. 1860 Jasper County, Texas Census, 491–92.

16. [Frank L. Britton] *Report of the Adjutant General of the State of Texas for the Year 1873*. (Austin: Caldwell & Walker, 1874), 128.

17. *San Antonio Daily Herald*, February 1, 1873; *Fugitives*, 70. Denson wrote a detailed account of the difficulty between himself and the Short brothers on January 30, which was published in the *Austin Weekly Statesman*, February 6, 1873. Ironically in the preceding column appeared a lengthy appeal to Governor E. J. Davis, requesting assistance from the State Police. "Lawlessness and crime is prevalent in our community," began the second paragraph, "and our civil officers are unable to enforce and execute the laws of the land. Our good, law-abiding citizens are in danger of losing their lives, should they attempt to assist the officers in executing the law." More than one writer has Denson being killed in this matter, most notably C. L. Sonnichsen in his influential classic *I'll Die Before I'll Run: The Story of the Great Feuds of Texas*, giving the date of

Denson's death as January 14, 1873. Sonnichsen cited his source as the *San Antonio Daily Herald*, February 1, 1873, which reported thusly: "We regret to learn that Sheriff Dennison [*sic*], of Lampasas, was fatally wounded in attempting to arrest some parties, in that place, on Tuesday, the 14th inst." In reality Sheriff Denson recovered from his wounds and continued with a productive life. He was born February 1, 1833. He was elected sheriff on December 3, 1869, and then on February 5, 1870, General J. J. Reynolds, by Special Order No. 22, appointed him sheriff. He served in that capacity until December 2, 1873. Tise, 319. Denson died on March 31, 1892, a Mason in good standing. His tombstone in the small Sparks Cemetery near Lampasas indicates he had earned the rank of captain, Company D, 17th Infantry, Texas Regiment, Confederate States of America. 1870 Lampasas County census, 394. His residence must have been close to the Higgins', as John H. Higgins and his family, including "Pink" and "Bud," are all listed on the same census page. A succinct sketch of Denson's life, "Shadrick T. Denson" by Jeff Jackson, is found in *Lampasas County History: Its History and Its People* compiled by the Lampasas County History Book Committee (Marceline, Missouri: Walsworth Publishing Company, 1991), 59.

18. J. M. Redmon to Adj. Gen. Frank L. Britton, February 17, 1873.
19. Frederick Nolan, *Bad Blood: The Life and Times of the Horrell Brothers* (Stillwater, Oklahoma: Barbed Wire Press, 1994), 24–27; *Galveston Daily News*, April 5, 1877, citing reports from the *Lampasas Dispatch*.
20. *Galveston Daily News*, January 30, 1877; *Lampasas Dispatch*, September 27, 1877.
21. *Galveston Daily News*, April 5, 1877, citing a report from the *Lampasas Dispatch*.
22. *West Texas Free Press* (San Marcos), May 19, 1877.
23. *Galveston Daily News*, June 28, 1877.
24. Major Jones to William Steele, June 14, 1877.
25. Gillett, 114. Sweet was elected sheriff on December 2, 1873, re-elected February 5, 1876, and served until November 5, 1878. Tise, 319.
26. Major Jones to Neal Coldwell, June 25, 1877.
27. N. O. Reynolds "Operation of Detachments . . . July 30, 1877" prepared at Lampasas July 31, 1877.
28. Major Jones to William Steele, July 11, 1877.
29. W. A. Blackburn, Judge 17th Judicial District to Major Jones, July 11; Jones to Blackburn and Jones to Steele, July 12, 1877. Presumably this is James Polk

Mason, although Blackburn refers to him as J. M. Mason while Reynolds in his July 31 report referred to him as J. B. Mason.

30. Major Jones to Adjutant General Steele, July 12, 1877.
31. N. O. Reynolds. "Operations of Detachments . . . July 1877; *Fugitives*, 16.
32. N. O. Reynolds, "Operations of Detachments . . . July 1877"; *Galveston Daily News*, May 19, 1877; *Fort Worth Democrat*, May 22, 1877; *Weatherford Exponent*, "Killed While Discharging His Duty—Death of Deputy Marshal M. R. Greene," May 26, 1877; Stewart Caffey, ed., *Comanche Country, Reflections of Our Heritage*, vol. 2 (Comanche, 1983), 8, which includes a bust photograph of Greene. Mastin Reynolds "Boss" Greene's body was interred in the Oakwood Cemetery of Comanche. The Bailey brothers were arrested in 1883 and jailed in Comanche. On the night of November 11 a mob estimated at between forty and fifty men overpowered the jail, took the brothers a mile north of town and hanged them from a tree near the southeast corner of the cemetery. The next day Dee Bailey's wife arrived from Coryell County, thinking her husband would be released on bond, but all she could do then was to take the bodies back to Coryell County for burial. The reports from Comanche indicated the mob was made up of men from Coryell County, but this is not likely. *Galveston Daily News*, November 13, and 15, 1883, citing reports from Comanche dated November 12 and 14.
33. N. O. Reynolds, "Report of Operations . . . July, 1877"; *Lampasas Dispatch*, July 26, 1877.
34. *Lampasas Dispatch*, July 26, 1877.
35. Petition to Major John B. Jones by C. L. Nevill, *et al.*, July 16, 1877. The men who signed the petition were Nevill, David L. Ligon, William T. Derrick, Samuel A. Henry, Lowe W. Rogers, Henry W. McGhee, Ben F. Carter, Vernon Coke Wilson, Henry B. Waddill, William Clements, J. H. Gibbs, Mervyn B. Davis, Jack Martin, Isham Harrison, A. B. Ward, Chris R. Conner, William P. Hughes, and N. O. Reynolds.
36. Major Jones to Adj. Gen. William Steele, July 25, 1887, from headquarters in Lampasas. The *Lampasas Dispatch*, July 26, 1877; the Austin newspaper also reported the killing of Graham—"shot by parties in ambush as he was leaving his work" —but made no suggestion it was part of the Horrell-Higgins feud. *Austin Daily Democratic Statesman*, July 29, 1877.
37. Major Jones to Adj. Gen. William Steele, July 31, 1877, from headquarters in Lampasas.
38. *Galveston Daily News*, August 8, 1877.
39. *Lampasas Dispatch*, August 9, 1877

40. N. O. Reynolds' "Operation of Detachment . . . July 31, 1877," prepared at Lampasas.

41. Ibid., and "Statement of Arrests and Attempts to Arrest, July 31, 1877," prepared at Lampasas. Alberry Higgins, the younger brother of Pink, has received little attention in the feud literature. The 1870 Lampasas County census shows the family: John H. and Hester, forty-seven and forty-one years of age, from Georgia and South Carolina respectively, farming and keeping house. Their children then were Julia A., age twenty-one; John P., age nineteen; Malinda J., seventeen and Alberry J., fourteen. They lived in Precinct No. 1 with their post office at Lampasas. 1870 Lampasas County census, 393. As far as known Bud Higgins took no active part in the shooting phase of the feud.

42. *Lampasas Dispatch*, August 9, 1877.

43. The original Horrell document is preserved in the Adjutant General's Papers at the Texas State Archives, document in file 401-395, folder 17. The original Higgins document is preserved in file 401-396, folder 1.

44. Gillett, 116–17. This terminology is from the first edition; in the Lakeside Classics edition the phrase "most desperate band of men that ever lived" became simply "the most desperate band"; the phrase "imperishable renown" became "great credit," 116.

45. *Galveston Daily News*, August 14, 1877, correspondence from "Winchester" at Lampasas, August 10.

46. Gillett, 119. In the first edition the name of John Gibbs is included but is absent from the Lakeside Classics edition, 118–19. He added "and four others whose names I don't remember."

47. *Lampasas Leader*, January 26, 1889.

48. Ibid.

49. Walter Prescott Webb *The Texas Rangers: A Century of Frontier Defense* (Austin: The University of Texas Press, 1935, 1965), 335.

50. Captain Daniel W. Roberts, *Rangers and Sovereignty* (Austin: State House Press, facsimile edition, 1987), 167–70.

51. C. L. Douglas, *Famous Texas Feuds* (Dallas: Turner Co., 1936; repr., Austin: State House Press, 1998), 140–42.

52. *Belton Journal*, December 19, 1878, reprinting an undated article from the *Waco Telephone*.

Chapter 8: A Prisoner Lost in Indiana

1. *Daily Democratic Statesman*, August 9, 1877. In 1870 the twenty-five-year-old Smith was living with his wife and two small children, his occupation given as farming. 1870 Hamilton County Census, 449. He was appointed sheriff on February 4, 1871, elected sheriff on November 8, 1872 and re-elected February 15, 1876. Tise, 230.
2. *Galveston Daily News*, August 15, 1877, reporting news from Hamilton County. The "old feud" had earlier been "quieted by Major Jones's men, and they ask for aid now. Major Jones ordered men from Lampasas to Hamilton."
3. C. K. Bell to Major Jones, August 4, 1877. Bell was a very young man to be involved in Hamilton County politics. He was almost twenty-four when requesting help from Major Jones. When enumerated in the 1880 census he was living with his mother and sister, all natives of Tennessee. 1880 Hamilton County Census, 357. Dr. Nicholson giving power of attorney to J. J. Tobin of Travis County, January 29, 1877, written at Jacksboro. The document was witnessed by Ranger L. B. Beavert.
4. Major Jones to Neal Coldwell, August 7, 1877.
5. Tise, 230. Tennessee-born George Washington Wade had served under Capt. Franklin Jones in the Frontier Forces from Mason County from August 25 to November 11, 1870. By 1880 he was a Hamilton County merchant with a wife and child. 1880 Hamilton County Census, 358. After locating in Texas in 1854 Wade made two trips to the California gold fields. The family moved to Hamilton County in 1876 where he was appointed sheriff. He died about 1907 in Cleburne, Texas. Amy Wade, "George Washington Wade," *A History of Hamilton County, Texas* (Dallas: Taylor Publishing Company, 1979), 296.
6. Major Jones to Neal Coldwell, August 7, 1877.
7. Margaret S. Peirce, "James Shackleford Gillett" in *New Handbook*, vol. 3, 169.
8. Major Jones General Order No. 16, August 9, 1877.
9. "Dock" Civils remains an elusive figure. This may not be his correct name, as a J. M. Sivils later was killed in Clay County. Civils' name may have been properly spelled Sivils, and J. M. may have been a relative. In late September 1876, W. T. Gee, the Clay County sheriff, shot and killed J. M. Sivils of Henrietta, the Clay County seat. Sivils had been drinking and acting in a disorderly manner when Sheriff Gee approached to arrest him. "They talked the matter over and Gee did not dream of resistance, when all at once Sivils drew a revolver and told Gee he would shoot him if he attempted to arrest him. Gee tried to talk him out of it, when Sivils commenced shooting. Gee called to an imaginary crowd to

not harm him, and thus gained time enough to draw his own pistol and fired." *Galveston Daily News*, August 8, 1876, reporting Clay County news.

10. J. W. Warren telegram to Major Jones, August 6, 1877, summary of operations for August, 1877 by N. O. Reynolds and "Report of Operations" by Reynolds, August 31, 1877, prepared at Burnet. No explanation is given as to why this Owens was called "Wild Bill." *Daily Democratic Statesman*, August 9, 1877.
11. G. M. Doolittle was born in about 1853 in Lorraine County, Ohio. He served under Capt. John R. Waller in Company A Frontier Men from Erath County, mustering in on May 25, 1874. He served under J. W. Millican in Company A of the Frontier Battalion from December 1 until December 25, 1874. On September 1, 1875, he mustered into Lieut. Ira Long's Company A as a private in Mason, serving until February 29, 1876. By August 1877 he apparently was a resident of Lampasas, and considered himself a detective, writing in one letter: "I am traveling hunting men all the time[.] I make it a business." Ranger Service Records, Texas State Archives, and letter from Doolittle to the adjutant general of the state of Kansas, August 21, 1877. Original in Gov. George T. Anthony's Correspondence Received, "Crimes & Criminals: Miscellaneous" at Kansas State Historical Society, Topeka.
12. N. O. Reynolds to Major Jones, August 11, 1877, written at Lampasas; *Daily Democratic Statesman*, August 14, 1877; *Dallas Daily Herald*, August 15 and 17, 1877, reprinting news from Travis and Lampasas County respectively; *Galveston Daily News*, August 27, printing a news item from Navasota, Grimes County, of August 23; "Reward Notice" for John D. McRae, from Record Group No. 307, Secretary of State Papers, Texas State Archives; G. M. Doolittle Service record, and "Record of Criminals by Co[unties], description" Ledger 401-1081, Texas State Archives.
13. "Statement of Arrests" August 31, 1877, prepared at Burnet, Records of District Court, Lampasas County. On April 3 Cornet was sentenced on case # 543, theft of cattle, to a term of five years at hard labor; case #544, theft of a steer, one year at hard labor; case # 545, theft of a cow and yearling, one year at hard labor. Sheriff Albertus Sweet with a guard of seven men arrived in Austin on April 7 with Cornet and other prisoners: Tom Benson, James Clark, E. A. Labbaite, Jack Fisher, Bud Perkins, Will Kincheloe, Charles Stewart and James Polk Mason. Cornet, Benson and Clark were delivered to Huntsville, while the others remained in the Travis County jail in charge of Sheriff Dennis Corwin. *Daily Democratic Statesman*, April 9, 1878. Huntsville prison records indicate that Cornet, # 6666, was received on April 10, 1878, with $1.70 in his possession. He was listed as being twenty-one, five-feet-seven and one-half inches tall, dark complexion with hazel eyes and brown hair. He was the fourth child

of Reuben and Susan Cornet, born probably in Falls County, Texas. In 1870 he was in San Saba County, "at home" living with his family and the family of John J. Long. Long's wife Elizabeth was probably a sister of Alf's mother. In the Long household were the five members of the Long family as well as the ten members of the Cornet family. 1860 Falls County census, 150; 1870 San Saba County census, 117.

14. N.O. Reynolds to Major Jones, August 11, 1877, from Lampasas. Ferguson's description appears in *Fugitives from Justice*, 25, and in a letter from Pike County, Arkansas Sheriff O. B. Owens to Hamilton County Sheriff W. R . Byrd of August 6, 1892. Extradition papers for Ferguson, Record Group # 307, Texas State Archives.
15. N. O. Reynolds to Major Jones, August 11, 1877.
16. Reynolds "Statement of Arrests" August 31, 1877, prepared at Burnet, and Reynolds to Major Jones, August 31; also Supplemental Monthly Return of Reynolds, August 1–14, 1877, prepared at "Headquarters Front. Batt. Lampasas, Texas."
17. The hanging of Reese resulted in considerable newspaper coverage. The *Statesman* presented a twenty-six-line statement about it, which was reprinted in the *West Texas Free Press* of San Marcos. It pointed out that Reese "was found dead, hanging to the limb of a tree, near that lively little frontier town [of Brownwood]." He had come from Highland, Ohio, four months previously and was known as "an industrious day laborer" and no cause could "be assigned to his horrible 'taking off.'" Those suspected of his lynching were identified and, commented the *Statesman*, "If men holding such positions be capable of such enormities what security can there be for life or property where they reign [?]" *West Texas Free Press*, June 24, 1876.
18. 1860 Hancock County, Indiana census, 711, and August 5, 1870, 423, post office Palestine, Indiana. In 1860 Tuttle was one of seven children enumerated with the Thomas C. and Elizabeth J. Tuttle family. *Hancock Journal* of Greenfield, Indiana, August 30, 1877.
19. *Brownwood Eagle* of May 3, 1876, newspaper clipping in W. S. Tuttle extradition file, Texas State Archives.
20. The reward offer of $250 by Governor Hubbard was for the arrest and delivery of Tuttle inside the door of the Brown County jail. The requisition on the governor of Indiana was that "the Reward must cover expense of Extradition." This notation was on the reverse of a letter from Brown County District Attorney Silas C. Buck to Hubbard, written April 8, 1877. Curiously, James C. White, in *The Promised Land: A History of Brown County, Texas* (Brownwood Banner Press, 1941), 77, wrote that Sol Tanner, "first mayor of Brownwood

[and] City Marshal Dave Breckenridge hanged a man named Pierce. . . . Mr. Tanner was born in Indiana, August 5, 1835, and was married May 20, 1858, in Blanco, Texas, to Miss Cinthia A. George." Tanner died in 1891. Did author White confuse Tuttle and Tanner in writing that the latter was from Indiana, when it was Tuttle?

21. This man should not be confused with the John Lackey who was severely wounded by John Wesley Hardin in Gonzales County in 1871.
22. According to an article in the *Fort Worth Democrat* of July 28, 1877, Lackey was "passed through here yesterday [July 27] securely manacled on horse back, in the custody of Corporal W. P. Roscoe, a member of company C, of the frontier battalion, stationed at Coleman City." He was to be turned over to civil authorities in Brownwood, where he was to await trial for the Bennett Edwards murder. *Fort Worth Telegram*, July 27, 1877; *Lampasas Dispatch*, August 16, 1877, printing an article from an undated issue of the *Brownwood Bulletin*; requisition from Governor J. M. Stone, July 13, 1877; warrant issued to Captain J. C. Sparks; *Dallas Daily Herald*, August 18, 1877. Sparks had risen to the rank of 1st Lieutenant during the war and then "achieved a brilliant reputation as a brave commander" in the Frontier Battalion. He then worked as a grain dealer in Waco, McLennan County, and then moved to Corsicana, Navarro County, where he was living when he and the Fuller brothers became embroiled in an argument over a yearling calf. Sparks attempted to arrest the pair but was shot and killed by Bigman Fuller the night of April 6, 1883. *Fort Worth Daily Gazette*, April 8; *Waco Daily Examiner*, April 10, 1883; 1880 McLennan County, Texas census, 11.
23. *Indianapolis Journal*, August 31, 1877; *Indianapolis Daily News*, September 1, 1877, printing a report from correspondent "Quiz" writing from Greenville on August 30; *Hancock Democrat*, September 6, 1877.
24. Supplemental Monthly return of N. O. Reynolds, August 1–24, 1877, prepared at "Headquarters Front. Batt. Lampasas Texas."
25. *Fugitives*, 177.
26. Major Jones to Adjutant General Steele, August 20, 1877.
27. *Galveston Daily News*, August 15, citing a letter from B.K.R. to editors of the *News*.
28. Governor Hubbard General Order No. 20, August 24, 1877
29. Reynolds, "Report of Operations [of] Cos. A C & E." August [27–31], 1877; *Galveston Daily News*, September 7, 1877; a summary of state news from Burnet as reported in the *Austin Statesman*; the *Weatherford Exponent*, September 29, 1877.

30. N. O. Reynolds. "Statement of Arrests and Attempts to arrest made by detachments of Co's 'A' and 'E' Frontier Batt[alion]" prepared on August 31, 1877, from Burnet.
31. Gillet, 120–22. Declaration for Pension of N. O. Reynolds, # 1,168,335.

Chapter 9: One Dublin Taken, One Dublin Escapes

1. Charles M. Webb (May 2, 1848–May 26, 1874) had served as 1st Lieutenant in Company C of the Brown and San Saba County Rangers under Captain J. G. Connell from January 6 to March 26, 1874. His death at the hands of John Wesley Hardin came exactly two months after leaving the Ranger service, on May 26, which was also Hardin's twenty-first birthday. Muster & Pay Roll Records, Texas State Archives. Webb is buried in Greenleaf Cemetery in Brownwood, Texas.
2. Jack Duncan's life is thoroughly defined in *Bounty Hunter* by Rick Miller (College Station, Texas: The Early West, 1988); Hardin has proved to be a much more popular subject for biographers. For his career in Florida see Jesse Earle Bowden and William S. Cummins, *Texas Desperado in Florida: Texas Outlaw John Wesley Hardin in Pensacola, 1877* (Pensacola Historical Society, 2002); Chuck Parsons, *The Capture of John Wesley Hardin* (College Station, Texas: The Early West, 1978); A. J. Wright, "John Wesley Hardin's 'Missing Years,'" *Old West* (Fall 1981): 6–11, and A. J. Wright, "A Gunfighter's Southern Vacation," NOLA *Quarterly* (Autumn 1983): 12–16. Excellent biographies of Hardin remain *The Last Gunfighter* by Richard C. Marohn (College Station, Texas: The Early West, 1995) and *John Wesley Hardin: Dark Angel of Texas* (El Paso: Mangan Books, 1996) by Leon C. Metz. A more complete biography is *A Lawless Breed: John Wesley Hardin, Texas Reconstruction and Violence in the Wild West* by Chuck Parsons and Norman Wayne Brown (Denton: University of North Texas Press, 2013). Duncan's partner in the arrest is in *John B. Armstrong: Texas Ranger and Pioneer Ranchman* (College Station: Texas A&M University Press, 2007). The "panther" quotation is in the *San Antonio Daily Express*, August 29, 1877, and other newspapers. The reward was not for Hardin "dead or alive"; the proclamation read "for the apprehension of John Wesley Hardin, and making an appropriation therefore, approved January 29, 1875, do hereby offer a reward of four thousand dollars for the apprehension and delivery of the said John Wesley Hardin within the jail house door." Records of the Administration of Richard Coke Governor of the State of Texas," January 15, 1874-January 14, 1879, 471, microfilm in Texas State Archives, Travis County.

3. *Galveston Daily News*, September 11, 1877, citing a "Special Telegram" from Austin, September 10.
4. N. O. Reynolds' Monthly Return, September 30, 1877; Reynolds to Jones, September 5, 1877, from Running Brushy Creek, Williamson County; C. L. Nevill, "Minutes of Co E Scouts etc. by C.L. Nevill 1st Sergeant," 2–3. Hereafter cited as Nevill, "Minutes."
5. Reynolds' Monthly Return, September 30, 1877, Comanche County, Texas; Mark Odintz, "Bagdad, Texas" in *New Handbook*, vol. 1, 333–34.
6. Reynolds to Major Jones, September 6, 1877; written at Running Brushy Creek, Williamson County; Jones to Reynolds, September 6, 1877; Reynolds' Monthly Return, September 30, 1877, Comanche County; Nevill, "Minutes," 4–5. A Sam Higgins is enumerated in the 1880 Lampasas County census, a twenty-eight-year-old farmer born in Georgia, with a wife and three children. They had been in Texas since at least 1873 as all the children were Texas-born. Apparently he was no close kin to the feuding Higgins clan. 1880 Lampasas County census, 319.
7. N. O. Reynolds to Major Jones, September 5, 1877.
8. Frank E. Wilson was elected sheriff the first time on February 15, 1876, and served until November 5, 1878, then was elected a second time on November 6, 1888, and served until November 4, 1890. Tise, 126.
9. N. O. Reynolds, "Statement of Arrests . . ." September 30, 1877; Nevill, "Minutes," 7.
10. Gillett, 125–26.
11. *Daily Democratic Statesman*, September 20, 1877.
12. *Lampasas Dispatch*, September 27, 1877. Incidents in the Horrell-Higgins feud were frequently reported in the *Galveston Daily News*. In the *News* of August 15, for example, it was Higgins, Mitchell, and Wren who were acquitted of the charge of killing James Buck Waldrip and assaulting the Horrell party on June 7. Further, they were discharged from the accusation of waylaying and shooting at Bud Higgins and Milam [?] Wren. *Galveston Daily News*, August 15, 1877, citing news from Lampasas County.
13. *Weatherford Exponent*, October 6, 1877.
14. *Dallas Weekly Herald*, September 29, 1877, written from Comanche, September 26, 1877.
15. John Wesley Hardin, *The Life of John Wesley Hardin, As Written By Himself*, Introduction by Robert G. McCubbin (Norman: University of Oklahoma Press reprint, 1961), 122–23. Hereafter cited as *Hardin*.
16. *Weatherford Exponent*, October 6, 1877.

17. *Hardin*, 123.
18. George B. Hendricks, *The Bad Men of the West* (San Antonio: The Naylor Company, 1941; revised edition, 1959), 160.
19. *Galveston Daily News*, August 21, 1895.
20. *Weatherford Exponent*, October 13, 1877, a report from W.A.F. written at Comanche, September 30, 1877.
21. *Galveston Daily News*, October 7, 1877.
22. George W. Campbell to Major Jones, October 15, 1877, from Camp Elm, Throckmorton County; N. O. Reynolds' Monthly Return, September 30, 1877, Comanche County.
23. *Galveston Daily News*, October 3, 1877.
24. N. O. Reynolds' Monthly Return and Statement of Arrests, 1876, from Kimble County; *Galveston Daily News*, December 5 and 15, 1877; Childers, having "skipped out" on his bondsmen, was later arrested by Robertson County Deputy Marshal Bishop on December 13 at Hearne. Bishop turned him over to Sheriff J. W. Jones.
25. Gray and Moore, *Mercantile and General City Directory of Austin, Texas—1872–73* (Austin: S.A. Gray, 1872), 107. *Mooney and Morrison's General Directory of the City of Austin, Texas for 1877–1878* (Austin: Eugene von Boeckman, 1877), 216. Tullis' six-year term, which would expire on December 28, 1883, was commuted to a five-year term by proclamation from Governor O. M. Roberts on December 16, 1880. Prisoner # 6479 was discharged April 28, 1882. "Convict Record, Texas State Penitentiary, 180. "The Schedule of Inhabitants in the City of Austin, County of Travis, State of Texas [1875]" shows Tullis as a forty-five-year-old American, his wife Laura and seventeen-year-old son T. W. Tullis, 43; *Daily Democratic Statesman*, January 8 and 19, 1878. The land forgery group was considerable. D. H. Francis was found guilty and sentenced to five years in prison. Others included Tullis, Ham, Hatch, and the two McCulloughs. The *Lampasas Leader* reported there were about twenty-five in all. Another probable member of the group was G. W. H. Martin, later arrested by the Hamilton County sheriff; he never stood trial as Sheriff G. W. Wade, former Ranger, reported that on December 31, 1877, Martin committed suicide by taking poison. *Galveston Weekly News*, January 11, 1878, reprinting an item from Austin, January 7.
26. N. O. Reynolds' Monthly Return, October 31, 1877; "Statement of Arrests," from Kimbleville.
27. Thomas Sieker, younger brother of Lamar P. Sieker, was born in New York on September 28, 1852. His Texas Ranger career began on November 13, 1876,

in Capt. Frank M. Moore's Company D. He also served under Captain D.W. Roberts. Sieker died in Dallas on January 13, 1935, and rests in Forest Lawn Burial Park. Robert W. Stephens, *Texas Ranger Sketches* (Privately printed, 1972), 146–47.

28. N. O. Reynolds' Monthly Return, November 30, 1877, from Camp Bear Creek; Nevill, "Minutes," 13.
29. *Galveston Daily News*, November 10, 1877, written November 5 at Menardville. The letters of Mervyn that were printed in the *Galveston Daily News* have been published in their entirety in "'Mervyn': A Poetical Correspondent" by Chuck Parsons in the *Brand Book* of the English Westerners Society, Winter 1988/89, 1–9.
30. N. O. Reynolds' Monthly Return, November 30, 1877, prepared at Camp Bear Creek; Nevill, "Minutes," 14.
31. *Galveston Daily News*, November 19, 1877.
32. N. O. Reynolds' Monthly Return, November 30, 1877; Nevill, "Minutes," 14.
33. *Galveston Daily News*, December 7, 1877, written at Llanotown, December --, 1877.
34. *Hardin*, 126.
35. Coryell County Sheriff James R. Raby to William Steele, April 4, 1873; "Record of Criminals by Co[unty] crime, description," Kimble County, 368–69, Ledger 401-1081, Texas State Archives.
36. 1880 Kimble County census, 266. For an authoritative treatment of the Dublins, see Peter R. Rose, *The Reckoning,* 45–46.
37. *Galveston Daily News*, December 12, 1877, reporting news from Kimble County; "Statement of Arrests . . ." November 30, 1877.
38. Gillett, 128–29.
39. Caleb Hall was the seventh child of Caleb and Lucy Hall, and was born June 15 or 16, 1849. 1850 Graves County, Kentucky census, 397; Johnson, 64.
40. *Galveston Daily News*, December 12, 1877, printing correspondence from "K.K." of Wortham dated December 8. K.K. intended his description of the killing to be a "true account of the horrible murder perpetrated in our midst . . . causing each citizen to recoil with horror at its barbarity and total lack of provocation." The physical description is from the Rushing extradition file, Record Group 307, Texas State Archives. The "wolfish look" is from a description printed in an unidentified newspaper clipping in the Rushing file.
41. N. O. Reynolds' Monthly Return, December 31, 1877, prepared at Camp Steele, Kimble County; Nevill, "Minutes," 17–20.

42. N. O. Reynolds' "Record of Scouts," December 31, 1877.
43. Gillett, 133; Nevill, "Minutes," 22–23.
44. Gorman replaced Sheriff J. M. Reynolds on May 3, 1877. He was then elected on November 5, 1878 and served until November 2, 1880. He was later elected again, on November 7, 1882, and served until November 4, 1884. Tise, 307.
45. N. O. Reynolds' Monthly Return, December 31, 1877; Nevill, "Minutes," 26–27; *Galveston Daily News*, January 21, 1878.
46. Rick Miller, *Sam Bass and Gang* (Austin: State House Press, 1999), 115–22.
47. *Galveston Daily News*, January 17, 1878, citing a special telegram from Austin to the *News* dated January 9. Ranger Service Record of Harry Cook. In January of the following year, Cook was captured, although no details have been uncovered. The only details available are Reynolds' report that on January 27 Pvts. Lowe Rogers and William Clements had returned from Austin to Frio City, being on detached service, escorting Harry Cook. "Record of Scouts," January 27, 1878.

Chapter 10: A Killing in Scabtown

1. *San Antonio Daily Express*, November 27, 1878, correspondence from Hans Mickle from Fort McKavett.
2. Ibid., and Jerry M. Sullivan, *Fort McKavett: A Texas Frontier Post* (NP: Texas Parks and Wildlife Department, [1981?]); Vivian Elizabeth Smyrl, "Fort McKavett" in *New Handbook*, vol. 2, 1111. William Lehne was born in Brunswick in 1837 and was in Texas by the late 1850s, living in Gillespie County when the 1860 census was conducted. By 1870 he was identified as a retired barkeeper, thirty-seven years old, living in Fredericksburg with his wife Theresa and four children, all Texas born. 1860 Gillespie County census, 5 and 1870 census, 316 respectively. William M. Lehne died April 5, 1877, according to Frederica Burt Wyatt, in *The Cemetery at Fort McKavett, Texas* (Junction, Texas: Kimble County Historical Museum, 1999), 12.
3. N. O. Reynolds, "Record of Scouts Continued," December 31, 1877, prepared at Camp Steele, Kimble County.
4. Two documents exist in the service record for Ben Johnson, one dated at Kimble County, Bear Creek camp, showing he was due $24.66 but owed Reynolds $4.50 and Thomas Sieker $5.50. The second document, prepared at Camp Steele, shows he had earned $53.37 but owed Reynolds $8.25 and Richard C. Ware $12.10. Nothing has survived regarding George Stevenson's service record.

5. Gillett, 130.
6. Sheriff J. H. Comstock to Editor, January 2, printed in Austin's *Daily Democratic Statesman*, January 12, 1878; Reynolds to Major Jones, January 3, 1878.
7. Charles Miller and Steve Saunders are both listed as "Soldiers" in the Fort McKavett census. Both were identified as being twenty-one years old, black, and from Kentucky. Neither could read nor write. 1870 Menard County census, enumerated by 1st Lieut. William Hoffman. Miller, 156 and Saunders, 157.
8. Gillett, 132.
9. J. H. Comstock to Editor, *Daily Democratic Statesman*, January 12, 1878.
10. Telegrams from N. O. Reynolds to Adj. Gen. William Steele, January 2 and 3, 1878, written from Fort McKavett.
11. N. O. Reynolds to Major Jones, January 3, 1878.
12. Henry McGhee to John McGhee, January 1, 1878. Private letter printed in the *Waco Weekly Examiner and Patriot*, January 11, 1878.
13. Major Jones to Captain Coldwell, January 7, and Major Jones to Reynolds, January 8, 1878.
14. *Galveston Weekly News*, January 21, 1878, printing news from Menard County.
15. In 1870 Ida Miller was enumerated as a resident of the "Peternales [*sic*] Settlement" in Gillespie County. She was twenty-six years of age and living in the residence of black farmer James Tinker and his wife, both from Kentucky. Ida Wallace, who later married Charles Miller, is not shown there to have any children. She is listed as a mulatto and from Tennessee. Her occupation is given as "Keeping House." 1870 Gillespie County census, 334; her post office was Fredericksburg.
16. Ida Miller to Fritz Tegener, written at Fort Concho, March 21, 1878, and notation by Tegener and Governor Hubbard on the same document.
17. Adjutant General Steele to Major Jones, March 27, 1878.
18. Ranger Service Record, Timothy McCarty. Little is known of McCarty's background. His parents' names are unknown, but the 1860 Culpeper County, Virginia, census shows him as a twelve-year-old residing with the John N. Griffin family. Griffin is shown to be a sixty-seven-year-old farmer with real estate valued at $24,000 and personal estate valued at $2,010. McCarty's place of nativity is shown to be Ireland. However, the 1870 census of Culpeper County shows McCarty, identified as a twenty-one-year-old farm hand, still residing with the John N. Griffin family, but now his nativity is shown to be Virginia. Thus not only are his parents' names unknown and his birth year uncertain—either 1848 or 1849—but his place of birth is either Ireland or Virginia. Why

and when he left Virginia and located in Texas is also unknown. 1860 Culpeper County, Virginia census, 999, and 1870 Culpeper County census, 634. McCarty apparently had family members living in Austin at the time of his death as an article in the *Daily Democratic Statesman* of January 13 mentions a letter from Reynolds, expressing "sympathy with the relatives and friends of Tim McCarty." Further, McCarty was a member of the Austin Fire Department, and resolutions were unanimously adopted at their January 6 meeting "to render a tribute of praise to the good citizen [Tim McCarty]." *Daily Democratic Statesman*, February 17, 1878. For a brief treatment of the Fort McKavett killings see Chuck Parsons' "Wild Shooting Kills Five" in *Chronicles of the Old West* 3, no. 2 (January 2003).

19. McCarty's name is on panel 9, column C, line 17. Clifford R. Caldwell and Ron DeLord, *Texas Lawmen 1835–1899: The Good and the Bad* (Charleston, South Carolina: History Press, 2011). The Memorial is located at 1601 South Interstate 35, south Austin.
20. Nevill, "Minutes," 28.
21. N. O. Reynolds Special Order No. 4, issued January 14, 1878.
22. N. O. Reynolds Monthly Return, January 31, 1877; Nevill, "Minutes," 31.
23. William Steele to N. O. Reynolds, March 22, 1878. A. T. Andreas, *History of the State of Kansas* (Chicago, 1883), 653. The date of the killing of Michael Pointing is from the *Burlington Osage County Chronicle* of Burlington, Kansas, September 4, 1874, "Trouble in Coffee County"; details concerning the reward are from the *Burlington Patriot*, January 18, 1878. According to Andreas' account McDonald was convicted of manslaughter in the second degree and was sentenced to the Kansas penitentiary for a term of twenty years. A. T. Andreas, *History of the State of Kansas*.
24. Jeff Jackson, "Langford Cove," Unpublished manuscript in authors' possession; *Houston Daily Telegraph*, February 1, 1873; "Record of Criminals by Co[unty] crime, description," Kimble County: 368–69; Coryell County: 408. Ledger in Texas State Archives.
25. Gillett, 129.
26. Gillett, 133.
27. Ibid., 133–34.
28. The 1880 Kimble County census shows two Potter families. The first was W. Potter, fifty-eight years old, residing with his wife Mary, and their seven children ranging in age from three years to eighteen years. The parents were born in Missouri; the children, all but the youngest, were all born in California. In the next household enumerated were living Mrs. Thomas Potter and her three

sons, Moses, William, and Thomas. Their occupation was given as "Cow Boy." 1880 Kimble County census, 268.

29. Gillett, 137. Curiously a reporter for the *San Antonio Express*—"Texan" — quotes "a little boy" as giving the warning to Dublin, saying "Richard look at the rangers." "Texan" was filing his report from Kerrville, January 25. He reported that after Dublin refused to surrender the Rangers fired a few shots in the air, "and that did no good. . . . the boys were ordered to 'pull down' on him, when he instantly fell, several shots having gone through him almost at the same moment." *San Antonio Weekly Express*, Supplement, January 31, 1878.

30. *Fugitives*, 15. The entry reads: "Dublin, Richard . . . Murder; indicted April 1873; supposed to be in Kimble county." His name is the first in the listing for Coryell County.

31. N. O. Reynolds Monthly Return, January 31, 1878.

32. *Lampasas Dispatch*, February 7, 1878. The date of Richard Dublin's death has been reported variously, as January 16, 17, and 18; also the year has been surprisingly given as 1877, 1878, and 1879. Nevill, in his memoranda book, in which he presumably recorded events within a day or so, echoed Reynolds' report when he wrote, "[January] 16 Corp. Gillett and five men went in pursuit of Richard Dublin and killed him while resisting arrest. distance marched 90 miles."

33. N. O. Reynolds to Major Jones, January 22, 1878; *Galveston Daily News*, February 11, 1878.

34. N. O. Reynolds to Jones, March 27, 1878.

35. Convict Register: Division of Prisons, Illinois Department of Corrections, Menard Division, microfilm roll # 21–22, located at the Illinois State Archives, Springfield, Illinois. Those convicted of the Pegleg Stagecoach robberies were Mack Potter, Bill Potter, Mathew Wilkens/Wilkins, and Dell and Roll Dublin, convicted in August 1880. The breaking up of the Dublin gang provided headlines far from Texas. The *New York Times* in its Sunday issue of March 17, reprinting an item from an undated *Austin State Gazette*, headlined its article: "Texas Miscreants Dispersed." Its local color, unusual for a newspaper, suggests a writer such as Mervyn. It also represented the first time Reynolds' name appeared in the *New York Times*, and is reprinted here in part.

> In the wilds of Kimble and Menard Counties, where rugged mountains are piled deeply on level plains, where the cat's claw and cactus make impenetrable barriers, except by narrow intricate paths, for years have dwelt a gang of white men as savage as the Indians, after whom they model in their modes of living. This gang for 9 or 10 years acknowledged Dick and Dell Dublin as leaders. They halted at no crime, they feared no

law. After they passed beyond the Pecos to return painted as Indians, to rob, murder and ravish on the credit of the red men. . . . Lieut. Reynolds has utterly destroyed these miscreants. One of the gang arrived in chains day before yesterday. Dick Dublin is dead, killed by the rangers in resisting arrest. Dell Dublin is in jail. Others of the renegade band are killed, and the rest are scattered into Mexico. Kimble and Menard Counties are quiet now.

36. 1880 Travis County census, 251.
37. N. O. Reynolds' "Record of Scouts" attached to Monthly Return, January 31, 1877.
38. Ibid.; Nevill, "Minutes," 32; *Daily Democratic Statesman*, December 20, 1881; "Rube Boyce, Ranger and Frontiersman," *Frontier Times* 4, no. 11 (August 1927): 57. This is an obituary for Boyce reprinted from the Coahoma, Texas *Herald* of May 26, 1927. The obituary gives his birth date as January 8, 1853, but his tombstone in the Coahoma Cemetery gives his life dates as 1852–1927. See also "The Boyce Family" in *Families of Kimble County*, Vol. 1, edited by Frederica Burt Wyatt, Chair, Kimble County Historical Commission (Junction: 1985), 68–69; see also "Adeline Boyce" by Frederica Burt Wyatt in *True West*, September-October 1974, 51 and 53.
39. The *Mason News-Item* noted the arrest with no drama: "The rangers, under Corporal Warren, arrived in Mason a few days after Christmas with John Ringo, who was tried by virtue of a writ of habeas corpus and the bond fixed at $2500." *Galveston Weekly News*, reprinting the item from Mason. Curiously Ringo received greater notoriety only after he left Texas, mainly given him due to his role in the feuds of Tombstone, Arizona Territory. Due to the popularity of the works of such writers as Walter Noble Burns and Stuart N. Lake, as well as highly successful Hollywood productions of the 1990s, Ringo's name is recognized world-wide. The definitive biography of Ringo is Dave Johnson's *John Ringo King of the Cowboys: His Life and Times from the Hoo Doo War to Tombstone*, 2nd ed. (Denton: University of North Texas Press, 2008).
40. Unfortunately we know nothing as to why this Nick Ware was arrested. Lieutenant D. W. Roberts had mustered a man named Nick Ware into his Company D on May 25, 1874, who later served under Lieutenant F. M. Moore. An "N. O. Ware" also served under Captain G. W. Baylor and also under Charles L. Nevill. Was the man rounded up by Nevill in early 1878 the same as Nick Ware/N.O. Ware? Were there one, two, or three men with the same or similar names?
41. Nevill, "Minutes," 34, February 28, 1878. *Austin Gazette* item reprinted in the *Dallas Daily Herald* of March 5, 1878. Darnell was the son of Samuel

and Mary Darnell, residing in Gonzales County when the 1860 census was conducted. Darnell began a career of creating trouble for lawmen and others. Andrew G. Darnell was shot and killed on July 4, 1898, by Frank Johnson, a former Texan like Darnell, in Cochise County, Arizona Territory. Johnson was cleared as it was determined the killing had been done in self-defense. Correspondence from Lynn R. Bailey to Parsons in undated letter.

42. Gonzales County District Court Records, Criminal Docket Book B, 342.
43. Gillett, 140–42.
44. John R. Banister, Hand written memoir, 1914; Nevill, "Minutes," 39; Leona Bruce, *Banister Was There* (Fort Worth: Branch-Smith, 1968), 24–25.
45. *Fugitives*, 131, 162. Gillett wrote in his personal copy that Stark Reynolds had been killed but provided no details.
46. *Houston Daily Telegraph*, November 20, 1874; *Daily Democratic Statesman*, November 20, 1874.
47. Gillett, 142.
48. *Galveston Daily News*, February 23, citing a telegram from Fort Mason dated February 23, 1878.
49. *Dallas Weekly Herald*, March 9, 1878.
50. *Galveston Daily News*, March 1, 1878
51. *Dallas Daily Herald*, March 1, 1878.
52. The historical marker is located eight miles east on U.S. Highway 377 near Junction, Kimble County.
53. *Fort Worth Democrat*, May 3, 1879.
54. Criminal Minutes, Book A, District Court Records, Milam County.
55. Rick Miller, *Sam Bass and Company* (Austin: State House Press, 1999), 126–30.

Chapter 11: Protecting the Man Killer

1. *Daily State Gazette* (Austin) October 4–5, 1871; *Journal of the House of Representatives of the Twelfth Legislature* (Austin: J. G. Tracy, 1871), 192–206; *Fugitives*, 63, 173; *Daily Democratic Statesman*, March 3, 1878. See also *The Governor's Hounds: The Texas State Police, 1870–1873* by Barry A. Crouch and Donaly E. Brice (Austin: University of Texas Press, 2011), 98–102.
2. 1870 Robertson County, Texas census, 241.
3. *Fugitives*, 173; reward proclamation of Governor Coke, February 24, 1874, Record Group 307, Texas State Archives.

4. Physical description of Cotton from reward proclamation, February 24, 1874.
5. *Daily Democratic Statesman*, March 3, 1878; Reynolds' Monthly Return, March 31, 1878; Nevill, "Minutes," March 3 and 13, 1878, 40.
6. The capture of Cotton was reported in the *Weatherford Exponent* of Saturday April 7, 1877. "Caught at Last" was the headline of the article reprinted from the *Mexia Ledger*. According to this report Cotton, along with brothers Wood and Giles Trammel, were "overhauled" at Shreveport, Louisiana. Also see Rick Miller, *Bounty Hunter* (College Station: Texas A&M University Press, 1988), 117–18, a complete biography of John R. "Jack" Duncan.
7. *Galveston Daily News*, March 26, 1878, citing a report from Kimble County in "State News" column. This later appeared in the *Galveston Weekly News*, April 1, 1878. Gillett, 145–46.
8. N. O. Reynolds to William Steele, March 21, 1878, from Fort McKavett.
9. John R. Banister, "Memoir."
10. Nevill, "Minutes," March 16, 1878; N. O. Reynolds Monthly Return, March 31, 1878.
11. Nevill, "Minutes," March 22, 1878; Ibid.
12. N. O. Reynolds to Adjutant General Steele, March 21, 1878.
13. N. O. Reynolds to Major Jones, March 27, 1878.
14. Major Jones to N. O. Reynolds, April 8, 1878.
15. Adjutant General Steele to Major Jones, March 27, 1878; "Letters Sent Wm Steele Adjutant General From Mch 4, 1878 To Jany 25, 1879," 36; Ledger in Texas State Archives, A.G.P.
16. N. O. Reynolds to Major Jones, March 27, 1878.
17. Ibid., April 15, 1878.
18. Nevill, "Minutes," April and May 1, 1878; Reynolds, "Statement of Arrests," no place.
19. *Weekly State Gazette*, April 27, 1878.
20. Major Jones to N. O. Reynolds, May 3 and 7, 1878.
21. E. G. Nicholson, Frontier Battalion surgeon to William Steele, May 24, 1878. Typescript copy of letter in the Walter Prescott Webb Collection, Briscoe Center for American History. Dr. Edmund G. Nicholson spent the remainder of his life in Frio and Val Verde Counties. The 1880 Frio County census shows him as forty years of age, a native of Maryland. He then was boarding at the house of Annie McGhee, along with Sheriff James C. B. Harkness and Deputy Francis E. Lister, and others. Through all the years in both Frio and Val Verde Counties he claimed a few acres of land, a buggy or carriage, a couple of horses

or mules and "tools and implements," which were no doubt his medical instruments. He was a victim of Bright's disease and after some time in Santa Rosa Hospital in San Antonio he went to Mineral Wells, Palo Pinto County, where he died on February 3, 1893. He had no family or known relatives. Frio County tax rolls, 1880–1881; Val Verde County tax rolls, 1885–1892; *San Antonio Daily Express*, February 4, 1893; *Texas Courier of Medicine* 10, no. 7 (March 1893): 209; *Galveston Daily News*, February 8, 1893.

22. Chuck Parsons, *James Madison Brown: Texas Sheriff, Texas Turfman* (Wolfe City, Texas: Henington Publishing Co., 1993), 65–70.
23. *San Antonio Daily Herald*, May 31, 1878; *Burnet Bulletin*, April 1, 1880, printing a lengthy review of the San Saba troubles from an undated issue of the *Austin Review*; *Belton Journal*, October 21, 1881, citing reports from Brenham of October 8 on the conviction of Kendall for murder in the second degree; Guion letter, May 23, 1878 in the Walter Prescott Webb Collection, Briscoe Center for American History. John Isaac Guion was born January 4, 1852, in the governor's mansion at Jackson, Mississippi, the son of Governor and Mrs. Cornelia Thankful (Hall) Guion. After receiving an above average education in private Mississippi schools Guion moved to Texas in the early 1870s and taught school in Austin prior to relocating in San Saba where he began his law practice. After four years in San Saba he moved to Dallas, then to Paint Rock, Concho County, then to San Angelo where he "devoted 33 years in practicing law and in developing the surrounding country." He was appointed a trustee of Texas A&M College by Governor Oscar B. Colquitt in 1910, elected president of the board in 1913, and served as such until resigning in 1918. He died October 27, 1920. Emory E. Bailey, ed., *Who's Who in Texas: A Biographical Directory* (Dallas: Who's Who Publishing Company, 1931), 276.
24. Major Jones to N. O. Reynolds, May 28, 1878.
25. Citizens of San Saba County petition to Major Jones, June 1, 1878.
26. N. O. Reynolds Monthly return, June 30, 1878; Nevill, "Minutes," June 2, 1878; Gillett, 152–54.
27. *Daily Democratic Statesman*, June 6, 1878; Gillett, 153–54.
28. *Galveston Daily News*, June 21, 1878.
29. Ibid., July 3, 1878.
30. Tise, 454. William Russell Doran was born February 7, 1832, in Jackson County, Mississippi, and moved to San Saba County after service in the Civil War. Besides his work as sheriff of San Saba County he ranched and operated a livery stable in San Saba until his death in 1904. Joyce Capps, et al., eds., *San Saba County History 1856–1983* (San Saba County Historical Commission, 1983), 77–78.

31. N. O. Reynolds Monthly Return, June 30, 1878, prepared at San Saba; Nevill, "Minutes," June 1–8, 1878; 1880 Walker County census, 266. Goodin's occupation was consistently listed as shoemaker. He was born in New York or Massachusetts about 1805 and arrived in Texas in April of 1839. He received a land grant of 320 acres and established his home in Jefferson County. Gifford White, compiler, *1840 Citizens of Texas: Land Grants,* vol. 1 (St. Louis, Missouri: Ingmire Publishers, 1983), 96. By 1880 he was listed as a prisoner in Huntsville, seventy-five years of age. Goodin was five-foot eight-inches tall, 148 pounds, fair complexion, blue eyes and white hair. He was convicted on November 5, 1879, in Orange County and received at the prison on November 8 with $4.25 in his possession. Additional remarks show "Death pardoned February 1, 1884." "Convict record: Texas State Penitentiary at Huntsville, Walker County," 27; 1850 Jefferson County, Texas census, 244; 1880 Walker County census, 266. His name was frequently spelled as "Goodwin" and occasionally was a cause for wordplay. One newspaper report indicated he had murdered a man named Ben Wolrath in Wilson County "about Christmas," was jailed in county seat Floresville but then had escaped by locking his jailer in his own cell, and was then reported to be in Oakville with a stolen mare in his possession. Commented the reporter: "He is a 'good one' sure enough—$1,100 reward was offered for his capture." *Victoria Advocate*, March 2, 1878, reprinting an item from the *Pleasanton Stock Journal.*
32. John Wesley Hardin to his wife Jane, June 23, 1878.

Chapter 12: Gunsmoke at Round Rock

1. N. O. Reynolds to Major Jones, July 4, 1878; *Fugitives*, 99.
2. *Lampasas Daily Times*, July 6, 1878.
3. Major Jones to N. O. Reynolds, July 7, 1878.
4. *Lampasas Daily Times*, July 8, 1878
5. Frederic Nolan, *Bad Blood: The Life and Times of the Horrell Brothers* (Stillwater, Oklahoma: Barbed Wire Press, 1994), 140–43.
6. N. O. Reynolds to Major Jones, July 13, 1878.
7. *Austin Weekly Democratic Statesman*, August 1, 1878. E-mail from Dave Johnson, January 22, 2014.
8. N. O. Reynolds Monthly Return, July 31, 1878, prepared at camp on the San Saba; Reynolds to Major Jones, July 13, 1878.
9. Gillett, 154.

10. Rick Miller, *Sam Bass and Gang* (Austin: State House Press, 1999), 13; Walter Prescott Webb, *The Texas Rangers: A Century of Frontier Defense* (Austin: University of Texas Press, 1935, 1985), 371; [Charles L. Martin], *A Sketch of Sam Bass, the Bandit* (Norman: University of Oklahoma Press, 1956 and 1997).
11. Wayne Gard, *Sam Bass* (Boston: Houghton Mifflin Company, 1936) provided details of the various robberies. Gard's minor errors have been corrected in Rick Miller's *Sam Bass and Gang*, a biography which has replaced Gard's and will remain the definitive one. The *Fort Worth Democrat* carried extensive reports of Bass' robberies, especially the issues of January 29, February 28, April 11 and 12 and July 23, 1878. The *Galveston Daily News* provided extensive contemporary coverage of the pursuit, capture, and death of Bass, in particular the issues of July 23–25, 1878. See also Webb, 374.
12. Gillett, 175.
13. Nevill, "Minutes," July 18, 1878; Gillett, 175. Some writers have questioned why Major Jones could not have found sufficient ranger support closer than where Reynolds was camped. The other companies were stationed as follows during the month of July: Company A was in Frio County under Capt. Neal Coldwell; Company B in Denton County under Capt. June Peak; Company C in Shackelford County under Lieutenant G. W. Arrington; Company D in Kimble County under Captain D. W. Roberts; Company F in Edwards County under Capt. Pat Dolan. Each of the companies was considerably farther from Round Rock than Lieutenant Reynolds.
14. Gillett, 176.
15. N. O. Reynolds Monthly Return, July 31, 1878.
16. Nevill, "Minutes," July 18, 1878; *Galveston Daily News*, July 29, printing a communication to the *News* from Round Rock, July 22, 1878.
17. [Charles L. Martin], 152. The street fight even received attention in the *New York Times*. Headlined on page one "A Texas Sheriff Murdered" the paragraph read: "A [Galveston] *News* [of July 19] special from Round Rock says Sam Bass, the noted desperado and train robber, and two others, who had come into town to perfect a plan for robbing a bank, were recognized by Deputy Sheriff Grimes, who attempted to arrest them. They shot him dead and retreated, closely pursued by Deputy Sheriff Maurice Mane [*sic*], who killed one of the outlaws and was himself wounded. Bass escaped. A body of State troops and citizens are in close pursuit." *New York Times*, July 20, 1878.
18. Gillett, 178–80.
19. *Galveston Daily News*, July 21 and 24, 1878. The description of Bass' wounds was provided by Dr. C. P. Cochran and A. T. Morris.

20. Charles L. Nevill, "Passing of Sam Bass, Bank Robber." This combination article-interview is from the *San Antonio Daily Express*, December 22, 1901. Reynolds kept a scrap book but of all the pasted-in articles from unidentified newspapers, this is the only one relevant to his Ranger career. Strangely, in this lengthy article, there is no mention of Reynolds, by then Nevill's brother-in-law, although there is discussion of the capture. San Antonio reporters found Nevill to be good copy; in the December 8, 1901, issue appeared "Last Indian Fight in Texas" based on interviews with Nevill and records pertaining to his experience fighting Victorio's band of Apaches.
21. *New York Times*, July 21, 1878.
22. John R. Banister to his mother, July 22, 1878. The complete postcard as well as a photograph of same is reproduced in *Banister Was There* by Leona Bruce (Fort Worth: Branch-Smith, Inc., 1968), 37–38. Ranger John R. Banister was the father of author Leona Banister Bruce.
23. *Belton Weekly Journal*, May 22, 1879.
24. *Belton News*, July 29, 1880.
25. Inscription per author Parsons' notes; *Galveston Daily News*, July 24, 1878; Webb, in 1935, wrote that the monument then at Bass' grave was the third as "the two original ones having been chipped away by souvenir hunters." *The Texas Rangers*, 389.
26. *Lampasas Daily Times*, July 31, 1878.
27. "How Sam Bass Was Killed" in the *San Antonio Daily Express*, September 12, 1895. The killing of John Wesley Hardin on August 19 prompted the *Express* reporter to interview Hall who took the opportunity to relate his version of the death of Bass.
28. "Last Fight of Sam Bass, Noted Texas Bandit" appeared in the *El Paso Herald* of August 12, 1902 and was reprinted in the *Lampasas Leader* of September 12 and the *Gonzales Inquirer* of September 26, 1902, and perhaps other newspapers as well. It was then reprinted in J. Marvin Hunter's popular *Frontier Times* 10, no, 2 (November 1932): 57–60.
29. N. O. Reynolds Monthly Return, July 31, 1878
30. *El Paso Herald*, August 12, 1902; *Galveston Daily News*, July 24, 1878.
31. For an opposing version of who killed Bass see Robert W. Stephens' *Texas Ranger Sketches* (Dallas: privately printed, 1972), 151–52. Supposedly Bass identified the man who shot him had lather on his face, and as Ware was in the barber shop it must have been his bullet which gave him the death wound. This statement appeared in a newspaper clipping pasted into Ranger Walter Durbin's scrapbook, but with no indication as to what newspaper. At the time

Stephens owned this scrapbook. Ware died in Fort Worth on June 25, 1902, but is buried in Colorado City. Ware had been informed by Major Jones that Bass and other gang members were expected and to be ready for them. It seems unlikely that at this time Ware would decide to get a shave.

32. James B. Warden, "I Saw the Shooting of Sam Bass," *Williamson County, Texas: Its History and Its People*, Mrs. Jean Shroyer, compiler and editor (Austin: Nortex Press, 1985), 45.
33. Rick Miller, *Sam Bass and Gang*, (Austin: State House Press, 1999), 376–77.
34. N. O. Reynolds to Major Jones, July 22, 1878; Reynolds Monthly Return, July 31, 1878.
35. Nevill, "Minutes," July 26, 1878.

Chapter 13: A Sheriff vs A Ranger

1. Major Jones to Reynolds, July 27, 1878; Reynolds Monthly Return, August 31, 1878; Robert W. Stephens, *Texas Ranger Sketches*, 59–61.
2. N. O. Reynolds Monthly Return, August 31, 1878; *Galveston Daily News* of June 29, 1877, had reported an item from the *San Saba News* that recently the district court had adjourned with thirty-nine indictments found. Some ten or twelve of the parties had been arrested and all given bail except George Hoy "against whom there are several indictments, and in default of giving bond in all has been sent to Austin for safe keeping." A change of venue was taken to Burnet County in all of his cases. Hoy's paperwork had been forwarded even though he was not in custody, so it would be ready when he was captured. It is not surprising he was not found as George Riddle Hoy was not even in Texas then, for on July 26, 1878, he and others were in Dodge City, Kansas, following a trail drive, and started to "hurrah" or "tree" the town. Officers Wyatt Earp and James Masterson, and perhaps others, fired on the cowboys inflicting a dangerous wound on Hoy. He died on August 21, 1878. Dodge City's *Ford County Globe* announced his death and pointed out that he "was apparently rather a good young man" although he was under a bond of $1,500 for his court appearance "on account of some cattle scrape, wherein he was charged with aiding and assisting some men in 'rounding up' about 1,000 head of cattle which were claimed by other parties." It is unknown if Joe Henry was one of his companions or if he were being hunted by Reynolds' men at the same time and their names were placed together by chance. See David Johnson, "George R. Hoy: Obscure Victim," NOLA *Quarterly* 14, no. 1 (1990): 8–9; see also *Why the West Was Wild: A Contemporary Look at the Antics of Some Highly*

Published Kansas Cowtown Personalities by Nyle H. Miller and Joseph W. Snell (1963 by Kansas State Historical Society; repr., Norman: University of Oklahoma Press, 2003), 154–55.

3. D. H. Bowen, who replaced Binford, was mustered into Reynolds' Company E on August 22, 1878, and remained with the Rangers for some time after his service with Reynolds. In the 1880 Howard County, Texas, census he is shown as a private in Capt. Ira Long's company, serving along with Sgt. Richard C. Ware, 2nd Corporal David L. Ligon and the two Banister brothers who had served with Reynolds but had left Company E after Reynolds' resignation. Besides Captain Long, Bowen served under commanders C. L. Nevill, June Peak, and John Hoffar. He apparently served with the Rangers through 1881, although the available record is not clear. The 1900 Runnels County census shows him as a widower with four children and born in South Carolina in January 1849. Bowen's oath to serve as a Ranger, on the other hand, shows him as a native of Walker County, Alabama. Obviously official records occasionally contradict themselves, depending on the informant. Runnels County Census, E.D. # 128, Sheet 11; Ranger Service Records, A.G.P., Texas State Archives.
4. N. O. Reynolds to Major Jones, August 17, 1878, from Camp Stockbridge; Reynolds Monthly Return, August 31, 1878.
5. N. O. Reynolds to Major Jones, August 21, 1878; Reynolds Monthly Return, August 31, 1878.
6. Nevill, "Minutes," August 24–26, 1878.
7. Major Jones to N. O. Reynolds, September 5 and Reynolds to Major Jones, September 8, 1878.
8. *National Police Gazette*, September 21, citing a report from Houston, September 10, 1878.
9. *San Antonio Daily Express*, September 12, 1878.
10. Ibid., September 20 and *Weekly Supplement* September 29, 1878.
11. *Burnet Bulletin*, September 28, 1878, citing a report from Liberty Hill, September 20, 1878.
12. John Wesley Hardin to Jane Hardin, September 24, 1878.
13. Thomas Ripley, *They Died With Their Boots On* (Garden City, New York: Doubleday, Doran & Company, 1935), 223. The three principal characters Ripley discussed were Hardin, Bill Longley, and Ben Thompson.
14. *Austin Weekly State Gazette*, October 12, 1878.
15. It is indeed unfortunate that there is no known complete file of the *National Police Gazette*. Some issues do have imaginative drawings but others have drawings based on photographs, which bear a close resemblance to the originals.

In Rick Miller's biography of Bill Longley for example, he includes the montage of drawings that appeared in the *Gazette* of October 26, 1878. *Bloody Bill Longley: The Mythology of a Gunfighter,* 2nd ed. (Denton: University of North Texas Press, 2011).

16. *Fort Worth Democrat*, October 4, 1878.
17. John Wesley Hardin to Jane Hardin, October 4, 1878, written at Tyler, Texas.
18. Ibid. Undated letter from Huntsville, probably written shortly after his arrival there, or possibly written upon arrival at Fort Worth. Even from the context it is impossible to determine which letter was written first.
19. Nevill, "Minutes," October 12, 1878.
20. *San Antonio Daily Express*, September 22, citing a report from Mason, September 20, 1878.
21. N. O. Reynolds Monthly Return, September 31, 1878.
22. N. O. Reynolds Special Order No. 9, September 21, 1878, from Camp Stockbridge.
23. N. O. Reynolds Special Order No. 10, revoking No. 9, September 24, 1878. Banister forfeited one month's pay for his lack of judgment. Reynolds to Adjutant General Steele, September 25, 1878.
24. N. O. Reynolds to William Steele, September 25, and N.O. Reynolds to Major Jones, October 14, 1878.
25. N. O. Reynolds to Major Jones, October 22, 1878.
26. Major Jones to N. O. Reynolds, October 24, 1878.

Chapter 14: An Outrage Upon Children

1. A. J. Sowell. "Frontier Incidents" from *Texas Indian Fighters*, in *Frontier Times* 25, no. 6 (March 1948): 162. 1870 Goliad County, Texas Census, 395. A Texas State Historical Marker was erected in 1979 to commemorate the tragedy.
2. *San Antonio Daily Express*, October 12, Correspondence from Adobe, written at Kerrville October 7, 1878.
3. Sowell, 162; Bob Bennett, *Kerr County, Texas 1856–1956* (San Antonio: The Naylor Company, 1956), 186–87; 1870 Goliad County census, 395.
4. *San Antonio Daily Express*, October 8, 1878, citing General Mason's report from Fort McKavett; *Washington Post*, October 10, 1878.
5. *Denison Daily News*, October 12, 1878.

6. Forrest Salter, "Historic Murder Story Rethought," *Kerrville Mountain Sun*, October 14, 1992.
7. Nevill, "Minutes," October 31, 1878.
8. *San Antonio Daily Express*, October 31, in "State News" column, dateline Austin, October 29, 1878.
9. *San Antonio Daily Express*, November 1, "Frontier Protection," a report from Adobe written at Kerrville on October 26, 1878; Gillett, 186.
10. Gillett, 186–87; Donaly E. Brice interview with William Dowdy, undated; authors' visit to the site of the massacre, courtesy Peter R. Rose.
11. N. O. Reynolds to Major Jones, November 1; Major Jones to Reynolds, November 13, 1878.
12. N. O. Reynolds to Major Jones, November 1, 1878.
13. Major Jones to N. O. Reynolds, November 13; Major Jones' Special Order No. 145, November 26, 1878.
14. Gillett, 187; N. O. Reynolds, "Operations of Company 'E' Front. Batt. From Nov. 1st 1878 to Nov. 15th 1878" and Nevill, "Minutes," November 3, 1878.
15. Gillett, 187–88.
16. Nevill, "Minutes," November 3 and 6, 1878.
17. *San Antonio Daily Express*, November 10, correspondence from Hans Mickle, written from Center Point, Kerr County, November 6, 1878.
18. Milam County, Texas census: 1850, 22; 1860, 53–54; 1870, 244–45.
19. *San Antonio Daily Express*, November 10, 1878, correspondence from Hans Mickle; also *Gonzales Inquirer*, November 16, 1878.
20. District Court Records, Milam County. Research assistance provided by Ms Dorothy Allison, Cameron, Texas.
21. John P. Kirk, Secretary Sheriffs' Association, *A List of Fugitives from Justice, Indicted for Felonies in the State of Texas and a Descriptive List of Escaped Convicts* (Austin: no publisher, 1886), 68.
22. Death Certificate # 28, Bee County, Texas, filed July 24, 1924. The cause of death was listed as organic heart disease. The certificate fails to show the age or date of birth of this Eli Wickson.
23. Gillett, 188.
24. *San Antonio Daily Express*, November 30, written November 28, 1878.
25. N. O. Reynolds, Special Order No. 11, November 24, 1878, written at Camp Contrary.
26. Major John B. Jones, Special Order No. 145, November 26, 1878, written at Camp Dowdy.

27. *Daily Democratic Statesman*, December 3, 1878.
28. N. O. Reynolds Special Order No. 12, December 1, 1878, from "Headquarters Co 'E' Front. Batt," Written at Camp Contrary, Kerr County.
29. N. O. Reynolds to Major Jones, December 4, 1878
30. *Belton Journal*, December 19, 1878. A similar lengthy report appeared in the *San Antonio Daily Express* of December 18 headlined "Lynch Law in Bosque." Because the parties composing the mob were "well disguised by masks" none was recognized by the jailer or the guards. Any other prisoner in the jail would have been too fearful of admitting to anything. The Meridian report concluded: "There is little doubt here of the guilt of the Horrells, though the manner of their punishment is regretted."
31. N. O. Reynolds to Major Jones, December 21, 1878.
32. *San Antonio Weekly Express*, January 23, 1879.
33. *Daily Democratic Statesman*, January 11, 1879. These Hardins have no known relationship to John Wesley Hardin.
34. Major Jones to N. O. Reynolds, December 30, 1878; Jones to Reynolds, January 13, 1879.
35. "Statement of Thefts and Robberies of Amos W. Perkins," January 10, 1879.
36. N. O. Reynolds Monthly Return, December 31, 1878.

Chapter 15: Dealing with Fence Cutters

1. Gillett, 189.
2. Oath prepared and signed January 1, 1879, at Camp Contrary; Reynolds Monthly Return January 31, 1879. The men who swore the oath under Captain C. R. Perry were C. L. Nevill, J.B. Gillett, L. R. Hughes, R. C. Ware, Abram Anglin, J. H. Bates, J. R. Banister, W. L. Banister, D. H. Bowen, William T. Clements, B. F. Carter, P. S. Carter, W. T. Derrick, G. W. Forbes, T. P. Gillespie, T. C. Jackson, Henry Maltimore, J. H. North, L. W. Rogers, H. J. Thomas, C. L. Ware and J. T. Gillespie. George M. Hughes and M. S. Moreland were discharged on the day prior to re-organization.
3. Major Jones to N.O. Reynolds, January 13, 1879.
4. Ranger Service Record: John M. Parks.
5. N. O. Reynolds to Major Jones, February 2, 1879.
6. Ibid., February 14, 1879.
7. The others who signed, besides Reynolds, were: P. C. Jackson, J. H. North, G. W. Forbes, J. H. Bates, D. H. Bowen, J. R. Banister, C. L. Ware, J. M. Parks,

William Clements, B. F. Carter, W. L. Banister, A. Anglin, L. R. Hughes, Henry Maltimore, R. C. Ware, and H. J. Thomas."Recommendation of Sergt. C. L. Nevill for appt as Lt. of Compy" to Major Jones February 28, 1879, A.G.P.

8. Gillett, 191–92.
9. The wording printed in the first edition of this work was copied from an original held in the possession of Reynolds descendants and copied by hand on July 12, 1988, at the home of Bernard Davis, Center Point, Texas. The *Galveston Daily News* of March 14, 1879, and other newspapers did print the resolutions, with only slightly different wording and punctuation. The copy presented to Reynolds himself remains in the possession of the family.
10. *San Antonio Daily Express*, March 16, 1879.
11. Gillett, 192–93.
12. *San Antonio Daily Herald*, September 10, 1879, citing a report from correspondent "Felix" writing for the *San Antonio Daily Express*. Felix wrote the piece while in Blanco City,
13. *Daily Democratic Statesman*, December 25, 1879; advertisement placed in the "Twenty-Five Cent Column."
14. Ibid., September 15, 1882; *Morrison and Fourmy, General Directory of the City of Austin, 1881–82*, 130.
15. Daniel P. Greene, "San Marcos, Texas," *New Handbook of Texas*, vol. 5, 867–88.
16. *San Marcos Free Press*, January 21, 1880.
17. 1880 Hays County Census, 31.
18. *San Marcos Free Press*, April 21, 1881.
19. E-mail from Donaly E. Brice to the late Al Lowman, San Marcos, June 9, 1999; and from James F. Greene, San Marcos, to Donaly E. Brice, June 10, 1999.
20. Adjutant General John B. Jones to N. O. Reynolds, August 23, 1880, "Letters Sent A.G.O. Texas from Jany 27 1880 to Sept 20 1880," 432, Ledger 401-628. Hereafter cited as A.G.O.
21. N. O. Reynolds to Adj. Gen. John B. Jones, August 28, 1880.
22. Adjutant General Jones to D. W. Roberts, September 13, 1880, A.G.O., 480.
23. L. B. Caruthers to Neal Coldwell, September 21, 1880.
24. Adjutant General Jones to Reynolds, September 22, 1880, "Letters Sent Adjutant Genl's Office from Sept 21, 1880 to April 1 1882 (incl.)," 5, Ledger 401-629, Texas State Archives.
25. Adj. Gen. John B. Jones to D. W. Roberts, October 4, 1880, "Letters Sent," 23.

26. Adj. Gen. John B. Jones to N. O. Reynolds, October 15, 1880, "Letters Sent," 15.
27. L. P. Sieker, Lieutenant Commanding, to Adj. Gen. W. H. King, October 9, 1881.
28. Robert W. Stephens, *Texas Ranger Sketches* (privately printed, 1972), 144–46. Sieker died in Houston, November 13, 1914.
29. N. O. Reynolds to Neal Coldwell, October 11. 1881.
30. *San Marcos Free Press*, January 20, 1881.
31. *New Orleans Times*, July 22, 1881.
32. *Austin Daily Statesman*, July 20, 1881.
33. *San Marcos Free Press*, May 25, 1882.
34. J. W. Martin to Neil Coldwell, March 3, 1882. Both Jackson and Martin were residents of Lampasas County as early as 1880. Jackson enumerated the county census in 1880. He was then thirty-three years old with an eighteen-year-old wife, F. R. He listed his occupation as farming. J. W. Martin was also farming, thirty-two years old with a wife and a one-year-old son. 1880 Lampasas County census, 331. "Society Jack" Martin, born April 18, 1848, at Tuskogee, Alabama, came to Texas "when quite young," and on February 6, 1878, married Mary E. Senterfitt. Soon thereafter they moved to Lampasas. Martin died on February 15, 1901, and is buried in the Lampasas City Cemetery. Obituary in the *Lampasas Leader*, February 22, 1901, copy courtesy Jeff Jackson, Lampasas.
35. *Galveston Daily News*, April 27, 1882. The spelling of the names used here is as they appear in the Order of Judgment of the Court in District Court Records, Lampasas County. The *News* identified the Crown brothers as "Meyer" and "Wilson" Crown.
36. Grand Jury Book, Lampasas County, 15. Little is known of this J. C. "Doak" Bradley. There is a Doak Bradley in the 1880 Wood County census, an eighteen-year-old black man, boarding in the John Ellis household. His occupation was given as a wood cutter. 1880 Wood County, Texas census, 286. The other witnesses besides Higgins and Kyle were D. C. Freeman, J. M. Moore, D. W. Phillips, John Phillips, J. N. Mitchum, George Bradley and A. M. McFarland.
37. Ledger: Grand Jury Book, 54.
38. "Election held in the city of Lampasas for Municipal offices," 5; *Houston Daily Post*, April 19, 1883.
39. Ledger: Grand Jury Book, 54, 65–67, 73–74. The spellings H. G. *Christain* and H. G. *Christian* both appear in the Ledger.
40. *San Antonio Daily Express*, July 19 and 20, 1883. Telegraph news from Lampasas to the *Galveston Daily News*, July 25, 1883, telegram from Lampasas July

24; Jonnie Ross Elzner, *Relighting Lamplights of Lampasas County* (Lampasas Hill County Press, 1974), 143.

41. *Galveston Daily News*, July 27 and 28, citing telegrams from Lampasas of July 26 and 27, 1883.
42. *Galveston Daily News*, July 31, 1883, citing telegrams from Lampasas of July 30; *San Antonio Daily Express*, July 31, citing telegrams from Lampasas July 30. Sheriff Wolf, a thirty-one-year-old native of Tennessee, resided in Lampasas with his wife Callaway V. and their six-month-old son Walter A. His brother, Elvis N. Wolf, twenty-five and born in Texas, lived in the same residence and acted as deputy sheriff.
43. *Galveston Daily News*, August 2, citing a telegram from Lampasas of August 1; and August 7, citing a telegram from Lampasas of August 6, 1883.
44. *Galveston Daily News*, August 8, 1883.
45. *Texas State Gazetteer and Business Directory 1884–5*, vol. 2 (St. Louis: R. J. Polk & Co., nd), 487–80. This book's actual publication date is unclear, as it states the city marshal was John W. Reeves. Reynolds took over the position in April 1883.
46. *Galveston Daily News*, August 19, citing telegrams from Lampasas, August 18, 1883.
47. *Galveston Daily News*, November 13 and 15, citing telegraphic specials from Comanche November 12 and 14, 1883.
48. *Galveston Daily News*, August 25, 1884; *Lampasas County History: Its History and Its People* (Marceline, Missouri: Lampasas County Historical Commission, 1991), 6.
49. *Brenham Daily Banner*, November 21, 1884.
50. The election was most interesting for Lampasas city and county citizens as it was a race between Wolf who had served many years, and well-known N.O. Reynolds who had made his mark on the county back in the 1870s during the Horrell-Higgins Feud. Of interest is that in Precinct # 1, the town of Lampasas, Wolf garnered 334 votes, Reynolds 281, and Fox only 21. But the vote was for the entire county and it was in the outlying precincts that Reynolds proved victorious. What might have been a surprise to some was that the areas where the Horrells lived chose Reynolds over Wolf or Fox. Record of Election Returns, No. 1. Lampasas County, Lampasas County Clerk's Office, Lampasas, Texas, page 21. Special thanks to Jeff Jackson who provided this detailed information on this election.
51. W. P. Beall and Marin V. B. Sparks, "Certificate of Election, Lampasas County," November 13 and 27, 1886.

52. Curiously Sam Horrell had been arrested once before by another Ranger captain, Ira Long. The Austin *Statesman* reported: "Capt. Long, of the rangers, has captured Sam Horrell and Gus Stanley, charged with murder and burglary in Lampasas county." *Daily Democratic Statesman*, July 14, 1880.
53. John P. Kirk, comp., Secretary Sheriff's Association, *A List of Fugitives from Justice, Indicted for Felonies in the State of Texas and a Descriptive List of Escaped Convicts* (Austin: no publisher, 1886), 55–56. Hubbard and Smith were farming on adjacent farms in Coryell County. In 1880 James Smith was a twenty-five-year-old farmer with his wife Martha, eighteen, and their two children. In the next dwelling is the family of father-in-law J. H. Hubbard, forty-years-old, a farmer from Virginia, with his wife, Elizabeth S. They had six children. 1880 Coryell County census, 456.
54. N. O. Reynolds to L. P. Sieker, January 19, 1887.
55. Oran M. Roberts, "The Political, Legislative, and Judicial History of Texas for Its Fifty Years of Statehood, 1845–1895," *A Comprehensive History of Texas 1685 to 1897*. Edited by Dudley G. Wooten (Austin: Texas State Historical Association Edition, 1986), 261; and Wilburn H. King, *Report of the Adjutant General of the State of Texas December, 1888* (Austin: State Printers, 1889), 48.
56. N. O. Reynolds to W. H. King, July 28, 1886; Reynolds to Sieker, July 29, 1886.
57. Dan L. Thrapp, "Ira Aten," *Encyclopedia of Frontier Biography*, Supplement vol. 4 (Spokane: The Arthur H. Clark Company, 1994), 19. Such writings include Aten's own *Six and One-half Years in the Ranger Service: The Memoirs of Ira Aten, Sergeant, Company D, Texas Rangers* (Bandera: Frontier Times Museum, 1945) and Harold Preece's *Lone Star Man: Ira Aten, Last of the Old Texas Rangers* (New York: Hastings House,), 1960. The most complete and certainly a work that will remain a near definitive biography of Aten is Bob Alexander, *Rawhide Ranger, Ira Aten: Enforcing Law on the Texas Frontier* (Denton: University of North Texas Press, 2011).
58. The names of two of the murderers of Braeutigam were identified previously as Collier and (occasionally) Bean. Their correct and full names are from *Rawhide Ranger, Ira Aten: Enforcing Law on the Texas Frontier* by Bob Alexander, 54.
59. "Operations of Front. Battalion and Report of Special Rangers From December 1, 1885 to November 30, 1892," Ledger 401-1084, page 84, Texas State Archives.
60. Ira Aten, "Fence-Cutting Days in Texas," *Frontier Times* 16, no. 10 (July 1939): 441–42.

61. Henry M. Holmes to Governor John Ireland, August 17, 1886; N. O. Reynolds to Ireland, December 24, 1886.
62. W. A. Patterson to Governor Ireland, December 24; Reynolds to Ireland, December 24, 1886.
63. Capt. William Scott Monthly Return, December 31, 1886, prepared at Brownwood, Brown County.
64. Ibid., January 31, 1886. For a comprehensive biography of Brooks see *Captain J.A. Brooks: Texas Ranger* by Paul N. Spellman published by University of North Texas Press, 2007.
65. Capt. William Banta and J. W. Caldwell Jr., "Life of Alexander Brown," *Twenty-seven Years on the Texas Frontier* (Council Hill: Oklahoma: L.G. Park, 1893), 170–71.
66. *Galveston Daily News*, January 11, 1887.
67. In 1880 Jerry Dugger was farming in Burnet County, age thirty-one, a native of Georgia. His wife Mary A., age thirty-one, was from South Carolina. At the time they had one child, an eight-year-old daughter named Geraline. 1880 Burnet County census, 173.
68. *Lampasas Leader*, November 17, 1888. Jerry Dugger was charged as an accomplice in the death of Brown. He was found guilty and sentenced to serve ninety-nine years in the penitentiary. On appeal Dugger's conviction was overturned and cause remanded. *Lampasas Leader*, February 2, 1889.
69. Banta, 175.
70. *Galveston Daily News*, January 11, 1887. Also a "Withdrawal Card" for Reynolds, showing his recommendation "to all lodges of our chivalric order, wherever located." Copy courtesy Stephen Reynolds Davis.
71. *Galveston Daily News*, May 31, 1887.

Chapter 16: The Cornett-Whitley Gang Emerges

1. John D. Templeton, *Report of the Attorney-General of the State of Texas For the Years 1885–6* (Austin: State Printing Office, 1886), 35; J. S. Hogg, *Report of the Attorney-General of the State of Texas For the Years 1887–8* (Austin: State Printing Office, 1889), 4; J. S. Hogg, *Report of the Attorney-General of the State of Texas For the Years 1889–1890* (Austin: State Printing Office, 1891), 26.
2. *Lampasas Leader*, October 6, 1888.
3. *Galveston Daily News*, December 13–14, 1887.

4. There is no full-length study of the Cornett-Whitley gang, although they were much more successful than Sam Bass and his gang. The 1860 census shows the Cornett household: L. E., a twenty-nine-year-old stock raiser born in Missouri as head of house hold. Seventeen-year-old Cordelia is enumerated next followed by her six-month-old son Braxton, the future gang leader. The 1870 Goliad Census shows the future train robber as nine years old, with a six-year-old sister named Cordelia and mother Cordelia, now listed as twenty-six-years-old, all living in the household of William McGinty, a stock raiser born in Georgia and uncle of young Braxton. At the age of eighteen Brack was convicted of horse theft and sentenced to a term of ten years in Huntsville penitentiary. He escaped but was quickly recaptured in December 1878; he then escaped again on November 27, 1880, and was never recaptured. During his time in prison he certainly became acquainted with John Wesley Hardin and others Reynolds would have known, such as George W. Gladden from the Mason County War days. The 1880 Walker County prison census shows him as "B. Cornett" then twenty-five-years old. 1860 Goliad County census, 54; 1870 Goliad County census, 369; 1880 Walker County census, 259; *Convict Record, Texas State Penitentiary*, 213. An authoritative account of the gang's major criminal activities, but not the entire career of Cornett, remains "A Great Man Hunt—Correspondence from 'W.B.S.'" [Walter Barlow Stevens] by Jeff Burton in the *Brand Book* of the English Westerners Society, London, 1975–1976, vol. 18 (1977): 11-34. This is an annotated reprint of Stevens' long article that originally appeared in the *St. Louis Globe-Democrat*, October 27, 1888, which in turn originated in Austin, Texas, on October 24, 1888.

    Barber was born about 1860, possibly in Williamson County. In 1880 he was living there with George W. Murray, a thirty-two-year-old Mississippi-born farmer with his wife and two small children. Barber is listed as twenty years of age. Census enumerator J. W. Ledbetter noted by his name "wife's son," certainly an impossibility as Mrs. Murray was only twenty-six years of age. Possibly Ledbetter meant "wife's brother." 1880 Williamson County census, 525; also Mary Whittington, "The Great Train Robberies of 1885 and 1887," *Plum Creek Almanac* 19, no. 2 (Fall 2001): 140–44.

5. *Austin Daily Statesman*, May 19 and 20, 1887. According to the *Statesman* of May 19 the posse included Marshal James Lucy, Deputy Sheriff Tom Platt, Marshal Rankin, Jacob D. "Jake" Platt, Walter Robinson, and three others identified only as Anglin, Bracken, and Montgomery. "Anglin" undoubtedly refers to former Reynolds ranger Abram Anglin. The others were John W. Bracken and Henry Montgomery, both mounted policemen. Bill Smith Price authored a book dealing with Whitley entitled *Bill Whitley, Outlaw* (Austin: Nortex Press,

1995). Therein Price identified the officers as "Rundell, Grissorway, Jack Platt, Anglin and Bracken Montgomery, brothers, Wattes [*sic*, Walter] Robinson and Sergeant Palmer," 42. "Palmer" was Charles C. Palmer, a sergeant of police. No other mention of Grissorway has been found, and certainly Anglin and Bracken were not brothers. *Morrison & Fourney's General Directory of the City of Austin, 1885–86*, and same 1887–88 and 1889–1890. According to a report from Waco there were a dozen men who "did the work" and the robbers netted "boodle" in the amount ranging from $21,000 to $55,000; the *Tombstone Epitaph* of Tombstone, Arizona, carried an item in its issue of May 21, citing the report from Waco, May 20, 1887.

6. *Austin Daily Democratic Statesman*, June 19, citing reports from Flatonia, Galveston, and San Antonio of June 18, 1887; a detailed report of the robbery appeared in the *Tombstone Epitaph*, June 22, 1887.
7. *Galveston Daily News*, October 7, citing a report from Grandview, Texas, of October 6, 1887.
8. *St. Louis Globe-Democrat*, October 27, 1888. Author Bill Smith Price, in *Bill Whitley, Outlaw*, strangely doesn't mention Sheriff Reynolds by name, writing this of Reynolds' unintentionally causing the plan to capture the gang to fail. "A sheriff who wanted to be famous [Reynolds] and wasn't asked to get in on the scheme intercepted Bill and Barber as they were riding across the country to meet the train at Temple [Bell County]. When they saw the sheriff they easily threw him off and abandoned their plans to pull Reeves off the train," 52. Bill Smith Price was a granddaughter of Whitley. There is nothing in the record of N. O. Reynolds to indicate that he "wanted to be famous" as author Price has written. It is also very doubtful that the outlaws so easily "threw him off" their trail.
9. Bob Alexander, *Rawhide Ranger Ira Aten: Enforcing Law on the Texas Frontier*, succinctly describes the death of Cornett, 142.
10. *Daily Democratic Statesman*, February 17, 1888.
11. John T. Olive had an extensive career in Williamson County. He was elected sheriff on November 4, 1884, re-elected on November 2, 1886, and served until November 4, 1888. Then he was elected a second time on November 4, 1890, and served until November 8, 1892. Tise, 544.
12. Sergeant Ira Aten to L. P. Sieker, August 6, 1887, A.G.P.
13. *Austin Daily Democratic Statesman*, August 10; *Galveston Daily News*, August 9, 1887; 1880 Williamson County census, 504. Stanley is buried in the Matsler Cemetery in Williamson County. His grave is marked. Stanley's name appears on the Lost Lawman Memorial monument, managed by the Texas Sheriffs

Association, panel 10, column A, line 5. The name of Ahijah W. "Hi" Grimes, another deputy of Williamson County who was killed by members of the Sam Bass gang, also appears on this same monument, panel 9, column A, row 15.

14. *Galveston Daily News,* August 8 and 9, 1887.
15. *St. Louis Globe-Democrat*, October 27, 1887.
16. *Lampasas Leader*, October 6, 1888, headlined its article "Whitley Downed At Last." According to the *Leader* Bybee was sent to Huntsville, but that name is not found in the Huntsville penitentiary records.
17. *Austin Daily Statesman*, April 27, 1888.
18. Burton, 28; *Austin Daily Democratic Statesman*, September 27, 1888.
19. *Austin Daily Democratic Statesman*, September 27, 1888, citing reports from San Antonio dated September 26, 1888.
20. Stanley Whitley, et al., "Whitley" in *Burnet County History*,2 , by Darrell Debo and the Burnet County Historical Commission (Burnet: Eakin Press, 1979), 332–33. Mahomet Cemetery is a small cemetery in rural Burnet County. The 1880 census shows Cordelia, fourteen years of age, with her parents, James and Elizabeth Cox. 1880 Lampasas County census, 347.
21. *Lampasas Leader*, October 6, 1888.
22. *Dallas Morning News*, November 10, 1888; *Austin Daily Statesman*, November 22, 1888; *Galveston Daily News*, December 8, 1888; *Dallas Daily Times-Herald*, December 9, 1889; *Indian Chieftain* (Vinita, Indian Territory), November 22, 1888; *Fort Smith Elevator*, December 13, 1889; Dewey Don Queen, "The Queen Family," *Round Rock, Texas U.S.A.* (Wolfe City, Texas: Henington Publishing Co, 1972), 243–44. Jeff Burton identifies Queen as Stanley Queen, whereas Dewey Don Queen identifies the outlaw as Samuel. The Queen family resided in Williamson County in1880 with sixty-eight-year-old Samuel as head of household with his wife Jane A., fifty-eight. The three children include Reubin A., thirty-two and suffering from epilepsy; Samuel D., twenty and working on the family farm; and Stanley P. nineteen and also suffering from epilepsy. It is doubtful if the son suffering from epilepsy would have found much success on the outlaw trail. For this reason we believe the outlaw Queen was Samuel D., agreeing with Dewey Don Queen. 1880 Williamson County census, 498.
23. *Lampasas Leader*, October 13, 1888. Whitfield Chalk Sr., according to the 1880 census, was a farmer and carpenter, sixty-nine years old, residing in Lampasas County with his wife Mary and two sons, Jefferson, twenty-one, and Whitfield Jr., sixteen, and attending school. 1880 Lampasas County census, 344.

24. *Lampasas Leader*, October 13, 1888. A later item pointed out that Mr. Brown had lived there nearly all his life and was relocating to Port Lavaca, Texas, with his wife and "family of excellent children." Besides serving for a number of years as a jailer he had been in charge of the county farm. *Lampasas Leader*, October 29, 1909.

25. Ibid., November 3, 1888.

26. Ibid., November 10 and 17, 1888.

27. Ibid., November 10, 1888.

28. Ibid.; Marriage Book D, 1886–1892, Lampasas County Marriage Records, September 15, 1886; 1880 McLennan County census, 249; District Court Records, Texas vs. Sam Neff, # 1729, horse theft, November 17, 1887. This was officially dismissed on May 12, 1890. Criminal Minutes District Court, Lampasas, Vol. 8; Ohio Penitentiary Register of Prisoners and Index, Vol. 15, February 1889-January 1891, 199–201. Microfilm copy provided through the courtesy of Carol W. Bell, Warren Trumbell County Library, Warren, Ohio. On October 13, 1891, Maggie L. Neff filed for divorce from her husband, which became final on November 8, 1891. Neff was released from the federal penitentiary on March 8, 1893. He returned to Texas where on June 7, 1894, he was arrested again on a warrant charging him with horse theft. The charge was dropped later for want of evidence. In March 1897 Neff relocated to Coke County where he married Donnie J. Cox on September 16, 1906. The couple lived in Coke County for years, and then on February 14, 1934, Neff died in Wichita Falls, Texas. Samuel Herbert Neff is buried in Tennyson, Coke County.

29. *Lampasas Leader*, November 27, 1888

30. Ibid., December 22, 1888.

31. Civil Minutes District Court, Lampasas County, # 1207, Lampasas County, November 11, 1889, 254 and November 5, 1890, Vol. 7, 254, 322.

32. Joyce Tomlinson, reviewing the history of the First National Bank's first hundred years. "First National Bank observes birthday" in the *Lampasas Dispatch Record*, July 12, 1984.

33. *Lampasas Leader*, June 29, 1889.

34. Ibid., August 31, 1889.

35. Handwritten notes in the collection of the Lampasas County Historical Commission.

36. Letterhead in Lampasas Museum.

37. Lampasas County Commissioners Minutes, Vol. 3, 480–81, including a diagram of the trees placed in the courthouse yard.

Chapter 17: A Loss and a Final Guard

1. *Lockhart Post*, June 9, 1899.
2. Vivian Elizabeth Smyrl, "Lockhart, Texas," *New Handbook*, vol. 4, 257.
3. Application for liquor license, June 1, 1899, Caldwell County Court Records.
4. *Lockhart Post*, June 9, 1899.
5. Ibid., June 16, 1899.
6. Deed Record Book 24, 516, Caldwell County Civil Court Records; Deed Record Book 25, 453–54, Lockhart, Texas.
7. *Lockhart Post*, September 15, 1899.
8. *Galveston Daily News*, August 14, 1877, printing a lengthy article "Texas Watering Places" written from Burditt's Well, a name by which it was also known, on August 8, by "Rusticus." The *Lockhart Post* reported that the Reynolds family visited Burdette Wells on Sunday, August 27, 1899.
9. "Burdette Wells, Texas" by Vanessa L. Davis, *New Handbook*, vol. 1, 828.
10. *Lockhart Post*, January 12, 1900. "Staples Store" today is simply Staples, with a population of less than one hundred. "Staples Texas" by Al Lowman, *New Handbook*, vol. 6, 61–62.
11. *Lockhart Post*, February 9 and March 2, 1900.
12. 1900 Caldwell County census, E.D. # 118, sheet 9, enumerated June 5, 1900.
13. *Lockhart Post*, September 21 and *Lockhart Weekly Post*, May 16, 1900.
14. *Lockhart Weekly Post*, May 15, 1901.
15. Application for Liquor License, March 1, 1902, Caldwell County Court Records, 113.
16. Ibid., September 12, 1902, 303.
17. Ibid., September 29, 1902, 307.
18. *Lockhart Post*, March 3, 1903. Application for Liquor License, August 25, 1903, 143.
19. *Lockhart Post*, September 10, 1903.
20. Ibid., August 13, 1903.
21. Ibid., December 17, 1903.
22. Ibid., February 4, 1904.
23. Ibid.
24. *Galveston Daily News*, August 9, 1877.
25. 1910 Orange County census, E.D. #117, sheet 8. "Orange, Texas" by Diana J. Kleiner, *New Handbook*, 1160-161.

26. *Bradford Star*, Towanda, Pennsylvania, March 28, 1912.
27. B. T. Reynolds obituary and photograph of her headstone courtesy Ms Pat Buck, Endicott, New York, June 2003.
28. Original letter in the Rieter Family Papers. The late Diane Davis Rieter was a great-granddaughter of N. O. Reynolds.
29. Diane Davis Rieter, "The Nelson Oscar [*sic*] Reynolds Family" in Gerald Witt's *The History of Eastern Kerr County* (Austin: Nortex Press, 1986), 206–07; Deed Record Book, # 36, Kerr County, 212–13; *Mountain Sun*, Kerrville, Texas, May 1, 1947; "Mrs. N. O. Reynolds, 84, Beloved Resident of Center Point, Dies."
30. *Lockhart Post Register*, April 21, 1921. To the right of Lula Blunt's marker is that of her husband, Charlie H. Blunt with dates November 24, 1885, to March 6, 1958; obituary in the *San Antonio Express*, April 17, 1921. Blunt was the son of Dr. Walter F. and Dora G. Blunt. Dr. Blunt died June 25, 1903. From 1875 to 1897 he held the position of quarantine officer at Galveston. In 1898 he was appointed State Health Officer by Governor Culberson. *Lockhart Register*, July 3, 1903.
31. The authors were privileged to examine this copy of Gillett's *Six Years* at the former home of Mr. and Mrs. N. O. Reynolds at Center Point, then the home of Diane Davis Rieter, great-granddaughter of Reynolds. Interview with authors in the home July 12, 1988.
32. Official death certificate # 8901 of Nelson Orcelus Reynolds.
33. Dates of children's births from application for pension dated April 3, 1915, at Orange; death certificate # 8901. He also listed Lula J. Reynolds born December 18, 1885.
34. Probate Record #499, filed March 24, 1922, Kerr County Court records, Kerrville.
35. *Kerrville Mountain Sun*, March 10, 1922.
36. Irene Reynolds to Washington Gardner, August 22, 1922.
37. Ibid., March 21, 1923.
38. Official death certificate of Irene Temperance Nevill Reynolds # 15019. *San Antonio Daily Express*, April 29, 1947, "Reynolds" in "Deaths" column; *San Antonio Light*, April 29, 1947. Reynolds family tree courtesy Stephen Reynolds Davis. Mrs. Reynolds' parents both had long and productive lives. Her father, Zachariah Lewis Nevill, was born April 7, 1838, and died on March 22, 1909, in El Paso, Texas. They are both buried in Angleton Cemetery, Brazoria County, Texas. Their graves are marked.

39. Official program, "Historical Marker Dedication—Center Point Cemetery," August 22, 1987; *San Antonio Express-News*, August 22, 1987; official program, "Texas Ranger Memorial Service—Center Point Cemetery," October 23, 1999; Zeke MacCormak, "Eternal Rest: Cemetery's 32 Texas Ranger graves marked for honor," *San Antonio Express-News*, October 6, 1999, 1,7B.

BIBLIOGRAPHY

PRIMARY SOURCES

Archives and Information Services Division, Texas State Library and Archives Commission:

Adjutant General Correspondence. Adjutant General Records.

Bierschwale, Charles, Collection.

Coke, Gov. Richard, Papers.

Convict Record, Texas State Penitentiary, Huntsville, Texas.

Executive Record Book. Govs. Coke and Hubbard. July 1875–June 1877.

Extradition Papers. Secretary of State Records.

General and Special Orders of Major John B. Jones and Adjutant General William Steele. Adjutant General Records.

Hubbard, Gov. Richard Bennett, Papers.

Letters, Adjutant General's Office, Dec. 9, 1876 to Aug. 28, 1877.

Monthly Returns, Muster and Pay Rolls: Captain C. R. Perry; Captain D. W. Roberts; Lieut. Ira Long; Captain J. M. Denton; Capt. Neal Coldwell; Capt. John C. Sparks; Lieut. Frank M. Moore; N. O. Reynolds.

Nevill, C. L. Minutes of Co. E. Scouts etc. Adjutant General Records.

Ranger Correspondence, Adjutant General Records.

Record of Criminals by Co[unties], Description. Adjutant General Records.

Reynolds, N. O. Report of Operations.

Texas Ranger Service Records. Adjutant General Records.

Texas County Records:

Bee County:

Wixon, Eli. Death Certificate #28. Court Records, Beeville, Texas.

Caldwell County:

Deed Records, Books 24 and 25.

Reynolds, N. O. Applications for Liquor License. Civil Court Records.

Frio County:

Tax Rolls, 1885–93.

Gonzales County:

District Court Records. Criminal Docket Book B. Gonzales County Courthouse Annex, Gonzales, Texas.

Hays County:

Police Court Record Book B. Hays County Courthouse, San Marcos, Texas.

Kerr County:

Deed Records, Book 36.

Reynolds, N. O. Probate Record, #499.

Lampasas County:

District Court. Criminal Minutes. Vol. 8.

District Court. Civil Minutes. Lampasas County Courthouse, Lampasas.

Grand Jury Book. Lampasas County Courthouse, Lampasas.

Marriage Book D, 1886–92. Marriage Records.

Milam County:

District Court Records. Milam County Courthouse, Cameron, Texas.

Record of Prisoners Confined in the County Jail.

Val Verde County:

Tax Rolls, 1885–93

Miscellaneous:

Britton, Frank L. *Report of the Adjutant General of the State of Texas, for the Year 1872*. Austin: James P. Newcomb & Company, 1873.

———. *Report of the Adjutant General of the State of Texas, for the Year 1873*. Austin: Cardwell & Walker, 1874.

Death Certificates: Nelson Orcelus Reynolds. Kerr County. March 1, 1922; #8901. Irene T. Reynolds. Kerr County, April 27, 1947, Bureau of Vital Statistics, Austin.

Declaration for Pension. Nelson Orcelus Reynolds. #1,168, 355. Civil War Service.

Gray & Moore Mercantile and General City Directory of Austin, Texas for 1877–78. Austin: Eugene von Boeckman, 1877.

"Historical Marker Dedication—Center Point Cemetery." Official program, August 22, 1987.

Hogg, J. S. *Report of the Attorney-General of the State of Texas for the Years 1887–8*. Austin: State Printing Office, 1891.

House Miscellaneous Document No. 127. 40th Congress, 2nd Session, May 11, 1868. Communication from Governor Pease Relative to the Troubles in That State.

Jones, John B. *Report of John B. Jones, Commanding the Frontier Battalion, Texas State Troops, March 1876*. Houston: A. C. Gray.

Journal of the House of Representatives of the Twelfth Legislature. Austin: J. G. Tracy, 1871.

Morrison & Fourmy's General Directory of the City of Austin, 1881–82.

Morrison & Fourmy's General Directory of the City of Austin, 1885–86.

Morrison & Fourmy's General Directory of the City of Austin, 1887–88.

Morrison & Fourmy's General Directory of the City of Austin, 1889–90.

Muster and Descriptive Roll: Orcelus Reynolds, National Archives, Washington, D.C.

Muster and Descriptive Roll: Thomas Polk Edmondson, National Archives, Washington, D.C.

Ohio Penitentiary Register of Prisoners and Index, Vol. 15, February 1889-January 1891.

Reece, J. N. *Report of the Adjutant General of the State of Illinois, Springfield, Illinois*. Springfield, IL: NP, 1900.

Templeton, John D. *Report of the Attorney-General of the State of Texas for the Years 1885–6.* Austin: State Printing Office, 1886.

Whiteside County, Illinois, Grantor Book 10.

UNITED STATES CENSUS RECORDS

Illinois: Whiteside County, 1870.

Indiana: Hancock County, 1860, 1870.

Kentucky: Graves County, 1850.

Missouri: Clay County, 1860.

Pennsylvania: Bradford County, 1850, 1870.

Texas: Austin: The Schedule of Inhabitants in the City of Austin, County of Travis, State of Texas [1875]
Blanco: 1870.
Burnet: 1870, 1880.
Caldwell: 1900
Coryell: 1880.
Dallas: 1860, 1870.
Falls: 1860.

Frio: 1880.
Gillespie: 1860, 1870.
Goliad: 1860, 1870.
Gonzales: 1860.
Hamilton: 1870, 1880.
Hays: 1870, 1880.
Howard: 1880.
Jasper: 1870.
Jefferson: 1850, 1860.
Kimble: 1870, 1880.
Lampasas: 1870, 1880.
McLennan: 1880.
Mason: 1880.
Menard: 1870.
Milam: 1850, 1860, 1870.
Orange: 1910, 1920.
Robertson: 1870.
San Saba: 1870.
Travis: 1870, 1880.
Walker: 1880.
Williamson: 1880.

VIRGINIA: Culpeper, 1860, 1870.

BOOKS, PAMPHLETS, AND ARTICLES

Alexander, Bob. *Winchester Warriors: Texas Rangers of Company D, 1874–1901*. Denton: University of North Texas Press, 2009.

———. *Rawhide Ranger, Ira Aten: Enforcing Law on the Texas Frontier*. Denton: University of North Texas Press, 2011.

Andreas, A. T. *History of the State of Kansas Containing a Full Account of Its Growth from an Uninhabited Territory to a Wealthy and Important State*. Chicago: Self published, 1883.

Anonymous: "The Boyce Family" in *Frontier Times*, August, 1927.

———. *The Texas Centennial Roster, 1836–1936*. San Antonio: Stationers Exchange, 1936.

———. *Terrace Cemetery, Garza County, Texas*. Typescript copy in Texas State Library.

———. *Proceedings of the First Annual Reunion of the Texas Rangers Association and Organization of the Texas Ranger Battalion at Austin, Texas, October 4th, 1897.*

———. *The War of the Rebellion: A Compilation of the Official Records of the Union and Confederate Armies.* Washington, D.C.: Government Printing Office, 1897.

———. *Menard County History: An Anthology.* San Angelo: Anchor Publishing Co., 1982.

———. *Historical and Biographical record of the Cattle Industry and the Cattlemen of Texas.* New York: Antiquarian Press, Ltd., 1959 edition.

———. *Kimble County Official Historical Markers.* Brochure. 1974.

———. *Lampasas County History: Its History and Its People.* Marceline, MO: Lampasas County Historical Commission, 1991.

Aten, Ira. *Six and One-half Years in the Ranger Service. The Memoirs of Ira Aten, Sergeant, Company D, Texas Rangers.* Bandera, Texas. *Frontier Times*, 1945.

Aten, Ira. "Fence-cutting Days in Texas." *Frontier Times*, July, 1939.

Bailey, Emory E., ed. *Who's Who in Texas: A Biographical Directory.* Dallas: Who's Who Publishing Company, 1931.

Banta, William and J. W. Caldwell Jr. *Twenty-seven Years on the Texas Frontier.* Council Hill, OK: L. G. Park, 1893.

Bent, Charles, ed. *History of Whiteside County, Illinois from its First Settlement to the Present Time.* Facsimile edition. Morrison, IL: Sterling-Rock Falls Historical Society, 1877.

Bradshaw, H. C. *History of Bradshaw County, Pennsylvania, With Biographical Sketches.* Chicago: S. B. Nelson & Company, 1891.

Bruce, Leona. *Banister Was There.* Fort Worth: Branch-Smith, 1968.

Burton, Jeff. "'A Great Manhunt'—Correspondence from 'W.B.S.'" in the *Brand Book* of the English Westerners Society, 1975–76. London: Vol. 18, 1977.

Caffey, Stewart, ed. *Comanche Country, Reflections of Our Heritage.* Vol. 2. Special Project by the Students of Stewart Caffey. Published in Comanche, Texas, 1983.

Capps, Joyce, ed. *San Saba County History, 1856–1893.* San Saba County Historical Commission, 1983.

Capps, Joyce, Compiler. *San Saba, Texas Cemetery Inscriptions*, pamphlet, 1992.

Carnal, Ed. "Reminiscences of a Texas Ranger" in *Frontier Times*, December, 1923.

Cox, Mike. *The Texas Rangers: Wearing the Cinco Peso, 1821–1900.* New York: Tom Doherty Associates, 2008.

Cox, Minnie. *Biography of Cicero Rufus Perry, Captain, Texas Rangers.* Johnson City: NP, 1985.

Didway, Charles, ed. *Wagon Wheels: A History of Garza County*. Seagraves, TX: Pioneer Book Publishers, Inc., 1973.

Douglas, C. L. *Famous Texas Feuds*. 1936. Reprint, Austin: State House Press, 1998.

Elzner, Jonnie Ross. *Relighting Lamplights of Lampasas County*. Lampasas: Hill Country Press, 1974.

Gamel, Thomas W. *The Life of Thomas W. Gamel, as Narrated to Glenn James and Henri Rupe Capps*. Mason: The Mason County Historical Society, 1994. With annotations by Dave Johnson.

Gard, Wayne. *Sam Bass*. Boston: Houghton Mifflin, Company, 1936.

Gay, Beatrice Grady. *"Into the Setting Sun" A History of Coleman County*. No place, 1936.

Gillett, James B. *Six Years with the Texas Rangers, 1875–1881*. Chicago: Lakeside Press, 1943.

Haley, James L. *The Buffalo War: The History of the Red River Uprising of 1874*. Reprint, Austin: State House Press, 1998.

Hardin, John Wesley. *The Life of John Wesley Hardin, as Written by Himself*. Introduction by Robert G. McCubbin. Norman: University of Oklahoma Press, 1961.

Hendricks, George B. *The Bad Men of the West*. San Antonio: The Naylor Company, 1941, 1959.

Heverly, Clement E. *Pioneer and Patriot Families of Bradford County, Pennsylvania, 1770–1800*. Towanda, PA: Bradford Star Printing, 1913.

[Holmes, Henry M.] "Attorney's Business Book," Book 4.

[Holmes, Lucie] *The Lucie Holmes Diary 1875–1876. The Hoo Doo War Years*. Mason: The Mason County Historical Commission, 1985.

Hunter, J. Marvin and Noah H. Rose. *The Album of Gunfighters*. Privately printed, 1951.

Hunter, J. Marvin [?] "Captain Dan W. Roberts," *Frontier Times*, August, 1927.

Jackson, Jeff. *Historical Guide to the Shootout on the Public Square*. No publisher, 1990.

Jackson, Jeff. "Shadrick T. Denson" in *Lampasas County Texas Its History and Its People*. Lampasas: The Lampasas History Book Committee, 1991.

Jackson, Jeff. "Langford Cove." Unpublished manuscript, copy in authors' possession.

Jackson, Jeff. *Law and Order Frontier Lampasas*. Lampasas: Lampasas County Chamber of Commerce, 2003.

Johnson, Dave. *John Ringo*. Stillwater, OK: Barbed Wire Press, 1996.

Johnson, Dave. *John Ringo King of the Cowboys: His Life and Times from the Hoo Doo War to Tombstone*. Denton: University of North Texas Press, 2008.

Johnson, Dave. *The Mason County "Hoo Doo" War, 1874–1902*. Denton: University of North Texas Press, 2006.

Johnson, Dave. ". . . about fifteen men stepped to the front." NOLA *Newsletter* 10, no. 1 (January–March, 1985).

Johnson, Dave. "George R. Hoy: Obscure Victim." NOLA *Quarterly* 14, no. 4, 1990.

Johnson, Dave. "Scott Cooley—A Byword for Terror." NOLA *Quarterly* 27, no. 3 (April-June 2003).

King, W. H. *Report of the Adjutant General of the State of Texas, December 1888*. Austin: State Printers, 1889.

Kirk, John P., compiler. *A List of Fugitives from Justice, Indicted for Felonies in the State of Texas and a Descriptive List of Escaped Convicts*. Austin: no publisher. 1888.

[Martin, Charles L.] *A Sketch of Sam Bass, the Bandit*. Norman: University of Oklahoma Press, reprint, 1997.

Miller, Nyle H. and Joseph W. Snell. *Why the West Was Wild: A Contemporary Look at the Antics of Some Highly Publicized Kansas Cowtown Personalities*. Topeka: Kansas State Historical Society, 1963; reprint by University of Oklahoma Press, 2003.

Miller, Rick. *Bounty Hunter*. College Station: Creative Publishing Company, 1998.

———. *Sam Bass and Gang*. Austin: State House Press, 1999.

———. *Bloody Bill Longley: The Mythology of a Gunfighter*. Denton: University of North Texas Press, 2011.

———. *Texas Ranger John B. Jones and the Frontier Battalion, 1874–1991*. Denton: University of North Texas Press, 2012.

Moursund, John Stribling. *Blanco County Families for One Hundred Years*. Edited by Mabel Stribling. Revised edition. Burnet, TX: Nortex Press, 1981.

Nolan, Frederick. *Bad Blood: The Life and Times of the Horrell Brothers*. Stillwater: Barbed Wire Press, 1994.

Parsons, Chuck. "Texas Ranger N. O. Reynolds' Lost Years." NOLA *Quarterly* 26, no. 3 (July-September 2002).

Parsons, Chuck and Gary P. Fitterer. *Captain C. B. McKinney: The Law in South Texas*. Wolfe City, TX: Henington Publishing Co., 1993.

Parsons, Chuck. "'Mervyn' A Poetical Correspondent" in the *Brand Book* of the English Westerners Society. Winter, 1988–1989.

Parsons, Chuck. *James Madison Brown: Texas Sheriff, Texas Turfman*. Wolfe City, TX: Henington Publishing Company, 1993.

Parsons, Chuck, and Norman Wayne Brown. *A Lawless Breed: John Wesley Hardin, Texas Reconstruction, and Violence in the Wild West*. Denton: University of North Texas Press, 2013.

Ponder, Jerry. "Captain John E. Clark." NOLA *Quarterly* 28, no. 3 (July-September 2004).

Preece, Harold. *Lone Star Man Ira Aten, Last of the Old Texas Rangers*. New York: Hastings House, 1960.

Price, Bill Smith. *Bill Whitley, Outlaw*. Austin: Nortex Press, 1995.

Queen, Dewey Don. "The Queen Family" in *Round Rock, Texas, U.S.A*. Wolfe City, TX: Henington Publishing Company, 1972.

Rieter, Diane Davis. "The Nelson Oscar [*sic*] Reynolds Family" in Gerald Witt's *The History of Eastern Kerr County*. Austin: Nortex Press, 1986.

Ripley, Thomas. *They Died with Their Boots On*. New York: Doubleday, Doran & Company, 1935.

Roberts, Luvenia Conway. *A Woman's Recollection of Six Years in Camp with the Texas Rangers*. Austin: Von Boeckman-Jones Company, 1928. Reprint by State House Press of Austin, 1987.

Roberts, Dan W. *Rangers and Sovereignty*. Reprint, Austin: State House Press, 1987.

Roberts, Oran M. "The Political, Legislative and Judicial History of Texas for its Fifty Years of Statehood, 1845–1895" in *A Comprehensive History of Texas 1685 to 1897*. Edited by Dudley G. Wooten. Austin: Texas State Historical Association, 1986.

Robertson, Walter M. "The Loss [*sic*] Valley Fight." *Frontier Times*, December, 1929.

Rose, Peter R. *The Reckoning: The Triumph of Order on the Texas Outlaw Frontier*. Lubbock: Texas Tech University Press, 2012.

Salter, Forrest. "Historic Murder Story Rethought." *Kerrville Mountain Sun*, undated clipping.

Shroyer, Jean, comp. and ed. *Williamson County, Texas: Its History and Its People*. Austin: Nortex Press, 1985.

Sinise, Jerry. *George Washington Arrington: Civil War Spy, Texas Ranger, Sheriff and Rancher*. Burnet, TX: Nortex Press, 1979.

Sonnichsen, C. L. *I'll Die Before I'll Run: The Story of the Great Feuds of Texas*. New York: Harper & Brothers Publishers, 1951.

Sowell, A. J. "Frontier Incidents." *Texas Indian Fighters in Frontier Times*, March, 1948

Speer, William S. *Encyclopedia of the New West.* Marshall, TX: United States Biographical Publishing Co., 1881.

Stamps, Roy, and Jo Ann Stamps. *The Letters of John Wesley Hardin.* Austin: Eakin Press, 2001.

[Steele, William] *A List of Fugitives from Justice.* Facsimile edition of *Fugitives from Justice: The Notebook of Texas Ranger Sergeant James B. Gillett.* Austin: State House Press, 1997.

Stephens, Robert W. *Texas Ranger Sketches.* Wolfe City, TX: Henington Publishing Company, 1972.

Stovall, Frances, et al. *Clear Springs and Limestone Ledges: A History of San Marcos and Hays County.* Austin: Nortex Press, 1986.

Sullivan, Jerry M. *Fort McKavett: A Texas Frontier Post.* NP: Texas Parks and Wildlife Department, 1981[?].

Thrapp, Dan L. *Encyclopedia of Frontier Biography.* Spokane: The Arthur H. Clark Company, 1994.

Tise, Sammy. *Texas County Sheriffs.* Hallettsville, TX: NP, 1989.

Tyler, Ron, Editor in Chief. *The New Handbook of Texas.* Six volumes. Austin: Texas State Historical Association, 1996.

"William Steele" No author given. Vol. 6, 79.

"John B. Jones" Thomas W. Cutrer. Vol. 3, 986.

"Cicero Rufus Perry" Thomas W. Cutrer. Vol. 5, 157.

"Burdette Wells, Texas" Vanessa L. Davis, Vol. 1, 828.

"Fort Mason" Julius E. DeVoss, Vol. 2, 1110–11.

"San Marcos, Texas" Daniel P. Greene, Vol. 5, 867–88.

"Orange, Texas" Diana J. Kleiner, Vol. 4, 1160–61.

"Bagdad, Texas" Mark Odintz, Vol. 1, 333–34.

"James Shackleford Gillett" Margaret F. Peirce. Vol. 3, 169.

"Fort McKavett" Vivian Elizabeth Smyrl. Vol. 2, 1111.

"Lockhart, Texas" Vivian Elizabeth Smyrl. Vol. 4, 257.

"Kimble County" Nolan Thompson.Vol. 3, 1100–01.

Utley, Robert M. *Lone Star Justice: The First Century of the Texas Rangers.* New York: Oxford University Press, 2002.

Wade, Amy. "George Washington Wade" in *A History of Hamilton County, Texas.* Dallas: Taylor Publishing Company, 1979.

Webb, Walter Prescott. *The Texas Rangers: A History of Frontier Defense.* Austin: The University of Texas, 1935, 1965.

White, Gifford, Compiler. *1840 Citizens of Texas: Land Grants*. Vol. 1. St. Louis, MO: Ingmire Publishers, 1983.

White, James C. *The Promised Land: A History of Brown County, Texas*. Brownwood, TX: Brownwood Banner Press, 1941.

White, Lucille. Letter to J. Marvin Hunter in *Frontier Times*, February-March 1976.

Whitley, Stanley. "Whitley" in *Burnet County History*, Vol. 2. Edited by Darrell Debo. Burnet, TX: Eakin Press, 1979.

Whittington, Mary. "The Great Train Robberies of 1885 and 1886." *The Plum Creek Almanac* 19, no. 2, Fall 2001.

Williams, David M. *The Vicious Murder of S. S. Brooks*. Paper presented to the Edwards Plateau Historical Association and printed in booklet form, 2002. Paper presented October 5, 2002.

Wyatt, Frederica Burt. "Adeline Boyce," *True West*, September-October 1974.

Wyatt, Frederica Burt. Chair. *Families of Kimble County*. Vol. 1, 1985; Vol. 2, 1998. Junction, TX: South Llano River Printing Company.

Wyatt, Frederica Burt. *The Cemetery at Fort McKavett, Texas*. Junction, TX: Kimble County Historical Museum, 1999.

NEWSPAPERS

All newspapers are from Texas cities unless otherwise noted.

Belton Journal, Belton

Belton News, Belton

Bradford Star, Towanda, Pennsylvania

Brenham Daily Banner, Brenham

Burnet Bulletin, Burnet

Daily Democratic Statesman, Austin

Daily Express, San Antonio

Daily Herald, San Antonio

Daily State Gazette, Austin

Tombstone Epitaph, Tombstone, Arizona

Dallas Morning News, Dallas

Dallas Daily Tribune-Herald, Dallas

Dallas Daily Herald, Dallas

Dallas Weekly Herald, Dallas

Denison Daily News, Denison
El Paso Herald, El Paso
Fort Smith Elevator, Fort Smith, Arkansas
Fort Worth Democrat, Fort Worth
Fort Worth Daily Gazette, Fort Worth
Galveston Daily News, Galveston
Hancock Democrat, Greenfield, Indiana
Houston Daily Post, Houston
Houston Daily Telegraph, Houston
Indian Chieftain, Vinita, Oklahoma
Indianapolis Journal, Indianapolis, Indiana
Kerrville Mountain Sun, Kerrville
Lampasas Leader, Lampasas
Lampasas Dispatch, Lampasas
Lampasas Daily Times, Lampasas
Lockhart Post, Lockhart
Lockhart Post Register, Lockhart
National Police Gazette, New York
New Orleans Times, New Orleans, Louisiana
New York Times, New York (reprint of an article in the *Austin Gazette*)
Prospect News, Doniphan, Missouri
St. Louis Globe-Democrat, St. Louis, Missouri
San Antonio Express, San Antonio
San Antonio Light-News, San Antonio
San Marcos Times, San Marcos
Waco Daily Examiner, Waco
Waco Daily Examiner and Patron, Waco
Weatherford Exponent, Weatherford
Weekly State Gazette, Austin
West Texas Free Press, San Marcos

INDEX

A

B

C

E

F

H

I

J

K

L

M

M

N

S

T

U

Y